THE A–Z OF GENDER AND SEXUALITY

*of related interest*

**Written on the Body**
Letters from Trans and Non-Binary Survivors of
Sexual Assault and Domestic Violence
*Edited by Lexie Bean*
*Foreword and additional pieces by Dean Spade, Nyala Moon,*
*Alex Valdes, Sawyer DeVuyst and Ieshai Bailey*
ISBN 978 1 78592 797 3
eISBN 978 1 78450 803 6

**To My Trans Sisters**
*Edited by Charlie Craggs*
ISBN 978 1 78592 343 2
eISBN 978 1 78450 668 1

**How to Understand Your Gender**
A Practical Guide for Exploring Who You Are
*Alex Iantaffi and Meg-John Barker*
*Foreword by S. Bear Bergman*
ISBN 978 1 78592 746 1
eISBN 978 1 78450 517 2

**The Gender Agenda**
A First-Hand Account of How Girls and Boys Are Treated Differently
*Ros Ball and James Millar*
*Foreword by Marianne Grabrucker*
ISBN 978 1 78592 320 3
eISBN 978 1 78450 633 9

# THE
# A–Z
## OF
# GENDER
## AND
# SEXUALITY

From Ace to Ze

*Morgan Lev Edward Holleb*

**Jessica Kingsley** *Publishers*
London and Philadelphia

First published in 2019
by Jessica Kingsley Publishers
73 Collier Street
London N1 9BE, UK
and
400 Market Street, Suite 400
Philadelphia, PA 19106, US

*www.jkp.com*

**Library of Congress Cataloging in Publication Data**
A CIP catalog record for this book is available from the Library of Congress

**British Library Cataloguing in Publication Data**
A CIP catalogue record for this book is available from the British Library

ISBN 978 1 78592 342 5
eISBN 978 1 78450 663 6

Printed and bound in the United States

*To everyone who breaks unjust laws.*

# ACKNOWLEDGEMENTS

Cosmic appreciation for all the people who have taught me, the friends and lovers who've supported me and encouraged me and sweetly demanded a signed copy of this book well before it was a real object.

Thank you Jo Marius Hauge for your friendship, your validation, your excellent performance art, your impressive knowledge of bottoming, your excellent advice, and the sitting with me and singing with me in the sad boy corner when I was heartbroken and homeless. I love you so much.

Thank you Christopher Gill, Kitty Richardson, MaréLua Açir, Pasha Blanda, Anna, Sofia Nikolaevna Aneychik, Tobias Slater, and Joe Isaac, for your invaluable insights, captivating conversations, your empathy and affection, and for sharing your joys and struggles and creative projects and resources and lives with me.

Thank you especially to Christopher, who gave me the idea for this book in the first place, for believing in me even though I'm stubborn. I love you.

Thank you to Kitty and the babes of Willow Coven—Jo Marius, MaréLua, Vicki Baars, Roo, and LucasDonna—for housing and feeding me in the spring of 2017, when I was evicted. Thank you to Lyra Dunseith for helping me secure new housing in London, and to Kitty and Christopher for later helping me move to Glasgow.

Thank you Angus Henderson, H Beverley, Jo Marius, and Kitty for your invaluable input and expertise with particular aspects of queer culture and history. Should there be any incorrect or problematic information included herein, the fault lies entirely with me.

Thank you Andrew James, my editor, for your boundless patience with me as I floundered and deadlines slipped past.

Thank you to my mother, Stacey Potts, the first queer I ever knew, for her boundless love and support. You are an absolute beacon of compassion who inspires me to constantly learn and better myself, and serve my communities through kindness and generosity rather than judgement, without compromising my values. Your activism in America fuels mine abroad. You have been the surrogate mother of many of my queer friends with less-than-understanding parents, and are personally responsible for sustaining my communities with your support, empathy, and optimism. I love you, Mom.

Thank you to my fathers for giving me daddy issues and teaching me to be my own dad.

Thank you to everyone who assisted with stabilizing my immigration status in the UK: to everyone who helped me navigate the labyrinthine bureaucracy, everyone who gave me money to cover the legal costs, everyone who supported my application with paperwork, and to my spouse for marrying me.

Thank you to all the activist groups I have had the privilege of working with, and those who have worked in solidarity with us. Thank you especially to everyone who works to support survivors of sexual violence, and all the survivors who have shared their experiences, their strength, and their anxieties with me. There is power in our mutual aid. (If your activism doesn't center the safety of survivors and hold abusers accountable, it's broken.)

Thank to you the queer activists of the past, whose work inspires us to be unapologetically ourselves and unwavering in our demands for dignity.

Thank you to the broader queer communities of London and Glasgow for welcoming me in, pushing me out, welcoming me back, and showcasing a multitude of glorious culture and infighting. I believe in our collective learning and healing through support groups, skill shares, safer spaces, dance nights, group chats, community gardens, mutual social media hyping, accountability processes, and drag shows.

Thank you to the wider queer community online, and to everyone who has called me in and called me out on Twitter.

Thank you to the secret underground of trans people who helped me navigate healthcare and gave me hormones when my doctors wouldn't.

Thank you to my therapist, and all my friends and lovers who have generously acted as surrogate therapists.

Thank you to everyone who's given me gender euphoria by using my given names and pronouns or chatted me up on Grindr.

Thank you to everyone who has ever asked me for help: there is nothing more empowering, and helping you helps me. Asking for help is hard and I'm flattered to be considered approachable enough to ask.

This project was only possible through funding and other material support from my family and friends, and ultimately the death of my grandfather and my subsequent inheritance. We don't often acknowledge the socio-economic barriers to creating art, but we should.

# INTRODUCTION

This is a book about queer language, designed to define queer and LGBT+ words and contextualize their histories. It will explore the intrinsic, complicated relationship between sexuality and gender, and illuminate the power in claiming (or rejecting) labels.

"Queer" is deliberately elusive but still has meaning, which will be threaded throughout this book. It is similar to, but distinct from, terms like "gay," "LGBT+," "homosexual," and "transgender"; it is more fluid and political, and it invites constant, critical reinterpretation. "Queer" is in opposition to "straight" and "cis," but can also find itself in confrontation with "gay" and "LGBT+." As a reclaimed slur it is not a universally embraced catch-all term, and it should not be coercively assigned to people. In this book, detailed in its own entry, I'll be using "queer" as an adjective to mean anyone whose identity is gender non-conforming and externally politicized. This includes, for example, a bullied gay teenager, but not a gay man with institutional power who assimilates into heteronormativity (homonormativity) by denying access to resources to the gay teenager. This is already a problematic definition because perhaps queerness should not be conditional on circumstance or privilege, but I think it is context-dependent and absolutely political. The same wealthy homonormative gay man may not be queer in San Francisco, but is absolutely queer in Chechnya where his sexuality would be literally policed. Queer is, if nothing else, a gendered Other. We cannot talk about queer without talking about a history of violence.

People, even queer and trans people, can feel overwhelmed with the current terminology around sexuality and gender. Yet, having the right word to describe yourself and your experience is extremely empowering.

More than anything, this book is for people who are exploring their gender and sexuality; second, I hope it is useful for significant others, family, friends, and allies (SOFFA), and professionals who work with trans and queer people.

May this book dispel anxiety around using the wrong words. Words are powerful, and our language reflects our cultural priorities. Yet I hope that we can find the nuance between insisting on inclusive language—on being recognized instead of erased, on having our pronouns used, on shifting away from problematic language—and knowing when to act on good faith and call people in instead of calling them out. I don't want to live in a world where using the "right" words is more important than doing the right thing. That said, anyone who is truly an ally will welcome being corrected when they use an inappropriate word or phrase.

We must accept—no, embrace—that all words are the wrong words, and the right words, depending on their context. Two people could describe the same experience but choose different words to identify themselves, and shun the label someone else would choose. Best practice for understanding someone else's identity or experience is to ask them to define it themselves, or better yet, listen to what they've already said about it.

The most important aim of this book is to help the reader navigate the relationship between gender and sexuality. The current discourse, even in academic trans/queer communities, is disappointingly muddled on this topic. Why is the "T" part of "LGBT+"? What is the relationship between gender identity and sexual orientation? The historical context of the LGBT movement was born out of centuries of discrimination and demonization of deviance from prescribed gender roles—sometimes expressed in same-sex attraction. Gender identity and sexual orientation are intrinsically linked though obviously not interchangeable. There are aesthetics and behaviors which are "gay" despite having nothing to do with sex or attraction, because they subvert traditional gender norms; for example, men who wear dresses are assumed to be gay and likely to be socially punished accordingly. I want to remind readers that sexuality as we understand it today is defined by gender and gender roles rather than love or sexual practices, contrary to narratives of the modern "love wins" LGBT+ rights movement, or the straight facets of the BDSM scene.

I also want to explain (and destabilize) such pervasive concepts as "man," "woman," "sex," "gay," and "gender." I want this book to offer context, somewhere to position these terms, but ultimately to raise questions about them. But this is not an academic book designed to further intellectualize gender and contribute to the discourse (though that would be a happy side effect). I am raising these questions to challenge the current modes of oppression which rest on assumptions about gender and sexuality. I want people to stop policing non-normative gender expressions, to stop invalidating gender non-conforming identities, to stop destroying (through negligence and murder) trans bodies. When there are "normative" genders and sexualities, those deemed to be "non-normative" are made unlivable through violence. We deserve to live with dignity.

This book will cover:

- Words which describe gender: for example, "man," "non-binary," "femme," "cis"
- Words which describe sexuality: "bisexual," "gray ace," "MSM"
- Words surrounding the above which are pervasive yet elusive: "gender," "queer," "sex (n.)," "sex (v.)," "sexuality"
- Gay, trans, and queer slang words of note: "passing," "camp," "chemsex"
- Basic words about drag: "cross-dresser," "queen," "king"
- Selective words around BDSM, because as a practice and culture it has distinctly "bent" (not-straight) origins: "kink," "top," "sadism"
- Words relevant to LGBT+ rights and anti-discrimination: "transmisogynoir," "cis gaze," "Pride," "LGBTQIA+"
- Words relevant to queer activism: "pinkwashing," "homonationalism," "transmilitarism," "patriarchy"
- Key concepts in politics, privilege, and oppression, which intersect with queer politics: "cultural appropriation," "anti-Blackness," "agism"
- Words relevant to gender-affirming healthcare and psychology (in the US and UK): "transition," "real-life experience," "T," "bottom surgery," "dysphoria," "AFAB"
- Slurs which have been reclaimed by groups they target: "tranny," "faggot," "dyke"
- Words relevant to historical queer culture: "Molly houses," "Polari"

These words will be presented in a glossary format, alphabetically. Each will offer a concise definition for quick reference, and a longer history and context where appropriate. The text can also be read as a whole, for both a brief history of queerness and as a modern history of current queer discourse, immediately obsolete but a snapshot of its time. As with all snapshots, the photographer has a responsibility to frame the subject in a way which reflects its "truth." But truth is a phantom, and, like a photographer, I am only able to show you my subject as I see and experience it.

My approach to language is post-structural and descriptivist (not prescriptivist); words do not have inherent meaning, they are signifiers of meanings and these meanings shift across time. I don't see this being an attempt to remain up-to-the-minute; it's not possible or desirable to release a new edition every time a word's connotations shift.

Regardless, this book would still offer a valuable context—both broadly speaking, and as a living history of the moment it was written— and I expect most words will remain relevant for several years or longer.

The shifting meaning of words isn't linear: a word can have many meanings at the same time, different in different contexts, even for the same speaker. There are often several labels used to describe the same identity, but different labels are preferred in different groups or contexts, and/or they have slightly different connotations which make them more or less appropriate for different contexts. Just because words don't have stable definitions doesn't mean they don't have meaning, history, and context.

Some of the words I seek to define (or rather, discuss) carry political or social legitimacy, while others are out of date, out of fashion, or problematic. Just because a word has more social or political currency doesn't mean it's the best word: often the more accepted words are reductive because they're easier to understand.

Language is a tool of empowerment but it's also a tool of violence, used to silence and oppress marginalized people. Many of these words are politically charged and were formed through the necessity of creating a group identity, either to demand civil rights, or to Other a group as deviants.

With the acknowledgement that language is malleable and ever-changing, I want to offer context for the words currently and formerly in use. People are beginning to learn that there are certain words that were once in use but are no longer "politically correct," and I want to demystify that and pre-empt the question "why?"

This book will only cover English-language terms (with a few exceptions), partly to limit the scope, and mostly because as a white American author with no cultural ties outwith the Anglosphere, I am not qualified to define non-English terms, or to fully understand their contexts. However, I want to stress that other languages and cultures have rich histories and wide spectrums of gender variance and sexuality outside the cisgender heterosexuality that is prized as the "default" in our culture. Many other cultures have a long history of third genders or what we might describe as transgender identities and experiences, from *hijra* to Two-Spirit to Onnabe. The gender binary as we understand it and its coded gender roles—including strict adherence to heterosexuality under punishment of anti-sodomy laws—were exports of European imperialism. English is a language of the colonizer and this book will implicitly reflect that. While I've done my best to be comprehensive with Anglophonic terms (though that task is impossible), I make no claims to being comprehensive full stop. I highly encourage readers to undertake independent research on other gender and sexuality terms in different languages.

Despite my best efforts, this book will inevitably be incomplete.

Queer histories are too often co-opted by cisgender straight people. I'm a trans and bisexual-queer author and I want to reclaim control of our narratives, and amplify the work (especially activist work in the past and present) of the most influential yet marginalized in our communities. Transgender people (and those who, in their time, would use different words to describe themselves based on their gender non-conformity) have always been at the forefront of queer liberation. There would be no modern LGBT+ movement if it weren't for trans women, and in fact all civil rights movements, from women's suffrage to present-day pro-refugee efforts, rest on the work of trans people. Trans people do not live single-issue lives: we are also disabled, people of color, poor, migrants, prisoners, sex workers, fat, homeless, old, and young, and we are at the front of these struggles as well as fighting for trans and queer liberation.

This book is ethnographic: it is a study of the self, of things I am and am not. I am writing from my own understandings of gender and sexuality, which I think of as relatively well-informed as a queer and non-binary trans person who has spent several years studying and inter-rogating gender. It reflects my personal experiences, my relationships with these words and with the people who use them, and my personal anarchist politics. It would be arrogant to suggest that these are definitive explanations, and that my definitions are simply correct. Language is context-dependent and there is no escaping my context. I'm a white American queer/bisexual non-binary trans femme Jewish mentally ill millennial boy of the precariat class who's lived in London and Glasgow and Twitter, and this book will no doubt reflect that. My work as a trans educator and activist, and my history as a sex worker, immigrant, and survivor of sexual violence, will come through; so will my privileges as a white able-bodied thin person.

These are things I know about, but I am not the only one who knows about them, and my experiences and opinions don't represent everyone with similar identities to my own.

There is no singular trans experience and I in no way represent an entire trans community; I fully reject the notion of being an authority, even on my own text.

Especially regarding transmisogyny, race, class, and dis/ability, I have done my best to amplify the points I've heard my more knowledgeable comrades stress. All faults of this book are my own, but its merits are the culmination of decades of theory and discussion which I have tried faithfully to condense.

As a trans person, I essentially get asked to write pieces of this book all the time, for both newly self-described trans people and their allies. I anticipate some resistance from queers who want to keep some of these terms secret. I'm not writing this to let outsiders into our safe spaces (and there will always be undergrounds within undergrounds), but for "new" queers and the people who support them. I appreciate the need for safer spaces and exclusion, but if we are to dismantle straightness and cisness and their inherent oppressions, then we must also expand queerness. But if you're straight and cis, you need to do the work of undoing your privileges! This book will help illuminate and challenge those privileges. Cisgender heterosexuals don't need more representation, but they do need help understanding the complicated relationship between sexuality and gender, so that they can be better allies and hopefully interrogate their own identities for further self-understanding. It can be daunting to critically engage with questions of gender and queerness once you realize that heterosexuality and "biological sex" are relatively recent concepts, and I hope these pages give everyone a safe space to explore other possibilities.

Please defer to your own lived experience when deciding what words are applicable to you. Regarding other people, we must acknowledge that they are the experts on their own lives and communities and so we should respect whatever terms they use to describe themselves.

The purpose of this book is not to "normalize" (read "neutralize") queer terms. I want to arm queer youth and newly identified queers with the language with which to describe themselves, so that they may articulate their needs, throw this book in the bin, set it on fire, and create new words and definitions from the ashes.

If you need permission, you are encouraged to cross out offending sections, make notes in the margins, and rip out entire pages.

# A

**A** — The A in LGBTQIA+ is for ASEXUAL, AROMANTIC, and AGENDER. It is not for "ally."

LGBT+ and the longer LGBTQIA+ are only useful as they group together people who are gender transgressors; they describe a broad shared experience of alienation under cisheteronormativity.

*see also:* LGBT+; CISHETERONORMATIVITY; GAY–STRAIGHT ALLIANCE; ALLY

**AAVE** — Acronym for "African-American Vernacular English."

The term AAVE itself is debated among Black people because it uses a colonial term for Blackness ("African American") which many Black people do not identify with.

AAVE is a variety of English spoken by many Black Americans and some Black Canadians. It has its own vocabulary, grammatical structure, and accents. Its roots are in Southern English; it is not derived from West African Pidgin English or Creole languages, though those have parallels with AAVE.

Because AAVE is seen as an inferior vernacular in connection with all the stereotypes of anti-Black racism, AAVE speakers are penalized if they don't speak Standard English in formal, business, academic, or public settings.

Lots of queer terms (and lots of terms in general) come from AAVE. Black people are often denied credit for creating culture, including language; they're punished for deviating from whiteness (which is impossible for them to avoid even if they wanted to); and when an aspect of Black culture is deemed the right level of edgy and desirable by whiteness, they're denied credit for it.

Examples in modern queer culture, which are appropriative when used by non-Black people, include:

- a look, serving looks, serving face
- as fuck, af
- basic
- boi
- drag (as in, "getting dragged")
- extra
- fierce
- fuckboy
- here for it
- looking like a snack
- mood, a mood
- on point
- read (as in, "read for filth")
- serving (serving shade, serving looks, serving tea)
- shade
- shook
- tea
- thicc
- thirst
- yaas
- the clapping hand emoji between words

AAVE isn't just a list of words; it has a tone and a rhythm which is distinct from Standard English.

It's appropriative and rude for non-Black people to speak AAVE, use AAVE terms, or use the tone or rhythm of AAVE.

*see also*: CULTURAL APPROPRIATION; WHITEWASHING; ANTI-BLACKNESS

**ABLEISM** — A totalizing system which oppresses disabled people and privileges abled people. Interactions which uphold this system.

Like all oppressions, ableism is both systemic and personal. Disabled people are more likely to suffer violences—physical, sexual, emotional, financial, and medical—and are less likely to be believed about their experiences. Disabled people are barred access to physical spaces which are not made accessible, and face discrimination which denies them socioeconomic and political access to opportunities and public life. Ableism intersects with other systems of oppression to further disenfranchise people with multiple marginalized identities: patriarchy, transphobia, classism, fatphobia, white supremacy, homophobia, and agism.

Ableism frames disabled people as a burden, on individuals and society. Crip theory—a critical perspective on disability which uses similar lenses as queer theory and focuses on the liberation of all disabled people—highlights that all bodies are interdependent: none are "independent" or more "dependent" (e.g., on carers).

Ableism stereotypes disabled bodies as being asexual or deviant in their sexuality. Disabled people are patronized and infantilized, which denies them sexual agency; or, they are fetishized, which also denies them their sexual agency as well as their personhood. This not only manifests in discrimination and lack of positive representation, but physical and medical violence like forced sterilization.

Ableist language is that which further entrenches the stigma of disabilities, including stigma around mental health (which many people consider to be disabling). For example, pejorative or hyperbolic use of the words "crazy," "dumb," "lame," "stupid," and "crippled" is rooted in ableism, even if that is not the conscious intent of the speaker. Ableist language often intersects with other oppressions: dismissing women as "hysterical" is a historical tactic of misogynists to ignore women's pain.

Disability is a diverse category. Making a space accessible does not just mean installing wheelchair ramps; it means considering and accommodating the needs not only of people in wheelchairs, but people with other mobility disabilities, people with cognitive and developmental disabilities, people with sensory disabilities, and people with chronic pain. Combating ableism means listening to the needs of disabled people and prioritizing their needs instead of centering the feelings (including guilt) of abled people.

*see also:* CRIP THEORY; DISABILITY; OPPRESSION; FETISHIZE; BODILY AUTONOMY; FASCISM

**ACCOUNTABILITY** — A process by which people take responsibility for their harmful actions, and make sincere attempts to mitigate the harm they caused and actively prevent causing future harm.

Accountability processes are difficult to navigate for all parties involved, but the effort is made through the belief that community alternatives to the criminal justice system are worthwhile, especially because marginalized people are likely to be failed by the criminal justice system.

*see also:* TRANSFORMATIVE JUSTICE; VIOLENCE

**ACE** — Short for ASEXUAL.

**ACEARO** — Short for ASEXUAL and AROMANTIC: someone who experiences neither sexual nor romantic attraction.

The acearo spectrum includes gray asexual and gray-romantic people, or people who fall between asexual and sexual, and aromantic and romantic.

*see also:* GRAY ACE; GRAY-ROMANTIC

**ACTIVISM** — A practice or philosophy of action, in support of, or in opposition to, a political issue.

Activism is central to discussions about gender and sexuality because activists combat stigma, discrimination, and violences suffered by people on the basis of their genders and sexualities; queer identities, lives, and bodies are apparently still controversial. We are still struggling for basic rights like access to healthcare and housing, and freedom from interpersonal and structural violences. LGBT+ activism and queer activism have some overlapping immediate objectives, but are at odds in their worldview and ultimate end-goals.

LGBT+ activism is focused on fostering tolerance and acceptance for LGBT+ people within cisheteronormative society. Some key LGBT+ activist aims are: better representation of LGBT+ in positions of political and economic power, equal access for LGBT+ people into social and legal institutions such as marriage and the military, and hate crime legislation. LGBT+ activism seeks to celebrate diversity of queer people and allow us entry into "straight" society as it is, but does not seek to change any aspect of society. A lot of LGBT+ activism is rooted in respectability politics: "Look, we're normal just like you," and "Don't worry, we don't want to cause disruption, we just want a seat at the table."

Queer activism focuses on empowering the most marginalized and vulnerable people. Queer issues are less about same-sex marriage and more about prison abolition, housing, poverty, border and migration, detentions and deportations, police abolition, free education, free childcare, and free and universal access to healthcare. Queer activism challenges corporate/consumer, "mainstream" LGBT+ aims and prioritizes empathy over pity, liberation over assimilation, and agency over essentialism. Queer activism shifts focus from essential identities to identities based on affiliation (e.g., men who have sex with men, groups affected by AIDS, and sex workers). This approach was born out of resistance to AIDS stigma and increased homophobia in the 1980s. Issue-based coalitions, rather than shared but abstract identity-based activism, prioritize material conditions of vulnerable people and work toward improving them.

Activism is multi-faceted. Direct action against oppressive structures, and collaborating with problematic institutions on the basis of harm reduction, are both valid tactics. Support work for activists is itself an aspect of activism; without support (be it emotional, domestic, financial, or otherwise), activists could not continue their work. Social and systemic change requires sustained pressure and a diversity of tactics.

Respectability politics is a facet of activism, and can be useful—if the goal is harm reduction, sometimes playing into the respectability of a polite and formally educated person who speaks "standard" English is the best option because it will garner the most positive public attention. Likewise, the use of celebrity to fund important work is another valid tactic. But respectability politics alone is not enough to engineer social and systemic change; civil rights are simply not won by being respectable.

Identity politics, though potentially reductive, also has utility. Strategic essentialism (a term coined by post-colonial theorist Gayatri Chakravorty Spivak) is the foregrounding of a specific group identity in order to achieve a goal, despite knowing and debating differences privately within the group.

Direct action is the most immediate, and often the most effective, tactic for an activist. It means identifying problems and materially enacting/constructing solutions rather than petitioning anyone else to make change. Direct action is not necessarily the same as "doing an action," which is not always appropriate; for example, you can't "do an action" against capitalism because capitalism is a set of social relations, not a single business or bank or piece of legislation. But we can do actions which undermine or momentarily interrupt capitalism.

There is valid criticism of "activist" as an identity: if activism is creating social change, then the activist is an expert and positions themselves as more appreciative of the need for social change, and more able to execute it. The activist label then privatizes social change, divides the labor and makes it only the responsibility of the activist. This assumes that people who aren't activists cannot, and are not, working toward social change by—perhaps in small ways, perhaps mundanely—disrupting the reproduction of oppressive social relations and undermining systemic violences. But struggles for liberation are happening all the time! "Politics" isn't just something we do when we protest or sign a petition; we do it literally all the time. Everything is political.

*see also*: TRANSFORMATIVE JUSTICE

**ACT UP** — An HIV/AIDS direct action group active in the late 1980s and throughout the 1990s and early 2000s. Its main goal was to address the public health crisis of the HIV/AIDS epidemic through prevention and accessible treatment.

ACT UP is an acronym for the AIDS Coalition To Unleash Power. It was formed in March 1987 in the Lesbian and Gay Community Services Center (now called the Lesbian, Gay, Bisexual & Transgender Community Center) in New York City. It also had decentralized chapters across the US, Europe, and one in Kathmandu, Nepal; some of them are still active. ACT UP was arguably the single most successful modern queer rights group to use direct action.

The group's motto was SILENCE = DEATH, and their visuals often featured a pink triangle, a symbol of queer resistance. Other slogans included "Act up, fight back, fight AIDS," and "AIDS is a political crisis."

The demands made by ACT UP were about the research on, and treatment of, people living with HIV/AIDS. AIDS was (incorrectly) seen as a "gay plague" which only affected queer men, and the political climate of the 80s and 90s was extremely homophobic—the public and governmental response to the health crisis was essentially to ignore it and allow people to die. The first ACT UP action in March 1987 was a demonstration on Wall Street which demanded greater access to experimental drugs for treating HIV/AIDS and called for a coordinated national strategy for addressing the public health crisis. Other issues of import for ACT UP were housing, homophobia, abortion and contraception, safer sex education, media coverage of the AIDS crisis, access to federal benefits for HIV/AIDS patients, the lack of public investment in the AIDS crisis, and the methodologies of research and data collection surrounding HIV/AIDS.

ACT UP tactics were based on direct action. One aspect of this was to directly educate people on HIV and safer sex: ACT UP created and disseminated public service announcement videos about how HIV is (and is not) transmitted.

But ACT UP was known for their highly visible, public demonstrations. In January 1988, ACT UP protested at the Heart building, the parent company of *Cosmopolitan* magazine, after *Cosmo* published a misleading article about heterosexual women can't get AIDS from unprotected vaginal sex. On 10 December 1989, more than 5,000 ACT UP members occupied Roman Catholic Church at St. Patrick's Cathedral in New York City to protest their homophobic and misogynistic stances against HIV education, condom distribution, and abortion. Members of ACT UP NY returned to St. Patrick's on 12 December 1999 to repeat the protest.

On 21 May 1990 ACT UP occupied the National Institute of Health in protest of the underrepresentation of women and people of color in clinical trials, and demanding more AIDS treatments. ACT UP Women's Caucuses targeted the Center for Disease Control (CDC) because the CDC definition of AIDS did not include symptoms that women with AIDS experienced, so women with AIDS were denied an AIDS diagnosis and were instead diagnosed with AIDS-Related Complex (ARC) or HIV; denial of an AIDS diagnosis meant that they did not have access to social security benefits. ACT UP protested the CDC definition in Washington DC on 21 May 1990, chanting "How many more have to die before they qualify?" and holding posters that read "Women don't get AIDS, they just die from it." Because of ACT UP's pressure on the CDC, the definition of AIDS was expanded in 1993 to include the symptoms of women and the access to federal benefits for AIDS patients was made easier; also, women were more likely to be correctly diagnosed with HIV/AIDS.

On 22 January 1991, ACT UP members stormed the CBS evening news to declare, "AIDS is news, fight AIDS not Arabs!" live on air during coverage of Operation Desert Storm. The next day there were coordinated demonstrations across New York City demanding "money for AIDS not war".

ACT UP in New York City was so effective because its members were a combination of experienced activists on issues like prisoners' rights and women's and reproductive rights, and wealthy, middle-class gay men who had resources at their disposal and were suddenly in the middle of a public health crisis.

The structure of ACT UP was leaderless and decentralized, with larger groups creating a support network for smaller "affinity" groups, caucuses, and committees. The affinity groups focused on specific issues and actions, often coordinated within a larger ACT UP action. ACT UP had no formal structure and the process for decision-making was generally reached through a vote.

The visual style of ACT UP was, and still is, extremely influential on queer and anarchist politics and aesthetics. The art and media for ACT UP were designed by anonymous art collective Gran Fury, whose work is characterized by appropriating commercial language for political impact, using bold typefaces and often including the faces of public figures. ACT UP and Gran Fury used art to bring attention to the HIV/AIDS epidemic on t-shirts, wheat-pasted posters, pins, postcards, flyers, billboards, banner drops, protest placards, and television.

ACT UP's legacy has been to dramatically improve healthcare for people living with HIV and AIDS, through better access to healthcare and improving the healthcare itself by putting pressure on institutions like the FDA, CDC, and NIH. ACT UP is also responsible for "radicalizing" a generation of queers to the effectiveness of anarchist direct action tactics, and highlighting the willingness of government and public institutions to abandon queer people in a health crisis.

There are also parallels to be drawn between securing healthcare for people living with AIDS/HIV, and trans people who need to access healthcare (trans-specific and otherwise).

Some direct action queer groups influenced by, or born out of, ACT UP are Bash Back!, Damned Interfering Video Activists TV (DIVA TV), Fed Up Queers, Fierce Pussy, Housing Works, Lesbian Avengers, and Queer Nation.

*see also:* HIV; AIDS; ACTIVISM; TRANS HEALTHCARE; BODILY AUTONOMY; PINK

**AESTHETIC** — A branch of philosophy which studies art, beauty, and taste. Informally used as a noun and adjective to indicate taste or a look.

Aesthetic is the artistic expressions you're drawn to, and which you create or reproduce. Your aesthetic could be defined by an outfit, a color, a period of art, a material, an Instagram filter, a sonic texture, a genre of film; it's anything artistically appealing, anything you find beautiful.

Aesthetic is a key part of gender. Structurally, gender is a set of norms surrounding behavior and aesthetics. Individually, gender is an identification with roles (community and behavior) and aesthetics.

Gender expression is also a matter of aesthetics and behavior. We read people's genders based on their appearance and the way they conduct themselves: the way they stand, walk, talk, and the things they say and do. Behavior is, generally, a stronger gender signifier than aesthetic: people will assume a gendered difference between people wearing the same outfit if their gendered behavioral cues are sufficiently strong. You can't see someone's gender with any certainty, but most people project theirs aesthetically, subtly or otherwise.

Aesthetics create and reproduce culture, and work as a signifier to flag to other people that you're part of a shared group. Is aesthetic the product of a shared identity or that which constructs and creates identity?

Queer culture has its own set of aesthetics: haircuts, colors, beauty practices, and shared artistic references to, and appreciation of, popular (and obscure, pop-cult) culture. The subcultures within queer culture also have their own aesthetic norms and cues.

*see also:* GAY CULTURE; GENDER EXPRESSION; GENDER

**AFAB** — Acronym for ASSIGNED FEMALE AT BIRTH.
*see also:* CAFAB; DFAB; FAAB

**AGENDER** — The absence of a feeling of gender.

Agender people might identify themselves as trans, non-binary, genderqueer, or by any other gender label. They might be gender fluid and only be agender some of the time, and a man, a woman, or any other gender at other times. Agender people may or may not pursue medical transition to change their body.

An agender person can have any sexual orientation or none, though their lack of gender disrupts the idea of sexuality as a spectrum of attraction to same and "opposite" genders.

Agender is one of the As in LGBTQIA+, along with aromantic and asexual.

*see also*: GENDER

**AGE OF CONSENT** — *see:* CONSENT.

**AGISM** — Fear of, or contempt for, people based on their age or the perception of their age. Behavior based on those feelings. A system of oppression in which the elderly and young people are marginalized and subject to violence.

Agism is reproduced in the queer community. Like in cisnormative society, queer beauty standards fetishize young people and reproduce harmful norms about weight and aging. The fetishization of youth harms both young people (who are more likely to be targeted by predatory people, and less equipped to protect themselves) and older people (who are stigmatized and desexualized).

Like all systems of oppression, agism intersects with other marginalizations: classism, racism, ableism, misogyny, queerphobia, transphobia, and fatphobia.

*see also:* OPPRESSION; QUEER TIME; TRANS TIME; CHOSEN FAMILY

**AIDS** — Acquired Immune Deficiency Syndrome, a medical condition which can develop following Human Immunodeficiency Virus (HIV) infection.

AIDS became a public health crisis in the 1980s and 1990s, but was largely ignored by public officials because of its association with the gay community.

*see also:* HIV/AIDS; ACT UP

**A**

**ALLISTIC** — Someone who is not autistic. Someone who is neurotypical.
  *see also:* AUTISM; NEUROTYPICAL; NEURODIVERSE

**ALLO, ALLOSEXUAL** — Someone who is not asexual. Someone who experiences sexual attraction.

Allosexual is an important word in queer discourse because without it, the opposite to "asexual" is assumed to be the default and "normal," which frames asexuality as deviant and abnormal.
  *see also:* ASEXUAL; NORMALCY

**ALLY** — Someone who is not part of an oppressed group but positions themselves as sympathetic to the struggles of that group, and is (hopefully) invested in their liberation.

The A in LGBTQIA+ is not for ally; it's for agender, asexual, and aromantic.

Allyship is also plausible deniability for queerness. If it's not safe for someone to be out, or if they just aren't yet ready to claim their queerness, allyship allows them to be in proximity to queerness, culturally and politically.

The role of the ally in activism should be to uplift the oppressed group, and to relinquish power (social, economic, and political) to the oppressed group to create a more equitable society.

However, allyship is often performative: allies will virtue signal to indicate that they are good, "progressive" people and to assuage their guilt. Allies often do what makes them feel good, or makes them feel like they're being good allies, rather than listening to what their comrades actually want or need. Allies can be obnoxious and entitled; they expect to be offered the world for doing the bare minimum and act defensively if their efforts aren't immediately lauded. Even well-meaning allies might center their own feelings when you come out: "I'll support you, but this is hard for me." This is why some people make a marked distinction between an ally and a comrade, or an accomplice. Ally is a word tainted with polite neoliberalism, of working within the confines of an oppressive system and never breaking the law, of marching peacefully and quietly and not striking or speaking truth to power. Allies tend to prioritize order and assimilation while the people they purport to support are invested in liberation, which inherently necessitates destabilizing current systems.

*see also:* GAY–STRAIGHT ALLIANCE; LGBT+; ACTIVISM

**AMAB** — Acronym for ASSIGNED MALE AT BIRTH.

*see also:* CAMAB; DMAB; MAAB

**AMATONORMATIVITY** — The assumption and expectation that romantic love is universally experienced and desired, and that romance is the most significant interpersonal bond.

Amatonormativity is perpetuated by cultural norms which imply, if not state explicitly, that we are incomplete before finding a romantic partner.

Amatonormativity undermines the importance of non-romantic intimacy, friendship, family, and the relationship with the self. It also reproduces unhealthy relationship norms, such as possessiveness over romantic partners and fear of being alone.

*see also:* AROMANTIC; GRAY-ROMANTIC; ASEXUAL; DESIRE; LOVE; QUEERPLATONIC

**AMBIPHILIA** — Attraction to men and women.

Ambiphilia is part of an alternative model of sexuality to heterosexual and homosexual which does not make any reference to the subject's gender, and instead focuses on the gender/expression of the people they're attracted to. While androphilia (attraction to men/masculinity) and gynephilia (attraction to women/femininity) have clear utility, ambiphilia's definition is already covered by the word "bisexual," which is in more common usage and has an important queer history.

*see also:* BISEXUAL; ANDROPHILIA; GYNEPHILIA; SEXUALITY

**ANDROGYNE** — A non-binary gender associated with androgyny.

Androgynes might define themselves as being transgender, genderqueer, non-binary, and/or any other gendered categories which are not exclusively masculine or feminine. They might have gender dysphoria, or not, and if they do, they may or may not choose to pursue medical intervention to change their bodies.

Androgyne has historically been used synonymously with "hermaphrodite," which is an outdated term (and reclaimed slur) for intersex.

*see also:* ANDROGYNOUS; TRANSGENDER; NON-BINARY; INTERSEX

**ANDROGYNOUS** — Neither decidedly masculine nor feminine.

Androgyny can be an ambiguous middle-ground between masculinity and femininity, or a combination of hyper-masculinity and hyper-femininity. Androgyny can refer to aesthetic, behavior, and internal sense of gender/self.

In our patriarchal society, which upholds masculinity as both the priority and the default, a soft masculine look is often labeled androgynous. Femininity is gendered, and masculinity is only named when it's taken to extremes.

*see also:* GENDER EXPRESSION; PATRIARCHY

**ANDROPHILIA** — Attraction to men or masculinity.

Part of an alternative model of sexuality to heterosexual and homosexual which does not make any reference to the subject's gender and instead focuses on the gender/gender expression of the people they're attracted to, along with gynephilia and ambiphilia.

*see also:* SEXUALITY; GYNEPHILIA; AMBIPHILIA

**ANTI-BLACK RACISM, ANTI-BLACKNESS** — A specific form of racism directed at Black people and Blackness.

Examples of anti-Blackness include: appropriating Black culture and Black liberation struggles; denial of Black identities which are not "simple" (e.g., Afro-Latinx, Afro-Caribbean, or any Black mixed race people); discrimination which positions Blackness as inferior to whiteness or non-Black people of color; institutional white supremacy, which benefits white people and, to a much lesser extent, non-Black people of color, at the expense of Black people; and denial of, and profit from, Black suffering. In short, anti-Blackness is racial injustice suffered by Black people.

In the aftermath of slavery, Blackness is still denied humanity, and by extension human gender and sexuality. To be Black is *a priori* to be gender non-conforming, because gender is constructed alongside/within white supremacy. Anti-Blackness also manifests as hyper-sexualization, fetishization, and tokenism.

Anti-Blackness is a queer issue and a queer problem. The LGBT+ image is whitewashed, and anti-Black racism is rife in queer communities.

Within and outwith queer communities, Black people and Black communities are falsely assumed to be more homophobic than non-Black people. The assumption that all Black people are monolithic in their attitudes about anything is itself racist, and this particular assumption manifests as erasure of Black queers, and justification for anti-Blackness in the name of queer liberation: that is, a white savior complex wherein white people see fit to educate Black people on queer culture and sensitivity. Blackness is painted as "uncivilized" for any iterations of homophobia while homophobic whiteness is euphemistically called "old fashioned."

*see also*: WHITE SUPREMACY; RACISM; OPPRESSION; CULTURAL APPROPRIATION; TOKEN; FETISHIZE; FASCISM

**ANTI-SEMITISM** — Hostility to, and prejudice against, Jews.

Anti-Semitism is a form of racialized oppression. Many Jews aren't white; and for white Jews, their whiteness is conditional. Jewishness isn't itself a race; it is both a religion and an ethnic group, but Jewishness is often racialized as an Other to whiteness. White supremacy targets Muslims and Jews as racialized groups and alleged threats to whiteness.

Anti-Semitism, like all bigotry, intersects with other systems of oppression. Anti-Semitism in the 20th century was closely tied to queerphobia; both Jews and queers were persecuted as undesirables during the Holocaust, along with the disabled, Romani people, ethnic Poles and other Slavs, Soviet citizens, Jehovah's witnesses, and anarchists and communists. Anti-Semitism was, and still is, a vehicle for policing gender and sexuality: any deviation from white, cisheteronormative gender and family structures is punished. The links between anti-Semitism, homophobia, transphobia, and fascism are deeply entrenched.

Queer Jews exist, though there is practically no positive representation of queer Jews. There is a false assumption that observant

Jews are forbidden from being queer, and that religious families are homogeneously queerphobic and will ostracize their queer children.

*see also:* ISLAMOPHOBIA; RACISM; FASCISM; OTHER

**APHOBIA** — Discrimination against asexual and aromantic people, particularly the exclusion of asexuals and aromantics from queer communities and discourses.

Aphobia is a particular strand of queerphobia: ace and aro people are at risk for the same violences suffered by other queer people, including discrimination, erasure, abuse, pathologization, and corrective rape.

On top of this, ace and aro people are assumed, by other queer people, to not experience oppression. Therefore asexuals and aromantics are denied entry into queer communities.

Amatonormativity—or the assumption and expectation that everyone seeks romantic love (which is generally, incorrectly, assumed to involve sexual desire by default) and prioritizes romance over other forms of intimacy—fuels aphobia.

Asexuals and aromantics are rendered invisible and their existence is denied.

Stereotypes about asexuals and aromantics are strikingly similar to other queerphobic stereotypes: "It's a phase," "You just haven't met the right person yet," "You're making it up for attention," "You just can't attract someone of the opposite sex." Ace and aro people are stereotyped as lonely, reclusive, nerdy, and socially incompetent.

Ace and aro people suffer specific kinds of discrimination based on their sexual and romantic orientations. Denying them access to queerness on the basis that it's "not the same" is weak, and implies, for example, that gay men and lesbians, don't have any shared struggle or oppression because they suffer different flavors of homophobic discrimination.

Ace and aro people are definitively queer, because their existence subverts heteronormativity. They eschew the expectations of their assigned gender roles—that they will fall in love with a person of the opposite sex, with whom they will reproduce—and like all queer people, they are punished for that deviance.

*see also:* ASEXUAL; AROMANTIC; AMATONORMATIVITY; INVISIBILITY

**ARO** — Short for AROMANTIC.

**AROMANTIC** — Someone who does not experience romantic attraction. Shortened to ARO.

Some aromantics are romance-repulsed, some aren't. Some aromantics are asexual, some aren't. Romantic attraction (or lack thereof) does not necessarily inform sexual attraction (or lack thereof).

Aromantic is one of the As in LGBTQIA+, along with asexual and agender. But there is contention about whether aromantic people who are both cisgender and heterosexual are part of the LGBT+ and queer communities.

The symbol for aromantic people is an (aro) arrow.

*see also:* AMATONORMATIVITY; QUEERPLATONIC; LGBT+; QUEER; ZUCCHINI

**ASEXUAL, ASEXUALITY** — A sexual orientation defined by a lack of sexual attraction. Often shortened to ACE.

Asexuality is an LGBT+ identity; the A in LGBTQIA+ is for asexual, agender, and aromantic. It's also a valid queer identity. Asexuals are not heterosexual, so they have a valid claim to LGBT+ and queerness. Cisgender hetero-romantic asexuals are still queer, and are not cishet. But, the queer community has a plurality of opinions and this is not consensus.

Asexuality is a form of gender transgression for not fulfilling the sexual aspects of their assigned gender role, which is why it is part of the LGBT+ group. Asexuality is contrary to cisheteronormativity, which implores a (usually/allegedly monogamous) sexual and romantic relationship between a cis man and a cis woman, which follows a particular love-marriage-children trajectory. The discrimination that asexuals (and aromantics) suffer is called "aphobia."

Asexuals do not always claim queerness, for the same reasons other LGBT+ people might not; plus, queer communities are often hyper-sexualized which, is alienating to aces. Many allosexual queers are rightly loud and proud of their sexualities, and being outspoken about it is subversive; but queer spaces tend to be dominated by cis white gay men, and are not made to be welcoming of asexuals (or people of color, or women, or trans people, or disabled people, or older people, or poor people).

Asexual people may or may not have sex, or masturbate; the term, like other sexualities, is defined not by practice but by (lack of) attraction. Asexuality is not synonymous with "abstinence" or "celibacy." It also doesn't mean that asexuals can't enjoy sex; it means they don't experience sexual attraction. Some asexuals enjoy sexual activity, and some are sex-repulsed. Arousal is not necessarily attraction; some aces have arousal and some don't. Lack of arousal is not a medical problem itself, though it can be a symptom of medical conditions. Because of this, asexuals are often pathologized.

There is an asexuality spectrum: allosexual (people who experience sexual attraction), asexual (no sexual attraction), gray asexual (rarely experience sexual attraction), and demisexual (only experience sexual attraction after an emotional bond is formed). Like other kinds of sexual identity, there is a lot of diversity among asexual people. Asexuals don't all experience sex and romance the same way, and their asexual identity will be informed by their other identities.

Sexual attraction or lack thereof should not be conflated with romantic attraction. Asexuals may or may not experience non-sexual forms of attraction: romantic, platonic, or aesthetic. Asexuals who experience romantic attraction will usually also identify with a sexuality label like "gay," "straight," "lesbian," or "bisexual" to describe their romantic attraction. Sexuality labels only work if they are self-defined; there is no "test" for asexuality. It's up to individuals to self-define and labels of asexuality should not be coercively applied to people.

Asexuals are just as whole, complete, and capable as everyone else of having fulfilling loving relationships, romantic or otherwise. Asexuals have emotional needs and form emotional bonds.

Asexuality is not a "choice," the same way being gay or trans isn't a choice—which is to say, it actually can be a choice, and that would be valid, but generally it's considered innate. Asexuality as a result of trauma, or doing sex work ("circumstantial asexuality") is also valid. Discovering "why" someone is queer (including ace) is a bad project which fuels eugenics and does nothing to help queer people. Asexuals don't need to be cured or "find the right person"; conversion therapy and corrective rape are extremely violent and harmful.

Asexuals suffer queerphobic discrimination and ace-specific discrimination: for example, the assumption that sexual attraction is an inherent part of romance or being human. In heteronormative culture, asexuals are made to feel broken or lacking. Asexuality is infantilized; asexuals are coded as immature because sexual attraction is part of the heteronormative narrative of growing up. Asexuals are assumed to be cold or uncaring because sex is hailed as the ultimate form of intimacy, in a false equivalence of sex and love. Asexuals are also assumed to be dorky because sexual prowess and seduction are "cool" and validating. There is basically no decent representation of asexuals in popular media.

*see also*: LGBT+; SEXUALITY; GRAY ASEXUALITY; DEMISEXUAL; APHOBIA; ALLOSEXUAL

**ASSIGNED FEMALE AT BIRTH (AFAB)** — A sex assignment given to newborns whose genitals are perceived to be female-typical, or whose genitals are "ambiguous" but "closer" to a vagina than a penis.

Alternative terms are "Coercively Assigned Female At Birth (CAFAB)," "Designated Female At Birth (DFAB)," and "Female Assigned At Birth (FAAB)."

Being assigned female at birth comes with social expectations of cisgender girlhood and heterosexual womanhood.

Using sex assignment at birth can be useful for grouping people together who have shared experiences, but this utility is limited: not everyone who is AFAB, and not even everyone who is trans and AFAB, or cis and AFAB, has a shared experience of gender. Grouping people together based on sex assignment is also alienating for many trans and intersex people who don't want their sex assignment to define them.

Alternatives for talking about the different experiences and struggles shared by trans people who were AFAB include "trans masc" or "trans masculine," and "transmisogyny exempt", but these phrases too have their own problems. Most of the time, especially when referring to an individual, it's more appropriate to mirror the self-described gender(s) of the people in question.

*see also*: COERCIVELY ASSIGNED FEMALE AT BIRTH; DESIGNATED FEMALE AT BIRTH; FEMALE ASSIGNED AT BIRTH; SEX (n.); GENDER; CISHETERONORMATIVITY; TRANSGENDER; TRANSMISOGYNY EXEMPT

**ASSIGNED MALE AT BIRTH (AMAB)** — A sex assigned to newborns whose genitals are perceived to be male-typical, or whose genitals are "ambiguous" but "closer" to a penis than a vagina.

Alternative terms are "Coercively Assigned Male At Birth (CAMAB)," "Designated Male At Birth (DMAB)," and "Male Assigned At Birth (MAAB)."

Being assigned male comes with social expectations of cisgender boyhood and heterosexual manhood.

Using sex assignment at birth can be useful for grouping people together who have shared experiences, but this utility is limited: not everyone who is AMAB, and not even everyone who is trans and AMAB, or cis and AMAB, has a shared experience of gender. Grouping people together based on sex assignment is also alienating for many trans and intersex people who don't want their sex assignment to define them.

Alternatives for talking about the different experiences and struggles shared by trans people who were AMAB include "trans femme" or "trans feminine," and "transmisogyny affected", but these phrases too have their own problems. Most of the time, especially when referring to an individual, it's more appropriate to mirror the self-described gender(s) of the people in question.

*see also:* COERCIVELY ASSIGNED MALE AT BIRTH; DESIGNATED MALE AT BIRTH; MALE ASSIGNED AT BIRTH; SEX (n.); GENDER; CISHETERONORMATIVITY; TOXIC MASCULINITY; TRANSGENDER; TRANSMISOGYNY AFFECTED

**ASSIMILATION** — The expectation that marginalized people emulate, rather than deviate from, the norms of the hegemonic group, including obscuring or erasing their differences.

Assimilation is a political tactic used by persecuted groups to make themselves seem palatable and "normal" to their oppressors, with the aim of gaining equal rights or ending discrimination. Assimilation maintains the status quo instead of challenging it: it further delineates who is "deviant" and excluded from rights or protections, instead of removing structures which deny people full personhood. Assimilation is also constantly encouraged by the oppressive groups, because deviance is considered threatening and is therefore punished on both systemic and interpersonal levels.

One key tactic of assimilation is for an oppressed group to distance itself from a more vulnerable oppressed group; for example, cis gay people distancing themselves from trans people despite an interlocked history. White, educated, middle-class cis gay and lesbian people have become the face of the LGBT+ movement, despite being both a minority within the group and the least vulnerable people in the group, and being the least instrumental in starting the political movement or fighting for LGBT+ rights. In short, assimilation is adjusting the hierarchies of an oppressive system without making any change to the system itself.

It's bad political praxis to focus on gaining rights and protections for the most palatable/least vulnerable people in the hope that it will "trickle down," or that it's only politically possible to focus on the most "acceptable" people of the out-group. Instead we must focus on protecting the most marginalized, the least acceptable members of society. This disrupts the cultural hegemony of the privileged rather than expanding it to include only-slightly-different people, as well as more dramatically shifting the Overton window of ideas tolerated in public discourse.

The assimilationist line of "It's not our fault we're like this, we'll do our best to be like you" frames difference as inferior and pitiable. Anti-assimilation is a political counter-tactic. The anti-assimilationist killjoy demands access to public life and equal rights without politely integrating themselves into the hegemonic culture which excludes them. The killjoy knows that there is no amount of assimilation which will make them, the Other, acceptable enough to be "worthy" of equal treatment.

*see also:* HOMONORMATIVE; TRANSMILITARISM; HOMO-NATIONALISM; LGBT+ RIGHTS; RESPECTABILITY; OTHER; ACTIVISM

**AUTISM, AUTISTIC** — A cognitive developmental difference, or a neurotype, pathologized as a mental disorder, characterized by difficulty with normative social interactions and communication.

Autistic is synonymous with "neurodivergent" or "neuroatypical," its opposite being "neurotypical." Autism is a non-linear spectrum. It is not a disease.

Autistic adults are assumed to be asexual and are infantilized, which is a form of ableism.

There is a lot of interest in the high correlation between autism and gender dysphoria. But, finding a "biological" connection or a gene for autism or transness is a bad project which benefits eugenists, not trans or autistic people.

*see also:* ALLISTIC; NEURODIVERGENT; NEUROTYPICAL; PATHOLOGIZE; FASCISM

**AUTOGYNEPHILIA** — A pathology given to assigned male at birth people who fantasize about being attractive to women. Used to delegitimize the womanhood of trans women.

This fantasy is extremely common among cis women, yet is only considered a "paraphilia" (mental illness) for trans women, AMAB trans people, and men, because the psychiatric community has historically seen women as not experiencing paraphilia and sees all AMAB people as men.

Autogynephilia appeared in the *DSM-5* under "transvestic disorder." It's used by TERFs to undermine trans women's identities as women, and suggest that trans women are perverse men who fetishize womanhood.

Autogynephilia fits into a broader transmisogynistic cultural narrative about trans women and trans feminine people being perverse threats to cis womanhood, and by extension dangerous to cis women. The pathology is used to deny trans people self-determination of the genders, and vilify trans women and AMAB trans people as predatory men, despite all evidence showing that trans people are far more likely to be victims than perpetrators of abuse and assault.

Both the term and the formal diagnosis have been discredited by the modern psychiatric community and the trans community more broadly. The notable exception is "gender critical" psychiatrists who use conversion therapy tactics despite them violating the norms of best practice.

A more accurate, less pathologizing and less stigmatizing term to describe erotic thoughts based on being a woman is "female/feminine embodiment fantasies," coined by trans writer and biologist Julia Serano.

*see also:* TRANSMISOGYNY; TERF; CONVERSION THERAPY; GENDER CRITICAL

# B

B — The B in LGBT+ is for BISEXUAL and BIGENDER. The B in BDSM is for BONDAGE.

**BATHHOUSE** — A gay public sex venue.

Before indoor plumbing was common, bathhouses were public spaces for people to bathe. As showers and toilets become the norm in homes, bathhouses became spaces for men to cruise. Sometimes they're saunas; sometimes they're bathrooms in gyms.

Bathhouses are not only public sex venues; they're also community and social spaces, many doubling as gyms, performance venues, and dance clubs. Bathhouses tend to be more social than other physical gay cruising spaces, like cottages or parks.

The role of bathhouses in modern gay culture is shifting as people increasingly use online spaces for cruising and private spaces for group sex. Public sex venues became less popular in the 1980s during the AIDS crisis, and although they experienced a short resurgence they are less popular again now. Monied queers are hosting private parties in their apartments and hired-out venues, or in private members' clubs which boast exclusive lists and membership fees of $150+. Bathhouses have connotations of shame and stigma and dark secret encounters; private parties are luxurious and are somehow both more exclusive and communal. The decline of genuinely public sex spaces locks out low-income people and anyone who lacks the social capital to network their way into an exclusive event.

Agism may also be a factor. Younger people have new modes of cruising and navigating anonymous sex, and are not necessarily invested in keeping physical spaces open because they don't have the same utility to them. Is it worth it, history for history's sake? Some young people reject everything tied with history because it's old, and old people are seen as gross.

But older queers still use bathhouses. Like gay bars, bathhouses are closing not because people aren't using them, but because gentrification and rising rents are making them unsustainable as businesses.

Bathhouses are also targeted by legislation which effectively criminalizes queerness and perceived sexual deviancy under the guise of sanity or hygiene laws.

*see also:* COTTAGING; CRUISING; GAY BAR

**BATHROOM BILLS** — Legislation which mandates that people use gendered public bathrooms which correspond to their gender assigned at birth, or the gender on their birth certificate.

Bathroom bills are designed to exclude trans people from public space, under the pretense of protecting cis women and children from predatory men (and trans women, who are maliciously conflated with men). Bathroom bills are an example of institutional transphobia, but they disproportionately affect trans women and other trans people who are read as gender non-conforming "males."

Bathroom bills are an example of the cis obsession with trans genitals. Moral panic about trans people being allowed access to bathrooms is based on the biological essentialist idea that trans people are not "really" their declared gender—especially the idea that trans women are "really" men—and that predatory men are eager to legitimately gain access to women's spaces (bathrooms) to assault "real" women and children. This legislation is premised on the assumption that the only barrier to dangerous men assaulting women in bathrooms is the social norms which deny them access to women's spaces; as though predatory men fear the consequences of crossing an abstract "no boys allowed" line more than the consequences of physically assaulting someone; as though allowing trans people to use the right bathroom will result in a flood of violent men storming women's spaces.

There is not a single recorded incident of a cis person being assaulted in a bathroom as the result of trans inclusivity. There are, however, many incidents of trans people being assaulted by cis people in bathrooms, demanding to see their genitals or the gender markers on their IDs. Butch cis women have also been assaulted in bathrooms by transphobes because they are gender non-conforming and were mistaken for trans women.

Bathroom bills cannot be effectively enforced, but they nonetheless contribute to a culture of transphobia where gender non-conforming people are targeted as deviant and dangerous, and trans people are unable to use public spaces. The most recent US Transgender Survey (2015) found that in the past year:

- 24% of trans people had their presence questioned in a bathroom.
- 9% were denied access to a bathroom; higher for people of color, up to 18% for Native Americans.
- 12% were verbally or physically assaulted in a bathroom; higher for multiracial people at 16%, and Native Americans at 24%.
- 0.6% were sexually assaulted in a public bathroom, most of them currently working in an underground economy and/or trans women of color.
- 59% avoided using public bathrooms for fear of confrontation. Trans men reported much higher avoidance of public bathrooms at 75%, compared to trans women and non-binary people, both at 53%. Undocumented trans residents reported avoiding public bathrooms at 72%.
- 32% limited their food and drink consumption to avoid using public bathrooms.
- 8% reported having a urinary or kidney-related problem as the result of avoiding using public bathrooms.

Bathroom bills are not about bathrooms, but about access to public space and policing gender non-conformity. The result isn't a "safer," trans-free environment for cis people, but increased violence directed at trans people and legitimate trans anxieties which contribute to disordered eating and kidney-related health complications.

see also: TRANSPHOBIA; TRANSMISOGYNY; CIS GAZE

**BAREBACK** — Gay slang for having sex without a condom.

There is stigma and slut-shaming for gay people who bareback because of the HIV/AIDS crisis, when HIV was transmitted largely through condom-less sex.

Condoms are one safer sex tool among several; they're very effective at preventing HIV transmission and transmission of other sexually transmitted infections (STIs), as well as preventing pregnancy. But, they are not the only effective method for preventing HIV transmission or pregnancy. For HIV-negative people, taking pre-exposure prophylaxis (PrEP) is as effective as using condoms in preventing HIV. And, if an HIV-positive person is undetectable (i.e., their viral load is undetectable), there is no risk of them transmitting HIV.

Condoms and other barriers like dental dams and gloves are the only safer sex method to prevent transmission of other STIs, like gonorrhea, syphilis, chlamydia, and herpes. People who report using condoms "sometimes" are just as at risk for STIs as people who report never using condoms. If you don't use condoms every time you have sex, you should consider using other methods of HIV prevention and birth control.

*see also:* CONDOM; SAFER SEX; PrEP; UNDETECTABLE

**BDSM** — Acronym for a set of kinky sexual power relations: B&D (Bondage & Discipline), D/s (Dominance/submission), s/M (slave/Master), S&M (Sadism & Masochism).

BDSM is a broad range of practices, fetishes, and subcultures, which relies on the informed consent of all involved partners and onlookers. While the BDSM scene is very queer, being kinky or interested in BDSM does not inherently make someone queer; cisgender heterosexual people who engage in BDSM shouldn't be claiming queerness on the basis of their kinks.

Same-sex attractions and behaviors were pathologized in 19th- and 20th-century psychology. All non-procreative sexual desire and behavior, along with gender non-conformity (which inherently includes any same-sex attraction), were moralized as "perverse," dangerous, and unhealthy. With that pathologization, queer people were denied intimacy in normative settings. While BDSM practices have probably been in use for as long as people have been having sex, BDSM as a social and semi-public scene in the US and Western Europe developed in the aftermath of World War I.

BDSM was a safe alternative for sexual intimacy without fluid exchange during the AIDS crisis. The BDSM scene in the 1980s campaigned to make safer sex (sex with condoms and barriers) kinky and sexy. In an erotic setting where there are already lots of accessories—harnesses, ropes, boots, uniforms, implements—rolling on a condom was framed as a sexy part of the process. BDSM was also a scene where people developed and popularized sex acts which didn't involve fluid exchange, such as fisting (penetration with a fist rather than a phallus), finger docking (fingering the inside of the foreskin, giving the effect of penetration), and sounding (penetrating the urethra).

BDSM was a very kinky, bent, not-straight scene until the 1990s when it was effectively co-opted by straight cis people looking to spice up their sex lives. BDSM was, and in many places still is, a safe scene to explore sexual and gender non-conformity, cross-dressing, and transness. For trans people who have dysphoria and need to basically dissociate from their bodies in order to make it through the day, there is something very liberating about being very physically present without having your gender questioned.

BDSM practices may be frowned upon in normative settings, but in kinky communities they're given a pass without any self-reflection or analysis of power. For instance, the language of "slave/Master" is pretty tasteless: kinky communities are overwhelmingly white and whitewashed because of this very insensitivity, along with racial fetishizations, and there are other words which can be used in place of "slave" which don't carry intergenerational trauma for people of color.

Similarly, the insistence of some kinky people that being kinky is a queer identity itself, even if you're cisgender and heterosexual, conflates private sexual deviance (BDSM) and structural violence against queer people. Cishets are not systemically punished, attacked, or denied access to public life for being kinky.

The assertion of kinkiness as a queer identity (like polyamory as a queer identity) often comes from straight cis men who enjoy dominating women, or cishet women who enjoy submitting to men; but neither of those practices deviate from cisheteronormative gender roles for men and women, so should hardly be considered kinky, let alone queer.

*see also*: KINKY; PERVERT; LEATHER; SAFER SEX; CONDOMS; SEX POSITIVITY

**B**

**BEAR** — A gay archetype: a queer man who is big and hairy.

Bearness is a combination of gender expression, gender identity, and sexuality, comparable to other "gay genders" like twink, otter, bulldyke, or lipstick lesbian. A straight man who is big and hairy isn't a bear, and neither is anyone who doesn't identify with the bearness.

Bears are their own distinct subculture within the gay scene, and have been holding bear-specific events and developing a bear culture since the 1970s. Bears tend to project an image of rugged masculinity, but there is intra-community debate on what exactly constitutes a bear, and on the acceptability of femininity among bears and gay men in general.

Being a bear implicitly means that the bear is a queer man or queer masculine person, but it does not indicate anything about preferred partners or sexual roles; that is, a bear can be a top, vers, or bottom.

*see also:* CUB; TWINK; OTTER; GAY CULTURE; GAY; MASC 4 MASC

**BEARD** — Slang for an ostensibly romantic or sexual partnership which is used to conceal one's deviance from cisheteronormativity.

Beards are socially necessary in times and social groups with compulsory heterosexuality, when queers would be punished if they were out or if they were "suspiciously" single.

There are different kinds of beard "arrangements." Some beards are facades arranged explicitly in solidarity between a straight-appearing couple, with the mutual understanding that they are not genuinely together.

Some beards don't realize that they are a beard because their partner is closeted; sometimes someone is called a beard if their friends or the public think that their partner is secretly queer. Closeted queer men in particular have been vilified for concealing their sexual orientation from the women they date, because both queer masculinity and unmarried womanhood are taboo.

*see also:* CISHETERONORMATIVITY; HOMOPHOBIA

**BENT** — An opposite term to "straight." Used in the UK as slang for "queer."

*see also:* STRAIGHT; KINK; QUEER

**BI** — Short for BISEXUAL.

**BI-CURIOUS** — Someone who considers themselves heterosexual but has a sexual or romantic "curiosity" toward the same gender.

Some people find it difficult to relinquish the label "heterosexual," because our society is heteronormative and punishes deviance from that norm. A person saying that they're bi-curious is a less committal choice than claiming bisexuality. The same person might also opt to call themselves "mostly straight" rather than bisexual, even though bisexuality does not necessarily mean an equal attraction to multiple genders.

*see also*: HETEROFLEXIBLE; BISEXUAL

**BIGENDER** — Someone who has two genders.

A bigender person's gender might be binary, man and woman; or they could be any combination of genders. Some bigender people experience their genders as distinct and discrete; others experience both their genders simultaneously.

Because bigender people are not solely and unambiguously the gender they were assigned at birth, they fall under the transgender umbrella label. Other gender labels which could describe a bigender person include: "genderqueer," "demi-boy," "demi-girl," and "non-binary." As with all gendered terms, it's up to everyone to self-define which labels fit their experience of gender.

*see also*: TRANSGENDER

**BINARY** — A division of two discrete groups which are considered to be opposites.

Binaries are sometimes helpful, but usually reductive. Binaries implicitly suggest that there are only two, distinct, ways of being; there is no space in-between the two categories, no spectrum, and no movement between them. Trans theory embraces the liminality—the ambiguous space between binaries—and intersectionality, the complex relationships between multiple identities.

Dualisms have long been used as justifications for hierarchy and oppression. Here are some binaries which underscore the cisheteronormative patriarchal capitalist white supremacy we all live in:

- man/woman
- straight/gay

- white/black
- rich/poor
- boss/worker
- masculine/feminine
- liberation/oppression
- dominant/submissive
- top/bottom
- West/East, or West/Orient
- North/South
- adult/child
- sane/insane
- abled/disabled
- neurotypical/neurodivergent
- cis/trans
- self/Other
- body/mind
- healthy/unhealthy
- thin/fat
- natural/unnatural
- natural/artificial
- citizen/immigrant
- privileged/oppressed

The binaries above are false dichotomies. There is no middle ground or gray area acknowledged between them; they are mutually constituted and defined in opposition to each other. One is normal and the default, and one is the Other. Normal is good, understood, knowable, correct; Other is weird, deviant, unknowable, wrong. Some of the hegemonic Selfs are so normalized that their words are not commonly used or understood, like abled, cis, and neurotypical.

*see also:* GENDER BINARY; SEX (n.); NON-BINARY; INTER-SECTIONALITY

**BINDER, BINDING** — A binder is a piece of clothing designed to bind the chest for a flatter appearance. Binding is the practice of flattening one's chest with clothing or bandages.

Binding is done by anyone who wants to flatten their chest or change their silhouette. Trans people, butches, drag kings, and cosplayers are some of the people who bind. Binding can help alleviate dysphoria for trans people, and so should be considered an aspect of trans healthcare.

It's important to bind safely to avoid damage to your ribs. Binders are a safer method of binding than using bandages. Bandages are designed to constrict and get tighter as you exhale, making it harder to breathe in again. Only wear a binder for a maximum of eight hours at a time, and avoid sleeping in it.

*see also:* TRANSGENDER; TRANS HEALTHCARE

**BIOLOGICAL ESSENTIALISM** — The notion that there is a biological reality or "essence" of gender and sex; that sex is a naturally occurring, rather than socially defined, truth innate to everybody. It relies heavily on the gender binary, and does not account for the spectrum of biological sexual characteristics.

Biological essentialists might concede that gender is a social construct, but they insist that biological sex is "real" and scientifically objective. Both gender and sex are social constructs, meaning that our understanding of them is socially constructed, not that they're fake, negligible, or immaterial.

Biological essentialism posits that all of our social experiences of identity can be explained by and reduced to our biology (hormones, brain, genes). It's objectifying and reductive, and incorrect. It's also fatalistic: it implies that our identities, and our experiences of gender and sexuality, are predetermined from birth by our biology.

"Nature versus nurture" is a false binary. Our biology influences the way people perceive us (which they are taught), which contributes to our social conditions. And, our biology isn't static: our experiences and environments change our brains, and many trans people change other parts of their bodies to be more aligned with their genders, including hormones which affect our moods and emotions. Our biology and our environment are constantly informing and shaping each other.

Mind–body dualism is rejected by most modern biologists, cognitive scientists, and psychiatrists. The "born in the wrong body" narrative to explain transness is unsophisticated and doesn't describe the experience of many trans people, but it was adopted because it was simple and gave us political traction.

B

Biological essentialism is used to bolster bigotry. It's been used to suggest that women are inherently inferior to men, that people of color are inherently inferior to white people, and to target queer and trans people.

Biological essentialists position queerness as "unnatural": they point to the "biological imperative" to reproduce, which is assumed to belong solely to straight cis people. Many queers can reproduce with their bodies, and many people, queer or not, reproduce the self through adopting children, or by means entirely unrelated to children.

Biological essentialism is used by so-called "radical feminists" to invalidate trans people, especially trans women and non-binary people affected by transmisogyny. They suggest that everyone assigned male at birth is afforded unalienable male privilege on the basis of their body, and everyone assigned female is oppressed on the basis of that assignment. This analysis assumes that all people assigned male at birth are always and forevermore perceived as male, and that they unconditionally benefit from the systemic oppression of women (patriarchy), and that their "male" bodies (i.e., their penises and testosterone-dominant hormones) make them inherently male and inherently violent toward women. This is the same logic which insists that sexual violence is inevitable because men "can't control themselves." All of these assumptions are weaponized to deny trans people civil rights, under the guise of protecting cis women. However, these arguments are extremely porous and don't hold up under scrutiny. Trans women and other AMAB trans people do not have male privilege, because they are not male; instead they suffer a combination of transphobia and misogyny (called "transmisogyny"), which includes additional threats of violence that cis women don't face.

Sexism and misogyny don't simply stem from a hierarchy of genitals. Having a penis does not mean having a "biological" privilege; any privilege arising from having a penis is conditional on being cis. There are some pro-trans rights arguments which say that genitals are un-readable in public, and therefore people aren't oppressed on the basis of their genitals, but this isn't strictly true. Many trans people make efforts to change the appearance of their genitals by packing or tucking, because it helps them pass. Feminine people with bulges in their skirts are treated like public fetish objects, in the same way that any feminine person in public becomes object, but amplified. Everyone who isn't a cis man will face degrees of medical neglect and social discrimination on the basis

THE A–Z OF GENDER AND SEXUALITY

of their gender. Likewise, they will have to fight for their reproductive rights and their bodily autonomy in general. Tying gender to body parts (usually, tying womanhood to vaginas, uteruses, menstruation, and the potential for pregnancy) looks suspiciously like misogyny.

Biological essentialists argue that trans people are not "genetically" their gender. Gender isn't genetic, and the gendered aspects of biology cannot be reduced to chromosomes. Biological essentialism basically asserts that a trans person is not possible: we cannot have both "female" reproductive organs and "male" hormone balances; we cannot have both penises and breasts. But we do.

An opposing approach to understanding sex and gender is bio-psychosocial, which posits that biology, psychology, and sociality are overlapping, and that it is not possible (nor desirable) to disentangle them. This is one aspect of queer biology. One example is Sari van Anders' work, which shows that our neuroendocrinology (hormone levels in our brains, such as testosterone) can both alter and be altered by our behavior.

The problem with biological essentialism is that it's reductive and perpetuates harmful myths, not that it denotes a physical difference between bodies. Trans people are not in denial about the differences between our bodies and cis bodies. Sometimes we use language to describe our bodies that cis people don't understand; but it is not to dilute meaning from the words, it's to more comfortably and accurately discuss our bodies.

Most of the time when you're talking about gender, you don't need to include comments about biology or body parts. So don't.

*see also:* SEX (n.); TRANSMISOGYNY; TERF

**BIOLOGICAL SEX** — *see:* SEX (n.).

**BIOPOLITICS** — The intersection of biology and politics. The social and political power over life. Politics of the body.

Biopolitics is a wide term encompassing biotechnology, eugenics, race theory and scientific racism, the body as a political weapon (e.g., suicide bombing), and environmentalism. Foucault used it to refer to the application and impact of political power on all aspects of human life.

The social contract—the state will protect and the citizens will participate, pay taxes, and sacrifice their bodies to war—is obsolete. There is no opting out, and the state will kill you if you try. Stateless people are extremely precarious: Palestinians, Kurds, any diaspora, refugees, and asylum seekers being some examples.

The state regulates the body: healthcare, sexual practices, environmental issues, and disaster relief (or lack thereof). The state has tried to regulate trans people and queer people out of existence, through lack of healthcare (AIDS crisis, trans healthcare), queerphobic adoption policies, and criminalizing queerness. The state also uses biopolitics to target people of color, women, poor people, and disabled people, and makes their lives less livable.

Biopolitical resistance is happening all around us. It's in indigenous movements, squatting, food banks, communal childcare practices, and queer porn. Any act which empowers marginalized people (including yourself) to live more full and dignified lives is an act of biopolitical resistance.

*see also:* HIV; TRANS HEALTHCARE; FASCISM

**BIPHOBIA** — Fear of, or contempt for, bisexuals. Behavior based on those feelings. A system of oppression in which bisexuals are marginalized and subject to violence.

Biphobia is the denial that bisexuality is valid, and the association of bisexuality with negative stereotypes or behaviors. It's also called "monosexism," which more broadly enforces a hetero/homo binary that alienates bisexuals and asexuals.

Bisexuals experience discrimination from both straight and queer communities. Biphobia takes the form of outright violence and discrimination, fetishization, and erasure. There are unique discriminations, stereotypes, and assumptions around bisexuality which make bisexuals vulnerable. Biphobia also affects people who are pansexual, polysexual, and other queer sexualities which are not asexual or exclusively monosexual.

Bisexuality is subject to many stereotypes and misconceptions. Bisexuality does not require an equal attraction to different genders: you can be bisexual if you're mostly attracted to one gender, but also occasionally attracted to others. Likewise, bisexuality doesn't require sexual experience with more than one gender (or any): it's about attraction, not behavior. Bisexuals are bisexual regardless of who they're in a relationship with. Bi people cannot be in a "straight" relationship because they are not straight—however, the dynamics of bisexuals being in a "gay," "lesbian," or "queer" relationship are more complicated, and a bi person may choose to describe their relationship that way whilst still asserting their bisexuality.

Biphobia is a particular aspect of homophobia/queerphobia, and shares many of the same characteristics as monosexual homophobia: assuming bi people want to pass as straight; assuming bisexuals are just seeking attention; fetishizing and objectifying bisexual women; lack of access to, and representation in, public life; and physical and emotional violence.

Like other queerphobias, there is the assumption that bisexuality is a phase; but both queer and straight communities perpetuate the idea that bisexuals will eventually "settle down" and "pick a side" of either being gay or straight. Bisexuals are assumed to be "greedy," promiscuous, and incapable of monogamy. This overlaps with stereotypes about gay men, but bisexuals are also assumed to be unsatisfied unless they are in sexual relationships with men and women. Of course, bisexuals are no more or less likely to be promiscuous or non-monogamous than other people.

Biphobia is gendered. Bisexual women are especially fetishized, and bisexual men are especially vilified. Bisexuality is more acceptable in women because it caters to heterosexual men's fantasy about women having sex with women; the existence of bisexual men is itself a threat to the fragile heterosexuality of the straight man, who is afraid of being hit on and seduced by another man. One common manifestation of biphobia is the "seeking bisexual unicorn girl" on dating apps, which fetishizes bisexual women as promiscuous fuck toys for straight-man-heteroflexible-woman couples to project their fantasies onto; she is a unicorn because she's not real, just a fantasy. In the 1980s and 1990s bisexual men were demonized for "spreading AIDS and HIV" to straight women, when their bisexuality was less of a factor than the complete lack of access to both healthcare and safer sex information about HIV/AIDS and women. Bisexual men are also fetishized by straight women, albeit to a lesser extent than bisexual women are fetishized by straight men.

Bisexuals are rarely represented in the media, and most representations are biphobic: bisexuals are portrayed as violent and mentally ill; ruthless seducers; or cheaters and betrayers to straightness, gayness, and their partners. The implication is that bisexuality is selfish, amoral, and hedonistic.

Bisexuals are also under-represented and under-served in queer communities, even though bisexuals (or, queer people who are not exclusively homosexual) outnumber gays and lesbians. Bisexuals lack our own community because we have such little and poor representation, so we tend to identify with a gay community or a straight community instead. We're also pressured, from straight and queer communities, to blend into monosexuality.

One key factor of biphobia is that bisexuals are erased when they're in relationships with people of the same gender and assumed to be gay, or a different gender and assumed to be straight.

When bisexuals are assumed to be straight, some people consider this "straight passing privilege," which allows bi people to avoid direct violence and discrimination; but erasure is its own violence, and the absence of violence is premised on denial of their bisexuality. Biphobia also includes telling bisexuals that they don't have a legitimate "queer experience" if they are assumed to be straight.

Being an outsider and rejected by the in-group of people who are supposed to be like you is more painful and emotionally damaging than being rejected by mainstream society. Bisexuals face this rejection from the queer community (as do queer people of color, fat queers, and queers who are alienated by queer culture such as poor queers, disabled queers, and sober queers). Some gay people assert that bisexual men are homophobic and afraid to claim their gayness. "Gold star" gays and lesbians are monosexual gays who have never had sex or relationships with people of the opposite sex; this positions bisexuality below monosexuality in a hierarchy of "authentic" queerness. Many gay people refuse to date bisexuals because they are "tainted" with a less legitimate queerness, or because the monosexual fears that the bisexual isn't earnest in their queerness and will eventually "return" to heteronormativity.

Bisexuals are more likely than gays, lesbians, and heterosexuals to suffer from: mood and anxiety disorders like depression; hypertension; smoking; risky drinking; and suicidal ideation. Bisexual women who are in a relationship with a monosexual person are more likely to suffer domestic violence. Bisexuals are less likely to come out to their healthcare providers, and by extension are more likely to get incomplete safer sex information. Bisexuals are likely to earn less than straight people, lesbians, and gay people; and they are more likely to live in poverty.

Bisexuals suffer these discriminations and violences regardless of whether they are read accurately as bisexual or inaccurately as monosexually gay or straight. Bisexuals don't have "straight privilege."

In the 80s bisexuality was excluded from research on sexuality, deemed to be "secondary homosexuality." In 2005, a study called "Sexual Arousal Patterns of Bisexual Men" allegedly "proved" that bisexuality in men does not exist. The media jumped on it, claiming to have "solved the problem of bisexuality."

Subsequent studies, including by the original author, have proved it wrong. Even today, cishet and LGBT+ publications alike fail to account for bisexuality, and bisexuals are often not included in research on sexuality. A recent trend is speculating why so many "straight" men have "gay" sex with other men, whist completely evading the possibility of bisexuality as an explanation.

In 2015, biphobia was added to the name of the International Day Against Homophobia, Biphobia, Intersexism, and Transphobia (IDAHOBIT), which falls on May 17 every year. It was previously named the International Day Against Homophobia and Transphobia (IDAHOT), and was started in 2005 as the International Day Against Homophobia (IDAHO).

The word "bisexual" is subject to unique scrutiny. People get fixated on "bi = 2" and implore that bisexuality is therefore a "binary" sexuality meaning attraction to the "same" and "opposite" genders, or men and women. Bisexuals do not reinforce the gender binary by claiming the label "bisexual." "Bi" can mean "two," but also means "twice," as in "bimonthly." Likewise, "oct" means eight but October is the tenth month in the year; we're able to appreciate that the meaning of words isn't necessarily anchored to their original meanings or etymologies.

Despite not really being any more problematic a term than "gay" and "lesbian," "bisexual" gets scrutinized, dissected, and problematized to a much higher degree. Biphobia pressures bisexuals (and people who aren't hetero or homosexual) to reject "bisexual" as a label and instead pick something less "problematic," to "pick a side" (hetero/homo), or to reject labels altogether. This further divides what could be a bisexual community. Extra scrutiny of "bisexual" forces us to constantly defend our label of choice.

There are other, newer words to describe bisexuality which some people prefer: "pansexual," "polysexual," and "omnisexual" among them. But "bisexual" is still extremely relevant and has a long history of activism. It's the most commonly understood sexuality to describe attraction which isn't limited to one gender. "Queer" also encompasses bisexuality. We should totally embrace having new words to describe things as complex as sexuality, but in activism and forming community there is value in highlighting similarities as well as differences, and building solidarity based on those similarities (e.g., "gay" or "queer" to encompass all LGBTQIA+ identities). Having an umbrella term is valuable when we face erasure and invisibility.

Like all systems of oppression, biphobia intersects with other marginalizations: classism, racism, ableism, misogyny, agism, transphobia, and fatphobia.

*see also:* BISEXUAL; ERASURE; REPRESENTATION; FETISHIZE; GAZE; PASSING; GOLD STAR GAY; PANSEXUAL

**BISEXUAL** — Someone who is attracted to more than one gender, someone who is attracted to two or more genders, someone who is attracted to the same and other genders, or someone who is attracted to people regardless of their gender.

Bisexual is both a noun ("She's a bisexual") and an adjective ("He's bisexual"). It's the B in LGBT+.

The definition of bisexual has shifted from its older meaning, "Someone who is attracted to the same and opposite genders." All major bisexual organizations now use an updated definition, which allows the term to include non-binary people.

Until the late 1800s, the word bisexual was interchangeable with "hermaphrodite" (a term now outdated and rejected in favor of "intersex"). The first use of bisexual to describe sexual attraction was in American neurologist Charles Gilbert Chaddock's 1892 translation of Richard Freiherr von Krafft-Ebing's *Psychopathia Sexualis* (1886). Alfred Kinsey's research in the 1940s and 1950s popularized the concept of bisexuality, even though he rejected the modern use of the word.

Bisexuals are the largest single group in the LGBT+ community.

Because of biphobia and bisexual erasure, bisexuality is often interpreted as homosexuality. In an American study from 2013, four in ten LGB adults surveyed identified as bi (with 30% identifying as gay men, and 19% identifying as lesbians).

Bisexuals were and are very involved in LGBT+ rights movements, and civil rights movements more broadly. Bi activist Stephen Donaldson (aka Donny the Punk) founded the Student Homophile League at Columbia University in 1966, and the university recognized it in 1967, making it the first officially recognized queer student group. Brenda Howard, an active member of the Gay Liberation Front and considered the "mother of Pride" for her role in coordinating a rally to commemorate the one-year anniversary in 1970 of the Stonewall riots, was a bi activist.

The modern bisexual political movement began in the 1970s. In 1972 the National Bisexual Liberation group was founded in New York City by bi activist Don Fass; they issued "The Bisexual Expression," most likely the earliest bisexual newsletter. The same year, a Quaker group called the Committee of Friends on Bisexuality issued their "Ithaca Statement on Bisexuality" in support of bisexuals. In January 1977, one of the first pieces of successful gay rights anti-discrimination legislation in the US was passed in Dade County, Florida, after successful campaigning by Alan Rockway, a psychologist and bi activist who co-authored the ordinance; this was a short-lived victory and the ordinance was replaced on 7 June that year following a national anti-gay rights campaign led by Anita Bryant and wasn't reinstated until 1 December 1998. In 1979, the first black gay delegation to meet with White House staff was organized by A. Billy S. Jones, who was a bisexual and a founding member of the National Coalition of Black Lesbians and Gays, and a core organizer of the 1979 National March on Washington for Gay and Lesbian Rights, as well as the first national conference for gay and lesbian people of color, the "Third World Conference: When Will the Ignorance End?" By the late 70s, activist and support groups for bisexuals had been created in Minneapolis, Chicago, Detroit, New York City, and the Bay Area.

The 1980s saw a number of "firsts": the foundation of the first explicitly bisexual political organization, BiPOL, (1983, San Francisco); the first bisexual rally (1984 outside the Democratic National Convention in San Fransisco, organized by BiPOL); the first regional bisexual conference in the US (1984, East Coast Conference on Bisexuality in Storrs School of Social Work at the University of Connecticut, with about 150 people participating); the first US-national bisexual newsletter (1988, Gary North, "Bisexuality: News, Views, and Networking"); the first non-heterosexual veteran to testify in front of Congress (1989, bisexual Cliff Arnesen, on gay, lesbian, and bisexual veterans' issues); and the first BiCon UK (1984, London). The Boston Bisexual Women's Network, the oldest bisexual women's group still running, was founded in 1983 when they began publishing their bi-monthly newsletter, BI Women, the longest-existing bisexual newsletter in the US.

Bisexuals were also active in combating the AIDS crisis in the 80s: doing safer sex outreach, and insisting that women, and bisexual men who have sex with men, be counted in AIDS statistics. Bisexual activist Veneita Porter, of the Prostitutes' Union of Massachusetts and Call Off Your Tired Old Ethics (COYOTE) advocated for women, trans people, and injection drug users living with AIDS in the mid-80s. Cynthia Slater, openly bi and HIV-positive, organized the first Women's HIV/AIDS Information Switchboard in 1985. One of the first needle exchanges in the US was set up by bi activist Liz Highleyman in 1991 with the founding of the Boston ACT UP IV League.

The 1990s saw yet more developments: BiNet US (the first and oldest national bi group in the US) was founded in 1990; the first academic course on bisexuality in the US was also established in 1990 (by Susan Carlton at UC Berkley); meanwhile, BiPhoria, the UK's oldest extant bi organization, was formed in Manchester. Bisexuality began to be included in large-scale surveys about sexuality as its own identity, and a subject worthy of its own research. The *Journal of Bisexuality*, the first academic journal on bisexuality, was founded by Fritz Klein in its current iteration in 1999, though some sources suggest Klein began collaboratively publishing the journal in 1982. The bisexual pride flag, designed by Michael Page, was unveiled on December 5, 1998: three horizontal stripes (magenta, lavender, and royal blue at a ratio of 2:1:2). Page explained the design on the now-defunct biflag.com:

> *The key to understanding the symbolism of the Bisexual pride flag is to know that the purple pixels of color blend unnoticeably into both the pink and blue, just as in the "real world," where bi people blend unnoticeably into both the gay/lesbian and straight communities.*

Current bisexual activist organizing is more likely to be explicitly queer in its approach than gay rights organizing. Ongoing bisexual issues include: fighting domestic and sexual violence; poverty; access to healthcare; and resisting the simple "inclusion" of bisexual people into positions of power, and instead challenging power structures which disenfranchise bisexuals.

Other words which have the same definition as bisexual, though they have different connotations, are "pansexual," "polysexual," and "omnisexual." Bisexuals might also call themselves "gay," "lesbian," and/or "queer," either in addition to bisexual, or alternatively.

There is a fascination with the difference between bisexual experience and bisexual identity. In a 2006 study, 73% of men in New York City who had sex with men identified as straight. However, bisexuality is defined by sexual attraction, not sexual experience; and like all gender and sexuality labels, it's up to each person to define their own experience and identity.

*see also:* BIPHOBIA; PANSEXUAL; GAY

**BITCH** — A derogatory word for women who are considered to be spiteful or overbearing, or for people exhibiting normatively feminine (and therefore "weak") characteristics.

It is also reclaimed by many women, and used affectionately as a term of familiarity.

Bitch is also used by, and arguably "reclaimed," by queer men and men who do drag and are targeted for deviating from hegemonic masculinity. However, many queer men seem to think themselves exempt from misogyny, which only contributes to them perpetuating it.

*see also:* MISOGYNY; HOMOPHOBIA

**BODILY AUTONOMY** — The self-determination of people over their own bodies.

Bodily autonomy is a key aspect of feminism and post-colonialism: the body is not property and cannot be owned by another person, and to deny someone agency and authority over their own body is a violation of their basic human rights. This includes sexual contact, reproductive choices, trans-specific healthcare, and medically unnecessary surgeries on intersex people.

*see also:* TRANSITION; CONSENT; REPRODUCTIVE RIGHTS; GATEKEEPING; INTERSEX

**BOI** — An AAVE alternative spelling of "boy," with additional gender-fuck meaning.

Boi has multiple meanings, but is generally used to describe young, assigned female at birth, queer butches or broadly masculine people. A boi might be a Sapphic woman, or a trans man. Some bois are very butch; some are effeminate. The utility of "boi" is mainly in describing a masculinity which is not cisheteronormative.

Bois might use a range of other gendered words to describe themselves, including: "lesbian," "dyke," "trans," "non-binary," "genderqueer," or "queer"; and they might use any pronouns. There are multiple possibilities, none mutually exclusive. Some cis men might identify as bois if they practice gender-fuckery.

The etymology of boi comes from East Frisian (modern-day Germany) for "young gentleman," and Middle English for "servant" and sometimes "devil, evil spirit."

*see also*: BOY; GENDER; AAVE

**BONDAGE** — *see*: BDSM.

**BORN THIS WAY** — A political slogan used to campaign for LGBT+ rights.

Insisting that queers are born this way has granted us political legitimacy, but it also pathologizes us and rests on biological essentialism.

Born this way is a modern adaptation of a century-old framing of queerness: queers (no matter their queerness, be it bi/homosexual or transness) are seen as "inverts" who were born in the wrong body.

Born this way implies that queers can't help the way they are, because they were born with their queerness; queerness is framed as an undesirable but unavoidable condition which must be pitied. The implication is that if queerness were a choice, we would choose instead to be cisgender and heterosexual so as to assimilate into "normal" society. Queerness is only deemed acceptable if it is innate, and if it is an apology. We're encouraged to reject and hate our bodies because it's the only way we can access healthcare and civil rights.

The biological essentialism of the born this way concept frames queerness as a medical problem to be solved or "cured," rather than a natural human variation or even a socialized identity and set of behaviors. Rather than entertain this essentialism, LGBT+ activism should insist that queer people deserve basic human rights and access to public life, regardless of how long we've been queer or "why" we're queer.

Born this way also frames gender and sexuality as static, rather than potentially fluid and dynamic. It's a crude reduction of queer experience, simplified to be understandable to cishets.

*see also*: SEXOLOGY; BIOLOGICAL ESSENTIALISM; INVERT; LGBT+ RIGHTS; ASSIMILATION

**BOSTON MARRIAGES** — A domestic relationship between two women, independent from men, in the late 19th and early 20th centuries.
*see also*: SAPPHIC; LESBIAN; BISEXUAL; GAY

**BOTTOM, BOTTOMING** — Bottoming is kink and gay slang for a complementary role to topping. Bottom is a queer identity.

Bottoming is associated with receiving penetrative sex and with being submissive—but these are not necessary aspects of bottoming. Bottoming is being responsive to the top and allowing them to lead the encounter, which may or may not involve a power exchange. Bottoming and topping are more like roles in a partner dancing: the lead and the follow have equal power, but an understanding that the lead will make decisions about what steps happen next. The follow can be active or passive, bratty, eager, submissive or dominant.

Bottoms are associated with femininity but are not necessarily feminine (or any other gender expression).

The language of "top/bottom/vers" is used by some as an identity label, but it doesn't have to be. The purpose of these labels is to make it easier for queer people to find sexual partners, not to define your identity (unless you want it to).

The term bottom is not used by straight people, despite its utility as a term across all genders and sexualities, because cisheteronormativity assumes that the man has a penis and will penetrate, and the woman who has a vagina will be penetrated, and that the man will lead the interaction.
*see also*: TOP; VERS; KINK; CISHETERONORMATIVITY

**BOTTOM SURGERY** — An informal name for a set of surgeries for trans people which changes the appearance of their genitals.

Bottom surgery is considered medically necessary for trans people with dysphoria relating to their genitals; but not all trans people want or need bottom surgery.

There are several types of bottom surgery:

- Metoidioplasty — a neopenis created from a clitoris, enlarged by hormone replacement therapy
- Phalloplasty — a neopenis created from donor skin
- Scrotoplasty — the creation of a scrotum, where prosthetic testicles can be inserted
- Vaginoplasty — a neovagina created from the penis
- Orchiectomy — the removal of the testicles

Other surgeries involving reproductive organs (e.g., hysterectomy) are considered part of trans healthcare, but "bottom surgery" is not. Each of these types of bottom surgery have their own variations.

Bottom surgeries are serious medical procedures which shouldn't be taken lightly, and they aren't; but they're often talked about as though trans patients have no appreciation of the gravity of them, and as though being post-op will mean resigning themselves to a sexless life where they're ugly but at least they don't have bottom dysphoria anymore. This kind of transphobia is perpetuated by both the medical establishment and the mainstream media.

Cis genitals are positioned as the ultimate, and we're told that if our genitals don't "pass" for cis that we are doomed to ugliness and self-loathing. It's entirely up to each trans person how they want their body to look and feel, and what their goals and priorities for their bodies are; these will dictate which, if any, bottom surgery they choose.

*see also:* GENDER REASSIGNMENT SURGERY; GENDER RECONSTRUCTIVE SURGERY; TOP SURGERY; TRANS HEALTHCARE

**BOY** — A masculine child. A term used patronizingly or endearingly for masculine adults.

A boy is anyone who feels affinity with boyishness or masculinity and chooses to call themselves boy. This might seem an unsatisfactory definition, but gender is elusive and self-defining.

The etymology of boy is interesting. The word entered English in the mid-1200s as "boie," meaning a servant, commoner, or knave, generally young and male. Other European languages also used it to mean a servant (e.g., French "*garçon*," Italian "*ragazzo*," Greek "*pais*," Old English "knave," Old Church Slavonic, "*otroku*"). Around 1300, boy meant a rascal, ruffian, or urchin. Boy possibly comes from "boi" ("evil spirit") and "bo" (a baby word for brother).

Its origin before the mid-1200s is unknown. Boy didn't mean "a male child" until the 1400s; "girl" was used as a gender neutral term for children from c.1300 to 1400. Boy was used to mean "Negro" or Asian servant or slave of any age from c.1600. Modern usage for people who aren't children reflects its racialized and class-patronizing etymology.

*see also:* GENDER; GIRL; BOI; MAN

**BOY PUSSY** — Gay slang for a bottom man's anus.

Many cis gay men will use words like "pussy" to describe their assholes but are vocally repulsed by trans boys and non-binary people who have vaginas. This is one example of cis gay men appropriating the feminine ("pussy" being associated with women in a cisnormative way) whilst still being extremely misogynistic.

*see also:* BOTTOM; PUSSY; GAY; TRANSPHOBIA; MISOGYNY

**BRAVE** — A patronizing, if well-intentioned, proclamation of approval.

"You're so brave" is something queers hear all the time. "You're so brave" for coming out, for being yourself, for daring to be yourself. It's meant as a compliment. It's meant as a recognition of strength, but most of us wish we lived in a world which didn't require such strength and resilience simply to have a comfortable gender expression or date who we want to.

Survivors of sexual violence are also called brave for speaking out about it. Queers are disproportionately likely to experience sexual assault or intimate partner violence.

Are straight cis people ever called brave for holding their lover's hand, or for wearing a skirt? By branding us "brave," it upholds the status quo that this is hard and important work which us brave queers need to do in order to change the world, rather than challenge the systems which privilege cishet people over us.

Our oppression becomes their inspiration porn. I want to see more cishet people be "brave" and stand up to patriarchy and transphobia instead of watching from the sidelines as we do all the work. "Brave" could usually be more appropriately substituted with "bitter."

*see also:* ALLY

**BREECHES ROLE** — *see:* TROUSER ROLE.

**BUGGERY** — English slang for anal sex, colloquially interchangeable with "sodomy." The literal equating, in legal terms, of anal sex to bestiality.

The buggery laws in England and Wales demonstrate the legal persecution of queerness, especially queer men. Though queerness is no longer explicitly criminalized in England and Wales, the social and legal consequences are still felt today not only in the UK but everywhere colonized by the British Empire.

In English law, buggery and sodomy are not defined in statutes but by judicial precedent. Buggery has come to be defined by the courts as: anal or oral intercourse with penetration by a penis; or vaginal intercourse involving a person and an animal (the court ruled that oral intercourse with an animal is not buggery, and there has been no case about anal intercourse with an animal). Regarding people, consensual sex between adults was not a defense against buggery.

The Buggery Act 1533 first made sodomy illegal in England under civil law (previously it was handled in ecclesiastical courts), though the Buggery Act does not define buggery beyond "the detestable and abominable Vice of Buggery committed with Mankind or Beast." The punishment for buggery was death, and government (crown) seizure of the offender's possessions rather than them going to the next of kin. Clergy were liable to be executed under the Buggery Act, though they could not be executed for murder, so the Act was used politically to execute inconvenient members of the clergy. The Buggery Act was repealed by Mary I in 1553, but was reenacted by Elizabeth I in 1563.

The Buggery Act was replaced by the Offences against the Person Act of 1828 and buggery remained a capital offense in England and Wales until 1861 when the death penalty was abolished. Buggery included anal sex between any gendered couple, but was most often used to target men having sex with men. The section "Sodomy and Bestiality" defined punishments for "the abominable Crime of Buggery, committed either with Mankind or with any Animal." Here we can see interchangeable use in law of 'sodomy' and 'buggery.'

The last people to be sentenced to death for buggery were James Pratt and John Smith, on November 27, 1835. The magistrate Hensleigh Wedgwood, who had committed the men to trial, wrote to the then Home Secretary Lord John Russel, commenting that the death penalty was an unfair sentence for buggery because it targeted the poor; avoiding arrest simply required renting a private room at a small (but for some, impossible) cost.

The punishment for sodomy was the death penalty, until 1861 in England and Wales, and 1887 in Scotland. In 1885, the Criminal Law Amendment Act made all "homosexual acts" illegal, including those carried out in private, which led to an increase in prosecutions of queer men. It was under the 1885 Act that Oscar Wilde was prosecuted and found guilty of "gross indecency" in 1895. Wilde's trial was highly publicized and influenced attitudes about homosexuality going into the 20th century.

In England, sex between women was never criminalized but was a matter of public "concern" after World War I, evidenced by the vilification of, and legal challenges to, Radclyffe Hall's 1928 novel *The Well of Loneliness*.

In the early 1950s, as many as 1,000 men were imprisoned every year for homosexuality; the high volume of prosecutions, several of which were high profile involving famous names, kept the repressive laws in the public eye. For fear of public disorder, a government committee was established to consider the criminalization of both homosexuality and prostitution. The 1957 Report of the Departmental Committee on Homosexual Offences and Prostitution, better known as the Wolfenden Report after the committee's chairman Lord Wolfenden, concluded that "homosexual behavior between consenting adults in private should no longer be a criminal offence." Despite the report's findings, there was no political will to decriminalize gay sex acts, but the report provoked debate, and The Homosexual Law Reform Society was formed in 1958 to campaign for legal reform. Homosexuality as a theme was becoming more common for theatrical plays being submitted for a license, and the policy toward the subject was begrudgingly being softened. In a memo dated October 31, 1958 Lord Chamberlain's Office (the official censor for all theatre performed in Britain) outlined changes to policy regarding portraying homosexuality on stage: the language is unsympathetic and states that excluding homosexuality from theatre has to that point been "to the public good," but it does say "we will allow the word 'pansy'."

The 1967 Sexual Offences Act, which only applied to England and Wales, partially decriminalized homosexuality by allowing sex acts in private between two men who were 21 or older, but it was still a criminal offense for men to have a same-sex sexual encounter in private in Scotland and Northern Ireland. The Scottish Minorities Group, founded in 1969, campaigned for legal equality in Scotland to match that of the Sexual Offences Act in England and Wales. After 1975, police did not prosecute offenses under the buggery legislation.

Until 1980, with the passing of the Criminal Justice Act (Scotland), it was illegal to have same-sex sex in Scotland. Some gay men migrated from Scotland to England to avoid persecution for being gay. Northern Ireland only saw the decriminalization of homosexuality in 1982 under a ruling from the European Courts, which effectively granted gay men the same decriminalization in Northern Ireland as the 1967 Sexual Offences Act in England and Wales. The Belfast Gay Liberation Society was the leading group campaigning for legal reform in Northern Ireland, coming into opposition from the "Save Ulster from Sodomy" campaign led by Reverend Ian Paisley in 1977.

The Campaign for Homosexual Equality (CHE) in the UK published *No Offence: The Case for Homosexual Equality in Law* in 1975 in response to the problems with the Sexual Offences Act, including the unequal age of consent (21 for men who have sex with men, and 16 for men and women having sex) and the erasure of gay women.

In 2003, the offense of buggery was deleted from the statutes in England and Wales.

*see also:* CONSENT; HOMOPHOBIA

**BUSSY** — *see:* BOY PUSSY.

**BUTCH** — A queer masculinity.

Butch was first coined by lesbians and other queer women in the 1940s, along with "femme." Butch was a rejection of the feminine gender roles by queer women. Butchness came to be associated with aggression—partly because butches would respond with protectiveness and righteous anger when queer bars were raided, and partly because any woman's gender expression which deviated from hegemonic cis femininity was a threat and therefore demonized—and by extension, lesbians as a group were seen as aggressive. Femmeness, which was also extremely political and present in the queer women's scene, went either ignored or unnoticed by mainstream culture.

While the modern labels of butch and "femme" only emerged in the 40s, they put words to an aesthetic and dynamic which had been practiced for a long time, and which does not (and never has) belonged only to lesbians. Butch and femme are the domain of all queers.

Butch and femme both have multiple facets and aesthetics, depending on what subculture they're being exhibited in. Queer butch is different from lesbian butch is different from cis gay men's butch. Butch makes room for queer people to embody an aesthetic and gendered way of relating which they find empowering, without necessarily identifying as men.

*see also:* MASC; FEMME; LESBIAN; GENDER EXPRESSION; GENDER

**BUTCH FLIGHT** — The false notion that trans men are actually butch women who attempt to escape misogyny by transitioning.

In this narrative, trans men and trans masculine people are painted as gender traitors, enablers of patriarchy, gender opportunists too weak to deal with the consequences of being a woman. The idea that trans men have an easier time than cis women in navigating their genders under cisheteropatriarchy would be amusing if it weren't so damaging. All trans people are subject to institutional transphobia; being trans is only "easier" in that it can ease dysphoria, but it does not position us in a position of relative privilege to cis women.

Butch flight is one aspect of transphobia, in which cis people (in this case, usually cis lesbians) objectify trans people (lamenting that all the butches that they fancy are now men) and speak over our experiences.

*see also:* BUTCH; TRANSPHOBIA; TRANSMISANDRY

**CAFAB** — Acronym for COERCIVELY ASSIGNED FEMALE AT BIRTH, a variation on "Assigned Female At Birth (AFAB)."
  *see also:* ASSIGNED FEMALE AT BIRTH; DFAB; FAAB

**CAMAB** — Acronym for COERCIVELY ASSIGNED MALE AT BIRTH, a variation on "Assigned Male At Birth (AMAB)."
  *see also:* ASSIGNED MALE AT BIRTH; DMAB; MAAB

**CAMP** — An aesthetic sensibility based on artifice and exaggeration. Camping is to add great affectation (e.g., to walk, talk, or dress affectedly).

Camp is a stylization which uses elements of drama, parody, hyperbole, grandiosity, irony, vulgarity, extravagance, and humor. Camp is "character."

Camp is a lens through which we can enjoy the sincere attempts and failures of "bad" art—camp is the good taste in bad taste. Everything gaudy and gauche has the potential to be camp. Camp is snob taste mixed with boredom, and so it is the domain of pretentious, self-proclaimed "tastemakers" and "influencers." But camp is generous: camp wants to appreciate and enjoy. It is not nihilistic. Nature is not camp; morality and politics and all things serious are not camp.

In her 1964 essay "Notes on Camp," Susan Sontag wrote that both androgyny and hyper-femininity/hyper-masculinity are camp. Sontag also tells us that "camp rests on innocence." Despite most camp things being contrived, things which are the most camp are naive and sincere, without the self-awareness that they are camp. Examples of camp canon include cabaret, Oscar Wilde, John Waters, Tiffany lamps, and Cher.

Camp was a key aspect of gay male culture in the 20th century; not all gays were camp, but gay aesthetics defined camp. Camp has since been filtered into and appropriated by mainstream culture.

*see also:* GAY CULTURE; MINCE

**CAMP TRANS** — An annual demonstration between 1992 and 2015 at Michigan Womyn's Music Festival (MWMF) to protest the festival's transmisogynistic "womyn-born-womyn" policy.

MWMF had a womyn-born-womyn policy since its inception in 1976. Camp Trans began protesting in 1991 when a woman was asked if she was trans, and when she refused to answer she was thrown out. The festival's informal policy has since been clarified by MWMF founder and organizer Lisa Vogel in 2013:

> *The Festival, for a single precious week, is intended for womyn who at birth were deemed female, who were raised as girls, and who identify as womyn. I believe that womyn-born womyn (WBW) is a lived experience that constitutes its own distinct gender identity.*

The focus of the organizers seemed to be on a shared experience of growing up as girls and women—many trans women share this experience, whether they were out as children or not. In 2005 Vogel drew an analogy between a womyn-born-womyn space and a people-of-color-only space:

> *I feel very strongly that having a space for women, who are born women, to come together for a week, is a healthy, whole, loving space to provide for women who have that experience. To label that as transphobic is, to me, as misplaced as saying the women-of-color tent is racist.*

A better analogy for the festival would be a women-of-color-only space which excluded Black women.

Camp Trans is a show of solidarity between trans and cis women who support the right of trans women to be in women-only spaces. Many LGBT+ groups boycotted the festival, and many artists refused to perform at MWMF. MWMF held its final festival in 2015.

*see also:* TRANSMISOGYNY; TERF; WOMYN

**CASTRO CLONE** — A gay male archetype; an idealized image of working-class masculinity, popularized in the Castro neighborhood of San Francisco in the late 1970s.

The Castro clone is masculine, muscled, and working class (or at least he adopts a working-class look), with a full mustache and sideburns, and tight trousers (leather or Levi's, with the top button undone). On top he wears a tight white t-shirt or tank top, or a plaid shirt; or, he's shirtless. The aesthetic's popularity was partly due to how accessible the "uniform" was: it was comfortable, inexpensive street wear which was suitable for gay bars and non-gay spaces, and considered attractive because it emphasized masculine attributes. The look was modeled on the greasers of the 1950s and 1960s, and heavily influenced punk, metal, leather, queer, and hipster fashion.

Gay magazines, gay porn (e.g., porn star Al Parker), and homoerotic artist Tom of Finland further entrenched the Castro clone in the canon of gay culture beyond San Francisco with images of buff construction workers, policemen, and bikers wearing the Castro clone look.

The Castro clone represents a "real" working-class masculinity: a push-back against the stereotype of queer men as effeminate aristocratic dandies. So, of course, it's been adopted by middle-class professionals who fetishize the gritty "authenticity" of working classness.

The Castro clone look remained popular throughout the 1980s, and is still popular today. Everyone was doing their best to look healthy and not infected with AIDS. The bear look is a spin-off of the Castro clone, where beards replaced mustaches; and the twink look is a contrasting response.

The Castro was one of the US's first gay neighborhoods. In 2018, it was officially established as an LGBT+ leather cultural district by the city of San Francisco, which reflects an appreciation for LGBT+ tourism more than for LGBT+ culture and history.

*see also:* GAY CULTURE; MASC 4 MASC; LEATHER; BEAR; TWINK

**CD** — Acronym for CROSS-DRESSER.

**CHASER** — Someone who fetishizes certain bodies or identities.

There are chasers who are attracted to trans women, trans men, non-binary people, people of color, and fat people, solely on the basis of their body or the chaser's assumptions about their body.

Chasers are only interested in pursuing their attractions based on fantasies, without any allowance that the bodies they are attracted to are complex individuals. A marginalized person who is attracted to people with the same marginalization (e.g., a trans man who is predominantly attracted to other trans men) is not a chaser.

*see also:* FETISHIZE

**CHEMSEX** — Sex between queer people (usually men) whilst on drugs. Drug use with the intention of having sex.

It's interesting that chemsex has become a named phenomenon, specific to the queer community. Straight people also take party drugs with the intention of having sex, but queerness is singularly associated with hedonism and excess. Mainstream media discussions on chemsex have largely contributed to a broader culture of scaremongering, shame, and homophobia.

The term also gained traction because queer people are perhaps more likely to explicitly discuss sexual intentions, sobriety, and drug use as part of a wider discussion on consent.

*see also:* CONSENT; SAFER SEX

**CHOSEN FAMILY** — The queer concept of an intimate group of people who are committed to supporting each other, as society expects our biological families to offer support.

Queers are alienated by hegemonic family structures, legally, socially, and personally. The legal family unit reflects cisheternormative monogamous family structures, and legally disenfranchises queer people. Marriage and its legal benefits are restricted to opposite-sex couples in most places; in some places, if a married trans person changes the gender marker on their birth certificate, the state legally divorces them. Marriage allows two queer partners access to each other in hospital, and access to each other's wealth and immigration status; also it often has tax benefits. But, marriage is not available to all queer people, and because as a legal contract it only allows for two parties, it reifies the privatization of emotional support and domestic labor into the couple unit.

Marriage is not the only area of struggle for queer families. Queer parents face greater difficulty in adopting children than straight parents, and it's extremely difficult to grant guardianship to more than two parents. Fertility is also difficult for trans people who use hormone replacement therapy (HRT). In the UK on the NHS, other medically necessary treatments which affect fertility (e.g., chemotherapy) qualify patients for storing their eggs or sperm before they undergo treatment; but if trans patients want to store their eggs or sperm before starting HRT, they must do so at their own expense.

Parents and guardians are legally able to control their queer children's lives and force them into conversion therapy or deny them hormone blockers. Queers are also at risk of being rejected by their biological families when they come out, regardless of how old they are.

There are lots of toxic ideas about family in hegemonic culture—for example, they're supposed to unconditionally love and support us (and if they don't, something is wrong with us), and we're expected to forgive them for anything because we're related (and if we don't, we're heartless). The family is an area of trauma for many queers, and sometimes it's better for us to remove ourselves than to forgive and continue enduring familial violence.

Because we're so often disowned or let down by our families, we create our own family from within our communities. Chosen family can be a group of friends and partners who live together, or a broader community network of people who you can count on for support.

*see also:* QUEER TIME; QUEERPLATONIC

**CIS** — Short for CISGENDER. Latin for "same."

**CIS GAZE** — The objectification of trans people by cis people.

Cis people will literally stare at trans people (and people who they perceive as trans), but the cis gaze refers more broadly to the objectification, dehumanization, tokenization, and fetishization of trans people by cis people.

The cis gaze commonly takes the form of sensationalizing transness, heralding distressing stories of trans people as "inspirational," consuming trans "trauma porn" in the media (especially the physical violence inflicted upon trans women of color), performatively parading a token trans person at an event (e.g., a panel discussion) to prove "progressiveness," and asking invasive questions to satisfy cis curiosity about trans bodies or experience.

"Cis gaze" is also an amusing play on the phrase "cis gays," who are regularly guilty of it.

*see also:* GAZE; FETISHIZE; CISGENDER; TRANSPHOBIA; ALLY; BRAVE

**CISGENDER (CIS)** — Someone whose gender identity unambiguously matches their assigned sex at birth. Someone who has not had a transgender experience or transgender history.

Cisgender is assumed to be the "default" identity; mainstream culture is saturated with cisness and cisnormativity. "Cisgender" is an important word because it removes the implication of normalcy in cisness and of abnormality in transness.

All cis people are in a position of structural privilege over trans people. They never need to defend or explain their gender in relation to their assigned sex at birth; their gender identity is not routinely invalidated; and they won't face medical neglect and barriers to healthcare, housing, jobs, and public space on the basis of their cisness.

Cis is not a slur. Transphobes think "cis" is applied coercively in a flagrant display of irony and lack of information and self-awareness.

Cis people regularly misunderstand what it means to be transgender by trying to imagine if their gender didn't match their assigned sex; a better insight is to imagine if their assigned sex didn't match their gender. An assigned female at birth cis woman who wants to understand what it's like to be trans should imagine that she was instead assigned male, and that everyone assumes she is a man to the extent that it's dangerous for her to correct them.

A minority of trans people view cis as a destination to be reached at the end of their transition. They see "trans" as a liminal state between their birth assignment and their "new" gender, which is "achieved" through social and medical transition, and when they are finished with their medical interventions, they no longer identify as trans. They might describe themselves as having a trans history. This narrative is mostly used by people who transitioned in the late 20th century before the word "cis" was used, and have now adopted a position of being cis.

However, this narrative is largely rejected by trans activists and younger trans people, on the basis that all trans people face oppression, even after "completing" medical intervention (which arguably never happens for people taking HRT).

*see also:* SEX (n.); TRANSGENDER; CISSEXISM; CISHET; TRANSITION; HORMONE REPLACEMENT THERAPY; PASSING; CISNORMATIVITY

**CISGENDERISM** — *see:* CISSEXISM.

**CISHET** — Portmanteau for cisgender and heterosexual. Refers only to someone who is both cis (cisgender) and het (heterosexual).

Cishet people are in an extremely privileged structural position relative to queer people; they do not face violence or discrimination on the basis of their sexuality or their cisness; cishet men have the added structural privilege of not facing violence or discrimination on the basis of gender as well. These privileges intersect with other identities like race, class, disability, and age.

Cishet people are not part of the "LGBTQIA+ community"; everyone else is, or at least has a legitimate claim to it should they choose to assert it. Cishet people cannot be queer, though some who are kinky or polyamorous or who do drag will try to claim otherwise.

There is debate within the LGBT+ community as to whether asexuals who are cis and hetero-romantic, and aromantics who are cis and heterosexual, have a claim to a queer identity. I suggest that asexuals are not heterosexual because they do not experience sexual attraction to the opposite sex, but some aces will choose to use "heterosexual" to describe their romantic orientation for simplicity. As for cis heterosexual aromantics, I suggest that their claim to queerness is much less defensible; there is no gender transgression in being cis and heterosexual with no romantic attraction.

*see also:* CISGENDER; HETEROSEXUAL; CISHETERONORMATIVITY

**CISHETERONORMATIVITY** — The combination of cisnormativity and heteronormativity. The cultural and legal hegemony of cisgender heterosexuals.

Under cisheteronormativity, the cisgender heterosexual identity is assumed to be the default. This is the basis for legal framework (e.g., legislation around marriage), social hegemony (e.g., sex education and cultural representation), and medical "normalcy" (e.g., assumptions about reproductive healthcare). Any deviation from cishetero-normativity—that is, any performance of gender non-conformity or a non-heterosexuality—is punished.

   see also: CISNORMATIVITY; HETERONORMATIVITY

**CISNORMATIVITY** — The assumption that cis people are "normal" and trans people are "abnormal."

   Cis people exist in a social environment which validates their genders and reinforces a gender binary which corresponds to their lived experiences, giving them relative privilege compared to trans people. Cis people therefore have a low tolerance for that which challenges their gender identities and their conceptions of gender more broadly. Cis fragility (drawing on white fragility in critical race theory) is rooted in a desire to restore and reproduce cisnormativity. It is a combination of lack of cis people's stamina in interrogating their conceptualizations of gender, as well as a resistance to challenging those conceptions.

   The very idea of trans people challenges the cisnormative notion of gender: gender is not easily defined by genitals or a falsely dimorphic understanding of "biology." Non-binary trans people further challenge cisnormativity simply by existing and refusing to define their genders in cisnormative terms.

   When cis people encounter challenges to their conception of a binary gender, they often react with defensiveness, forcing trans people to do the emotional labor of comforting the cis person in addition to educating them and explaining basic concepts about gender or divulging personal experience to satiate cis curiosity and confusion. This derails conversations about trans experiences with oppression and devolves them into assuages of cis guilt and potential violence.

   The too-familiar "I'm sorry I misgendered you—singular 'they' is hard for me," places cis difficulty in remembering a new name or pronoun over the discomfort and disrespect toward the trans person they misgendered. This is an attempt to redirect social resources (time, attention, emotional labor), prioritizing cisness over transness: a reinforcement of cisnormativity.

   Cis fragility is so delicate that cis people seek to reaffirm their genders in every step of their lives: everything from clothing to beverages to occupations is gender coded. This serves the interests not only of cisnormativity, but of patriarchy and heteronormativity in an extremely boring but ubiquitous triple threat. Cis gender expressions are not named as such: women wear feminine clothing, men perform masculinity, and these behaviors go unnoticed and unexamined until there is deviance from them, as though these norms are "natural" rather than dynamic and constantly redefined and reproduced.

Trans identities are not afforded the level of complexity that cis ones are assumed to have. Trans people are presumed to be constantly shaped and defined by their transness as though it is the primary, if not singular, aspect of their selves. Cis people, however, are just people. Because they occupy an identity of "normalcy," it is not considered an identity at all, and they presume that they have an objective perspective on gender uncolored by their own experiences of it.

Trans people are also expected to be "ambassadors" of transness. Cis people feel entitled to trans people's time in educating them and indulging their invasive questioning without considering that the trans person they're interrogating might not have an academic interest in gender. Trans people are presumed to know everything about all things trans and to accurately represent all other trans people, which is both impossible and exhausting. While trans people experience transphobia and cissexism on a regular basis, they may not have the vocabulary or framework to analyze their experiences at the systemic level. This contributes to trans people creating or leaning on existing hierarchies of palatable transness fit for anti-critical cis consumption in order to survive an interaction unscathed, even if it means sacrificing other, "more deviant," expressions of transness to do so.

Cis people who pride themselves on being "progressive" might learn correct terms and make efforts to use the right pronouns, but will still be unlikely to confront cissexism and transphobia as it manifests in their lives. They will congratulate themselves for asking the pronouns of a "visibly" non-binary person (whatever that means), but refuse to examine why their gender identity needed clarification when those of the apparently-cis people around them didn't. Or perhaps they'll never assume anyone's pronouns, but they also won't intervene in street harassment and violence directed at gender non-conforming femmes.

Privilege deflects the responsibility of accountability. There is no neutrality in issues of oppression, only complacency and antagonism.

The burden of interrupting cissexism and transphobia belongs with cis people, but trans people have already proven that we are more than capable of disrupting the power structures which oppress us whether cis people are interested in helping or not. There is power in challenging cis fragility. There is power in protesting cisnormativity by refusing to center cis experiences or use cis frames of reference. There is also power in survival, which is often opposed to confronting cisnormativity. Transness is antagonistic by nature; it is enough just to be.

see also: TRANSPHOBIA; QUEERPHOBIA; RACISM

**CIS PASSING** — see: PASSING.

**CISSEXISM** — The systemic oppression of trans people through the idea that cis genders and cis bodies are more legitimate than trans genders and trans bodies.

Cissexism intersects with other forms of oppression, and is a key aspect of patriarchy and heteronormativity.

see also: TRANSPHOBIA; GENDER BINARY; PATRIARCHY; CISNORMATIVITY

**CIVIL UNION, CIVIL PARTNERSHIP** — A legal recognition of a relationship, similar to marriage but not necessarily having all of the same benefits and protections.

Same-sex civil unions are an alternative to marriage that is seen as more agreeable to homophobes. Civil unions offer tax benefits and rights to partners; the specifics depend on where their union is recognized.

Civil unions are seen by some LGBT+ rights advocates as a first step to marriage equality. The focus on marriage equality as the key LGBT+ issue has been criticized for prioritizing the least vulnerable people in the community: middle-class, cis couples who have access to wealth, healthcare, stable jobs, housing, and the benefits of citizenship. Civil unions and marriage can both be seen as consolidating wealth and other resources in the hands of people who already have them, rather than expanding basic resources and making them available to everybody. Civil unions and same-sex marriage are also criticized for modeling

LGBT+ rights on assimilation into heteronormative society: if we can prove that we are just like straight people, that we too want a romantic, domestic, and sexual relationship with a life-long partner, then we will finally be deserving of basic rights.

In 1993, the Hawaii Supreme Court determined that denying marriage licenses to same-sex couples was discriminatory; in 2000, Vermont was the first to offer civil unions; and in 2015 same-sex marriage became federally recognized. In the UK, civil partnerships became legally recognized in 2005; and same-sex marriage in 2013.

*see also:* MARRIAGE EQUALITY; LGBT+ RIGHTS; HOMO-NORMATIVITY; ASSIMILATION; LOVE; SAME-SEX MARRIAGE

**CLASSISM** — Fear of, or contempt for, poor or working-class people. Behavior based on those feelings. A system of oppression in which poor people are marginalized and subject to violence.

Working-class people and poor people (two distinct groups, though there is obviously overlap) do not have the same access to gender transgressions or queerness as middle-class, upper-class, and rich people do. This manifests in multiple ways: material—if you're poor you simply cannot afford new clothes, access healthcare, or be "too" visibly queer because it could cost you your job or housing; legal—it costs money to change your name and/or your gender marker; cultural—working-class people are under more scrutiny for their "lifestyle" choices, including their gender expression and sexuality.

Still, working-class aesthetics and culture are appropriated by wealthier queers because they are deemed desirably "edgy" and "authentic." The very things that working-class people are punished for become the means for richer people to gain social capital.

Like all systems of oppression, classism intersects with other marginalizations: racism, ableism, agism, misogyny, queerphobia, transphobia, and fatphobia.

*see also:* CULTURAL APPROPRIATION

**CLAUSE 28** — *see:* SECTION 28.

**CLOCK (v.), CLOCKY (adj.)** — Clock is when someone realizes you're trans. Clocky means feeling like you'll be clocked.

Being clocked is a source of anxiety for many trans people because the reaction of the person who's realized you're trans is unpredictable. They might treat you differently, out you to other people, or become violent.

Getting clocked is a common trans fear, but cis people are actually terrible at clocking trans people despite many of them thinking otherwise.

*see also:* PASSING; OUTING; STEALTH

**CLOSET, CLOSETED** — Not telling people, or actively denying, that you are something other than heterosexual and/or cisgender.

"The closet" is something to "come out" of, placing the onus on queer people to declare our genders and sexualities as Other from the default cishet.

The closet is positioned as a self-imposed prison and as our fault for not living "authentically." The focus should instead be on creating a world in which it is totally safe to be queer, where there is no need to come out of the closet because there is no expectation of disclosure and no assumption of cisheteronormativity.

Lots of people, understandably, stay closeted for safety and survival, or stay selectively closeted.

*see also:* COMING OUT; STEALTH; GAY SHAME

**COERCIVELY ASSIGNED FEMALE AT BIRTH (CAFAB)** — A variation on "Assigned Female At Birth (AFAB)," highlighting the coercion inherent in gendering infants and young children.

Cis people probably shouldn't say they were "coercively" assigned a gender at birth because they don't suffer the coercion of an assigned gender on the same scale as trans people; it would be bad form.

*see also:* ASSIGNED FEMALE AT BIRTH; DFAB; FAAB

**COERCIVELY ASSIGNED MALE AT BIRTH (CAMAB)** — A variation on "Assigned Male At Birth (AMAB)," highlighting the coercion inherent in gendering infants and young children.

Cis people probably shouldn't say they were "coercively" assigned a gender at birth because they don't suffer the coercion of an assigned gender on the same scale as trans people; it would be bad form.

*see also:* ASSIGNED MALE AT BIRTH; DMAB; MAAB

**COMING OUT** — Declaring your sexuality or gender identity to be other than cisgender and heterosexual.

Coming out relies on cisheteronormativity: it implies a secret, seedy, troubled "double life," deception, and deviance from the assumed norm of being cisgender and heterosexual. Cisheterosexuality is given the central place in the narrative (inside), and anything Other (outside) needs to be disclosed.

Coming out is framed as a confession. There is pressure for queer people to follow a prescribed narrative and perform the traumas of being queer for cishet people, especially authority figures like medical professionals. That "being queer is painful but I can't hide who I am anymore" narrative is designed to make cishet people feel comfortable, take pity on us, and see us as brave and inspiring—because when we come out, we don't know how the cishet audience will react.

The narrative is designed to keep us safe.

Coming out is not a single moment. Queer people have to choose whether or not they want to come out all the time, with every new person they meet and every interaction where they're assumed to be straight or they're misgendered. The alternatives of being closeted or stealth are less confrontational in the short term, but equally exhausting in the long term. Queer spaces are so valuable because they offer respite and remove the burden of making that choice.

Coming out can be a powerful tool. Being visibly out can help other queer people feel less alienated, but it also stigmatizes and further marginalizes people who don't (or can't, for safety) come out. People shouldn't be critiqued for their personal choice to come out, or not.

*see also:* CISNORMATIVITY; HETERONORMATIVITY

**COMMUNITY** — A group with common characteristics or struggles and a shared social network.

There is no monolithic queer community, LGBT+ community, gay community, or trans community. LGBT+ communities are diverse and full of subcultures, but can broadly be described as celebrating identity and offering support to combat widespread queerphobia and cisheteronormative pressures. Not all LGBT+ individuals consider themselves part of a LGBT+ community, and not every LGBT+ person has access to a LGBT+ community.

These communities are based on shared experiences and struggles, but oppressive hierarchies are still (re)produced in LGBT+ and queer spaces. Some examples of intra-community oppressive dynamics are: racism and agism and fatphobia in all queer communities; transmisogyny in the lesbian community; transphobia in the "gay male" community, which carries the unspoken assumption of "cis" before "gay male"; misogyny in gay male and "trans masc" spaces; trans histories being erased from the wider LGBT+ movement; biphobia everywhere; classism everywhere; ableism everywhere.

see also: GAY CULTURE; PRIDE; CHOSEN FAMILY

**COMPTON'S CAFETERIA RIOT** — A riot of transgender sex workers fighting back against police brutality in San Francisco.

This was one of the first LGBT+ riots in US history, predating the Stonewall riots. It took place at Gene Compton's Cafeteria in August 1966 (exact date unknown because police records don't exist, and newspapers didn't cover it) in San Francisco. Compton's was on the corner of Turk and Taylor Street in "The Tenderloin," a gay ghetto where all the queens and sex workers and queers lived and worked, and corrupt policemen patrolled.

The differences between gay and drag and trans at the time were blurry: all gender transgression was described as "gay"; some liked to dress as women (and would today be called "cross-dressers" or "drag queens"), some "lived as" women (and would today be recognized as trans women). In 1966 endocrinologist Dr. Harry Benjamin published *The Transsexual Phenomenon*. He wrote that gender identity was fixed but that the body could be changed, and legitimized the use of hormone replacement therapy and gender reassignment surgery for trans women; several of the queens who frequented Compton's saw him.

Compton's was full of trans queens, many of whom were sex workers, often because they couldn't access other work. Some professional "female impersonators" earned a proper living, but most queens were sex workers and there was toxic whorearchy (sex work hierarchy).

Working on the street was violent. Police would trawl Compton's and arrest queens and trans women for "female impersonation" for wearing makeup, or having long hair or buttons on the "women's" side of a blouse. When jailed they were in lockdown, and put into solitary if they wouldn't let wardens shave their hair.

Police raids were common, especially as sex work increased as the Vietnam War escalated. Gentrification meant The Tenderloin was the only affordable area in the city, so it became overpopulated as more people moved in. Tenderloin activists brought sexuality onto the civil rights agenda at a time when racial and economic discrimination were just starting to be taken seriously during the so-called "war on poverty."

Police and Compton's management were regularly harassing queens, so a "vanguard" activist group picketed Compton's on July 18, 1966; but the conflict between cops and queens remained unresolved.

In August at Compton's, a policeman grabbed a queen and she threw coffee in his face. Tables were flipped; sugar shakers were thrown at cops and through glass doors and windows. The cops retreated and called for backup, and the queens kicked and beat cops in the street with heavy purses. A police car was destroyed and a corner store set on fire. It was the first known instance of militant collective queer resistance in US history.

Police attitudes changed after Compton's. Elliot Blackstone, a police community relations officer, worked with trans activists to get anti-cross-dressing laws changed. The Center for Special Problems, a unit of the San Fransisco health department, provided trans people with photo ID cards that reflected their correct gender, because state IDs could not have gender markers changed. The cards read: "This is to certify that is under treatment at the Center for Special Problems for transsexualism." Attitudes toward trans women began to shift too; trans women could be women, so long as they didn't do anything unrespectable like sex work.

As a result of the riot, Compton's started closing at midnight. A pornography shop took its place in 1972.

*see also:* STONEWALL

**CONCERN TROLLING** — Framing bigotry as "concern" in order to legitimize it. Derailing discussions of oppression with "concerns" about the respectability of the oppressed group, or the wellbeing of individual members of the oppressive group.

Concern trolling is used to bolster anti-trans narratives about trans women being predatory men who shouldn't be allowed access to women's spaces due to "concern" for the safety of cis women and girls, despite all evidence showing that trans people (especially trans women and girls) are more likely to suffer violence in gendered spaces than cis people;

further, there are no reported incidents of assault by a trans person in gender-segregated spaces. Cis femininity is positioned as innocent and in need of protection from a deviant and dangerous trans femininity, and the violences suffered by trans people and gender non-conforming cis people are dismissed or ignored.

Concern trolling is also an old, and ongoing, anti-queer tactic, shifting discussions about queer sexual education to "concern" for the innocence of straight children and some shadowy "gay agenda" to ostensibly convert them into queerness through inclusive education. The latest evolution of this is "concern" about children being "indoctrinated" into transness, or the "transgender ideology," when in reality trans children are simply allowed to express their genders.

Fat bodies are policed through concern trolling over health, both by doctors (fat people are likely to be undiagnosed or misdiagnosed by doctors who see their fatness as an inherent health problem) and the public who profess to know that all fat bodies are "unhealthy." The "concern" that a fat person might be unhealthy is used as an excuse to shame them for their (perceived) lifestyle and diet, and to police their clothing choices and their taking up space in public.

Concern trolling is also weaponized against people of color. For instance the "concern" for "Black on Black crime" is used as a diversion in discussions about police brutality, despite not being statistically relevant. Islamophobia takes on similar manifestations of concern trolling in discussions on protecting the civil rights of Muslims (and people racialized as Muslims or immigrants from Muslim-majority countries), where the "concern" is the "violence" of Islam as a religion. In both these cases, the civil rights of minority groups are disregarded, and genuinely legitimate concerns about the violence of majority groups (e.g., the overwhelming majority of mass shootings in the US are carried out by white men) are ignored.

Sex workers are also subject to concern trolling: anti-sex worker activists will espouse "concerns" about the sanctity of women's bodies, whilst speaking over the affected sex-worker women (and ignoring the involvement of non-women in sex work altogether). They likewise discuss "concern" over trafficking victims, conflating sex work with trafficking and again ignoring both sex workers and trafficking victims, presumably because sex work makes them uncomfortable.

Unfortunately their discomfort and the legislation which flows from it puts both sex workers and trafficking victims at risk of violence from the state, the police, predatory brothel and strip club managers, and clients.

Concern trolling is either done out of ignorance or bad faith. Engaging with concern trolling should be done selectively, if at all, because any engagement distracts from more urgent and meaningful discussions and lends credibility to bad faith arguments.

*see also:* TROLL; RESPECTABILITY; SOCK PUPPET

**CONDOM** — A barrier used to prevent transmission of sexually transmitted infections (STIs) and pregnancy.

Free condom schemes are an important aspect of queer sexual health activism. Free condoms allow everyone to access condoms as a safer sex tool, regardless of income. They promote safer sex and give people greater agency over their sexual practices.

Until very recently, condoms were the only reliable way to prevent transmission of HIV—now PrEP is an effective alternative. Condoms are still the most reliable method of not transmitting other STIs like chlamydia, gonorrhea, and syphilis.

Condoms are also highly effective at preventing pregnancy.

Female condoms, gloves, and dental dams are also safer sex tools and work in the same way (as a barrier to fluid transmission), but are given a lot less attention because they are associated with women's sexual health rather than men's. But condoms are not only for men: they help everyone who has a penis, and everyone who has sex with people who have penises; and free condom schemes are especially beneficial for sex workers and poor people.

People who report using condoms sometimes face the same risk level for STIs as people who report seldom or never using condoms. If you only sometimes use condoms, consider alternative methods of HIV prevention and birth control to use in addition.

The wholesale cost of a condom is about $0.08. As usual, the cost of the preventative medicine (the condom) is far less than the cost of treating the diseases it prevents. Some people use free condom schemes as a vehicle to criticize the price of menstrual products (which should also be free), and in doing so undermine the radical activism of giving away condoms for free.

Condoms have been in use for STI prevention since at least 1564, recorded by physician Gabriele Falloppio in his treatise on syphilis. The first rubber condom was produced in 1855 in New England, and by the late 19th century "rubber" had become a euphemism for condoms around the anglophone world. The first latex condoms were produced in the US in the 1920s. The first recorded use of condoms for birth control was 1605, which was recorded because a Catholic theologian declared them immoral. The English Birth Rate Commission in 1666 noted a decline in births due to the use of "condons," which is the first documented usage of that word or any spelling variations. Until the 1800s, condoms were only used by the upper classes, as they were the only people who had access to them and to sex education.

*see also:* SAFER SEX; REPRODUCTIVE HEALTHCARE; HIV; AIDS; BAREBACK; ACT UP; PrEP

**CONSENT** — To actively agree. Mutual agreement on what happens next.

Consent is relevant to sex, other kinds of touching, and anything to do with bodily autonomy such as food and healthcare. It's also relevant to exposure to information and images.

Consent is not as simple as "yes" and "no," because to truly consent to something means to agree to it without conditions of coercion. Affirmative consent is meaningless if saying "no" is not a safe or realistic option.

Consent can be verbal or non-verbal. In gay men's spaces, non-verbal consent is the norm, due to hundreds of years of repression from the state. Men in gay bars and bathhouses might signal interest by putting their hand on your genitals or butt; the expected response is to either brush their hand away to indicate disinterest, or leave it there and look them in the eye to reciprocate interest. In queer and lesbian spaces, explicit verbal consent is the norm.

The age of consent is the age at which people are legally deemed competent to consent to sexual activity; it is designed ostensibly to protect young people from coercive sexual advance from adults, but age of consent laws have also criminalized consenting same-sex activities. The age of consent in the UK for men who have sex with men was addressed in Parliament in 1994, but not equalized at 16 (like for different-sex couples) until 2001 for England, Scotland, and Wales; and not equalized in Northern Ireland until 2009.

The defining difference between sex work and sex trafficking is consent. Sex workers choose their job (albeit possibly under coercive conditions like needing money to survive, but this is true of all waged labor) and consent to sell sexual services to clients. The worker might unenthusiastically consent to sex with the client, but lack of enthusiasm does not negate informed, active consent. Sex-trafficking victims do not consent to the sex they have, and they should not be considered sex workers.

Informed consent is a key aspect of healthcare. Patients need to understand their treatment in order to give informed consent. Access to trans healthcare is gatekept under the supposition that trans patients cannot give informed consent to access hormone replacement therapy, so instead they need the approval and recommendation of several doctors and psychiatrists; likewise they allegedly cannot give informed consent about trans-specific surgeries without living for at least one year "in role" during the so-called "real-life experience" test. In many places trans people cannot even give informed consent to change their names and the gender markers on their documents, and instead rely on a panel of "experts" or judges to grant them access to these changes. This is all extremely patronizing, expensive, and time-consuming; and while we're waiting because cis doctors are squeamish about transness, we suffer serious psychological (and legal) consequences. The supposed lack of ability of trans people to give informed consent rests on transphobic tropes: that we're unreliable witnesses in our own lives because our genders are based in deception and delusion, and that being trans is "just a phase."

*see also:* TRAUMA; TRANSFORMATIVE JUSTICE; BUGGERY; GROSS INDECENCY; SEXUAL OFFENCES ACT; SECTION 28; SEX POSITIVE, SEX NEGATIVE; TRANS HEALTHCARE

**CONVERSION THERAPY** — Attempts to convert people from queerness into cisheteronormativity under the guise of spirituality or pseudoscience.

Conversion therapy has the aim of turning gay, lesbian, bisexual, and asexual people into heterosexuals; and of transgender and gender non-conforming people into cisgender, gender-conforming people.

Conversion therapy is extremely damaging emotionally and psychologically, and sometimes physically. It is premised on the assumption that being queer is a problem to be cured. Conversion therapy is widely believed to be not only unnecessary and harmful, but ineffective.

Queers have been subject to conversion therapy techniques like chemical castration, electric shock therapy, corrective rape, and ice-pick lobotomies. Other, "softer" methods include social pressure, counseling, psychoanalysis, and group prayer.

Anti-trans conversion therapy for children (sometimes called "reparative therapy") is generally seen as more acceptable today than conversion therapy on the basis of sexuality. Trans and gender-variant children are coerced into conforming to the gender norms of their assigned sex at birth under the pretense that their lives will be easier if they are cis than if they are trans or gender non-conforming; but this fails to account for the distress of their gender identity being dismissed and their gender expression being labeled as wrong. This position is usually bolstered by a thorough misunderstanding of hormone blockers and the misconception that children are having trans-related surgeries.

Anti-trans conversion therapy sometimes positions itself as "gender critical," suggesting that trans people are just acting out outdated modes of femininity or masculinity, and that they don't need to transition to alleviate their dysphoria. While it's true that not all trans people have dysphoria or seek medical intervention to address it, for trans people who do want to medically transition there is no appropriate or effective alternative to treating gender dysphoria.

Anti-trans conversion therapy also places heavy emphasis on the possibility that the trans person might "actually" be homosexual rather than trans. This is an inversion of the view that was taken by early sexologists, who thought that homosexuals were transgender "inverts." Either way, conversion therapy causes individual harm, as well as broader social harm by reproducing the idea that queerness needs to be cured, through science, religion, or otherwise.

In most places, there is no legal ban on conversion therapy. The exceptions are: Argentina, Brazil, Ecuador, Fiji, Malta, Taiwan, Samoa, Switzerland; and some states, provinces, and municipalities in Australia, Canada, and the US.

see also: HOMOPHOBIA; TRANSPHOBIA; CORRECTIVE RAPE; VIOLENCE; TRAUMA; TRANS HEALTHCARE

**CONVINCING** — An alternative way of saying that someone passes as cisgender.

Trans people, especially trans women and trans feminine people, are often told they're "convincing" as women: that they look traditionally feminine and their transness is not visible. It's framed as a compliment but suggests that they are deceptive, that they are not actually women or not "real" women, or that transness is shameful and should be hidden.

*see also:* PASSING; CISNORMATIVITY; ASSIMILATION

**CORRECTIVE RAPE** — Sexual violence used as a weapon with the specific aim of punishing, or "correcting" queerness, and "converting" the victim into being cisgender and heterosexual.

Queers are more likely to experience sexual violence than cisgender and heterosexual people; corrective rape is one facet of the violence that we face in a homophobic and transphobic society.

Corrective rape is normalized by comments like "You think you're a lesbian but you just haven't found the right man yet," as though "the right man" will free you from the fate of queerness, as though "all you need is a good dicking."

The narratives around this violence differ depending on the perceived gender infraction of the victim—in the case of anyone who "should be" a straight cis woman (AFAB trans people, queer cis women) it's framed as a "lesson" to show us that we "really are" women who like, or will at least "take," dick from cis men; in the case of anyone who is AMAB, corrective rape is usually framed as punishment for being beyond redemption into cisheteronormativity—but the physical violence is the same, and it's horrifying. It is homophobia and transphobia taken to its extreme but logical conclusion.

Like conversion therapy, corrective rape is a multi-layered act of physical and psychological violence. And, it does not make victims less queer. It's probably not even meant to; it's primarily a demonstration of violence and power over queer bodies.

*see also:* CONVERSION THERAPY; SURVIVOR; TRANS PANIC

**COTTAGING** — Cruising for or having anonymous sex in a public bathroom.

Cottaging is UK gay slang, and especially refers to men having sex with men; the term originates from the cottage-like appearance of public lavatories in England. Lavatory buildings have been called cottages in England since the Victorian era, but by the 1960s this usage was exclusively in the domain of gay slang. Public bathrooms in the US used for anonymous sex are called "tea rooms."

Cottages exist near universities, bus stations, train stations, and airports. Cottagers would use foot-tapping signals to express interest in each other; some more popular cottages had "glory holes" drilled between the stalls where people would have anonymous oral sex or handjobs through the wall between them. Cottages also served an important social function for queer men to meet other queer men, especially if they were too young to get into gay bars.

Cottaging is no longer as popular as it was in the 20th century, unsurprisingly due to the internet and the use of hookup apps.

In the UK, having sex in a public bathroom is illegal, regardless of how discreet you are. To discourage cottaging, the doors in some cottages have been shortened to be below shoulder level, or removed entirely; or, the stalls have been extended to the floor to prevent foot signaling.

So-called "pretty police" officers would go to known cottages as "bait" to entrap the public into soliciting sex or engaging in lewd conduct.

*see also:* CRUISING; POLICE (n.)

**CRIP THEORY** — A critical perspective on disability studies which aligns disability studies with queer theory.

Crip theory takes on "cripple" as a reclaimed slur to subvert the linguistic framework which positions disability as suboptimal at best. Like queer theory, crip theory highlights the construction of normalcy, desire, and identity.

*see also:* DISABLED; QUEER THEORY; NORMAL; DESIRE; IDENTITY

**CROSS-DRESS, CROSS-DRESSER** — Someone who dresses as a gender "opposite" to their own. Interchangeable with "transvestite."

Cross-dresser is not to be confused with "transgender" or "transsexual." Cross-dressing is about a cross-gender gender expression; transgender and transsexual people have a "cross-gender" gender identity from the one they were assigned at birth. A trans person can also be a cross-dresser, dressing as a gender which they aren't. That said, the current terminology around trans identities is very new, and many people who could be categorized as trans might call themselves cross-dressers instead because it reflects the vocabulary they prefer or have access to.

Cross-dressing is not monolith style. It assumes some clothes "belong" to some gender and we all agree what these are through our social norms, when actually hotly contested. Cross-dressing also assumes a gender binary.

Cross-dressing is (now) a relatively safe avenue for exploration of gender identity and gender variance: lots of trans people experiment with drag or other explicitly performative gender roles and expressions before coming out.

Cross-dressing can be used to signal queerness, or sexual availability. Cross-dressing laws targeted trans people (who were not cross-dressing, but dressing as their genuine gender) and queers who used gender variance to signal queerness. Very specific sexual preferences and roles could be communicated through cross-dressing: it's long been a way to find available queer partners. Now there are still queer modes of dressing, but the need to find sexually compatible partners through dress is diminished with the internet and apps.

During the California gold rush (1848–1855) in San Francisco, men who sold sex would wear women's clothes to advertize their services, and women who sold sex would wear men's clothes for the same purpose.

Cross-dressing was historically criminalized. People were required to be wearing a certain number of articles of "correctly sexed" clothing to avoid being charged. Trans writer Katelyn Burns suggests that "this was done to protect the feelings of cisgender heterosexual people, and to ensure that they would never unknowingly compromise their sexualities by expressing attraction to a trans person or a gay man in drag."

Cross-dressing laws in the US are all local; there has never been federal legislation against cross-dressing. Cross-dressing laws passed in over 40 cities in the US between the Civil War and World War I lasted until the 1970s. They were used to reinforce not only normative gender and bodies, but to police the boundaries of sex, sexuality, race, citizenship, and access to public space. Cross-dressing laws were used to police queers: for example, in raids of bars when they couldn't find evidence of other offenses like selling sex.

Laws don't just police the boundaries of normalcy; they produce norms. Cross-dressing laws, and the modern bathroom laws, assume that gender is binary and discrete and knowable. They parallel race laws on interracial marriage and Jim Crow segregation laws, in that gender and race are both socially constructed categories with no clear boundaries, yet people were gendered and racialized as if their identities were immediately visible and obvious. Cross-dressing laws were used to police immigrants for deviating from white American norms of gender; to define what kinds of bodies and practices belonged in the nation-building project, and what bodies and practices belonged in the "man" and "woman" gender categories. Cross-dressing laws reinforced inequalities and exclusion from public life. Policing what bodies are acceptable in public space is dehumanizing; it redefines humanity to exclude some people. Cross-dressing, selling sex, public lewdity and exposure, and disability were all criminalized under the same legislations: as threats to public order; as urban blight.

Despite its historic criminalization, cross-dressing has a long theatrical pedigree, from Shakespeare to vaudeville, the saloon show, and modern drag shows.

Cross-dressers have also been a thriving subculture in cities like San Francisco since the mid-1800s.

Defining the identities of historical cross-dressers is pointless because for the most part we do not have documentation of them defining themselves, and identity labels have evolved considerably: "trans" and "homosexual" and "queer" didn't exist as words until relatively recently, but that doesn't mean they didn't exist as practices. We could, with sensitivity, use those words to describe many historical figures.

*see also:* DRAG; TRANSVESTITE

**CRUISING** — Actively looking for casual sex partners (often strangers) online or in a public space.

Cruising grounds are open spaces such as parks where people (usually queer men) look for anonymous sex partners. Dating apps can also be considered cruising grounds.

Cruising culture has developed out of the necessity for discretion, because if queers (especially queer men, or people perceived to be men) were "caught" soliciting sex, they could be subject to physical violence and arrest.

In the UK, public sex is not illegal as long as the public cannot see you having sex and is unlikely to come across you having sex; this does not including cottaging, which is illegal regardless of how discreet you are.

*see also*: GAY; COTTAGING; BATHHOUSE

**CUB, BEAR CUB** — Gay slang for a young bear.

*see also*: BEAR; GAY

**CULTURAL APPROPRIATION** — The commodification of Otherness in order to normalize it and sell it back to the Other.

Cultural appropriation is a big problem for LGBT+ communities: queer culture is being appropriated by cishetero culture; and white, middle-class queers are deeply guilty of appropriating Black and working-class cultures.

Straight cis people co-opt queer culture (e.g., femme as an identity and the cishet consumption of drag). People who aren't sex workers appropriate the fashion and political aesthetics of sex workers. White people appropriate, and colonize, the cultures of people of color. All marginalized groups are at risk of their culture being appropriated, bastardized, and profited from by the hegemonic group.

Is this because white, cishet, wealthy people who aren't disabled or sex workers, don't create their own culture? Or is it because marginalized people are disenfranchised, with less access to mainstream "respectable" culture, and therefore develop their own cultures and subcultures, which are then seen as both threatening to the mainstream but also coveted, edgy, interesting, and "quirky"? The insult of cultural appropriation is not only the lack of credit given to the people who develop the culture which is being stolen, but that the same expression of culture from its original source is dismissed or punished until it's appropriated and then celebrated on a privileged body.

*see also*: FETISHIZE; RACISM; ANTI-BLACKNESS; PRIVILEGE; AAVE; OTHER

**D** — The D in BDSM is for Dominance, opposed to the S for submission.
*see also:* BDSM

**DADDY** — Gay slang for a man who takes on a leadership, mentorship, or caregiving role in a relationship.

While the daddy is assumed to be an older man, they are not necessarily older, and not necessarily a man. But, the daddy is in charge. More than an age, daddy is a power relation; daddy is a mindset.

The daddy role is not really about age play, though there is all kinds of subtle age play happening in gay scenes; for example, twinks pretending to be younger than they are, and daddies pretending to be older. They might actually be the same age, but they're adopting different roles around intimacy.

Daddies are also associated with the leather scene, which is full of "leather daddies."
*see also:* KINK; LEATHER; GAY; AGISM; TWINK

**DEADNAME, DEADNAMING** — The use of a trans person's birth name or old name, which they don't use anymore.

When you know someone's name, using their deadname is extremely disrespectful, comparable to misgendering.

Changing names is something already common in our culture: many people change their last names when they get married or their parent gets married. Just as it would be inappropriate to use someone's old name in that case, it's inappropriate to use someone's deadname.

Unlike name changes due to a marriage, deadnames can be painful, and their use is unnecessary in nearly every situation.

A trans person might continue to use their deadname for legal purposes, or in specific situations where they are not out as trans. This doesn't mean that it's always okay to use their deadname; if you're not sure, ask them.

Everyone's relationship to their deadname is different: it could be stressful, ambivalent, or indifferent. Lots of trans people don't change their names when they come out; in that case, their birth name isn't a deadname, it's just their name.

The media has a tendency to report on trans people's deadnames under the pretense of "providing all the facts," but the majority of the time a deadname is not relevant information. This is especially disrespectful when the media reports on the death of a trans person.

*see also:* NAME; PRONOUNS; TRANSGENDER; MISGENDER; COMING OUT; TRANSITION

**DEMI-, DEMIGENDER, DEMI-GIRL, DEMI-BOY** — Someone who is partially, but not entirely, a girl (demi-girl) or a boy (demi-boy).

People with demigenders fit within the broader categories of transgender (because they do not identify unambiguously only with the gender they were assigned at birth) and non-binary (because their gender is neither exclusively man nor woman). But, like with all gender labels, it's up to each individual to choose how they define their gender, and someone with a demigender might not identify with transness or being non-binary.

*see also:* TRANSGENDER; NON-BINARY

**DEMIROMANTIC** — *see:* GRAY-ROMANTIC.

**DEMISEXUAL** — Sexual attraction only to people with whom you have an emotional connection.

Demisexuals are on the asexual spectrum. Despite the prefix "demi" for half, and demisexuality falling (to be reductive) halfway between sexual and asexual, demisexuals do not have a "half sexuality" and in no way are lacking wholeness.

Like all sexual orientations, demisexuality is defined by sexual attraction (or lack thereof), not by behavior. A demisexual person might have sex with someone they are not emotionally connected to, but this doesn't negate their sexuality. It's up to everyone to define their own sexuality, and the only accurate definitions of sexuality come from the subject themselves.

Demisexuals may prefix another sexual orientation label to more accurately describe their sexuality, such as "demi-bisexual."

*see also:* ASEXUAL; GRAY ACE

**DESIGNATED FEMALE AT BIRTH (DFAB)** — A variation on "Assigned Female At Birth (AFAB)."

*see also:* ASSIGNED FEMALE AT BIRTH; CAFAB; FAAB

**DESIGNATED MALE AT BIRTH (DMAB)** — A variation on "Assigned Male At Birth (AMAB)."

*see also:* ASSIGNED MALE AT BIRTH; CAMAB; MAAB

**DESIRE** — To hope for. Longing. Sexual, romantic, or aesthetic attraction.

Desire can be harnessed as a becoming. "Do I want you or want to be you?" What we truly desire is unknowable; we can only approach it. Through closeness ("radical sameness"), we conduct an exploration of the self. I knew I identified with queer masculinity (boys desiring boys) before I knew I was a boy.

Desire is used as a weapon to delegitimize trans experience: "You only want to be a woman so you can be a lesbian, you sick pervert." Well, maybe! So what!

Desire as a force of motivation for sexual and gender exploration is harmless and hopefully results in knowing yourself better, which is a worthwhile project.

Desire shouldn't be moralized but should be politicized. Yes, your "preference" for white people is racist; no, you shouldn't punish yourself for having problematic desires in some misguided act of self-flagellation seeking absolution. Don't force yourself to have sex with someone you don't fancy; instead investigate why you only fancy people who are pale and thin and young and cis. Diversify your media intake and your social group; but don't date or seduce people as if they are stepping stones on your personal journey toward enlightenment. It isn't sexy, but we are all steeped in patriarchy—there is no escaping it; we can only manage its material effects. This is systemic, not individual. You can't hate yourself for a lifetime of conditioning which dictates your desires; you can only mitigate the harm caused to the people marginalized by them. Problematic desires are produced and reproduced. But we can do our best to undermine and interrupt that process.

*see also:* SEXUALITY

**DESISTANCE** — When patients stop seeking medical support in transitioning.

Sometimes they stop being trans and consider themselves cisgender; sometimes they are still trans but have decided to stop pursuing the "medical" aspect of their transition (i.e., hormone replacement therapy and trans-specific surgeries).

The rate of desistance is extremely low (less than 5% at the highest estimates), and should not be confused with the (even lower) rate of "transition regret."

*see also:* TRANSITION; DETRANSITION; TRANSITION REGRET

**DETRANSITION** — When someone who previously considered themselves transgender stops their medical transition.

Sometimes the person realizes they are happier with the gender they were assigned at birth. Sometimes trans people cease their medical transition and are therefore counted in "detransition" statistics, but they continue to be their trans gender without ongoing medical aspects of transition (e.g., hormone replacement therapy).

Detransition as a concept is based on simplistic misunderstandings about transitioning. Transition is not a single moment or operation. Cis people will ask, "Have you transitioned?" or "Have you had the surgery?," which is not only invasive but an annoyingly incorrect framing. Transition is a variable process for each trans person, which may or may not include socially transitioning (changing names, pronouns, or gender expression) or medically transitioning (hormone replacement therapy, top surgery, bottom surgery, laser hair removal, or other surgeries like tracheal shave). For anyone who wants to change their name or gender marker, or do any medical transitioning, there is a lot of paperwork and often mandatory counseling involved in transitioning. If the act of using hormone replacement therapy is transitioning, many trans people will be "transitioning" for the rest of their lives.

As trans writer and activist Juno Roche put it, transition isn't a journey to a trans gender; trans is the destination.

see also: TRANSITION; TRANSITION REGRET; DESISTANCE; TRANS HEALTHCARE

**DEVIANT, DEVIANCE** — Behavior, gender expression, and sexual preferences outside the scope of "normal."

Deviance is punished. "Normal" is a moving target, and not necessarily healthy, or desirable, or interesting, or moral (though it is imbued with morality).

Deviant sexual behavior is a broad tent which groups together everything from light role play to extreme sexual violence. Trans genders, and queer sexualities, are painted as abhorrent, and equated to pedophilia, necrophilia, bestiality, and rape.

Deviant is used as an insult, and reclaimed by some queer people.

see also: NORMATIVITY; PERVERT

**DFAB** — Acronym for DESIGNATED FEMALE AT BIRTH, a variation on "Assigned Female At Birth (AFAB)."

see also: ASSIGNED FEMALE AT BIRTH; CAFAB; FAAB

**DISABILITY, DISABLED** — Impaired physical, cognitive, mental, or developmental function.

The scope of what is considered a disability depends on who you ask. Chronic pain and mental health problems like depression are considered by some to be disabling. Some trans people see their transness as a disability, either because it disables them in cisnormative society or because they see their transness as a mental disorder.

The legal status of disability is rightly the subject of extremely controversy: disability is defined as the inability to work, and so disabled people are forced to prove that they cannot work in order to receive government assistance. This is all the more difficult for people who are not deemed respectable, like people of color, sex workers, and queers.

see also: ABLEISM; MENTAL ILLNESS

**DISCREET** — Someone who doesn't want to be outed. Someone who is actively looking for hookups, but wants to be quiet about it due to apprehension about being outed or for other reasons.

Discreet is a common term on hookup apps. Materially this might mean the person doesn't show their face on the app, or that they cannot accommodate a hookup where they live, or simply that they need their partners to be subtle about the nature of their business when arriving and leaving.

Motivations for discretion range from modesty, to the safety of the closet, to cheating on a partner.

Some people are not comfortable having a hookup with a partner who is discreet because they don't want to feel like a "dirty secret." There are trends both of shaming people who are discreet for not being out and proud, and shaming people who are out and proud for being confrontational or "too in your face" about their sexuality. Both of these positions are dangerous, reinforce queerphobia, and lack empathy.

*see also:* STRAIGHT ACTING; CLOSET; HOMOPHOBIA

**DISORDER OF SEX DEVELOPMENT (DSD)** — A relatively new term used to replace "intersex," introduced by intersex activist Cheryl Chase in 2005 to improve medical care for intersex people. It is fraught with problems, however, because it pathologizes intersexuality as a "disorder" instead of noting it as a difference.

Intersex researcher Georgiann Davis (who is intersex herself) writes that the medical establishment was quick to adopt DSD nomenclature because it reasserts medical authority over intersex bodies after intersex activism in the 1990s put medical authority on intersex under jeopardy, and the DSD language allowed them to sidestep their tainted history of medical malpractice, and non-consensual and medically unnecessary intervention on intersex bodies.

DSD language suggests that intersex people have an abnormality, or worse, are abnormal. In her research, Davis found this pathologizing language to affect both people who have been surgically altered and those who haven't been. According to Davis, people who reject DSD language are less likely to receive support from the medical world and from family, but are more likely to report positive senses of self because they do not see themselves as abnormal. Shared terminology allows access to community and appropriate medical care, and there are costs for not adopting the current nomenclature. Of course, many people will selectively and situationally employ different rhetorics depending on their immediate circumstances and goals.

The tensions between pathologization, medicalization and medical "expert" outsiders, legitimacy, activism, and anti-assimilation in intersex activism mirror those in trans activism.

see also: INTERSEX; TRANSGENDER

**DMAB** — Acronym for DESIGNATED MALE AT BIRTH, a variation on "Assigned Male At Birth (AMAB)."

see also: ASSIGNED MALE AT BIRTH; CAMAB; MAAB

**DRAG** — An exaggerated performance of gender. Anyone can do drag, regardless of their gender, so anyone can be a drag queen, and anyone can be a drag king.

Drag is hyperbole, playful self-aware critique, and gleeful mockery of what is assumed to be "natural." Drag is sometimes about illusion, becoming as "passable" as possible; but it is sometimes about highlighting or parodying gender roles.

Drag is not about deception, but about spotlighting how malleable and ridiculous gender performance is. A woman is just as capable of being an over-the-top drag queen as a man, with a full face of makeup, false lashes, a blown-out wig, long white gloves, a push-up bra and a sparkly dress. Drag is no less authentic a performance of gender than any other. A woman who asks the drag queen, "Why do you dress up like a woman?" could be asked the same question in response.

Drag is not inherently transphobic. There are lots of trans drag performers, and you could say that all gender expressions are drag. But there is controversy about including (cis) drag performers (or those assumed to be cis) at LGBT+ events, because some people feel like drag mocks gender (it does, but this is not a bad thing). Drag complicates our understandings of "gender non-conforming," just like cross-dressing does. Drag is also a safe, non-committal way for people to explore different gender expressions.

Drag is a well-established art form with a long theatrical history, and has deep connections with the queer community. Until the late

20th century, there was little, if any, distinction made between drag performance on stage, cross-dressing off-stage, being gay, and being trans; all these people were grouped into the same community, because they all subverted gender expectations.

Drag has historically been a form of embodying, and exaggerating, qualities of femininity, sometimes at the comedic expense of women—especially trans women and women of color. Though most attention to drag is paid to white cisgender men, they are by no means the only ones "allowed" to do drag in general or be drag queens in particular. For cis men to suggest that they "own" drag is the height of entitlement.

*see also:* CROSS-DRESS

**DRESS (N.)** — A one-piece outer garment with covers the body from the chest to the legs or the feet.

While almost all other clothes are thought to be gender neutral, dresses are strongly associated with femininity. Wearing a skirt or a dress is one of the strongest gender cues—or cues of gender non-conformity—that you can send.

Until relatively recently, all children used to wear dresses, and all children used to be called "girls."

*see also:* GENDER EXPRESSION; GIRL

**DYKE** — A reclaimed slur for lesbian.

Dyke was first used in print in Claude McKay's 1928 *Home to Harlem*, as a derogatory word for a gender non-conforming woman. It referred to her masculinity, butchness, and attraction to other women.

Dyke is still used pejoratively by homophobes. In queer circles, dyke can mean a butch lesbian, or can be a value-neutral term for any lesbian, depending on the context.

*see also:* LESBIAN; BUTCH; AAVE

**DYSPHORIA** — *see:* GENDER DYSPHORIA.

*see also:* TRANS HEALTHCARE

**E** — Short for ESTROGEN.

**EFFEMINATE** — A boy or man—or anyone "supposed" to be masculine—who is perceived as feminine, unmanly, delicate, or overly refined.

Effeminate men are ones who look feminine, or behave femininely: for example, having expressive hand gesturing, or an interest in fashion (or basic grooming and hygiene) and decorating. Aesthetics generally are associated with femininity—masculinity is also highly invested in aesthetics, but it doesn't have the self-awareness to realize it. Men insecure in their masculinity will loudly reject anything associated with femininity lest their masculinity (or heterosexuality) be brought into question.

Effeminate boys are punished for their gender non-conformity with bullying from their peers and adults. Gender non-conforming boys are seen as much more culturally threatening than gender non-conforming girls, which is a manifestation of traditional sexism and the cultural inferiority of femininity to masculinity.

Effeminance (also known as "effeminacy") is a gender expression and not necessarily indicative of sexuality, but is strongly associated with gay men and trans women. This is a reductive fetishization of femininity on bodies which are "meant" to be masculine.

Effeminance carries gender and class connotations. Effeminate men are seen as too delicate and weak to do "masculine" tasks which require physical labor, getting dirty, or being socially assertive. Extravagant dress and concern with appearances made wealthy men "effeminate";

foppishness and dandyism, the domain of the rich, are associated with a limp-wristed over-refinement.

Effeminance is very different from a woman's femininity: While the characteristics may be the same, the gendered context of "male femininity" versus "female femininity" make it, and the reaction to it, different.

*see also:* FEMININE; FEMME; FEM; GAY; PANSY; NANCY; PONCE; MASC 4 MASC; FEMMEPHOBIA

**EGG** — Someone who has recently realized that they are transgender, or someone who trans people suspect is trans because they express dysphoria or cross-gender ideation, though they have not (yet) come out.

Egg is an intra-community term of endearment used by trans people to describe other trans people.

*see also:* TRANSGENDER

**EIR** — *see:* SPIVAK.

**EM** — *see:* SPIVAK.

**EMOTIONAL LABOR** — The work of managing other people's emotions, often involving downplaying your own feelings and needs.

Emotional labor is a structural imposition, not a personal one. Doing basic kin-keeping, calling your family, being a good friend or partner, are not necessarily examples of emotional labor. Emotional labor is, for example, the expectation that a woman sends the holiday cards for her husband's family, or that women smile at men on the street, or that service workers become surrogate therapists for customers, or that marginalized people are constantly expected to empathize with people actively oppressing them. We do emotional labor not because we are "naturally" more empathetic or nurturing, but because it's easier than dealing with the consequences of not-doing it, which can range from inconvenient to violent.

Emotional labor falls on all marginalized people. We not only suffer structural oppression, but we have to be careful how we talk about it so as not to upset privileged people and make them feel guilty, or defensive, or sad. Queer emotional labor includes: coming out; explaining your gender or sexuality; fielding invasive questions about your gender or sexuality; allowing cis people to "mourn" your pre-transition self; gently, carefully correcting people when they misgender you; gently correcting people when they say something queerphobic; reassuring people that no, they're not bad like those other cishet people, they're a good ally.

Emotional labor is also the (usually uncompensated) labor of workers in the service, childcare, caretaking, and domestic industries.

*see also:* ALLY; BRAVE

**ENBY** — Phonetic writing of NB, short for NON-BINARY.

**ERASURE** — When your identity is dismissed as not real, or your cultural history and contributions are ignored.

Erasure is alienating, and prevents people from finding others like them; it quells their culture. Queer erasure is the denial that queerness is real or valid, the assumption that queerness is just a phase, and the assumption that no one is queer. The queerness of historical figures often goes ignored, which is an act of queer erasure. The contributions of queer culture to mainstream culture (which could also be framed as the appropriation of queerness by the mainstream) are erased and "straight-washed." Within queer communities, bisexual people and trans people are often erased; likewise people of color, disabled people, and older people are glossed over or ignored entirely while white, abled queers in their 20s and 30s are the default "face" of the queer community.

Erasure and hyper-visibility are two sides of the same coin. Bisexual women and trans women are both ignored and erased from queer history and the modern LGBT+ movement, and hyper-visible in mainstream culture as fetish objects and threats to cisheteronormative culture.

*see also:* CISHETERONORMATIVITY; VIOLENCE; VISIBILITY

**ESTROGEN** — A hormone used in hormone replacement therapy (HRT) to alleviate dysphoria, feminize the body, and/or de-masculinize the body. It is used by some trans women and other trans people who were assigned male at birth.

Estrogen is taken as part of a HRT regimen for AMAB people who want to change their hormones from being androgen-dominant (testosterone); along with it there are anti-androgens (T blockers) and progestogens. HRT is one aspect of medical transition which some, but not all, trans people choose to pursue.

The effects of feminizing HRT include growing breasts, feminine fat distribution and body hair pattern, thinner and softer skin, lessened muscle retention, rotating the pelvic bone slightly forward, mood changes, smaller genitals, and different erectile function and experience of orgasm. Some trans women develop symptoms associated with menstruation, without the menstruation itself, which recur roughly every month: bloating, soreness of breasts, abdominal pain, hot flashes, migraines, nausea, back pain, and diarrhea.

HRT will not "undo" all of the effects of puberty, if an androgen-dominant puberty has already happened: HRT will not change height, shoulder and ribcage width, length of limbs, and facial bone structure; nor will it reduce the Adam's apple, or un-thicken the vocal chords for a higher voice. Facial hair is only minimally affected by HRT. But, most of these things can be changed through other avenues of medical transitioning, if desired: facial feminization surgery, tracheal shave, vocal training, vocal surgery, and laser hair removal.

HRT is proven to alleviate gender dysphoria for trans people who want to alter their secondary sex characteristics, and gives many trans people a more comfortable sense of self.

*see also*: HORMONE REPLACEMENT THERAPY; TRANS HEALTH-CARE; TRANSITION; GENDER DYSPHORIA; HORMONE BLOCKERS

**EQUALITY** — Having the same access to civil rights and social security, regardless of identity.

Equality is premised on the assumption that everyone will benefit from the same access to resources. The American neoliberal dream is based on the idea that the ideal society is one where anyone who works the hardest and smartest can succeed; that it is acceptable for everyone to "start at the bottom" and "work their way up."

Equality, in a queer and civil rights context, also assumes that the marginalized people want to assimilate into society as it is rather than change it into something better and more equitable.

Universal basic income (UBI) is an example of equality, rather than equity. The premise that everyone is entitled to a living income, regardless of how much they work, is good. But the idea that this income could be the same for everyone and we'd have a just society is flawed. The living wage is different in different places; some people need more access to healthcare and other costly accessibility aids like wheelchairs and hearing implements; many people are carers with dependents and so have higher costs; and access to public transportation, the cheapest option, is limited by location, mobility, and safety in public space. Still, UBI is potentially good as a harm reduction tactic, but it can't be our only welfare.

*see also:* LGBT+ RIGHTS; ASSIMILATION; LIBERATION; EQUITY

**EQUITY** — Fairness or justice.

In an activist or civil rights context, equity is distinct from equality because it acknowledges that justice cannot be achieved by simply giving everyone the same access to resources; some people need more resources than others in order to live a dignified life.

In a simplistic example, someone with a chronic health condition will require more healthcare treatment, which costs money, than someone who doesn't have any chronic health conditions. In an equal system, every person would be entitled to the same number of doctor visits, the same medication costs, and the same waiting times for treatment; but this is clearly not equitable.

Different people have different needs. It is important to recognize (and celebrate) our differences rather than pretending that we're all the same.

*see also:* EQUALITY; TRANSFORMATIVE JUSTICE

**EUNUCH** — Associated with a historic social group, a boy or man who has been castrated, typically early in life and with significant hormonal implications as he reaches puberty.

Eunuchs were castrated, usually without their consent, so that they might perform particular social functions—functions which were deemed unfit for a non-castrated man (because he is virile and threatening) or a woman (because she is deemed unfit generally). Eunuchs were their own gendered class; an interesting, and horrifying (non-consensual castration is horrifying), example of the emphasis placed on genitals as an indication of gender and power.

The practice of castrating boys so they become eunuchs is ancient. Today, men who are castrated for medical reasons (e.g., prostate cancer patients) are not generally considered eunuchs because their castration does not fill a particular social or religious function, but some embrace the term.

*see also:* MISOGYNY

**EY/EIR** — *see:* SPIVAK.

**F** — A gender marker for female.

   *see also:* FEMALE; SEX (n.); X

**FAAB** — Acronym for FEMALE ASSIGNED AT BIRTH, a variation on "Assigned Female At Birth (AFAB)."

   *see also:* ASSIGNED FEMALE AT BIRTH; CAFAB; DFAB

**FACIAL FEMINIZATION SURGERY (FFS)** — A set of procedures to "feminize" facial features.

   FFS includes bony and soft tissue procedures, such as a brow lift, hairline correction, forehead recontouring, orbit recontouring (adjusting placement of the eyes), rhinoplasty (changing nose shape), cheek implants, lip augmentation, chin and jaw recontouring, and Adam's apple reduction.

   Facial feminization is considered medically necessary for trans patients with dysphoria who want to change their face.

   *see also:* TRANS HEALTHCARE; FEMININE

**FAG, FAGGOT** — A slur for queer men and queer people who are read as men, reclaimed by some of the queer people it targets.

   Faggot is an insult intended to name and shame men who have sex with men, but actually it labels anyone who's seen as a gender non-conforming man as a failure of (or traitor to) masculinity.

   Because it names a particular type of gender transgression, faggot almost feels like a gender itself. In reclamation, faggot allows for something more complicated than a binary between man/woman, oppressor/victim, and cis/trans.

*see also:* GAY; MASCULINITY; GENDER

**FAILURE** — Lack of success; deficiency.

A normatively successful life is measured by a stable career with a comfortable income, home ownership, a happy marriage, and children. Social and financial success are inaccessible (and undesirable) to many queers.

Embracing failure allows for escape from punishing norms. Refusing to conform to cisnormative ideals of beauty, body, sex, and sexuality is liberating; the same is true about eschewing milestones which ostensibly measure success.

The metrics for success were not designed with queers in mind. Being, or choosing to be, queer—to reject cisheteronormativity through your body, your romantic relationships (or lack thereof), and your sexual encounters (or lack thereof)—is seen as a deficiency. We must be lacking, wanting, because it's inconceivable that someone would happily shun the norms we're told are the building blocks of a fulfilling life.

Queer failure is: failure to fuck properly; failure to form cisheterosexual monogamous reproductive relationships which follow the courtship-marriage-mortgage-children model; failure to conform to respectability politics and be "productive" members of society; and failure to have a "right" (cisgender) body and use it (fuck) the "right" way. These failures are compounded for disabled, fat, old, poor, and non-white people.

Who is afforded failure? Failure is a protest, but also a "quirky," "alternative" indulgence—a luxury.

*see also:* GAY SHAME; HETERONORMATIVITY; QUEER TIME; ASSIMILATION

**FAN FICTION, FAN FIC** — Fictional stories written by fans rather than the original writers. Stories which exist outside of the canon of a fictional universe.

Fan fiction is an opportunity for fans to see themselves represented in popular media, often by literally inserting themselves into the story. This is especially true in genres with particularly bad representation of women and queer people, like science fiction and fantasy. Fan fic allows fans a space for identifying with characters they love, without compulsive cisheterosexuality.

Slash fic is the pairing of characters with interpersonal attraction and sexual relationships. The first published slash fic was of *Star Trek* characters Captain Kirk and Mr. Spock in the story "A Fragment Out of Time" by Diane Marchant in the 1974 fanzine *Grup*, Issue 3. The pairing came to be written as Kirk/Spock or K/S (hence the "slash").

In addition to queering, fan fiction is also the site of increased positive representation for people of color, disabled people, and fat people. Fan fic authors might exploit a canon of ambiguity and write a popular character as being explicitly marginalized, or they might write an entirely new character who exists within the fictional universe.

There are many subgenres of fan fiction, each with their own histories, etiquette, and tropes.

*see also:* QUEER STUDIES; QUEERING; QUEERBAITING; REPRE-SENTATION

**FASCISM** — A political ideology which prioritizes the nation and racial purity, with strictly regimented socio-economic policies, governed through a centralized dictatorship with opposition quelled by force.

Fascism is about creating (and policing) a nation. Nationhood is shared culture, ethnicity, and territory, and gender norms are a key part of culture. Because we subvert gender norms and thus threaten the homogeneity of the nation, queer people are targeted by fascism.

Ethnic minorities, disabled people, and the mentally ill are also targeted by fascists. Fascism functions and gains traction by manufacturing enemies and scapegoats. Because fascism is entirely focused on the nation and building a coherent nationality, it is inherently invested in Othering people who don't conform to the ideals of the nation, despite the flimsiness of "racial purity" as a concept.

Gender non-conformity, including homosexuality, is policed and punished under fascism. Homophobia and transphobia are key facets of fascism. Feminisms which exclude the most marginalized women— like women of color and trans women and disabled women—are fasc-adjacent because they uphold and reproduce the same exclusionary ideals of fascists.

The Nazi persecution of queers involved: creating a culture of homophobia and violence, claiming that homosexuality is a disease and homosexuals must be destroyed; banning organized gay groups; destroying research on homosexuality and transsexuality; criminalizing homosexuality; raiding gay bars; targeting and arresting gay men (and queer people assumed to be men), and sending them to concentration camps for "extermination through work"; and castrating gay men across Europe.

In Nazi concentration camps, the pink triangle signified the crime of homosexuality, and the black triangle was for "asocials." Lesbians were classed as asocials, because the criminalization of homosexuality was specific to "male homosexuality," but the "asocial" label was used broadly for anyone whose lifestyle did not conform to Nazi ideals. Gay men suffered harsher treatment and were more likely to die in concentration camps than other "asocial" prisoners, reflecting the homophobia of both the Nazis' guards and the other prisoners. Gay men were also subject to medical experiments to "cure" them of homosexuality. Imprisoned gay men and gay women were forced to have sex with each other and other prisoners.

Restricting bodily autonomy and policing morality are key to building a fascist state. The Nazis created a Reich Central Office for the Combating of Homosexuality and Abortion. Eugenics are also a key tool of fascism. Selective human breeding is intended to "breed out" undesirable qualities; this is usually done either through killing "undesirable" people or forcibly sterilizing them.

After the Holocaust, queer people were not recognized as victims. The Holocaust was seen to "belong" to Jews, and other groups which were targeted and systemically murdered were not immediately recognized (e.g., Romani people, ethnic Poles and other Slavs, Soviet citizens, the disabled, the mentally ill, Jehovah's witnesses, and anarchists and communists). Studying the persecution of gay people by the Nazis was further impeded by the continuation of institutional and cultural homophobia in Germany and the West at large. The criminalization of homosexuality in Germany remained on the books until 1994; gay Holocaust victims were not allowed access to pensions or other reparations before then because they were still classified as criminals. Homosexuals who were imprisoned by the Nazis and survived the concentration camps could be re-imprisoned for "repeat offenses," and some were forced to serve the anti-gay sentences given to them by the Nazis, regardless of the time they spent in camps. The Nazis' anti-gay policies and their targeting of the early gay rights movement in Germany was not considered suitable subject matter for Holocaust historians until the 1980s.

see also: VIOLENCE; OTHER; HOMOPHOBIA; POLICE (n.); RESPECTABILITY; TERF; SEXOLOGY; PINK; BODILY AUTONOMY

**FATPHOBIA** — Fear of, or contempt for, fat people. Behavior based on those feelings. A system of oppression in which fat people are marginalized and subject to violence.

Fat people are more likely to be unemployed, to face medical discrimination, to be subject to traumatic bullying in schools from a young age, and to be poor. Fat people, as a group, suffer medical abuse through neglect; their health problems and complaints and pain are likely to be dismissed or blamed on their weight. This is worse for fat women, trans people, and people of color, who are also less likely to be believed by doctors and have historically been subject to medical abuse.

Fatphobia is also a function of capitalism and a vehicle for consumerism: the shame or fear of being fat pressures us to buy dietary products, "control top" clothes, and gym memberships. Most clothing retailers don't make clothes for fat bodies—not because it isn't cost-effective, but because they don't want fat people wearing their clothes and tarnishing their brand.

Fat-shaming and body-shaming are part of fatphobia. Fatphobia intersects closely with ableism, misogyny, and classism. Fatphobia attaches moral value to dieting, eating "healthy" foods, and exercising, which are less accessible to disabled people and poor people. There is also more pressure on women than men to conform to thin beauty standards and the socially acceptable amount of consumption fueled by self-hatred.

Fatphobia is systemic but also manifests in individual interactions, including: making comments about someone's weight or appearance on the premise that being fat is undesirable ("You look great. Have you lost weight?"); assuming that "fatness" and "unhealthiness" are synonymous; unsolicited dietary advice; moralizing about food, diets, or eating; "before and after" pictures which do not address fatphobia; confusing one fat person for another; commenting on who is "allowed" to wear certain clothes; political or community organizing which does not account for accessibility for fat people (seating, capacity, weight limits); talking about "guilty" food or exercise habits where a fat body is the feared or implied negative outcome; and assuming that fat people have the same levels of access to medical care without institutional discrimination or neglect.

Fatphobia is also sexualized: presuming that fat people (especially fat women) are more sexually available or should be grateful for sexual attention; presuming that fat people are asexual or celibate because of their fatness; and fetishizing fat people as sex objects.

Gay culture hypersexualizes bodies, but only conventionally attractive bodies, and fatphobia is a major problem in gay communities and in discourse around attraction.

Fatphobia contributes to the normalization of eating disorders, which are already very common for queers and trans people. Talking about fatness (including your own) as ugly or undesirable is also a facet of fatphobia. Many people, especially trans people and queers, have discomfort with their bodies and many have internalized fatphobia. It's not helpful to be harsh on yourself for feeling fat and wishing you weren't, but we should be mindful of how and who we're talking to about this: if we tell our fat friends that we "feel fat and gross," then we're implying that they are gross because they're fat, especially if we are less fat than them.

Like all systems of oppression, fatphobia intersects with other marginalizations: classism, racism, ableism, misogyny, agism, queerphobia, and transphobia.

*see also:* MISOGYNY; OTHERING

**FEM** — An alternative spelling of femme.

Fem is preferred as a broader, distinctive term to femme by some who see femme as an exclusively lesbian identity, though the boundaries of femme and who has claim to it are both hotly contested within the queer community.

*see also:* FEMME

**FEMALE** — Characteristic of women and girls.

Femaleness and maleness have traditionally referred to ostensibly dimorphic biological sexual characteristics, but are by no means separate from gender.

Human biology is not dimorphic, so to insist that there are clear boundaries between "male" and "female"—and, further, that these boundaries are visible and obvious—is incorrect.

Female is gendered to an extent that it doesn't even suppose to refer to a biological "reality." It's used to police the boundary of womanhood and femininity, and weaponized against trans people to insist that they are not "really" their gender—the fact that this happens regardless of what medical interventions trans people have shows that it's not a question of "biology" at all.

Trans women (women who were incorrectly assigned male at birth) are female, regardless of any medical transition they have had (or not had). Trans men (men who were incorrectly assigned female at birth) are not female, regardless of their possible reproductive capabilities.

Female has been in use as an adjective to describe people since c.1300.
*see also:* SEX (n.); MALE

**FEMALE ASSIGNED AT BIRTH (FAAB)** — A variation on "Assigned Female At Birth (AFAB)."
see also: ASSIGNED FEMALE AT BIRTH; CAFAB; DFAB

**FEMALE TO MALE (FTM, F2M)** — An outdated shorthand for a trans man, or other trans person, who was assigned female at birth.

The FTM terminology positions maleness as an objective and a destination, with transition being a journey to that point; but this is extremely reductive, and most trans people do not experience their transition this way. Many trans people never identified with their assigned gender: a trans man, despite being assigned female, may have always been a man, whether or not he had the vocabulary to explain that experience.

This nomenclature also suggests that female and male are discrete categories, and that after a particular medical intervention (euphemistically called "the surgery" by ignorant cis people), maleness is achieved. The reality is that many trans people don't have trans-related medical intervention; and there are those who pursue a wide variety of treatments, some of them ongoing for the rest of their lives.

Rather than describe themselves in terms related to their transition, most trans people prefer to use words which accurately describe their genders, like "demi-boy," "gender fluid," or "man."

see also: TRANS MAN; TRANSGENDER; TRANSITION; BINARY; SEX (n.)

**FEMININE, FEMININITY** — Characteristics associated with women and girls, in opposition to men and boys. These include behaviors, aesthetics, and character attributes, as well as objects and professions which are gendered as being "for girls."

The "ideal" femininity—as prescribed by patriarchy, white supremacy, and capitalism (these three are inseparable)—is white, thin, wealthy, and cis. Failure to be these things is failure to be feminine, and if you're a woman (trans or cis) or assigned female at birth, that failure is punished.

Femininity is treated differently in different contexts: on stage, on the street, in the home, in the workplace. These contexts each have "acceptable" prescribed expressions of femininity which are rewarded, and deviance from them is punished, often with violence (e.g., street harassment, or employment discrimination if you don't wear makeup). In many contexts, femininity (and feminized behavior) is more likely to be rewarded if it's performed by men, such as men being nurturing, or men making an effort with their personal style.

When a body is read as feminine it becomes a public object, subject to the gaze and the physical reactions of the people around it. Women, feminine or not, experience this all the time because they are deemed inherently feminine; and men who are effeminate are "relinquishing" the privilege of their anonymity, their invisibility in public space. Trans women face a particular kind of invisibility and erasure in public space when they are read as masculine men; rather than a privilege, being read as a man is invalidating and can trigger dysphoria. There is a large spectrum of violence faced by all women, all feminine people, and all people who are read as women.

Along with bodies, work is extremely gendered. Care work, working with children, domestic work, cleaning, nursing, and service work are all considered to be "feminine." There are also fields which are thought to be "frivolous" and feminine, which women and effeminate men are mocked for enjoying, but which are dominated by men, whose profits in these industries far exceed women's: fashion and cooking are two examples.

Femininity is often pushed on people who don't want it, like trans men and gender non-conforming kids. They are "feminized" in the same way that trans women are coercively masculinized.

*see also:* FEMME; GENDER; WOMAN; GIRL; MASCULINE; MISOGYNY; FEMMEPHOBIA

**FEMINISM** — A diverse political movement which purports that men and women have equal value. There are so many strands and "waves" of feminism that a less vague definition of the movement as a whole becomes ineffective. Modern feminism is notably divided on a few axes: between third-wave and fourth-wave feminists, and progressive neoliberal feminists and post-colonial anti-capitalist feminists.

Feminism as a political movement began with the suffragettes with the goal of giving (white) women equal rights to (white) men; it has since moved on to goals of liberation of everyone oppressed under patriarchy.

Third-wave feminism is premised on the idea that the personal is political. This idea is largely premised on an individualist notion of oppression rather than a structural one. "Feminism is the theory; lesbianism is the practice," a phrase coined by trans-exclusionary radical feminist (TERF) Ti-Grace Atkinson encapsulates this. This challenges us as legitimate subjects of feminism if we are not lesbians (and implicitly, if we are not cis women). And if we are, then we are criticized if we are too hegemonically feminine: too appeasing of the male gaze, too willing to do housework, too comfortable wearing the bra we should be burning. The question becomes "Does doing _____ make me a bad feminist?," when the real discussion shouldn't be about individual choices but rather systems of oppression which make individual choices coercive, or remove the possibility of choice entirely. People are calling each other "bad feminists" for wearing makeup or kitten heels, but not for detaining and deporting pregnant women seeking asylum. Third-wave feminism is also notoriously transphobic, and modern TERFs uphold this tradition whilst ignoring both the shared struggles of trans people with cis women, and the progression that feminist discourse has made over the past 50 years.

Fourth-wave feminism is focused on identity politics, and how our identities inform our material conditions. But feminism itself is action, not an identity. When people (especially men, or cishet white women) claim, "I'm an intersectional feminist," it's prudent to ask, what is your feminism doing to undermine the effects of patriarchy on the most vulnerable? This is an example of the limits of identity politics: claiming a feminist identity is more about virtue signaling than it is about changing the material effects of patriarchy.

Progressive neoliberal feminism (appropriately called "white feminism") upholds white supremacy through a feminist rhetoric: by prioritizing the voices and the lesser struggles of white women over women of color; by painting white women as perpetual victims of racialized masculine aggression à la King Kong; and by advocating "solutions" which further disenfranchise people of color (e.g., prison, policing, voting for the white woman in the 2016 US presidential elections who enjoyed slave/prison labor in the Arkansas governor's mansion and thought of black teenagers as "super predators").

White feminism, when trans-inclusive, tends to prioritize getting pronouns right rather than, for example, reducing the danger to trans women who are street-based sex workers. White feminism is also known as carceral feminism, which views criminalization as the most legitimate way to end gendered violence. This upholds and justifies prisons, police, and war as "feminist" institutions. A perfect example of this is the proposed "non-binary prisons" in England.

Decolonial and anti-capitalist feminism instead focuses on the liberation of all marginalized people; the struggles under patriarchy, capitalism, and white supremacy are seen as inextricable. The carceral state with its policing and surveillance apparatuses and its imperialist foreign policies are directly oppositional to the goals and ideals of liberation. Therefore the goals of white feminism and decolonial feminism are often at odds.

*see also:* INTERSECTIONALITY; TRANSFEMINISM; TERF; WOMEN'S LIBERATION

**FEMME** — A queer femininity. A queer identity.

Femme is distinct from feminine.

Femme arose out of working-class lesbian bar culture, as a counterpoint to butch. Femme meant "a lesbian whose appearance and behavior are traditionally feminine." There is heated intra-community debate and speculation on exactly what femme means and who is allowed access to it. I suggest that anyone who is queer and feels an affinity toward femmeness has a legitimate claim to it.

There are many femme aesthetics: soft femme, high femme, hard femme, messy femme, and more. Aesthetic is the first site of punishment for femmes but it isn't the only or even necessarily most significant aspect of femmeness. Femme aesthetics (like all aesthetics) are interfered with by capitalism, which means that it's more expensive to be femme. Who has the luxury of affording how they want to look, and who has the safety to look the way they want to look? Capitalism loves a trans femme aesthetic on stage because it's "fierce" and "edgy" and fits into a certain kind of marketing and branding, but does not even pay lip service to the personhood of trans women and trans femmes who worry about getting home safely. Capitalism also prescribes the femmeness and femininity that we can access (e.g., through what clothing sizes are available). There are only certain types of femmeness which are celebrated, and even then only in specific contexts (e.g., on stage or online). Even in queer circles, the word femme gets used interchangeably with feminine. Femme has a lot of currency in queer scenes right now, and is at risk of being co-opted by mainstream cishet culture: there are currently high-street retailers selling "femme forever" graphic tees; they're co-opting, butchering, and then trying to sell femme back to us.

Fat femmes are held to a much higher standard of femininity in order to be visible. When different bodies wear the same femme look, it's perceived very differently: a thin white woman might be considered "high femme glam" but a person of color or a fat person or a poor person might be labeled something racist or classist in the same outfit. So people of color, fat people, poor people, and sex workers all develop their own version of femme, which are then appropriated by the mainstream. White wealthy cis femmes—even if they are actively unlearning their classism, racism, and transphobia—are still oppressors. Their femmeness will be rewarded in more contexts than the femmeness of black and brown femmes, trans femmes, and poor femmes.

Some femme signifiers are very queer and decidedly not performed for the straight male gaze: dark lipstick, "witchy" aesthetics, and girly tattoos.

Femme isn't only aesthetic; it's also relational (like all gender identities and expressions). Femme can be the allowance, by yourself, to love and feel vulnerable and nurture, and find strength in all these "weak" feminine emotions. But this is complicated, because women (and people assigned "womanhood") who are not femme are also expected to be "feminine" in these ways, and are more likely to take on feminized labor like care work.

Femme is rebellion, doing anything for yourself and for other femmes rather than for straight men or the male gaze. It's communication, how we engage with our world and how we ask for things, and flagging interest in each other—in other words, it's consent. It's using "femme4femme" to uplift and empower and validate ourselves.

Femme can be a resistance to the failure to live up to or embody prescribed femininity, but it is also regarded as a failure itself by patriarchy, regardless of its embodiment: hard femme is a failure because it is not "correct," but high femme is also a failure because it is assumed to be performed for the male gaze.

The etymology of femme comes from the Italian "*femminiello*," a non-derogatory term for feminine people who are assigned male: trans women, feminine gay cis men, cross-dressing cis men. "*En femme*" is French to describe cross-dressers.

Femme has always been queer, and not binary.

The debate right now on femme and who's allowed to claim femme isn't very nuanced, and has lots of unexamined transphobia and transmisogyny. The people who bear the brunt of the violence of this debate are trans women and other transmisogyny affected people. Sapphic women in the West popularized the "butch" and femme labels in the 1940s, but the practice is much older; and the recorded history of femme is whitewashed and mostly told through the male gaze. We should, hopefully, be reflecting on our material experiences when deciding who "gets" to use a word like femme.

Femmeness is often invisible (on people read as women) because it is mistaken for cishetero femininity. This is reflected in the Sapphic complaint of not knowing if a girl is straight or queer because she's femme/feminine, and of straight women appropriating queer culture and looks. While femme is made invisible in queer communities, it's hyper-visible in wider society where femininity is subject to constant gaze and judgement. Femme can be empowering for assigned female at birth (AFAB) people who have been prescribed a very narrow femininity: it can seem that the only way to subvert patriarchy is to reject femininity altogether, but femme is a subversive alternative to hegemonic femininity. Femme allows us to re-engage with femininity on our terms, instead of in the limited ways it's been forced upon us.

Femme can be very empowering, especially for assigned male at birth (AMAB) people who have been denied femininity. Performing femme when you're read as a man by the public is an inherently political and hyper-visible act, because of the way society treats men who are "feminine" or "dressing like women." The cultural context of wearing lipstick or dresses is extremely dependent on how the public perceives you.

Femmeness is subject to an objectifying gaze and blatantly disregards gender expectations, and is therefore subversive.

Femme is a queer identity and a gender itself, for queers: "My gender is 'femme.'" Pronouns do not indicate femmeness or lack thereof; femmes can use any pronouns, and not everyone who uses the traditionally feminine "she/her" pronouns is a femme.

In French, "*femme*" has different meanings depending on its context: it can mean woman, wife, feminine lesbian, or feminine queer person. In English, the word does not mean woman or wife: "*Elle est une femme*" ("She is a woman" in French) and "She is a femme" (English) do not mean the same things. Lots of English words are borrowed and adapted from French (and other languages), and their meaning is different in English!

see also: BUTCH; ASSIGNED FEMALE AT BIRTH; ASSIGNED MALE AT BIRTH; TRANSMYSOGYNY

**FEMMEPHOBIA** — The marginalization of femmes. The devaluation of femininity.

This is perhaps better understood as misogyny (when directed at women) and queerphobia (when directed at men and other people who aren't women).

The concept of femmephobia conflates misogyny with femininity and implies a "masc privilege." Masculine women, butches, and mascs who aren't men do not benefit from femmephobia. On the other hand, men have male privilege and benefit from the devaluation of femininity (i.e., misogyny). Cishet, masculine men also benefit from the oppression of feminine men (i.e., queerphobia).

Still, there is a legitimate need to examine the different manifestations of misogyny and queerphobia, how they punish us, and how we can undermine them.

There is the assumption that femininity is more performative than masculinity; that masculinity is the "default" and femininity is artificial, extravagant, indulgent, fussy, and fake. Rituals of femininity (e.g., doing your nails) are scrutinized and shamed, while the beauty rituals of masculinity (e.g., going to the gym) are lauded.

Patriarchy devalues or delegitimizes everything which is perceived as femme or feminine. It's easier to attack "fake boobs" (they're not fake) and acrylic nails than to attack patriarchy because as a system of oppression it isn't tangible in the same way. But this does a massive disservice to feminism as a movement: people marginalized by patriarchy should not be policing which facets of femininity are permissible, trying to delineate a boundary which positions them on the "good" side and breast implants on the "bad" side. Deriding things which are coded as feminine as weak—like makeup or feminized labor or being sexually submissive—does not ascribe a contrary "strength" to feminism as a movement.

*see also:* MISOGYNY; FEMME; QUEERPHOBIA

**FETISH** — The sexual arousal from a non-sexual object, body part, or scenario.

Fetishes fall beneath the kink tree: fetishes are kinks, but not all kinks are fetishes (some kinks are explicitly sexual, and are seen as just spicier expressions of a "normal" sexuality).

The very idea of a fetish raises questions about what is sexual versus non-sexual, and the bounds of normalcy.

*see also:* FETISHIZE; KINK

**FETISHIZE** — To make into a fetish. To objectify and sexually covet.

Fetishizing someone denies them agency or full personhood, because it reduces them to a single aspect of their bodies or selves which is sexualized.

Being fetishized is a consequence of so-called "visibility" while being a marginalized person, and with it comes the possibility for physical violence from the people who fetishize you should you reject them, or should their desire cause them to question and violently defend their masculinity or heterosexuality.

see also: FETISH; DESIRE; TRANS PANIC; GAY PANIC

**FFS** — Acronym for FACIAL FEMINIZATION SURGERY.

**FLAMING** — Overtly queer; flamboyantly and flagrantly flying in the face of gender norms.

Flaming is usually reserved to describing effeminate queer men (and people perceived as men), but could also describe butch queer women (and people perceived as women). It is used as both a neutral descriptor and an insult, depending on context.

see also: EFFEMINATE; GAY

**FRIEND OF DOROTHY** — 20th-century US queer slang for a gay man, referring to Dorothy in *The Wizard of Oz*.

Where queer sexualities and sex acts are criminalized, people develop euphemisms and covert ways of discussing their identities and behaviors without incriminating themselves.

Judy Garland is a gay icon. She's idealized for her skills as an artist, the way her personal struggles were seen to mirror those of queer men in the 20th century, and for her value as a camp figure. *The Wizard of Oz* books explore queer themes (without explicitly naming them as such), like queer love and lesbian separatism.

In the early 1980s, the US Navy was investigating homosexuality among service members in Chicago, and discovered that a lot of gay servicemen called themselves "friends of Dorothy." The Navy misunderstood and attempted to locate a woman called Dorothy, thinking she was the center of an insidious ring of homosexual servicemen, hoping to convince her to snitch on her gay friends.

Dorothy was never found.

Judy Garland died on the night of June 27, 1969, coincidentally several hours before the Stonewall riots began.

see also: POLARI; CAMP

**F**

**FRONT HOLE** — Alternative term for vagina, used by trans people who were assigned female.

It is preferred by some because it gives them less dysphoria or feels less clinical. The implied "back hole" is the anus.

*see also:* BOY PUSSY

**FRUIT, FRUITY** — Synonymous with "effeminate," "gay," "queer." Polari slang for "queen."

*see also:* POLARI; QUEEN

**FTM, F2M** — Acronym for FEMALE TO MALE.

**FURRY, FURRIES** — A fandom subculture interested in fictional, anthropomorphic animal characters.

Some, but not all, furries have a sexual interest in furry; this is distinct from a sexual interest in animals, which the furry fandom generally frowns upon. Furries who are sexually interested in furry are not queer just for being furries; furry is a kink, not a sexual orientation.

*see also:* OTHERKIN

**FUTCH** — "Feminine butch." On a spectrum between butch and femme. A queer identity and aesthetic.

*see also:* BUTCH; FEMME; ANDROGYNOUS

**G** — The G in LGBT+ is for GAY.

**GAL, GAL PAL** — Slang for a girl, in recorded use since 1795 as a vulgarism.

Gal pal is a phrase used without irony by media outlets and people who comment on romantic relationships between women, seemingly unaware that they are romantically or sexually involved with each other. It's now used ironically between queers, lightheartedly mocking straight people's inability to see a pair of women as anything other than friends.

*see also:* GIRL; WOMAN; SAPPHIC; ERASURE; SCISSORING

**GATEKEEP, GATEKEEPER** — Gatekeep means to arbitrarily delay or prevent access. A gatekeeper is someone who acts as a barrier to access.

The boundaries of queerness are deliberately blurry, but some people actively police them to keep others out. Any notion of gatekeeping, such as "not trans enough" or "not queer enough," should be challenged.

Trans healthcare and access to public life are heavily gatekept. Trans people are only allowed access to vital treatment after we've "proven" ourselves to a panel of so-called "experts," who often don't even know what "transgender" means. Our ability to change our names and gender markers on IDs often relies on a letter from a psychologist and a formal diagnosis of mental illness, rather than a self-declaration. Medical transition is only allowed after a long, arbitrary period of counseling and "real-life experience," which is more to assuage the doubts of cis practitioners than to ensure that trans patients are giving truly informed consent.

*see also*: POLICE (v.); TRANS HEALTHCARE; BODILY AUTONOMY; ERASURE; TRUSCUM; REAL-LIFE EXPERIENCE; LIVING AS; CONSENT

**GAY** — An umbrella term for homosexual, same-sex attracted, and LGBT+. A reclaimed slur.

Gay has come to be shorthand for all non-heterosexual people— sometimes it also includes heterosexual trans people—and the culture they create. Its use as an umbrella term is good because it's inclusive and usefully reductive; but it's also bad because it prioritizes homosexual men, erases difference within the queer community, and is justification for gatekeeping non-homosexual queerness (bisexuality, pansexuality, asexuality, and non-homosexual transness).

Gay has been, and continues to be, the umbrella term under which LGBTQ+ people politically organize. Gay is also a unifying cultural term through which all queer people can find representation and shared experiences.

Gay is a gendered term as much as it is about sexuality. Gay has a historic connection with trans: until the 20th century, gay and trans were regarded as the same, because both gay and trans were defined by being gender transgressions. Even throughout the 20th century, gay and trans culture were indistinguishable until the 1990s.

The modern relationship between gay men (as a group) and non-homosexual queer groups is fraught. Gay spaces are transphobic and misogynistic. There are LGB people campaigning to push the T out of LGBT+. The assumption that gay culture is all about sex—that the gay community is a massive orgy—means that aces and trans people (and anyone who doesn't fall into hegemonic cisnormative beauty standards, i.e., young, cis, thin, white, rich) can't participate in gay culture. Gay culture is all about playing with gender norms (e.g., drag, wearing makeup, calling each other "girl"); but when trans men do it, they're "invalidating" themselves as men.

Homosexuality has long been seen as deviant and criminal, so accusations of being gay were very serious and insulting. Gay continues to be used as a slur to describe all things bad, or all things perceived as gender transgressions: failures of masculinity and femininity. In the 1990s and 2000s, gay replaced queer as the ubiquitous homophobic slur.

Though it encompasses all non-heterosexual groups, gay is distinct from queer and other sexuality terms. Gay has connotations of homo-normativity, assimilation, and respectability. But an otherwise queer-identified person might still choose to call themselves gay in certain contexts where it's simpler and safer to say "I'm gay" rather than get into the nuances of sexuality or gender identity. Other times, they'll say, "I'm not gay as in happy, but queer as in fuck you."

see also: HOMOSEXUAL; LESBIAN; QUEER; BISEXUAL; LGBT+; TRANSGENDER; GENDER; INVERT

**GAY AGENDA** — A demonizing term used by the religious right to suggest a monolithic and nefarious gay community, usually one driven toward corrupting youth and destroying "family values."

It is also used with levity by gay people.

Levity aside, the LGBT+ rights movement does genuinely have a gay agenda. The foremost issue has been marriage equality, but a comprehensive gay agenda would also include: prison reform, sex education which is inclusive of queer and trans bodies and relationships, more hate crime laws, and full inclusion of trans and queer people in the military.

A queer agenda, however, would prioritize prison and police abolition, universal healthcare, ending homelessness (which disproportionately affects queer youth), abolishing borders and abolishing detention centers (which cage queer migrants and asylum seekers), and abolishing the military.

see also: HOMOPHOBIA; QUEERPHOBIA; ASSIMILATION

**GAY BAR** — A bar which welcomes or caters to queer people, explicitly or implicitly. The site of queer culture, with queer performances, music, and dancing.

Weimar Germany had thriving gay/trans culture, and in World War I US soldiers who went to Germany saw it and brought it back to America. The German influence, along with the rise in modern living, nightclubs, and youth living away from their parents, sparked the creation of the first major gay urban communities. Class distinctions were eroding because everyone went to the same gay clubs: "slumming" was popular among the rich, who went to places like Harlem's Cotton Club (a segregated, prohibition-era cabaret nightclub) and hooked up with street queens.

Some lived in butch or femme "drag" all the time, especially the lower classes who had less social status to lose for deviating from prescribed gender norms.

There were lots of gay clubs in America in the 1920s. Many were shuttered during the Depression in the 1930s, but more opened again during World War II when all the men went away to fight. Women weren't allowed into bars at all before World War I, but with suffrage they were allowed to access more parts of public social life. When the men left for war in the early 1940s, queer women took over the gay spaces; and when the men returned, the women stayed.

Gay bars are closing again because gentrification and rising rents force them to shut down. Gay culture happens in low-income areas because queers are more likely to be poor and disenfranchised; gentrification happens around gay bars because straight people find gay culture "edgy" and "arty" and desirable.

*see also:* GAY; GAY CULTURE

**GAY BASH** — Bullying or physical violence directed at queer people, or people perceived to be queer.

*see also:* HATE CRIME

**GAY CULTURE** — A diverse culture built and reproduced by queers through a shared alienation by cisheteronormativity.

All culture is infused with queerness because queers are everywhere and are leading on most aspects of culture. There is a meme which follows the format "Gay culture is _____" and the blank is filled in by anything from a niche fashion reference to symptoms of mental illness.

White queers steal from Black culture, and cishets steal from gay culture. The lines between queer culture and Black culture are blurry because Black queers create so much of what becomes Black culture, queer culture, and mainstream culture.

*see also:* GAY; QUEER; CULTURAL APPROPRIATION; CAMP

**GAY FOR PAY** — A straight person, usually a man, who has transactional "gay sex."

Sexual identity isn't about action, it's about attraction, so their straightness is not in question; but gay for pay might also be a way to safely explore gayness without confronting difficult issues about self-image and identity as a not-straight person.

*see also:* SEX WORK

## GAY LIBERATION FRONT (GLF), GAY LIBERATION FRONT WOMEN (GLFW) — A decentralized group of activist organizations

advocating for sexual liberation and connected issues of racism and anti-capitalism, formed immediately after the 1969 Stonewall riots. There were GLF groups in the US, the UK, and Canada.

The GLF in the US was started in July 1969, with the aim of continuing the momentum of the Stonewall riots and ending state and police persecution of queers. It supported a number of other groups, including the Black Panther Party. In 1970, the drag queen caucus of the GLF created the splinter group Street Transvestite Action Revolutionaries (STAR), which focused on supporting queer and trans street youth, especially people of color.

The GLF in the UK was founded by students Bob Mellors and Aubrey Walter at the London School of Economics, and its first meeting was held on October 13, 1970. The GLF demands were more radical than those of the UK's Homosexual Law Reform Society of the 1960s, which as the name suggests advocated for legal reform. Women were a minority in the UK's GLF and so formed their own social and activist groups to escape the misogyny and chauvinism of gay men. Many men in the GLF experimented with drag and gender bending, which made some of the women in the GLF uncomfortable; the issue of drag was divisive and caused the group to splinter into the GLFW, which is ironic given that the Stonewall riots and the GLF group in the US were both led by drag queens and trans women. The GLF group in the UK was disbanded at the end of 1973—with so many factions, consensus was impossible.

Many subsequent gay rights activist groups have their roots in the GLF.

*see also:* STONEWALL; ACTIVISM; HIV/AIDS

## GAY PANIC — A legal defense used to justify violence against queer people, especially against queer men.

Gay panic defense is taken to suggest that an assailant or murderer was "temporarily insane" whilst they attacked a gay person, driven momentarily mad by the possibility (and perceived threat) of receiving same-sex sexual advances. The mere existence of gay people is alleged to "provoke" violence against us, as if the presence of homosexuality requires heterosexuals to kill queers in "self-defense."

Gay panic is rooted in homophobic misinformation about gay people being sex-crazed, and prioritizes the fragile heterosexuality of violent men over the lives of gay people. It is used as a legal defense when the guilt of the suspect is not in question, in order to play on the homophobia of the judge and jury and get a lenient sentencing.

Gay panic is still considered a permissible legal defense in South Australia, and in every US state except California and Illinois.

*see also:* TRANS PANIC

**GAY PRIDE** — *see:* PRIDE.

**GAY SHAME** — An anti-Gay Pride movement which rejects the consumerism, corporate sponsorship, and celebrity focus of Pride. A reaction to the depoliticization of Pride.

In 1998 in San Francisco or Brooklyn (depending on who you ask), events and protests started being organized under the name Gay Shame; they have since fizzled out, then re-emerged and fizzled out again.

*see also:* QUEER; ACTIVISM; ASSIMILATION; PINKWASHING

**GAY–STRAIGHT ALLIANCE (GSA)** — A student- or community-based organization with the goal of providing support and a safer space for LGBT+ youth.

The first GSA was started in 1988 in Concord, Massachusetts. There are now over 4,000 decentralized chapters, and while most are in the US, they also exist in the UK, Canada, Mexico, the Netherlands, New Zealand, Hong Kong, Australia, Bulgaria, and India.

GSAs are reported to positively impact the mental health and academic achievements of queer youth, who might not have other support networks at school or at home.

GSAs are not really about an "alliance" between straight and LGBT+ people. GSAs are often college campus groups formed for gay people to organize, with the plausible deniability that any individual member could be a straight ally if it's not safe for them to be out.

*see also:* PROJECT 10; ALLY; ACTIVISM

**GAZE** — The act of seeing and being seen. The power dynamics of being watched.

As described in Foucault's panopticon metaphor, we live in a self-policing society where we could always be being watched, and where we are in fact usually being watched or recorded. We adjust our behavior, without prompting, to assimilate and act "normal."

The gaze comes not only from the state, but from individuals who police those around them. People who feel pressure from the gaze are encouraged to be insecure, docile, and to consume more. They also face mental-health problems and alienation.

The gaze is fetishistic and dehumanizing.

*see also:* MALE GAZE; CIS GAZE; STRAIGHT GAZE; FETISHIZE; ASSIMILATION

**GENDER (N.)** — A nebulous set of cultural norms surrounding behavior, community, and aesthetic. A relationship to power under patriarchy.

Gender is a feeling of affinity, a set of relations (hierarchy), and an alleged mark of biological difference (sex) and social difference (sexuality, under heteronormativity).

Gender is a social code; a set of norms which are culturally produced and ever-shifting. Gender is, in many cultures, a primary identity, so challenges to it can be extremely uncomfortable. Gender is internal (self) and external (society). It is neither possible nor desirable to try to distinctly separate these.

Gender is produced and reproduced through hierarchy, which is reinforced by compulsory heterosexuality which enforces gender roles and reifies that hierarchy. That hierarchy may begin with an assumption on gender based on the perception of genitals at birth, but it is mainly enforced through adherence to, or deviation from, gender norms and roles (i.e., appearance and behavior). Do you act like and look like the gender you are assumed to be, or not? Deviation invites punishment, but adherence is to be punished too. Everyone suffers, to varying degrees, under cisheteropatriarchy.

According to Simone de Beauvoir, "One is not born, but rather becomes, a woman." Some gender theorists think that our genders are "made" through privileged/oppressed relations: a person might be made into a woman when she is harassed on the street by someone who is made into a man as he harasses her. But gender policing doesn't only enforce hierarchy; it also enforces gender normativity and punishes deviation from the norm.

Gender is something we do, not a fixed or essential aspect of the self. Gender is a performance. But gendered performance isn't a single act; it is repetition and ritual, it is habit. It is the way we walk, the timbre of our voices, the way we interact with each other based on assumptions we make about other people's genders without realizing we're doing it. This performance is constant and so becomes naturalized, though there is nothing natural about it (and we can see how different it has been throughout history and across cultures). And, we are limited in the performances we're able to do, based on our other (perceived) identities and what is considered intelligible by current cultural norms around gender.

Gender is performative, but it is not just performance. Emphasizing the performative aspect of gender is reductive, and does not leave room for exploring why certain gender roles are more comfortable or natural. Performance doesn't explain dysphoria (physical or social). Saying simply that "gender is performative," or "all gender is drag," implies that gender is somehow not real. But of course it is real. It is elusive but extremely material, with concrete consequences.

In addition to performance, gender is an interior sense of self, aligning with or against cultural norms of gender. A person isn't a woman because she has a body gendered that way, but because she identifies with "womanhood," which can include aesthetics, behaviors, characteristics, and relationships to other genders.

Some types of feminism think that gender should be eradicated because its only purpose is to subjugate women, or women and queers; but for many queers and trans people, gender is positive and powerful. We want to eradicate gender hierarchies, but not the beautiful diversity of gender.

Gender is assumed to be a stable category, and upon gender "sexuality" is built. The current mainstream modes of describing sexuality—heterosexual and homosexual—depend on both the gender of the subject and the gender(s) of the people they're attracted to. This assumes that the gender of the subject is stable, and that the genders of the people they're attracted to are both stable and immediately recognizable.

Gender is flimsy and elusive when subject to interrogation. For lots of trans people who spend a lot of time thinking about it, it's hard to pinpoint why we are our gender and not some other genders. Gender for trans people can be extremely specific ("My gender is sassy Spock raising his eyebrow") and extremely vague ("My gender is obscurity"). Media portrayals can help people articulate their "gender feels" by providing a template from popular culture. It's not within the scope of this book (nor my ability as a theorist) to fully explore the implications of "self," "selfness." Suffice to say that gender is about a sense of self, and that maybe it does not need to be further explained.

Gender is elusive but it is also material, with material consequences. It is produced through external material conditions and experience (e.g., sexism, privilege). However, the affects of an internal sense of gender are also material: to try to separate external "material experience" from internal experience of gender (e.g., a trans woman who is gendered as a man, who ostensibly then does not experience sexism where cis women do) would be an error. Her material experience includes internalized misogyny and transmisogyny and constant erasure, and her lack of direct transmisogyny is conditional on her hiding and denying a key aspect of herself.

Gender is also reproduced through relationships to others: the way I act in different gendered relationships reaffirms (and actually creates, day by day) my gender. A girl is a girl partly because she adopts the role of "girl," and acts "like a girl" instead of "like a boy" or like both, or like neither. Our gender is reproduced by how we see ourselves, how our social group sees us, and how society sees us. We constantly signify our genders in order to "establish" or re-create them. What happens when people fail to see our gender despite the signals we send?

Failure. The production of gender norms means there are inverse gender failures. That there is gender at all means we are doomed to fail at it.

Gender norms define which bodies are legitimate, which are intelligible and "real"; bodies which defy these norms are illegitimate, unintelligible, and "fake."

Normative, "proper" gender is underwritten by racial codes of purity and taboos against miscegenation.

Gender is constructed, produced, and reproduced within existing power structures, which are totalizing and inescapable. Therefore, there is no "authentic" gender against which to compare ours. All gender is a performance, but some gender can leverage performance and subvert the power structures of patriarchy, capitalism, white supremacy, and so on, by challenging or questioning the gender binary, or cultural beauty norms.

Gender is constructed within other systems of privilege/oppression and other hierarchies, like white supremacy. The default gender template is heterosexual, cis, white, wealthy, and able-bodied. People who don't fit within those narrow categories are doing gender "wrong" already, before they've done anything, and we will not gain access to rights or resources by trying to cram ourselves into a box that can't contain us. Assimilation may afford you some safety, some invisibility, but it will not give you, or Others like you, liberation.

*see also:* SEX (n.); AMAB; AFAB; CISGENDER; TRANSGENDER; PATRIARCHY; QUEER; HOMOSEXUAL

**GENDER (v.), GENDERED** — To assign a gender to a person, aesthetic, object, or behavior. Names, colors, occupations, clothing, and bodies are all gendered.

It is not possible to extricate gender from our experiences, because it is constantly imposed upon us, similarly to white supremacy and other systems of oppression. Everything is infected with gender. We must aim to contest the normative gendering with something better.

Gender abolitionists are not interested in erasing all things which are currently gendered from humanity, nor do they want a single gender to replace the current wealth of gender diversity we have now. Gender abolitionism instead aims for the eradication of an asymmetric power system based on gender (or, more specifically, traits and bodies which have gender imposed upon them). Gender abolition must constantly evaluate itself to ensure that it isn't simply thinly-veiled misogyny, especially transmisogyny, which targets femininity as "gendered" while masculinity is prized as "androgynous."

*see also:* GENDER NEUTRAL LANGUAGE; CISSEXISM; PATRIARCHY

**GENDER AFFIRMING SURGERY** — Any surgery which "affirms" the patient's gender.

The term usually refers to chest surgeries (top surgery), genital reconstruction surgery (bottom surgery), and other surgical procedures which alleviate dysphoria.

While it's a useful phrase because it encompasses a range of trans-related surgeries, it's generally preferable to use the specific term for the surgery you're referring to. If using a blanket term is unavoidable, the phrase "transgender-specific surgery" is an alternative, though even that is not without its problems because cis people also get some of the same surgeries for different reasons (e.g., mastectomy).

This phrase is widely in use because it encompasses any surgery related to easing dysphoria for trans people. But, trans people's genders don't (necessarily) need to be "affirmed" through surgery.

Former terms to describe this include "gender reassignment surgery" and "sex change operation."

*see also:* TOP SURGERY; GENITAL RECONSTRUCTIVE SURGERY; BOTTOM SURGERY; TRANS HEALTHCARE

**GENDER BINARY** — A classification of gender. A power structure.

The gender binary is the binding of gender, biological sex, and gendered behavior together, and into two opposite, distinct, fixed categories, with no liminality, cross-over, or alternative: woman/female/feminine and man/male/masculine.

Gender is a spectrum, and so is biological sex and gendered behavior. Smashing the gender binary means challenging the idea of what it means to be a "woman" or a "man." Seeing gender as a binary reinforces power structures within patriarchy. The gender binary dictates not only what genders are permissible, but what ways of performing our genders are allowed.

Contrary to the claims of "gender critical" feminism, trans people do not "reinforce" the gender binary by existing. No genders "reinforce" the gender binary; the gender binary is not an individual choice of gender expression, it's a system of sorting, prioritizing, and vilifying people and behaviors. Trans people, by definition, challenge the gender binary because they challenge the "fixedness" of gender to sex, even if they "fully transition" (whatever that means) to an "opposite" gender.

Gender critical feminism, it turns out, isn't critical of gender; it's critical of trans people. For trans people, there is no winning in this game. There is no gender expression a trans person can adopt which will satisfy the call, seemingly put only upon trans people, to "smash the binary" rather than reify it. By naming themselves in opposition to the default binary, they are allegedly reproducing it.

What are we to do instead, other than simply be born in a different time? There is no possibility for existing fully outside of cisheteronormative patriarchy; to oppose it is to undermine and hopefully undo it.

Bisexuals are also accused of reinforcing the gender binary, based on the misconception that bisexuality is attraction to "the same and opposite" genders. Bisexuality has always included people outside the gender binary, and most modern bisexual groups have updated their definitions of bisexuality to "attracted to the same and other genders, attracted to two or more genders, or attracted to people regardless of gender." If anything, homosexuality and heterosexuality are more "binary" sexualities than bisexuality, though they are likewise not absolutely rigid.

If the gender binary were an accurate representation of human biology and gender, no one would ever deviate from a single column on the chart below:

|  | Female/Woman/Feminine | Male/Man/Masculine |
|---|---|---|
| *Chromosomes* | XX | XY |
| *Dominant hormones* | Estrogen/Progesterone | Testosterone |
| *Genitals* | Vagina | Penis |
| *Sex organs* | Uterus, ovaries | Testicles |
| *Gametes* | Egg | Sperm |
| *Gender identity* | Woman | Man |
| *Gender expression* | Hegemonic femininity | Hegemonic masculinity |

In reality, human biology, gender identity, and gender expression are extremely diverse.

The gender binary is not "real" (tangible, infallible, ultimate); it's a social construct. But it is real in the sense that it has significance, cultural weight, and consequences.

*see also:* PATRIARCHY; CISSEXISM; NON-BINARY; BINARY; TRANSPHOBIA; BIPHOBIA

**GENDER CRITICAL** — An anti-trans ideology which suggests that trans people are inherently reinforcing the gender binary.

Gender critical people argue that being trans is conforming to and reproducing outdated gender modes and the gender binary. The entire premise is based on a conflation between gender norms, and gender identity and dysphoria. When trans people conform to traditional gender norms, it's often because they need to in order to be gendered correctly, or to be taken as "serious" about their transition.

Rather than criticize the strategies that trans people use to navigate the world comfortably, we should be subverting systems of cisheteropatriarchy which prescribe the "correct" ways to do gender.

*see also:* TERF; GENDER DYSPHORIA

**GENDER DYSPHORIA** — A feeling of incongruence between the gendered self and the body, or how the body is gendered.

Gender dysphoria can be social, physical, or both. It can be relieved by using a different name or pronouns, feeling like people see you as the gender you want to express, and/or medical intervention to change your body.

Gender dysphoria is a medical term which pathologizes and medicalizes transness; it also lends credibility to the status of trans people as a protected political class. Gender dysphoria is a mental health disorder classified in the *DSM-5*, replacing gender identity disorder (GID). Unlike GID, gender dysphoria doesn't pathologize gender non-conformity; instead it focuses on the distress caused by an incorrect sex assignment at birth. This is a slight but important improvement, but we should ideally be moving away from pathologization and the institutions which require a medical diagnosis for trans people to be given basic rights. Trans healthcare should be treated as an issue of bodily autonomy, not "treatment" for a "condition."

Many, but not all, trans people experience physical dysphoria. Dysphoria is not a prerequisite for transness: transness is defined by not feeling unambiguously aligned with the sex you were assigned at birth.

Gender dysphoria cannot be relieved through conversion therapy, and attempts to make people not-trans, through coercion or otherwise, are abusive.

*see also:* TRANS HEALTHCARE; GENDER; TRANSGENDER

**GENDER EUPHORIA** — An opposite to gender dysphoria. The trans joy of experiencing your gender.

Gender euphoria is a sense of joy, exhilaration, and excitement experienced when you feel happy with your gender or gender expression. It's so named to highlight trans joy and to combat the mainstream narrative that to be trans is to be constantly miserable.

*see also:* GENDER DYSPHORIA

**GENDER EXPRESSION** — The gender(s) that someone is expressing with their outward appearance, including their body language, vocal mannerisms, makeup, accessories, clothes, and the way they relate to other people.

Gender expression is related to, but distinct from, gender identity and sex.

We are implicitly taught to gender different expressions, and how to perform the gender expressions for the gender we're assigned at birth. Performing these things is one way to send gender cues.

With practice, you can change the gender cues you send to people and it will change the way they gender you. This is not to suggest that you should conform to any gender expression in order for your gender to be legitimate, or to deserve respect for your gender: you deserve respect for your gender regardless of how you express it. Still, these descriptions might be useful if you're struggling to get people to "see" your gender. They're crude, but most people's ideas of gender are crude.

The strongest gender cue is facial and body hair; then body language and how you interact with other people; then vocal mannerisms; then cosmetic/"superficial" things like clothing, voice pitch, body shape, makeup, and hair style.

People also gender each other based on the perceived gender of the person they're with. If your gender expression is androgynous and you're having dinner alone with someone whose gender expression is traditionally masculine, you'll likely be assumed to be feminine based on the larger context of heteronormativity.

With regard to clothes, dresses, skirts, bows, high heels, overt makeup, showy jewelry, low necklines, and bright colors are all feminine modes of dress; trousers, button-up shirts, ties, suits, and no makeup are all "androgynous" but still masculine-coded. Still, clothes are arguably the least important gender cue we send to people: a woman in a masculine suit is instantly recognizable as a woman, and a man in a skirt is immediately recognizable (and lambasted) too. Of course we can't "recognize" people's genders just by looking at them. But the point is that we don't use clothes to "decide" what gender someone is nearly as much as we use other gender cues. Also note that it is acceptable for a woman to wear masculine clothes, but unacceptable for a man to wear feminine clothes, because being "like a man" is admirable but being "like a woman" is detestable.

Sitting with legs crossed at the knees or the ankles is feminine; legs crossed with one ankle on the other knee is masculine. Sitting with legs close together is feminine; sitting with legs wide apart is masculine. Folding hands together, or holding your own hands is feminine; sitting with hands on your knees and your chest open is masculine. Taking up space is masculine.

Standing upright like a pencil is feminine; leaning is masculine. Fidgeting or nervous-appearing behavior is feminine (maybe because women and femmes are rightly nervous in public space that constantly scrutinizes them at best or targets them for physical violence at worst). Stoicism and calm confidence are masculine (maybe because men get to move through public space with ease). Hands on hips is feminine. Hugging yourself is feminine. Arms crossed is masculine/androgynous. Elbows in close to your sides (with biceps pushing breasts inward) is feminine; elbows out is masculine.

Walking with your head down is feminine; walking with your head up is masculine. Walking with swaying hips is feminine; walking with swaying shoulders is masculine. Walking gracefully and smoothly is feminine; walking with a clunky "waddled" John Wayne-esque stride is masculine. Walking quickly is feminine; walking slowly is masculine. Walking with your arms across your chest or closely to your sides is feminine; walking with arms loosely at your sides, or with your hands in your pockets, is masculine.

Vocal mannerisms are a much stronger gender cue than vocal pitch. Speaking with an upward inflection at the end of sentences (or, ending sentences with a question mark?) is feminine; speaking in a monotone is masculine. Asking questions is feminine; stating "facts" is masculine. Speaking quickly is feminine; speaking slowly is masculine

THE A–Z OF GENDER AND SEXUALITY

(maybe because women and femmes need to speak quickly in order to say what they want before being interrupted by a man).

Gesticulating is feminine; not gesticulating is masculine. Women are taught to communicate by building emotional bonds and empathizing, which gives them worth in society as "nurturers"; men are taught to communicate through giving demands, stating information, and "teaching" (usually patronizing), which gives them social value as "leaders."

Disturbingly, but not surprisingly, these gender cues are basically synonymous with projecting "weakness" (feminine) or "strength" (masculine).

Gender expression is used to infer people's sexualities. Performing gender cues of what's perceived to be the "opposite" gender will result in people assuming that you're gay, much to the chagrin of trans people just beginning to change their gender expressions.

There are an infinite number of gender expressions, none of which is more correct or incorrect than another.

*see also:* GENDER (n.)

**GENDER FLUID** — A gender which is not static.

A gender fluid person could move seamlessly between two or more genders—this could be more like steps than seamless movement, but as a whole it feels "fluid."

Gender fluid falls within the "transgender" category, regardless of medical transition or lack thereof.

*see also:* NON-BINARY; TRANSGENDER

**GENDERFUCK** — To actively antagonize gender norms and the gender binary.

*see also:* GENDER NON-CONFORMING

**GENDER IDENTITY** — Could also just be called "gender." Cis genders are also gender identities but are never called that.

Gender (including an absence of gender) is common to all people. Gender identity, for cis and trans people, is believed by pediatricians to be developed by the age of four. However, gender identity is often more fluid. The World Professional Association for Transgender Health (WPATH) also acknowledges that "conditions specific to individual lives may constrain a person from acknowledging or even recognizing any gender dysphoria they may experience until they are well into adulthood."

Trans people are expected to justify their gender not only with academic texts on feminism, on queer theory, on sexuality and patriarchy and performance and power, but also with psycho-medical material on hormones, surgery, depression, trauma, autism, childhood anxiety, and a catalogue of every single violence we have suffered which has "made us" trans. Fuck that. I transitioned because I'm drawn to queer boy culture; because after years I still get a thrill being called "he"; because my body feels better on testosterone. Gender identity is personal and should not need to be explained; it's an issue of bodily autonomy and social respect.

see also: CISSEXISM; TRANS HEALTHCARE; TRANSPHOBIA; GENDER DYSPHORIA

**GENDER IDENTITY DISORDER** — see: GENDER DYSPHORIA.

**GENDER NEUTRAL** — Neither asymmetrically masculine nor feminine. Either genderless, or balanced between masculinity and femininity. Unisex.

Being gender neutral is not actually "neutral," politically or socially; it's very contentious. Everything from androgynous gender expressions to using gender neutral language is antagonistic and challenges the gender binary. Gender neutral parenting is seen as especially threatening to the reproduction of gender norms.

see also: GENDER (v.); GENDER BINARY

**GENDER NEUTRAL LANGUAGE** — Language which does not gender its subjects.

Examples of gender neutral language are "they" pronouns instead of "he/she" or "he or she"; the "x," Latinx and Chicanx; and any language which does not assign gender to its subjects. "Hello everybody" is gender neutral, while "Ladies and gentlemen" is not.

But, gender neutral language is not actually neutral. The use of gender neutral language is a political act, and one often met with resistance. Planned Parenthood (PP) recently adopted gender neutral language for describing its gynecological services, thereby acknowledging that people who aren't women have vaginas and need to access PP's services: some men and non-binary people have ovaries and a uterus, menstruate, and give birth. This is also a larger statement about the separation between gender and sex. Predictably, PP was met with both praise and venom.

Not everyone agrees or feels things like "mate" or "comrade" are actually gender neutral, because they're masculine coded. So if someone says they don't like these words to describe them, don't use them. "But I call everyone 'dude'" is not a good excuse.

It's usually best practice to use gender neutral language when addressing an audience or describing a hypothetical subject. This could also be called "inclusive" or "trans inclusive" language. However, there are times when it may be more appropriate to deliberately use gendered language; for example, in the *Dungeons and Dragons* handbooks, the hypothetical player is always gendered "she" in an attempt to normalize and welcome women and girls into playing the game, and in recognition that women and girls are socially excluded from tabletop gaming.

| Feminine | Masculine | Gender neutral |
|---|---|---|
| Sister | Brother | Sibling |
| Mother, Mom, Mommy, Motherhood | Father, Dad, Daddy, Fatherhood | Parent, Ren, Renny, Parenthood, Rentherhood |
| Aunt | Uncle | Ankle |
| Niece | Nephew | Nibling, Niblet |
| | | Cousin |
| Girlfriend | Boyfriend | Partner, Lover, Enbyfriend, Date mate, Babe, Amour |
| Girl | Boy | Kid, Child |
| Woman | Man | Person, Adult |
| Gal | Dude, Guy, Man, Bro, Mate (masculine coded), Comrade (masculine coded), Buddy (masculine coded) | Friend, Pal |
| Ladies | Gentlemen | Everyone<br>Kind audience<br>Esteemed guests<br>Friends<br>People<br>Y'all<br>Youse |

Using gender neutral language can also be reductive; it can also be erasure; it can also be violence. Using "they/them" to describe a trans woman but no one else, when she's made it clear her pronouns are "she," is a violent denial of her womanhood. This is disappointingly common in lesbian spaces where trans women are implicitly excluded.

*see also:* PRONOUNS

## GENDER NON-CONFORMING, GENDER NONCONFORMING (GNC) — Anyone who does not conform to hegemonic gender roles.

The scope for nonconformity for boys and men is greater than for girls and women, because girls and women are afforded some masculinity (because being masculine is good), whereas boys and men are not afforded any femininity (because being girly is bad); acceptable masculinity is much narrower.

There is a difference between bucking gender stereotypes (expression) and being trans (identity). Gender non-conforming can be a comfortable label in-between "cis" and "trans," for people who aren't cis but don't feel "trans enough" to claim transness.

*see also:* GENDER VARIANT

## GENDER REASSIGNMENT SURGERY (GRS) — A set of trans-specific surgeries, most often referring to "genital reconstruction surgery," which is the preferred term.

It was formerly called "sex reassignment surgery," or a "sex change."

*see also:* GENITAL RECONSTRUCTIVE SURGERY; BOTTOM SURGERY; GENDER AFFIRMING SURGERY; TRANS HEALTHCARE

## GENDER RECOGNITION — The legal recognition of a trans person's gender.

Requirements for gender recognition differ depending on where your identification documents are from, but commonly include: letters from therapists; deed polls or judge approval for name changes; letters from medical doctors; "real-life experience"; proof of "clinical treatment"; and in some places, genital reconstruction surgery or sterilization.

Self-determination is the best practice. Denying trans people the right to declare their own genders is patronizing and violent.

*see also:* TRANSGENDER; TRANS HEALTHCARE; REAL-LIFE EXPERIENCE; BODILY AUTONOMY; FASCISM

**GENDER VARIANT** — Anyone who strays from the norms of hegemonic masculinity and femininity.

Gender variant is a "softer" term than "transgender"; it's somehow less committal. It is often used for children who are gender non-conforming.

*see also:* GENDER NON-CONFORMING; TRANSGENDER

**GENDERED VIOLENCE** — Violence which targets people based on their gender. Punishment for gender deviance.

*see also:* PATRIARCHY; MISOGYNY; VIOLENCE; HOMOPHOBIA; TRANSPHOBIA; TRANSMISOGYNY

**GENDERFLUID** — *see:* GENDER FLUID.

**GENDERLESS** — *see:* AGENDER.

**GENDERQUEER** — A term for people who feel that "man" or "woman" are insufficient to describe their gender.

Genderqueer is an expansive term to describe anyone who doesn't fit comfortably as either a man or a woman. Genderqueer people are queering gender. The term originated in the 1990s. It is the predecessor to the newer term "non-binary," which is less politically charged.

Genderqueer people might use gender neutral pronouns such as "they/them" or "ze/zir," or they might use "he/him" or "she/her."

*see also:* QUEER (v.); QUEER (n.); TRANSGENDER; NON-BINARY

**GENITAL RECONSTRUCTIVE SURGERY (GRS)** — A set of medical procedures to alter or reconstruct the genitals, with the goal of alleviating dysphoria.

Genital reconstructive surgery is the term preferred by many trans people because, unlike "gender affirming surgery," it doesn't imply that their gender is "unaffirmed" before or without surgery. It is also called "bottom surgery."

*see also:* GENDER AFFIRMING SURGERY; BOTTOM SURGERY; TRANS HEALTHCARE

**GID** — Short for GENDER IDENTITY DISORDER.

*see also:* GENDER DYSPHORIA

THE A–Z OF GENDER AND SEXUALITY

**GIRL** — Someone who identifies with girlhood and femininity. A gender identity so culturally ubiquitous that it evades definition.

Girl is used for feminine children, adult women (often patronizingly), and by queer men for other men.

Girl is a Germanic word, in a grouping with others which begin with G or K and end in R. The L at the end of the word is a diminutive suffix. The g...r form denotes "young animals, children, and all kinds of creatures considered immature, worthless, or past their prime" (Liberman 2008).

Girl entered English c.1300 as a gender neutral word for a child or young person. In the late 1300s it acquired a gender-specific meaning, "female child"; in the 1400s it came to mean any young woman who was unmarried. From the 1640s, it was synonymous with "sweetheart." "Old girl" has been used to refer to a woman of any age since at least 1826.

*see also:* WOMAN; GENDER; GAY

**GIRL-DICK** — A term of endearment for a trans woman or trans femme's penis.

*see also:* TRANS WOMAN

**GIRLFRIEND** — A favored companion or sweetheart.

The predecessor to girlfriend was "she-friend," which was used in the 1600s to describe a girl romantically involved with a boy, or (presumably platonically) attached to another girl. By 1859, girlfriend had replaced she-friend and was used primarily to describe female friendships— which may or may not have been purely platonic. By 1922, it was a signifier of romantic attachment to a man, shifting to describe a girl–boy relationship.

*see also:* GIRL; LESBIAN

**GLBT** — *see:* LGBT+.

**GLF, GLFW** — Acronyms for GAY LIBERATION FRONT, and GAY LIBERATION FRONT WOMEN.

**GNC** — Acronym for GENDER NON-CONFORMING.

**GOLD STAR GAY, GOLD STAR LESBIAN** — A gay man who has never had sex with a woman, or a lesbian who has never had sex with a man.

People who proclaim to be gold star gays or gold star lesbians are usually resting on a foundation of biphobia and transphobia.

*see also:* GAY; LESBIAN; POLICE (v.); TRANSPHOBIA; BIPHOBIA

**GRAY ACE, GRAY ASEXUAL, GRAY ASEXUALITY** — Someone who falls on a spectrum between asexual and sexual. Someone who experiences sexual attraction very rarely, or at such a low level that it is ignorable.

A gray ace person is on the asexual spectrum and has a legitimate claim to an LGBT+ identity.

*see also:* ASEXUALITY; DEMISEXUAL; LGBT+; SEXUALITY

**GRAY-ROMANTIC** — Someone who falls on a spectrum between aromantic and romantic, also called "demiromantic."

Gray-romantic can mean someone who experiences romantic attraction, but only rarely. Alternatively, it can mean someone who experiences romantic attraction but does not desire romantic relationships. It can also describe someone who desires relationships which are not quite platonic and not quite romantic.

*see also:* AROMANTIC; QUEERPLATONIC

**GRINDR** — An ostensibly gay men's hookup app.

Grindr is notable because it reproduces gay culture and narratives on a large scale.

It's allegedly for gay men, but it includes: bisexual and bicurious men, straight men, straight trans women, queer trans women, and non-binary people who are deemed "close enough" to being "men" or "trans women." In other words, it's a queer space for all men, and women who are trans. Anyone who is read as a cis woman (e.g., lots of trans men and trans mascs) is not welcomed.

Grindr has popularized the terms "discreet," "straight-passing," and "convincing" within gay culture.

*see also:* GAY; DISCREET; STRAIGHT ACTING; CONVINCING

**GROSS INDECENCY** — A crime under the Labouchere Amendment (Section 11 of the 1885 Criminal Law Amendment Act in Great Britain), which policed sexual relations between men, including touching, kissing, and inviting or facilitating sex.

Gross indecency was a crime in the UK and its colonies. The term was first used in law in 1885 in the UK to criminalize sexual activity between men which did not quite constitute sodomy (penetrative anal sex), but it was never defined in any of the statutes which used it, in any country. Gross indecency was repealed in the UK with the 2003 Sexual Offences Act. It is still a crime in South Australia; Michigan, US; and Kenya—though only in Kenya is it still used to criminalize homosexuality, an inheritance from the British Empire.

Because the penalty for sodomy was so severe (death until 1861, and then life imprisonment), it was rare to get a prosecution; the Labouchere Amendment made it much easier to prosecute people, especially men. Courts relied on a "common sense of society" notion of what was "indecent." This made it easy to police and prosecute people. The text of the Labouchere Amendment states:

> Any male person who, in public or private, commits, or is a party to the commission of, or procures, or attempts to procure the commission by any male person of, any act of gross indecency with an other male person, shall be guilty of a misdemeanour, and being convicted thereof, shall be liable at the discretion of the Court to be imprisoned for any term not exceeding two years, with or without hard labour.

Between 1885 and 1967 (when the Act was replaced by new legislation, the Sexual Offences Act), 75,000 men were prosecuted for "gross indecency." Oscar Wilde was prosecuted for gross indecency in 1895 and imprisoned for the maximum sentence of two years of hard labor. Wilde's prosecution meant he had to pay the legal fees of the prosecution, the Marquess of Queensbury, which left him bankrupt. Wilde's sentencing severely affected his health and contributed to his death in 1900.

Alan Turing was convicted in 1952 for gross indecency when he reported that his lover's acquaintance had burgled his house. Turing was given the option of hormone therapy or imprisonment. He chose hormone therapy, which is widely considered to have contributed to his suicide in 1954.

In Canada, sex between men was criminalized as gross indecency in 1892, punishable by whipping and five years' imprisonment. In 1906 the intention to commit gross indecency was given the same maximum punishment. Canada had several subsequent gross indecency statutes, but all "gross indecency" laws were repealed, effective from 1987.

In South Australia, gross indecency is currently a felony: it requires involvement of a minor (under 16) and sexual acts, in public or private, which "a decent person" would find shocking, revolting, or disgusting.

Michigan is the only state in the US with a current gross indecency law, where it is a felony. Gross indecency between men was criminalized there in 1931; and between women, and men and women, in 1939. Through the decisions of the state court, the definition of gross indecency has been narrowed to: public sex acts, sex involving a minor, sex with the application of force, and sex work. Despite having separate laws to address each of these specifically, gross indecency remains on the books.

*see also:* BUGGERY; SODOMY; SEXUAL OFFENCES ACT; SECTION 28; CONSENT

**GRRL, GRRRL** — A girl or woman who participates in the feminist subculture of punk. "Riot grrl" has been in recorded use since 1992.
*see also:* FEMINISM

**GRS** — Acronym for GENDER REASSIGNMENT SURGERY and GENITAL RECONSTRUCTIVE SURGERY.

**GSA** — Acronym for GAY–STRAIGHT ALLIANCE.

**GYNEPHILIA** — Attraction to women or femininity.
Part of an alternative model of sexuality to heterosexual/homosexual which does not make any reference to the subject's gender and instead focuses on the gender/gender expression of the people they're attracted to, along with androphilia and ambiphilia.
*see also:* ANDROPHILIA; AMBIPHILIA; SEXUALITY

**HATE CRIME** — A crime which the victim or witnesses perceive as being motivated by the victim's actual or perceived race, religion, disability, non-heterosexual sexual orientation, or transgender status.

Hate crimes include physical violence, verbal abuse, sexual violence, and incitement to hatred (e.g., through anti-queer leaflets, harassment, blackmail, and refusal of goods or services).

Many queer people are unable to report hate crimes to the police because the police criminalize them, if not for their queerness then in other ways. The victim of the crime becomes the accused. Naming the problem makes you the problem. In fact, hate crime legislation does less to protect vulnerable people than it does to criminalize already marginalized people and funnel them into the criminal justice prison system. Privileged people who commit hate crimes do not get convicted; oppressed people do.

*see also:* RESPECTABILITY; POLICE (n.); LIBERATION; VIOLENCE; TRANSFORMATIVE JUSTICE

**HE/HIM** — A third-person pronoun.

Not everyone who uses he/him is a man, and not every man uses he/him. Pronouns do not necessarily indicate gender identity.

In Old English (which was spoken c.450–1100), "he" was a genderless pronoun used for everyone. In Middle English (spoken c.1100–1500), "she" emerged c.1100 and there was a gendered difference in pronouns.

*see also:* PRONOUNS

**HEGEMONIC MASCULINITY** — The dominant masculinity, which justifies and reproduces conditions of patriarchy and the subordination of women and other non-men, and punishes men who fail to embody the dominant masculinity.

Hegemonic masculinity is a gender studies concept which recognizes multiple masculinities across cultures and time, and the hierarchy among them. In our culture, hegemonic masculinity is misogynistic, queerphobic, aggressive, entitled, dominant, competitive, risk-taking, angry, emotionally repressed, fragile, unapologetic, and violent.

*see also:* PATRIARCHY; MASCULINITY

**HER** — *see:* SHE/HER.

**HERMAPHRODITE** — An outdated term, often regarded as a slur, for intersex people. It has been reclaimed by some intersex people.

*see also:* INTERSEX

**HETEROFLEXIBLE** — A sexual orientation which is "mostly" heterosexual but "flexible."

Heteroflexible is easier for some to embrace than an explicitly queer label like "bisexual" or "pansexual." The attachment to straightness provides safety and familiarity in a heteronormative culture.

*see also:* BI-CURIOUS

**HETERONORMATIVITY** — The assumption that heterosexuality is normal and natural, and that other sexualities, or lack of sexuality, are abnormal and unnatural. The expectation that sex is exclusively defined by vaginal penetration by a penis. The assumption that everyone is heterosexual until proven otherwise. The conditions which reproduce compulsive heterosexuality.

Heteronormativity is a concept coined by Michael Warner in 1991. Compulsory heterosexuality is an adjacent concept, coined by Adrienne Rich: women are coerced into heterosexuality by being rewarded for adhering to it and punished for deviating from it. I'd take it further and suggest that everyone, not only women, is coerced into compulsive heterosexuality. Heterosexuality as an institution.

In her writing "The Straight Mind," Monique Wittig notes that relationships between men and women are obligatory, and hetero-sexuality as an institution is invisible and taken as "natural" while queer people are asking themselves, "Why am I like this?" but straight people don't. Wittig argues that "woman" as a category only makes sense in a heterosexual context, that lesbians aren't women, that womanhood is an oppressive position defined by relationship to men.

Heteronormativity reinforces gender roles within a romantic relationship: the division of labor, different norms and "languages" and behaviors, different aesthetics, and different emotions allowed for each partner depending on their gender. This is rooted in misogyny; women are property whose primary function is to mother.

The effort which goes into reproducing heterosexuality betrays its fragility. If it was simply natural, we wouldn't need to work so hard to buttress it, and it wouldn't be so threatened by alternatives.

Heterosexuality deserves at least, if not more, critical scrutiny as LGB and other queer sexualities and performances of gender, given the presumption that heterosexuality is "normal," "natural," and "default," which prioritizes it and makes it seem a priori. Heterosexuality is seen as the "original" term, with the additional terms "homosexuality," "bisexuality," "asexuality" resting upon it; but actually, "heterosexuality" depends on these "supplement" terms in order to define itself (Derrida, built upon by Diana Fuss). The supplements are seen as inferior, but without them, the original could not exist.

Heteronormativity presumes everyone is straight unless otherwise proven, especially children. It also presumes that gay and queer people wish they were straight, and are interested in performing straightness.

Heteronormativity also presumes that animals are "straight," despite heaps of evidence that animals can be both homosocial and homosexual. Many animals masturbate, have sex when already pregnant, have same-sex sex, and engage in other non-procreative sex acts. Sex, for animals as well as people (we're animals too), has a social function, not just a reproductive one. Over 4,000 animal species reproduce asexually, and many species change sex throughout their lifetime.

The straight white cis man is the default subject in cultural discourse: people of color, women, and queer people are deviations from this "norm," even though they greatly outnumber him. There are bars and gay bars, hockey and women's hockey, histories and black histories, movies and LGBT+ movies.

There is plenty of research on the social and "biological" "reasons" for why people are gay or queer, but straightness is not brought into question. What are the social and biological reasons for hetero-sexuality? This is even more interesting when we consider that heterosexuality is defined by its exclusion of same-sex attraction, and that queer couples are entirely capable of reproduction.

*see also:* STRAIGHT; NORMATIVITY; PIV; HETEROSEXISM; STRAIGHT ACTING

**HETEROSEXISM** — More insidious than homophobia, heterosexism is discrimination against queerness or same-sex attraction in favor of opposite-sex attraction. It's the assumption that straight is the default. Heterosexism props up (produces and is produced by) heteronormativity.

*see also:* HETERONORMATIVITY

**HETEROSEXUAL, HETEROSEXUALITY** — Someone who is attracted to the opposite gender from their own. Heterosexual is interchangeable with "straight."

Heterosexuality rests on the assumption that the gender of the subject is known, that their gender has an "opposite," and that the gender of the desired person is also known and is in fact "opposite" to the subject's.

Heterosexuality is a relatively new identity category. It emerged along with other "sexual orientations" in the 1890s, as a "normal" contrast to homosexuality, which was newly invented as a label and pathology.

*see also:* HETERONORMATIVITY; STRAIGHT; SEXOLOGY

**HIM** — *see:* HE/HIM.

**HIR** — *see:* ZE/ZIR.

**HIV/AIDS** — Human Immunodeficiency Virus (HIV), and Acquired Immune Deficiency Syndrome (AIDS). Together these are a spectrum of conditions for patients who are HIV-positive.

AIDS does not only affect gay men, but its association with the gay community meant the homophobic public was negligent during the AIDS crisis in the 1980s and 1990s. The first HIV-related deaths in the UK were in 1982, and disproportionately affected gay and trans communities. Government was indifferent and community-based organizations of queers formed in response. HIV/AIDS strongly politicized queer identity, with groups like ACT UP using the slogan "SILENCE = DEATH" and a pink triangle (reclaimed from Holocaust imagery).

Public misinformation about transmission, and the strong association of HIV with gay men, fueled stigma and homophobia. In 1986, the UK government responded to the AIDS crisis with a public information campaign called "AIDS: Don't Die Of Ignorance." They released a leaflet, published by the Central Office of Information and posted it to every household in the UK, which further contributed to fear and confusion; accompanied by a television campaign which featured a falling tombstone labeled "AIDS," which scared people living with a positive diagnosis, essentially saying that AIDS is a death sentence with no cure or treatment.

HIV/AIDS is transmitted through sexual fluid exchange, and blood exchange. Contrary to popular belief in the 1980s and 90s, it is not transmittable through skin contact, kissing, or drinking from the same glass as someone who is HIV-positive. HIV can only be passed on if the viral load of the positive person is "detectable"; with ongoing treatment, many HIV-positive people have "undetectable" viral loads, which means they cannot transmit the virus. HIV transmission can also be prevented through the use of barriers (condoms) during sex, PrEP, and clean needles for intravenous drug users.

If untreated, AIDS is fatal. There is no cure or vaccine for HIV or AIDS, but if treated, patients have the same life expectancy as people who test negative. HIV/AIDS remains stigmatized but there are strong activist groups resisting this.

*see also:* POZ; ACT UP; PrEP; SAFER SEX

**HOMONATIONALISM** — The association of gay and LGBT+ civil rights with nationalism, especially colonialism and xenophobia. The assimilation of queers into nationalist ideology. The appropriation of queer struggles into furthering an imperialistic "national interest," allegedly to protect queers at home and defend the human rights of queers abroad.

Homonationalism is queer inclusion into colonial legacy sold as "progress." It's assimilation into imperialism, nationalism, white supremacy. Us gays can kill foreigners just as well as the straights! It's the preposterous assertion that Western, white, Christian nations are queer-friendly, safe places for LGBT+ people and that we must "export" our tolerance just as we "export" democracy.

Gay civil rights movements' discourse is being used to justify imperialism and colonialism of other allegedly "backward" homophobic countries and cultures, without recognizing the rife homophobia within the white, Western imperialist nation itself—and not acknowledging that most anti-queer legislation across the world reflects British colonial legacy. Homonationalism is often virtue signaling and performative allyship rather than any sincere attempt to welcome queer people into heteronormative society.

The UK posthumously pardoning Alan Turing and other queer men—whilst still criminalizing homelessness and denying trans people access to healthcare—is one example of this. When then-Prime Minister David Cameron suggested that "Muslims throw gays off rooftops" to justify imperialism, he ignored the issues of queers at home, did nothing to help the queers abroad, and fueled a nationalistic white savior complex. Homonationalism is using the perceived homophobia of other countries to justify anti-immigration policies, while detaining and deporting queer asylum seekers and refugees who face genuine threats of violence if deported for being queer.

Homonationalism as a term was coined by gender studies scholar Jasbir K. Puar in 2007.

*see also*: HOMONORMATIVITY; TRANSMILITARISM; ASSIMI-LATION; ISLAMOPHOBIA

**HOMONORMATIVITY** — The assimilation of homosexuals into heteronormativity. The hierarchy of queer lives and issues based on respectability.

Homonormativity prioritizes the "inclusion" of respectable queer people in straight society, without disrupting the homophobic status quo that mostly punishes less respectable queers. It nestles gayness into every oppressive power structure in our society, including homophobia and its misogynistic roots.

Homonormativity was was first articulated by trans activists in the 1990s in exploration of the exclusion of trans people by cis LGB activists, and the prioritization of cis gay interests over more urgent trans concerns..

*see also*: RESPECTABILITY; ASSIMILATION; HOMONATIONALISM; HETERONORMATIVITY

**HOMOPHILE** — A movement to decriminalize homosexuality in the 1950s and 1960s. It used assimilationist tactics and education, with the aim if decreasing homophobia.

Notable homophiles include the Mattachine Society, Harry Hay, James Gruber, the Daughters of Bilitis, Phyllis Lyon, and Del Martin.

Homophiles tended to accept that homosexuality was a pathological condition, either genetic or a "biological accident" for which people should be pitied, not persecuted; but they also campaigned against the "cures" for homosexuality.

It is possible that the homophile movement was respectable when public facing but more radical in private.

*see also:* ASSIMILATION; RESPECTABILITY

**HOMOPHOBIA** — Fear of, or contempt for, people who are gay, lesbian, LGBT+, or queer. Behavior based on those feelings. A system of oppression in which LGBT+ people are marginalized and subject to violence.

Homophobia is a manifestation of misogyny: the hatred or devaluation of women and anything associated with women and femininity. Homophobia is directed at all queers for failing to conform to heteronormative gender expectations, but is especially bad for queer women (particularly trans women), feminine queer men, and all non-binary people.

Like all systems of oppression, homophobia intersects with other marginalizations: classism, racism, ableism, misogyny, agism, transphobia, and fatphobia.

*see also:* MISOGYNY; PATRIARCHY; HETERONORMATIVITY; FEMMEPHOBIA

**HOMOSEXUAL** — Someone who is attracted exclusively, or overwhelmingly, to people of the same gender. Someone who is attracted to the same gender, without exclusivity. Someone who is LGBT+ or queer.

Sexuality became an identity category in the 1890s when sexologists pathologized same-sex attraction as a disease, and an "inversion" of gender identity—homosexuals were thought to be inverts, or the opposite sex trapped in the wrong body. The identity category heterosexual only came into existence in opposition to homosexuality.

Today homosexual is used by all types of queers to describe themselves, often tongue in cheek, including homoromantic asexuals. Homosexual is also the preferred umbrella term of some bigots.

see also: HOMOSEXUALITY; SEXOLOGY; GAY; LESBIAN; SEXUALITY; TRANSGENDER

**HOMOSEXUALITY** — An enduring pattern of sexual or romantic attraction to the same gender.

Homosexuality as an umbrella term includes all same-sex attracted people, and can be used to describe romantic attraction as well as sexual attraction.

Until 1990, homosexuality was a "disease," classified by the World Health Organization (WHO) as disease 302.0 in the *International Classification of Diseases*. Musician Tom Robinson wrote a song, "Glad To Be Gay" (written to be performed at Pride 1976 and released on the EP *Rising Free*, 1979), which discussed homophobic policing and police brutality, the particular kinds of violence faced by feminine queers, and assimilation. Robinson was in the habit of dedicating the song to the WHO.

see also: HOMOSEXUAL; SEXOLOGY; SEXUALITY; GAY; LESBIAN

**HORMONE BLOCKERS** — Medical intervention to delay puberty for transgender and gender-questioning children.

Hormone blockers are safe, and have no irreversible effects. They do not make children sterile; they simply delay puberty.

see also: TRANS HEALTHCARE

**HORMONE REPLACEMENT THERAPY (HRT)** — An aspect of medical transition for trans people which changes their dominant hormones, and by extension some of their secondary sex characteristics.

HRT is medically necessary for trans people with dysphoria who want to change their hormones; but, not all trans people want or need HRT.

see also: ESTROGEN; TESTOSTERONE; MONES; TRANS HEALTHCARE

**HRT** — Acronym for HORMONE REPLACEMENT THERAPY.

**HYPER-VISIBILITY** — see: VISIBILITY.

**I** — The I in LGBTQIA+ is for INTERSEX.

*see also:* LGBT+

**IDENTIFY AS...** — A clunky way of saying someone "is." Used exclusively to describe transgender and queer people when describing their genders and sexualities.

The phrase "they identify as..." is thick with condescension. The implication is that they "identify" as, but aren't "really," what they say they are. They "identify as" agender, but they are really "male." They "identify as" pansexual but really it's just a phase. It plays into a narrative which says that queers are confused and demanding that people enable our delusions which contradict reality.

"Identify as" creates a relationship between the subject and their identity: identity as process, as goals. It can be especially useful in highlighting the difference between who we are (how we identify) and how we are perceived.

There is a difference between "identify as" and "identify with." "With" suggests stronger separation—we identify with media, avatars, lovers, ideas.

*see also:* IDENTITY POLITICS; TRANSPHOBIA; HOMOPHOBIA; OTHER

**IDENTITY** — A sense of self, often aligned with groups of people with shared backgrounds or experiences.

Identity is a practice. It is ongoing, constantly shifting, and reproduced. In order to be reproduced, identity must be signified repeatedly. It is not static and must be regularly re-upped. Identity is performative.

Identity is context-dependent. A cis person, in a cisnormative society, in a room full of cis people, does not identify as "cis" because they don't have to—their identity is taken for granted. Queer identity might take on different terms depending on the situation, and how nuanced and understanding the audience is.

*see also:* IDENTITY POLITICS; OTHER

**IDENTITY POLITICS** — The politics surrounding group identity categories, including: race, gender, age, class, sexuality, ability, body size, and religion. Sometimes, often pejoratively, it is shortened to "idpol."

"Political correctness" is just a new way of saying that we acknowledge and respect a diversity of identities. Everything is political; even the claim to be apolitical is extremely political, and in making that claim the subject casts off any responsibility for the political conditions they are producing and reproducing. The creation of identity categories, the separation of people into allegedly discrete groups, is political.

Our separation is meant to divide us, but, the differences between different groups are real. Our lives are complex with intersecting identities and conditions, and we should strive to acknowledge difference whilst fostering community and solidarity, not flattening experiences or erasing difference.

Identity politics purports to fight for rights on the basis of identity, but there is not enough room in that conversation for the un-fixedness of identity. There needs to be a better balance struck between the identity labels people use/choose, and their material experiences of oppression.

There is a multitude of identities which already exist, which have existed for as long as people have. We use new words to describe them now, and that vocabulary will continue to change and adjust and hopefully acquire more nuance, but it does not mean that the identities which we are describing are new. By tweaking—or inventing—language to describe our identities, we make them (our identities, our selves) intelligible to others, to society. We humanize ourselves, explain ourselves, by having words which accurately (or, "this-is-the-best-I've-found-so-far") describe our identities. This is a valuable task. Identity labels also enable us to find other people like us and form community built around shared experience. Labels and categories allow us space to be seen and understood.

Many identities are thrust upon us; labeling them as we choose is an act of resistance.

Identity labels are valuable but we want to exist outside of (Black, LGBT+) history months, outside of a laundry list of marginalizations.

*see also:* TOKEN

**IDPOL** — Short for IDENTITY POLITICS. It is often used pejoratively.

**INCLUSION, INCLUSION THEATER** — Performative allyship with negligible material support for the people allegedly being "included."

Inclusion theatre is inclusion for the sake of appearing inclusive rather than for making sincere attempts at increasing positive representation or undermining structural oppression. It's also called "virtue signaling."

*see also:* ALLY; TOKEN; REPRESENTATION

**INTERGENERATIONAL TRAUMA** — Trauma transferred from survivors to subsequent generations through post-traumatic stress disorder mechanisms.

Children are directly and indirectly affected by the trauma of their parents. Sources of intergenerational trauma include slavery, genocide, war, domestic abuse, sexual violence, poverty, natural disasters, and terrorism, and can apply to any form of trauma.

The most substantial empirical evidence for intergenerational trauma comes from the trauma-surviving parents' child-rearing behaviors as altered by their traumas; but there is also evidence that trauma is epigenetically transferred to children through the parents' stress hormones.

There is also a wider cultural trauma when groups of people are collectively traumatized: slavery continues to have traumatic effects for Black people; the Holocaust continues to be a source of trauma for Jewish, Roma, Polish, Slavic, Russian, disabled, and queer people; and the AIDS crisis and the Nazi destruction of trans medical archives continue to be traumatic for queers. We are living in a time when trans women of color are, as a group, targeted and subject to extreme violence; this too is collectively traumatizing.

*see also:* VIOLENCE; SEXOLOGY; FASCISM; TRAUMA

**INTERMEDIATE SEX** — An early term used by Edward Carpenter in the early 20th century to describe trans people. Intermediate sex was a newer term for "uranian" and "invert," and a predecessor for "transsexual" and "transgender."

*see also:* URANIAN; SEXOLOGY; INVERT

**INTERNALIZED OPPRESSION** — Adopting stigmatized views of yourself from steeping in a culture of oppression (e.g., a sex worker holding whorephobic views, directing those views at themselves and other sex workers).

Like privilege, it is impossible to completely unlearn internalized oppression and be a "blank slate," because we will never live in a vacuum of power relations. However, it's still helpful and worthwhile to untangle our negative self-images from the socio-political structures which undermine our worth.

*see also:* OPPRESSION

**INTERSECTIONAL, INTERSECTIONALITY** — The understanding that no one axis of oppression can be regarded separately from all of the others.

Intersectionality as a term was coined by Black feminist and legal scholar Kimberlé Crenshaw in her 1989 piece "Demarginalizing the Intersection of Race and Sex: A Black Feminist Critique of Anti-discrimination Doctrine, Feminist Theory and Antiracist Politics"; but as a concept, intersectionality has been a hallmark of Black feminism since at least the 1800s.

All of our identities and perceived identities interact and determine how much structural power we have, but these are context dependent and there is no clear hierarchy of these categories. It's complex, not simple.

"Intersectional" is not shorthand for "inclusive." A conference panel is not "intersectional" for having people of multiple genders, sexualities, races, and economic backgrounds speaking on it: it's diverse. A second panel made up entirely of straight, white, cis, wealthy men is as intersectional as the first: the intersections of those privileges gives those men vast institutional power and an amplified voice which is assumed to be legitimate.

Intersectionality has gathered a morally righteous tone. "Intersectional feminism" is a term often used, to mean a feminist approach which acknowledges the intersections of oppression; that womanhood is not a single experience; and women of color, trans women, queer women, poor women, and disabled women suffer more misogyny, compounded with their other marginalizations. It might be pedantic but I'd gently remind "intersectional feminists" that "white feminism" is intersectional too: feminist movements led by white women who fail to account for racism and misogynoir are a perfect example of the intersection of race and gender, and the way white privilege operates to position the white experience as universal.

*see also:* OPPRESSION; PRIVILEGE; IDENTITY POLITICS; FEMINISM

**INTERSEX** — One of several contested terms to describe someone born with a combination of physical characteristics typically associated with exclusively maleness or femaleness (e.g., chromosomes, genitalia, and gonads).

There are multiple traits which could manifest as an "intersex condition"; for example, androgen insensitivity syndrome (AIS), which prevents the body from responding to androgen (testosterone), and Swyer syndrome, which is the presence of testes and a uterus. Both syndromes can lead to people having a phenotype (external appearance, in these cases of genitals or gonads) which does not "match" their sex chromosomes.

There is no single, universally agreed upon definition of intersex, and it is not a universally accepted term. Other terms, all contested, include "disorder of sex development (DSD)" and "hermaphrodite."

Intersex activism and communities are not monolithic. There are multiple stakeholders (intersex people, the parents of intersex children who are making medical decisions for them, and medical experts on intersexuality), and intersex activists disagree on how to, or whether to, collaborate with the medical establishment. Medicalization and pathologization are avenues to medical care and civil rights, but they also bolster assumptions about deviance from the gender/sex binary as a "disorder," with the implication that it can be medically rectified so the patient might live as closely as possible within the gender/sex binary.

Statistics on intersexuality are fraught because there is no widely used single definition. The most frequently used statistic is that 1 in 2,000 people are born with intersex traits, though this has been criticized by intersex activists such as Peggy Cadet. Data on intersexuality is also tricky because it either relies on reporting from doctors (rather than patients) whose patients might not even know they have intersex traits; or on patients' self-reporting, which is better, but only patients with social capital are able to seek out information and communities (and therefore research projects) on intersexuality. Georgiann Davis, an intersex researcher (both intersex, and a researcher on intersexuality) discusses this in her 2015 book *Contesting Intersex*.

Intersex people are likely to face medical neglect and lies, be labeled as "abnormalities" and imbued with stigma, and may suffer non-consensual and medically unnecessary surgery or intervention: removal of undescended testes, or circumcision to create a vagina. Often the medical opinion is that the patient is better off not knowing about their intersex condition, despite the ethical implications for the patient's bodily autonomy and informed consent.

It is common practice for parents of intersex children to be presented with an intersex diagnosis as though it is an immediate medical emergency, and a "state of exception" is created. Doctors can then suggest medically unnecessary surgery to "correct" the intersex characteristics so the patient is more closely aligned with a binary sex/gender, and the responsibility for this decision is placed with the parents and based on guilt, instead of lying with the doctor and the usual due diligence required for consenting to surgery, especially to a medically unnecessary surgery. For parents who are not familiar with intersexuality, or a non-essentialist understanding of sex and gender, the intersex condition is positioned as an urgent threat to the child's wellbeing.

DSD language is preferred by the medical establishment, which implicitly sees intersex conditions as abnormalities to be fixed. "Intersex" language instead positions intersex conditions as a natural biological variation.

One oppressive dynamic facing intersex people is the insider/Outsider binary in research, which places legitimacy with the voices of "experts" on intersexuality who are not themselves intersex, while intersex patients are positioned as "subjects" (objects) rather than people with valuable lived experiences, never mind their own research qualifications. The patient is denied agency and their experience is considered to cast doubt on their objectivity, while the non-intersex researcher is ostensibly objective and untainted by bias.

The medicalization of intersex perpetuates medical authority over intersex bodies (Katrina Karkazis). The primary stakeholder on issues about intersexuality must be intersex people, not their non-intersex doctors. Non-intersex "experts" might have something to offer to scholarship around intersexuality, but more often than not their contributions are insensitive and paternalistic, and they treat intersex people like a problem that needs to be fixed.

Intersex status is not relevant to gender identity and sexuality: the same as non-intersex people, intersex people can be any gender or sexuality. Some intersex people are trans.

Why is I part of LGBTQIA+? Because there is a shared denial of agency and "normalcy" over our bodies, and a shared failure to fit into hegemonic binaries of sex. Intersex is a "problem" because it challenges the gender binary and its biological essentialism.

Similarly to trans people, intersex people face stigma and difficulty accessing services, especially medical services, in a way which prioritizes their agency rather than treats them like an object of intrigue. Likewise, both intersex and trans people tend to develop a highly specialized knowledge of their conditions, regardless of their interest in medicine as a field, because their doctors are often under-informed and making medical decisions based on stigma and misconception, and are gate-keepers to proper medical care. The patient then must carefully toe the line between gently informing the doctor, and undermining the doctor's credibility as the "expert" lest they feel insulted and deny care entirely.

There are medical and social shared struggles between intersex people and trans people; it's useful to make these connections, but we shouldn't conflate them.

The goals of intersex activism today are, again, not monolithic, but include: the elimination of medically unnecessary surgeries; interrupting stigma, silence, and shame surrounding intersex bodies; collaborating with medical allies; building community within intersex organizations;

addressing inequalities within intersex communities, and including more diverse voices; and amplifying the voices of, and validating the experiences of, intersex children.

Intersexuality is not a sexual orientation, despite sounding similar to homosexuality, bisexuality, heterosexuality, and so on.

*see also:* DISORDER OF SEX DEVELOPMENT (DSD); HERMAPHRODITE; SEX (n.); BIOLOGICAL ESSENTIALISM; GENDER BINARY

**INVERT, INVERSION** — A late 19th-century psychology term for homosexual.

Havelock Ellis coined the concept of the "invert" in his 1897 work *Sexual Inversion*. Ellis argued that homosexuality was a congenital condition, which he called "sexual inversion": a physical or psychological state whereby the invert was possessed of a female soul in a male body (gay men), or a male soul in a female body (lesbians). Gender characteristics were aligned with sexual preferences and behavior. This is an interesting early example of how heterosexuality was seen to be more fundamental than a fixed biological sex.

This conceptualization and pathologization of queer people as inverts in the "wrong" gender is one example of the longstanding link between cis LGBQ+ people and trans people. Any attempts to culturally separate homosexuality and transness (or sexuality and gender identity) ignore the shared pathology and cultural history of all non-heterosexual and all transgender people.

*see also:* HOMOSEXUAL; TRANS; GAY; BORN THIS WAY; HETERONORMATIVITY

**INVISIBILITY** — Lack of representation. Incredulity about your existence.

*see also:* ERASURE; VISIBILITY

**ISLAMOPHOBIA** — Fear of, hostility to, or prejudice toward, Muslims.

Islamophobia is racist because—even though Islam is a not a race—people are assumed to be Muslim based on perceptions of their race. Islam has become racialized.

Islamophobia is very much a queer issue. "Islam hates gay people" is expression of racist colonialism and misinformation about Islam. Islam is based on the same holy books as Judaism (the Torah) and Christianity (the New Testament), plus the Quran. Islam doesn't "hate" gay people any more than the other Abrahamic religions do.

Islamophobia is used as a liberal excuse to invade and Other the countries of brown people. It's used to justify the oppression of Muslims through war and terror and military occupation in Muslim-majority countries like Iraq, Afghanistan, Libya, Syria, Yemen, and Palestine. Israel, pinkwashed as a "safe haven in the Middle East" for queer people, is an imperialist state occupying Palestine. Islamophobia is a convenient tool to garner public support for Israel and Western imperialism in the Middle East, a project fueled mostly by oil money.

Muslims are a diverse group of about 1.6 billion people from all over the world; Muslims are not a monolith. There are many queer Muslims. Suggesting that Islam is hostile to queer people is an insult to them, forcing them to choose between their identities and only affording them a two-dimensional self. There is great diversity in experience of acceptance of Muslim queer people from their communities, just like all queer people. There is no single "coming out" narrative for queer Muslims.

It's very convenient to divide groups of oppressed people. When someone says they support "LGBT people," it's important to ask which of us have enough humanity to count.

*see also:* PINKWASHING; ANTI-SEMITISM; HOMONATIONALISM; RACISM

**IT** — A third person, gender neutral, singular pronoun. It is used to dehumanize people, especially trans people, but has been reclaimed by some trans people.

It/its pronouns are commonly used to discuss objects, animals, or babies; that is, people or animals or things without agency or full personhood. Using it/its pronouns for queer and trans people is a tactic to dehumanize us and justify hurting us.

It/its pronouns are used by some people to describe themselves because "they" doesn't indicate a gender. It/its is also used by people whose languages don't have an equivalent of "they."

"It" comes from Old English "hit," a gender neutral pronoun which came to encompass all non-human nouns as gendered nouns faded from the language. The h- was lost due to being in an unemphasized position, as in modern English the h in "give it to him," "ask her," is some-times dropped. "It" meaning "the sex act" is from 1610s. "It" meaning "sex appeal" (especially in a woman) first appeared in 1904 in the works of Rudyard Kipling, and was popularized with Elinor Glyn's novella *It* and the subsequent film *It Girl* (both 1927) starring silent-film star Clara Bow. In children's games, the meaning "the one who must tag or catch the others" is attested from 1842.

*see also:* PRONOUNS; TRANS; TRANS PANIC

**IT'S JUST A PHASE** — A phrase used to delegitimize trans and queer people.

"It's just a phase" is a standard anti-queer narrative which implies that we're not "actually" queer; we're just confused and we'll soon see sense and grow out of it, assimilating into and meeting the "normal" and "natural" cisheteronormative expectations. This narrative should be challenged if not dismissed outright.

But, so what if it is a phase? That doesn't make it not "real." We're allowed to change and grow and go through phases. Without the allow-ance for "phases" we're unable to self-examine and adjust. As if we must know exactly who we are from the moment we're born, and remain that way for our entire lives!

*see also:* ERASURE; IDENTIFY AS...

**JOCK** — An athletic archetype of masculinity, usually associated with team sports, muscled bodies, and the gym.

The jock is assumed to be anti-intellectual in a false mind/body binary. He is expected to engage in "locker room talk" (casual misogyny) and use his physical strength violently. As a stereotype, the jock represents peak masculinity: physical dominance, competitiveness, hyper-sexuality, and a disinterest in all things feminine (except sexual conquests, who are indeed viewed as "things"). The jock doesn't cry or express any emotional vulnerability, but his repressed insecurities betray him through a short temper and the constant need to prove his masculinity.

The jock's archetypal "opposite," in another false binary, is the geek, who is weedy, bookish, and "sensitive" (the masculine geek's alleged sensitivity must be viewed critically, as it's often an excuse for his toxic "misunderstood" behavior, or demands for emotional labor from women).

In gay culture, just like straight culture, the jock is revered as embodying a standard of masculine beauty. His beauty ritual is his strict exercise regime and diet, which is just as performative (and "vain" and "frivolous") as any feminine beauty ritual. Maybe he waxes his chest and oils his body; maybe he takes topless selfies. His indulgence in his appearance is seen as more acceptable than a woman's.

From c.1650–c.1850 jock was slang for penis. Jock in its current usage is thought to be derivative of the term "jockstrap," an assless undergarment used to protect the penis and testicles during athletics. Jockstraps were invented in Chicago in 1874. The earliest recorded use of jock to mean "athletic man" is 1952. Jockstrap has its etymological origins in jockey-strap, referring to horse jockeys. Before being associated with horses in the 1660s, "jockey" meant "boy," and in Scotland and Northern England was a diminutive of "Jock" as an alternative given name to "Jack."

Jockstraps are functional for athletics, and their strappy but masculine nature makes them the staple in masculine lingerie.

The jock is a good example of how patriarchy enforces strict gender norms and punishes everyone, to different degrees. Jocks have the luxury of moving through the world with relative ease, so the consequences for deviation from hegemonic gender norms (e.g., being a man who is sexually attracted to men) are great. A jock might be queer, but his performance of masculinity fits so comfortably within the cisheterosexual norms that he is assumed to be straight. Because his performance of gender is praised, he may feel he has more to lose by declaring queerness. The more "respectable" masculinity is (i.e., the less threatening it is to patriarchy), the more fragile it is. Jocks are portrayed as being especially fearful of appearing gay, which of course makes them a popular gay porn category for consumption by both gay and straight viewers.

Women and other people who aren't men or masculine can be jocks too. Women jocks are assumed to be lesbians because sports are seen as inherently masculine, and masculine women are assumed to be lesbians. Being on a women's sports team is doubly gay because the women are both butch and surrounded by other butch women. Performance-based sports, like dance, cheerleading, and gymnastics, are not so strongly associated with butchness, gayness, or jockness. (Men who do performance-based sports, on the other hand, are not considered jocks but are considered gay.)

In being butch, women are punished for failing to perform hegemonic femininity. This can be compensated for by the jock if, outside of sports or the gym, they perform hyper-femininity. The burden of "proving" femininity is greater the more one deviates from it. Jocks who are masculine but not men will be assumed to be men, and so will be punished with erasure of their genders.

*see also:* MASCULINITY; BINARY; RESPECTABILITY; GAY; LESBIAN; FEMMEPHOBIA; BUTCH; PATRIARCHY

**KING** — Someone who does an exaggerated performance of masculinity.

Drag kings create personas which might use machismo and chauvinism or other tropes of masculinity. Their performances might include singing, lip syncs, stand-up comedy, acting, and dancing.

The term "drag king" was first published in 1972, but "male impersonation" is a much older tradition, and women have played male characters throughout the history of theater and opera.

Most drag kings are cis women, trans men, or non-binary people, but anyone can be a drag king.

*see also:* QUEEN; DRAG; TROUSER ROLE

**KINK, KINKY** — Unconventional or deviant sexual practices.

The term kinky comes from "bent," or an opposition to straightness in the broader sense of the word. Kink is no longer exclusive to straight people (if it ever was), and its opposition now lies in so-called "vanilla" sexual preferences.

Kinky practices include bondage, power play, pain, and humiliation for sexual pleasure, cross-dressing, unconventional role-playing, and anything widely considered non-normative.

Polyamory is not an oppressed group identity. It's not "kinky" to be a straight man who wants to fuck multiple women; that's a normative desire within patriarchy. Depending on your social context, it may be assumed that either monogamy or polyamory is the "natural," socially dominant mode of relationships. There is no "natural" mode—just do your best to communicate your boundaries and expectations.

*see also:* BDSM; FETISH; SEX POSITIVE; SEX NEGATIVE

**KINSEY SCALE** — A scale of 0 to 6 designed to represent where on a spectrum between "exclusively heterosexual" and "exclusively homosexual" someone is at the time when they respond. It was developed by Alfred Kinsey and first published in 1948.

| 0 | Exclusively heterosexual |
|---|---|
| 1 | Predominantly heterosexual, only incidentally homosexual |
| 2 | Predominantly heterosexual, but more than incidentally homosexual |
| 3 | Equally heterosexual and homosexual |
| 4 | Predominantly homosexual, but more than incidentally heterosexual |
| 5 | Predominantly homosexual, only incidentally heterosexual |
| 6 | Exclusively homosexual |
| X | No socio-sexual contacts |

The scale shows sexual diversity on a spectrum, not just a binary between gay and straight. It focuses on sexual behavior rather than identity, so your place on the Kinsey scale can shift depending on what you do—there's no interest in who you "are" or who you are attracted to. The Kinsey scale was explicitly designed to represent the sexual orientation of an individual for a given period of their life, with the implicit understanding that sexual orientation is not necessarily static throughout a lifetime.

The Kinsey scale assumes a single axis between "heterosexual" and "homosexual," and does not explicitly describe bisexuality or asexuality (which is defined by lack of sexual attraction, not sexual behavior like on the Kinsey scale) or account for non-binary people. Since its development, other scales for sexual orientation have been developed.

Kinsey himself was, by the modern understanding of the word, bisexual. However, he rejected that label because at the time the psycho-medical community still loosely associated it with "hermaphroditism" (an outdated term for intersex).

*see also:* GAY; BISEXUAL; BIPHOBIA; BINARY; BICURIOUS; APHOBIA

**KWEEN** — An AAVE alternative spelling of "queen," and a genderfuck mashup of "king" and "queen."
*see also:* AAVE; QUEEN; KING; DRAG

**L** — The L in LGBT+ is for LESBIAN.

**LAVENDER SCARE, LAVENDER MENACE** — A Cold War purge in the 1950s of queer people (and people suspected to be queer) from public office and public life under the pretense that they were communist sympathizers and posed a security threat. The civil rights activism that occurred in response.

The Lavender Scare was part of a wider culture of homophobia in the US during the second half of the 20th century. Queer people were expelled from public life and public office—they were fired from jobs in politics, the military, and education in coordinated efforts to remove them. They also suffered informal discrimination from employers across sectors. The 1953 Executive Order 10450 which barred homosexuals from working in the federal government remained in effect on paper until 1994; it was replaced with the "Don't Ask, Don't Tell" policy, which prohibited discrimination toward closeted queers but still banned gays, lesbians, and bisexuals from openly working in the military.

The response to the Lavender Scare is considered the start of the LGBT+ civil rights movement. Astronomer Frank Kameny was fired from the US Army Map Service for his homosexuality in 1957, and he picketed the White House in 1965 in one of the first demonstrations for gay rights.

The color lavender is associated with queerness and LGBT+ culture, along with pink and the rainbow.

*see also:* ACTIVISM; HOMOPHOBIA; LGBT+; HOMONATIONALISM; TRANSMILITARISM

**LGBT+, LGBTQ, LGBTQIAP** — Acronym which groups together everyone who is not both cisgender and heterosexual.

The long-form acronym stands for: Lesbian, Gay, Bisexual, Bigender, Transgender, Transsexual, Queer, Questioning, Intersex, Asexual, Agender, Aromantic, and Pansexual. It also implicitly includes: other non-monosexualities (e.g., omnisexuality); genders which fall under the transgender and non-binary umbrella; and sexualities which are on the asexual spectrum. All of these groups have a legitimate claim to queerness, should they choose to self-describe with that label. Other sources offer variations on the acronym's expanded definition, usually omitting the less commonly known labels.

Contrary to popular misconception, cross-dressers, drag performers, polyamorous people, and kinky people are not LGBT+ on the basis of those identities alone.

The LGBT+ acronym has utility in describing the shared struggles of all non-cis and non-heterosexual people under conditions of cishetero-patriarchy. However, the LGBT+ community (if such a community exists) is not homogenous, and we can't accurately discuss LGBT+ issues without also talking about classism, racism, fatphobia, ableism, agism, and colonialism.

Frustratingly, the least vulnerable LGBT+ people have become the face of LGBT+ culture and the struggle for LGBT+ rights: wealthy, white, cis gay men and lesbian women. There is minimal representation of bisexuals and other non-monosexuals, trans people, asexuals, and aromantics, which is why some activists joke that the B and T are silent.

LGBT+ has different connotations than queer, and than more specific identity categories (e.g., bisexual). LGBT+ is associated with palatable respectability politics and a neoliberal trickle-down approach to civil rights, whereas queer is associated with more radical left-leaning politics and less "respectable" tactics like direct action. LGBT+ is also preferred by people who feel the violence of queer as a slur; but the violence and negligence of corporate LGBT+ organizations also makes LGBT+ an alienating term for many.

Amusingly, the press has recently taken to calling individuals "LGBT," as in, "She's LGBT" rather than referring to the subject's specific relevant identity. This is likely to be because "LGBT" is a "safe" label to give people: it's politically correct and broad, which allows some laziness and ignorance about the person you're talking about. Is she bi or a lesbian? It doesn't matter, she's LGBT. It also excuses them from saying the words "lesbian," "gay," "bisexual," and "transgender," which apparently feel like insults to cishets, because cishets use them as insults. It keeps these specific identities as dirty words. Saying an individual is "LGBT" doesn't make sense though, because most queer people aren't all of those things at once. A more correct approach would be "She's a member of the LGBT community," which has the same problem of vagueness and additional problems about queerness being portrayed as a monolith—as if we all live in Rainbow Land together as a single community with a hegemonic culture and identical struggles.

*see also:* GAY; QUEER; ASSIMILATION; HOMONATIONALISM; COMMUNITY

**LGBT+ RIGHTS** — Laws and civil rights affecting LGBT+ people.

LGBT+ rights and activism are focused around marriage equality, hate crime legislation, and anti-discrimination legislation; in other words, assimilation into heteronormativity. It focuses on individual coming out and being "true" to your identity rather than disrupting or removing existing harmful social structures, including the legislator and judiciary.

*see also:* LGBT+; ASSIMILATION; RESPECTABILITY; HOMO-NORMATIVITY; HOMONATIONALISM; TRANS MILITARISM; TRANS HEALTHCARE

**LGSM** — Acronym for LESBIANS AND GAYS SUPPORT THE MINERS and LESBIANS AND GAYS SUPPORT THE MIGRANTS.

**LEATHER** — A queer subculture with a strong aesthetic.

The leather subculture was born out of World War I. It was an extremely homosocial group of men in uniforms (leather trench coats) experiencing group trauma. At the same time, women were becoming more present in social spaces which were previously only accessible to men. Men wanted their own spaces, so they set up bars and veterans' clubs. World War II further consolidated the culture, with more men, more uniforms, more homosocial group trauma, and more machinery. Men returned from the war knowing how to spit shine leather and chrome, and work on engines which went very fast; so they started motorcycle clubs and car clubs.

Lots of these clubs were based in bars, which were already extremely homosocial. These were bars full of men who were eager to take on the same roles they had in the war, with officers who made sense of things and bossed you around. The masquerade of masculinity, with the leather and uniforms and hierarchy, is appealing because it is familiar.

Leather and tight uniforms are paragons of the first half of 20th-century masculinity. You can see it in the superhero and cowboy comics of the time, which were of course consumed by soldiers. Gay culture was inseparable from leather throughout the 1950s, when queerness was coded. In the 1960s queerness became more overt, and bikers, military uniforms, police uniforms, and cowboys—all archetypes of masculinity—were part of the gay scene.

Dykes on bikes have been around for just as long as men—the leather culture is about masculinity and leather and power relations, not bodies or genitals.

Since the 1970s the Castro clone has kept leather a relevant part of the gay scene, and it continues to represent a rugged, butch, (fetishized) working-class masculinity.

*see also:* KINK; DADDY; DYKE; CASTRO CLONE

**LESBIAN** — A woman who is sexually or romantically attracted to women.

Lesbian can mean women who are attracted exclusively to other women, but it is also a broader term for women and femmes who are attracted to other women and femmes. This includes bisexual and pansexual women, asexual women who are romantically attracted to women, and non-binary people who identify with womanhood. All queer women share a culture with lesbians because mainstream distinctions between Sapphic women have been relatively recent, and many of the struggles between queer women surrounding their queerness and their genders are the same.

Some trans men who were lesbians before they claimed a trans identity retain their lesbian identity after they transition. This is especially true for older trans men, who may have spent most of their lives as part of a lesbian community, and may not have access to other queer communities. The blurriness and complexity of queer terminology should be embraced, not policed and erased.

Lesbians have their own culture and subcultures within the larger queer community.

*see also:* GAY; MISOGYNY; PATRIARCHY; FEMME; WOMAN; SAPPHIC

**LESBIANS AND GAYS SUPPORT THE MINERS, LESBIANS AND GAYS SUPPORT THE MIGRANTS (LGSM)** — Lesbians and Gays Support the Miners were an activist group of lesbians and gay men who raised money to support the South Wales mining community during the 1984–1985 miners' strike. The Welsh chapters of the National Union of Miners (NUM) because the first non-LGBT organization to march in the London's Pride Parade, and in 1985 the alliance saw between the NUM and LGSM contributed to formally committing the Labour Party to a platform of LGBT+ rights. Lesbians and Gays Support the Migrants is a modern activist group of queers who campaign in solidarity with migrants in the UK.

Both the historic and the current LGSM groups are founded on the principle of solidarity and shared liberation.

*see also:* SOLIDARITY; ACTIVISM

**LESBOPHOBIA** — The specific combination of misogyny and homophobia faced by lesbians and Sapphic women, and other women-attracted people who are not men.

Bisexual women, women who love women, and women who have sex with women also have a claim to lesbianism. Anyone who has a claim to lesbianism can experience lesbophobia. Women and non-men who don't date or have sex with men might not call themselves lesbians, but they are still subject to lesbophobia.

There is some contention surrounding the idea that Sapphic women who are also attracted to men can experience lesbophobia, or if they instead experience biphobia. There is also a very valid discussion to be had on whether the material effects of this violence are any different depending on the different labels we give it.

Lesbophobia is a particular manifestation of homophobia, and shares the general dismissal of lesbian sexuality as unreal or disgusting. Lesbophobia is being dehumanized on two fronts: being hyper-sexualized and fetishized, and being told you're disgusting and unnatural.

Lesbians face more pronounced fetishization than queer men experiencing homophobia, because female sexuality is culturally treated as existing for male consumption. Expressions of lesbian sexuality are seen to be spectacle, or to invite commentary. There is an assumption that expressions of lesbian sexuality (e.g., a woman kissing her girlfriend) are titillating performances for the male gaze.

Lesbophobia can also look like dismissing or haranguing lesbians for being undesirable and gross and wrong: that they are too ugly to get a man and just need to find good dick. The suggestion that lesbians just need to find the "right" man, or be fucked in the "right" way, bolster rape culture and implicitly encourage corrective rape.

Lesbophobia stems from the misogynistic idea that women can't reject men without having been rejected by men first. Male entitlement to women is subverted by lesbians, because men can't be lesbians or be with lesbians. Patriarchy's way of dealing with lesbians is to either say that they are wrong, or their sexuality is still "for" men, for men's pleasure as a viewer.

Lesbophobia can also come from queer men who are not sexually interested in women, and apparently think their lack of interest absolves them from all forms of misogyny.

We never see butch lesbians represented in the media because we only see lesbians who are palatable to the male gaze: lesbians whom men deem fuckable.

see also: OPPRESSION; MISOGYNY; HOMOPHOBIA; MALE GAZE; BIPHOBIA

**LIBERATION** — Liberation aims to restructure society for the benefit of everyone, and to empower everyone to live a dignified life with agency. This is in contrast to assimilation, which seeks to incrementally afford rights and protections to people from within the existing institutions.

see also: ACTIVISM; SOLIDARITY; ASSIMILATION

**LIFESTYLE** — A word used to imply that queerness is a choice or a bourgeois decadence.

Lifestyle is also used in kink communities (e.g., BDSM, cross-dressing, swinging, furries) to describe people who live in their kink role full-time ("lifestylers").

see also: GAY AGENDA; BDSM; FURRIES; KINK

**LIVING AS A WO/MAN** — A description of a trans person's pattern of gender expression.

The phrase "living as a woman" or "living as a man" doesn't make sense. How does a woman live? Its function is to euphemistically refer to transness: to either claim that a closeted trans person is not living "authentically," or to imply that an out trans person is masquerading.

This phrase also implies that the trans person wasn't living "as" their gender before they came out. This is a contentious claim; many trans people describe themselves in different terms, saying they have always been their gender, and therefore have always been "living as" their gender because it's not possible that they ever lived "as" something else.

Some trans people may self-describe using this language, which is their prerogative, but it's not good practice to employ when referring to other people.

Tellingly, cis people are never "living as" men or women; they simply are men or women.

*see also:* REAL-LIFE EXPERIENCE; TRANSPHOBIA; TRANS HEALTHCARE

**LOVE** — An emotion of strong affection or devotion. It is an important facet of the discourse surrounding LGBT+ identity and rights.

While sexual-romantic love is prioritized as the highest form of affection and the closest interpersonal bond, there are other forms of love: familial love, platonic love, self-love.

Mainstream LGBT+ groups used the slogan "love wins" to celebrate marriage equality; this implies that it was an issue of love, rather than assimilation.

*see also:* AMATONORMATIVITY; HETERONORMATIVITY; SAME-SEX MARRIAGE

**M** — A gender marker for male. The M in BDSM is for MASOCHISM.
  *see also:* MALE; SEX (n.); GENDER (n.); BDSM; X

**MAAB** — Acronym for MALE ASSIGNED AT BIRTH, a variation on "Assigned Male At Birth (AMAB)."
  *see also:* ASSIGNED MALE AT BIRTH; CAMAB; DMAB

**MALE** — A sex assignment or descriptor, associated with masculinity in opposition to femininity and "femaleness."

Male and female are defined by their opposition to each other.

Maleness is purported to be an exclusive and complete set of sexual characteristics: penis, XY chromosomes, testes, androgen-dominant hormonal makeup, masculine gender identity. However, human biology is not dimorphic, so to insist that there are clear boundaries between male and female—and further that these boundaries are visible and obvious—is incorrect.

Male is an allegedly biological, scientific term, but it is coded with gender. When people suggest that trans women are male, they are implying that there is a biological reality which stops them from being female and women.

Trans men are male; trans women and other AMAB trans people are not.
  *see also:* SEX (n.); FEMALE

**MALE ASSIGNED AT BIRTH (MAAB)** — A variation on "Assigned Male At Birth (AMAB)."
  see also: ASSIGNED MALE AT BIRTH; CAMAB; DMAB

**MALE GAZE** — The objectification of women and non-binary people by men.

The male gaze refers to the gaze of individual men, male-dominated institutions, or patriarchy at large.

The objectification of non-men can take many forms, from negative comments on their appearance and the implication that they are disgusting, to "positive" comments and fetishization and the assumption that they exist purely for male consumption. In all cases their lives and gender expressions are policed. Men, by contrast, are not subject to a gaze on the basis of their gender—though they might be subject to one on the basis of other marginalized identities.

*see also:* GAZE; PATRIARCHY

**MALE PRIVILEGE** — The lack of structural oppression from patriarchy. Freedom from misogyny and sexism.

Trans women and other assigned male at birth (AMAB) people who aren't men don't have male privilege. If they are assumed to be men, they might be afforded an absence of certain direct violence, or even a presence of benefits for their perceived maleness; for example, they're more likely to be hired if they have a masculine name and gender expression. However, this comes with a significant caveat because in being told constantly that maleness is desired and superior, they are being told that their femaleness and femininity are bad. On top of that, they're also told (as we all are) that transness, specifically trans femininity, is disgusting and bad and unnatural. For a trans woman or other AMAB non-man to perform hegemonic masculinity—and to repress their femininity—well enough to survive isn't a privilege.

*see also:* PRIVILEGE; PATRIARCHY; ERASURE; TRANSMISOGYNY

**MALE TO FEMALE (MTF, M2F)** — An outdated term for trans women and other trans people who were assigned male at birth.

The MTF terminology positions femaleness as an objective and a destination, with transition being a journey to that point; but this is extremely reductive, and most trans people do not experience their transition this way. Many trans people never identified with their assigned gender. A trans woman, despite being assigned male, may have always been a woman whether or not she had the vocabulary to explain that experience.

This nomenclature also suggests that female and male are discrete categories, and that after a particular medical intervention (euphemistically called "the surgery" by ignorant cis people), femaleness is achieved. The reality is that many trans people don't have trans-related medical intervention; and there are those who pursue a wide variety of treatments, some of them ongoing for the rest of their lives.

Rather than describe themselves in terms related to their transition, most trans people prefer to use words which accurately describe their genders, such as "demi-girl," "gender fluid," or "woman."

*see also:* TRANS WOMAN; TRANSGENDER; TRANSITION; BINARY; SEX (n.)

**MAN** — An adult who identifies with the cultural and social norms of masculinity and feels an affinity for manhood.

Gender is messy and elusive, and difficult to define. Man is defined in opposition to woman, and is not a monolithic category or experience. Manhood is not defined by body parts or assigned sex at birth.

*see also:* GENDER (n.); MASCULINITY

**MAN OF TRANS EXPERIENCE** — The preferred term for many men who are not cis, but who don't necessarily center their transness in their manhood.

Alternative terms include "trans man," "assigned female at birth" or "assigned-female," "transmasculine," and "trans masc." The terms any individual uses to describe themselves will be based on personal preference and subcultural connotations, and should be respected.

*see also:* TRANS MAN; TRANSMASCULINE

**MARGINALIZED** — Disenfranchised, structurally discriminated against, and disallowed access to public life.

Marginalization and its associated kinds of violence exist on a scale: some are more marginalized than others. But attempting to quantify marginalizations is a bad project which creates a false hierarchy of oppression, rather than working toward our shared liberation.

*see also:* OPPRESSION; INTERSECTIONALITY

**MARRIAGE EQUALITY** — The right for adults to marry, regardless of their genders.

Marriage equality has been the focus of LGBT+ rights in the past decade, despite it not doing much to help the most vulnerable in our communities.

Marriage equality was an important issue during the AIDS crisis when same-sex couples could not get married and were dying young, which meant that their partners had no legal rights to visit them in hospital, or to their life insurance policies or to inheritance. Marriage equality became an LGBT+ issue so partners could have legal rights and control over their partners' care, funeral, and estate.

Marriage equality is also a trans issue, though this is often overlooked. In some places, the state will legally divorce a couple if one of them changes their gender marker; and in others, the spouse of a trans person has the so-called "spousal veto" and can deny the trans spouse the right to change their gender marker.

Marriage is a tool of the state to consolidate power and resources: wealth, property, citizenship.

*see also:* LGBT+ RIGHTS; ASSIMILATION; HOMONORMATIVITY; SAME-SEX MARRIAGE

**MASC** — Short for masculine; a queer masculinity.

Masc has its cultural and aesthetic roots in butch, both of which are defined in their opposition to femme.

*see also:* MASCULINE; FEMME; BUTCH

**MASC 4 MASC, MASC4MASC** — Shorthand on dating and hookup apps to indicate that the subject is masc and looking for other masc people.

It is often accompanied by phrases such as "no fats, no femmes" and a list of acceptable or unacceptable races.

There has been a pushback against masc4masc within the gay community in an effort to appreciate femmeness, but mascness is still prioritized in general—and femmeness might be "appreciated" but it is also commodified.

*see also:* STRAIGHT ACTING; FEMMEPHOBIA; FATPHOBIA; GAY CULTURE

**MASCULINE, MASCULINITY** — A set of cultural norms and behaviors. An aesthetic. A power structure based on subjugating the feminine Other.

Any deviance from hegemonic masculinity is to invite punishment. Masculinity is fragile and constantly needs to be reasserted, often by degrading the feminine.

Masculinity is not inherently oppressive, but most iterations of masculinity (especially hegemonic masculinity) are.

Masculinity is seen as gender neutral compared to an allegedly more performative femininity. Even in queer spaces, queer masculinity is prized over queer femininity.

*see also:* GENDER (n.); MAN; BOY; FEMININE; TOXIC MASCULINITY

**MASOCHISM** — A sexual interest in relinquishing control and being subject to the will of another person, possibly including the use of pain, humiliation, and/or abuse.

Masochism was first popularized in Richard von Krafft-Ebing's 1886 *Psychopathia Sexualis*.

*see also:* SADISM; BDSM; PERVERT

**MEDICAL TRANSITION, MEDICAL INTERVENTION** — *see:* TRANSITION.

**MENTAL ILLNESS** — A cognitive or behavioral pattern which causes significant distress or impairment of personal functioning.

Queerness has long been pathologized as a mental illness, despite not being a problem on an individual level—it is only a "problem" in so far as it threatens the cisheteronormative status quo. It wasn't until 2001 that the American Psychological Association declared that "homosexuality and bisexuality are not a mental illness."

Viewing queerness as a mental illness, especially transness today, affords queers some legitimacy as a protected political class, to be pitied and supported rather than discriminated against. Some queers do see their queerness as mental illness because they are unable to comfortably function in a society which hates them, and so their anxiety, depression, and stress are directly tied to their being queer. It should be obvious here that the problem though is society, not the individual.

*see also:* DISABILITY; TRANS HEALTHCARE; NEURODIVERSE

**MEN WHO LOVE MEN (MLM)** — Men who are sexually or romantically attracted to men, sometimes called "Men who have Sex with Men (MSM)."

MLM is different from gay, bisexual, and queer because it's centered on behavior instead of identity. This makes room for men who are hesitant to claim queerness to describe their sexual and romantic life, and is especially important in a sexual health setting.

It also flattens out different queer identities, which is useful for solidarity and describing the shared experience of being a man who loves men.

*see also:* MAN; GAY; IDENTITY POLITICS

**MINCE** — To walk affectedly or effeminately—from Polari slang.

Mincing is an aspect of gender performance, and highlights the weight placed on non-verbal gender cues.

*see also:* POLARI; GENDER (n.)

**MISGENDER, MISGENDERING** — To incorrectly gender someone, by calling/referring to them with the wrong pronouns or an incorrectly gendered word.

Deliberate misgendering is an example of transphobia.

*see also:* GENDER; PRONOUNS; DEADNAME

**-MISMIA (SUFFIX)** — "Hatred of," used as a more accurate suffix to replace -phobia.

Rather than implying a "fear of," -mismia names bigotry as hatred. Examples include transmismia, homomismia, Islamomismia, bimismia, lesbomismia, queermismia, and fatmismia.

Using -mismia instead of -phobia eliminates the possibility of conflating mental health problems with bigotry—homophobia is not an illness, agoraphobia is.

This represents a shift in language and using deliberate language, but language is slow to evolve and -mismia is not yet in popular usage.

*see also:* -PHOBIA

**MISOGYNY** — The hatred of, and discrimination toward, women and things associated with womanhood and femininity; the subjugation of women and non-men under patriarchy.

Misogyny takes many forms: discrimination against women; the assumption that women are less qualified than men; slut-shaming and body-shaming; double standards and extra scrutiny of women over men; street harassment; expecting women to be beautiful and unconditionally emotionally supportive; only valuing women for their beauty or the emotional support they give you rather than as complex people; and gendered and sexual violence.

The gendered division of labor is another example of misogyny. Feminine labor is devalued literally and figuratively: most unpaid labor (i.e., domestic work and care work) is feminine-coded. Further, everything done by women is considered less legitimate and less credible, even when that labor is supposedly "women's work." Fashion, for example, is derided as frivolous and not treated seriously as an art form, but the people who profit most from it are men—the top designers are men, and the top stakeholders in the industry, like in every industry, are men.

Internalized misogyny positions women against each other, high-lighted in the "I'm not like other girls" attitude. It makes femininity a competition where everyone loses.

Misogyny is compounded when it intersects with other oppressions: racism, classism, transphobia, queerphobia, agism, and fatphobia.

*see also:* SEXISM; GENDER (n.)

**MLM** — Acronym for MEN WHO LOVE MEN.

**MOGAI** — Acronym for "Marginalized Orientation, Gender Identities, And Intersex."

MOGAI is a long, ever-expanding list of new "sexualities" based on increasingly specific particulars (e.g., gerontoqueerplatonic: the queerplatonic attraction to elderly people). MOGAI includes, among other things I'm no doubt oblivious to, being otherkin, having mental illness, being a furry, enjoying erotic fiction, and morally unacceptable sexual inclinations like pedophilia, necrophilia, and bestiality. All of these have (usually hilariously poorly designed) "Pride flags."

Being allegedly marginalized for a sexual preference—while also being straight and cis—is apparently appealing. "Cishet" is not a very nuanced term to describe gender and sexuality, and many cishet people are quick to suggest that being polyamorous or into kink is comparably marginalized to being queer—or that being polyamorous or into kink means they too are queer.

MOGAI conflates other marginalizations with marginalization based on gender identity and sexuality. Mental illness is stigmatized, but having mental illness does not make someone LGBT+. There is an interesting discussion to be had about the ways that sexuality and gender identity are policed in people with mental illness, and about what queerness is and its intersections with mental illness, but those are not the discussions happening under MOGAI.

Human sexuality is complex, and we don't necessarily need to categorize every individual type of attraction or repulsion. It's okay that not every queer woman is attracted to the same women in the same ways, under the same circumstances. Having a language to describe sexual preferences is wonderful, but shaping identity around it is misguided. There is utility in telling prospective partners what your sexual inclinations are (e.g., are you a top or a bottom or vers, what are your kinks, what are your boundaries?), but these things are preferences, and even where they are uncommon preferences, they are not marginalized identities.

Many of the MOGAI labels are created by sock puppets who aim to delegitimize the queer community (e.g., by inventing a pedophilia "sexuality" to bolster the narrative that queers are immoral, dangerous, and perverse).

*see also:* MARGINALIZED; SOCK PUPPET

**MOLLY HOUSE** — A place where queer men could meet other queer men—in use in 18th- and 19th-century England.

Molly houses could be pubs, coffeehouses, taverns, or private residences. Though there was sometimes a heavy undercurrent of having sex and finding sexual partners, Molly houses were not necessarily brothels.

The Molly house was an important part of queer subculture, and can be seen as the precursor to gay bars in a time when homosexuality was criminalized.

*see also:* GAY BAR

**MONES** — Short for hormones; *see:* HORMONE REPLACEMENT THERAPY.

M

**MONOSEXISM** — The assumption of a hetero/homo binary that everyone must be attracted to either (and only) the same or opposite gender as themselves.

Monosexism alienates bisexuals and asexuals, and agender and non-binary people. Monosexism contributes to the erasure of different genders. When ace or bi people are in relationships they're assumed to be either gay (in an exclusively homosexual way) or straight.

Monosexism as a term risks conflating heterosexism with homosexuality by placing heterosexuality and homosexuality in the same "privileged" group. Obviously, homosexuality does not occupy a privileged position like heterosexuality, but it does benefit from the reductive assumptions of monosexism in ways which other sexualities do not.

*see also:* MONOSEXUAL; BIPHOBIA; SEXUSOCIETY

**MONOSEXUAL** — Sexual attraction to only one gender.

Monosexual as a term implies an equal leveling between being exclusively homosexual and being straight, which is obviously not true; but it also highlights that bisexuals, pansexuals, asexuals, and other non-monosexuals experience specific issues of erasure and fetishization.

*see also:* POLYSEXUAL; BIPHOBIA; GAY; LESBIAN

**MSM** — Acronym for "Men Who Have Sex With Men."
*see also:* MEN WHO LOVE MEN

**MTF, M2F** — Acronym for MALE TO FEMALE.

**MUFFING** — Gently massaging or pushing the testicles in and out of the inguinal canals for sexual pleasure.

Sex for people with penises, whether they are trans or not, is focused on erections and penetrating and ejaculating, which is a very narrow understanding of sex.

Muffing is one way for people who have penises and testes to have receptive sex, along with receptive anal sex or oral sex. Assigned male at birth trans people might feel dysphoric if they have penetrative sex with their penis, and trans people who take feminizing hormone replacement therapy might not get or sustain erections.

Like most sex acts, muffing should be done gently and slowly at first, and may take some practice to get right.

Putting the testes into the inguinal canals is also a tactic used to tuck.

Muffing is a term coined by Mira Bellwether in the 2017 zine *Fucking Trans Women (FTW)*, which is about sex acts for pre- and non-op trans women.

*see also:* SEX (v.); TUCK

**NAFF** — Polari slang to describe being bad, drab, heterosexual, or boring. Possibly an acronym for "Not Available For Fucking."

*see also:* POLARI; HETEROSEXUAL

**NAME** — The particular word used to distinguish an individual.

The name is a site of gender; for trans people who change their names, it's a site of declaration and reclamation. Choosing a new name is an informal rite of passage for many trans people. Naming yourself is an act of self-definition and can be very empowering.

The legal name is not a stable category. People can have different names on their birth certificates, their photo IDs, their marriage certificates, and what they use in daily life. The concept of a "real" name is generally used to undermine trans people with invasive questions about their past.

Names are different for different scenarios. Sex workers usually use aliases and may have multiple personas; trans people tend to try out names with a small, safe social group before using them with the wider public; drag performers have names which often bleed into their non-performance life; and in the 20th century the gay community used "camp names" for each other (e.g., "Mary").

*see also:* PRONOUNS; DEADNAME; DRAG

**NANCY, NANCY BOY** — Pejoratives for a queer or effeminate man, sometimes reclaimed by the people they target.

Nancy and nancy boy are intended to be insults to masculinity, and are indicative of failure to correctly perform it.

*see also:* NONCE; EFFEMINATE; GAY

**NATURAL, UNNATURAL** — An arbitrary distinction used to assign value to identities, behaviors, aesthetics, and hierarchies.

There are not objective "facts of nature." Nature is the name we give to our wider environment, which predates us and will outlast us. Our facts are tainted by our biases and constantly need re-evaluating if they are to be useful.

Nature is not balance or order. Nature is chaotic and indifferent to human life, and we cannot untangle ourselves from it. We exist in nature; we are natural.

Race, sex, gender, and class are all social constructs; none are "natural" (i.e., created outside of human reasoning), but that doesn't mean they aren't real or material. Science has always been subject to personal and social bias, and has never been objective.

Natural versus unnatural is an arbitrary distinction, used to delegitimize "undesirable" behaviors. People use "natural" to imbue behaviors and identities with morality, and they usually mean "like me" or "how I should be." "Unnatural" is wielded to mean "unrelatable" or "bad." If humans are "natural" at all, everything we do is natural. There is no "unnatural."

*see also:* NORMAL; CISNORMATIVITY; HETERONORMATIVITY; BIOLOGICAL ESSENTIALISM; AESTHETIC

**NB** — Acronym for NON-BINARY.

**NE/NIR** — A gender neutral neopronoun.

Like ve/ver, ne/nir is derivative of both he/him and she/her, to create a gender balanced, gender neutral pronoun.

Like all pronouns, the use of ne/nir doesn't necessarily indicate anything about the user's gender; anyone can use gender neutral pronouns. Here are some examples:

| Ne is good | I called nem | Nir face lit up | That's nirs | Ne loves nemself |
|---|---|---|---|---|

*see also:* PRONOUNS; NEOPRONOUNS; GENDER NEUTRAL LANGUAGE

**NEM** — *see:* NE/NIR.

**NEOPRONOUNS** — "New" pronouns, as opposed to the more traditional he/him, she/her, and they/them.

In this book I've included several neopronouns in the entry on PRONOUNS, but that list is not exhaustive.

Other neopronouns might take the form of bun/buns/bunself (like a bunny), or mer/mers/merself (like a mermaid). They sound cutesy and like they're not to be taken seriously, but there's really no reason why we shouldn't respect any pronouns someone chooses for themselves.

see also: PRONOUNS; SPIVAK; GENDER NEUTRAL LANGUAGE; TRUSCUM; RESPECTABILITY

**NEUROATYPICAL, NEURODIVERSE, NEURODIVERGENT** — Being on the autism spectrum. The terms are sometimes used to describe other mental illnesses, disorders, and conditions.

see also: NEUROTYPICAL; AUTISM

**NEUROTYPICAL** — Being allistic, not autistic.

see also: ALLISTIC; NEURODIVERGENT

**NEUTROIS** — A non-binary gender or lack of gender. A feeling of neutral gender, neither male nor female.

Neutrois is similar to agender. Neutrois falls under the transgender, and non-binary, umbrella terms.

see also: NON-BINARY; AGENDER; TRANSGENDER

**NIR** — see: NE/NIR.

**NO HO** — Short for "No Hormones." Trans people who don't want or need hormone replacement therapy.

No ho is a resistance against the medicalization of transness, and the cis expectations that trans people "fully transition" to be as close to cisness as possible.

There can be an implied superiority of no ho trans people—when comparing themselves to people who do go on hormones—which is unfounded. Trans people should not create a hierarchy of "better" transition choices amongst ourselves; instead we should support each other to transition (or not) however best suits each of us. There is no single "correct" way to be trans or to transition.

see also: HORMONE REPLACEMENT THERAPY; TRANS HEALTH-CARE; TRANSGENDER; NON-OP

**NON-BINARY (NB, ENBY)** — A gender identity which does not fit within the gender binary.

Non-binary can be used to describe anyone whose gender isn't exclusively "man" or "woman," and anyone whose gender isn't either "man" or "woman." Anyone who is gender fluid, agender, demi-gender, genderqueer, neutrois, a mix of man and woman, or any gender which isn't unambiguously "man" or "woman" could call themselves non-binary. There isn't one single way to be non-binary.

Non-binary people fall within the definition of "trans," but some non-binary people don't call themselves "trans." Some people don't claim transness because they don't have dysphoria and feel like trans implies dysphoria or transition. Alternatively, it might be because they still feel aligned with some part of the gender they were assigned at birth. Take, for example, an assigned female at birth person who is a non-binary woman; her gender isn't unambiguously the same as the one she was assigned at birth, so she is trans. However, she is also a woman, which is her assigned gender, which may mean she doesn't feel trans, because the implication may be that she's a woman and trans, but not a trans woman. Other people policing the terms she uses to describe her gender are unhelpful at best and can cause harm—declaring that someone is cis if they refuse to call themselves trans is coercive and bad practice, and forces them to be quiet about the difficult nuances of their gender and experience.

While non-binary is a relatively new term, genders outside of the gender binary have existed and been celebrated for thousands of years, and in many cultures. Possibly the earliest known example of a non-binary gender on record is *hijra*, mentioned in the ancient Hindu text *Mahābhārata* (c.400 BCE).

see also: GENDER BINARY; GENDER DYSPHORIA; TRANSITION

**NONCE** — Pejorative slang for "queer." A child sexual abuser.

The connection between queerness and sex crimes is long and

painful, and has left queers with a collective inter-generational trauma that is regularly reified by current queerphobia. On top of that, many queers have been victims of child sexual abuse. To use a term which suggests that queerness is comparable—in immorality, in pathology, in "unnaturalness"—to pedophilia and child sexual abuse is extremely offensive to queers generally and survivors of childhood sexual violence specifically. Such a comparison shows absolutely no solidarity with some of the most vulnerable people in society.

Nonce is a slang term for a sex offender or child sexual abuser which arose from prison usage among inmates in England in the 20th century. Possibly it came from "nancy," though the etymology is unclear. In 1970 during an interview with researcher Tony Parker, a prisoner explained nonce as being short for "nonsenses": "sex cases, professional mental patients who live in a world of their own, they never really talk to anyone." The earliest known source to make a link between "nonce" and "nancy boy" was a 1984 article from *Police Review*, a weekly UK magazine for police officers—the connection being that both pedophiles and homosexuals are "perverts." This not only reflects a general culture of queerphobia at the time, but betrays police prejudice in particular against queer people.

Like all "accusations" of queerness, nonce is used to express disgust, discomfort, or the threat of violence. Nonce is directed toward anyone who fits a particular profile of gender non-conformity: quiet, feminine men, especially if they have skills relevant to childcare.

In prisons, inmates may request to be voluntarily isolated from the general prison population for their own safety. Sex offenders are likely to do this, as they are held in especially low regard by other prisoners; hence a separate vulnerable prisoners' unit might get called "the nonce wing" by the majority inmate population. However, it won't only be sex offenders who are unsafe in prison (let us pause and consider if any inmate is safe in prison). Vulnerable prisoners who might be singled out for their sexualities or genders are physically and conceptually grouped together with pedophiles and prisoners alleged to be pedophiles.

In civilian usage outside of prisons, likely exacerbated by widespread moral panic over pedophilia in the 1990s, nonce took the place of queer as the vilified sexual deviant.

*see also:* NANCY BOY; POLICE (n.); GAY; PERVERT; TRAUMA; SURVIVOR

**NON-OP** — A trans person who doesn't seek any surgical intervention as part of their transition.

Don't talk unprompted to trans people about their surgeries.

see also: PRE-OP; POST-OP; TRANSITION

**NORMAL, NORMATIVITY** — Normal means conforming to the patterns of the dominant social groups. Normativity is that which reproduces the hegemonic culture.

Normal is another way of saying "dominant." It is the cultural default—not necessarily the most common one. The hegemonic mode is given a privileged position of "naturalness" but is actually just as constructed as minority cultures and groups (e.g., masculinity, cisness, whiteness).

Normalcy is a tactic for shame and punishment. Normalcy is the status quo; any threat to that, to power, is "abnormal," wrong, and punished.

see also: OTHER; ASSIMILATION; PRIVILEGE; NATURAL

**OFFENSIVE, OFFENDED** — Disagreeable or upsetting due to insensitivity, rudeness, or denial of empathy or personhood. To be upset by something offensive.

Queer people are often accused of being too sensitive and too offended when we challenge language or norms which reproduce violent hierarchies. Apparently, we're meant to be more respectable and politely acquiesce to being denied healthcare, housing, and personhood. Being told we're being too offended is a derailing tactic to distract from the issues being raised by the "offended" party by focusing on their reaction to the offensive thing, rather than the offensive aspects of the thing itself.

We shouldn't stop using "bad" words because they're "offensive"; they're offensive not because people are too sensitive, but because those "bad" words uphold and reproduce harmful stereotypes, stigmas, and systems of oppression. "Bad" words and slurs are used as weapons to remind marginalized people of power dynamics.

Intra-community policing of what terms are offensive is counterproductive. When queer people tell each other that we cannot reclaim the slurs which have been weaponized against us, or that our preferred identity label is outdated and now "offensive," we're erasing our histories and denying ourselves the possibility of naming our own experience. This is especially relevant in talking to queer people without access to intra-community discussions on language, like older queers and queer people who live in rural areas.

No word or phrase is inherently offensive or oppressive; language is context dependent. Who is saying the potentially offensive thing, and to what audience? A good guideline is to ask if the "offending" person is speaking on their own marginalized identity and culture, if they're punching up (poking fun at groups or individuals with more structural power than them), or if they're punching down (further entrenching stereotypes about a group which has less structural power than them).

*see also:* TROLL; TONE POLICING

**OPPRESSION** — Structural violence against a group of people based on their identities and perceptions of their identities.

Structural oppression exists on several axes: ableism, sexism, cissexism, homophobia, classism, racism, agism, and fatphobia. Within these are other oppressions, such as anti-Blackness (a specific form of racism), whorephobia (a manifestation of misogyny and classism), xenophobia (where the immigrant is racialized as Other), Islamophobia (racialized oppression against Muslims), and anti-Semitism (ethno-religious oppression of Jews). An exhaustive list of oppressions based on identity, and perceived identity, is not possible. Because our identities intersect, so too do our oppressions and privileges. It is not possible to analyze these oppressions distinctly, because they do not exist distinctly.

Because everyone is indoctrinated into oppressive structures, like patriarchy and capitalism and white supremacy, everyone is by default sexist and classist and racist. Everyone has the potential to be oppressive, even oppressed people; for example, a woman may try to distance herself from femininity by claiming she's "not like other girls," which is an expression of internalized misogyny based on the idea that girls are inferior. Being oppressed does not give you a pass ("I can't be oppressive, I'm gay"), and having proximity to oppression through marginalized friends/partners/children certainly does not ("I can't be racist, I have a Black friend").

*see also:* PRIVILEGE; RESPECTABILITY; INTERSECTIONALITY

**OMNISEXUAL** — Sexual attraction to all genders, or sexual attraction regardless of gender.

Omnisexual could be used interchangeably with bisexual, pansexual, and polysexual; the choice of which term to use is a matter of personal preference.

*see also:* BISEXUAL; PANSEXUAL; POLYSEXUAL; BIPHOBIA

**OTHER, OTHERING** — In opposition to "self" or "I," or the dominant identity group. To make someone feel, or portray them as, negatively alien, strange, and fundamentally different.

Straight is I, queer is Other; cis is I, trans is Other; white is I, person of color is Other; Western is I, "Oriental" is Other. Other is outside, unknown and unknowable, or only known and defined in opposition to I. Society is designed for the ease of the I and the discomfort of the Other, not only through negligence but in a deliberate attempt to exclude the Other, for the I only understands itself in policing its boundaries and excluding the Other. Without trans there is no cis, and cis would not be prized and superior without an inferior to subjugate.

I and Other rely on the (flimsy, false) presumption of stable binary categories of identity. Despite the assumption of inherent I-ness or Otherness, the I must constantly reassert itself and prove its position as superior. Hegemonic masculinity is a good example. The I, the privileged identity, is fragile; it cannot withstand an interrogation of its construction ("What is a man?") or its "naturalness," nor can it stand a challenge to its superiority ("Why is masculinity better than femininity?"). It is also too fragile to withstand tension around its privilege, and it easily collapses from guilt (often masked in anger and "resolved" through violence). The I is constantly seeking to establish the boundaries around it, so that it can find comfort in knowing that it is included in privilege and is excluding the Other—men tease each other and challenge each other's masculinity to this end.

*see also:* FETISHIZE; FASCISM; BINARY

**OTHERKIN** — Someone who socially or spiritually identifies as non-human, or not entirely human.

Otherkin, as a group identity, grew out of online elvin subculture from the 1990s. But so-called "species dysphoria" is much older, pathologized as lycanthropy.

Otherkin communities tend to be subdivided into kintype, and overlap with the vampire and therian communities. Some otherkin identify as animals, and some as mythical creatures like angels, demons, aliens, dragons, and faeries.

Otherkin is not the same as trans, despite some otherkin using trans language like "trans-species dysphoria."

Otherkin are pathologized, and excessively bullied, especially online.
*see also:* FURRIES

**OTTER** — Gay slang for a man who is thin, youthful, and hairy.
*see also:* TWINK; BEAR; GAY CULTURE

**OUT** — Being openly gay, queer, or trans. It can also mean to be open about another marginalized status (e.g., sex worker).

Choosing to be out is a luxury, only available to people who won't suffer serious homophobic or transphobic consequences. Some people are not given a choice because they don't pass as cisgender or heterosexual, or because they are outed by someone else.

The dominant narrative is that being out is "living authentically." Shaming people who aren't out puts the onus for social change—eradicating queerphobia—on the people affected by the bigotry.

People can be selectively out (e.g., in their personal life but not at work). This may entail using different names or pronouns depending on what situation they're in. It's important to respect people's decisions to be, or not to be, out.

Cisgender and heterosexual people don't need to come out or be "out" about their genders and sexualities, because theirs are taken as normal and the default. This normalcy should be disrupted.

*see also:* COMING OUT; OUTING; CLOSET; BRAVE; STEALTH; PASSING

**OUTING** — To disclose someone's LGBTQ+ status without their permission. It is also used for sex workers, and (problematically) abusers.

Outing people (except abusers) is dangerous and rude. It removes agency about something deeply personal, and makes the outed person vulnerable to homophobic, transphobic, or whorephobic violence and discrimination.

Outing abusers is dangerous too, for the people who they have abused. Any action taken against abusers must be survivor centered and insulate the survivor(s) from harm as much as possible.

*see also:* COMING OUT; CLOSET; STEALTH; TRANSFORMATIVE JUSTICE

**OUTRAGE!** — A British queer direct action group, stylized as "OutRage!"

OutRage! was active between 1990 and 2011. They formed in response to escalating queer-bashing, including homophobic murders, and the persecution of queer men having consensual sex.

OutRage! was an anti-assimilationist, non-violent, non-hierarchical group. They focused on homophobic attitudes, especially in policing, and their tactics were non-violent civil disobedience. Their actions included: invading the Vatican's embassy in London to protest against the Pope's support for anti-gay laws in 1992; ambushing the Prime Minister's motorcade in response to Parliament voting to maintain the unequal age of consent for same-sex sex in 1994; and invading police stations and protesting the prosecution of queer men cruising and cottaging, throughout the 1990s.

OutRage! was possibly the longest-running grassroots, volunteer LGBT+ direct action group in the world.

*see also:* ACTIVISM; ASSIMILATION; ACT UP

**P** — The P in the long-form acronym LGBTQIAAP is for PANSEXUAL.
*see also:* LGBT+

**PACKER, PACKING** — Wearing objects to simulate a penis.

Packing includes everything from stuffing underwear with a sock to wearing a realistic prosthetic penis. Trans people may pack to relieve dysphoria; anyone might pack to genderfuck. Packers should be considered an aspect of trans healthcare when they're used to alleviate dysphoria.

Some (but not all) packers are made of body-safe materials which can be used for sex.
*see also:* STP; TRANS; TRANS HEALTHCARE

**PAN** — Short for PANSEXUAL.

**PANGENDER** — Someone who has more than one gender; sometimes, all genders. Pangender falls under the broader labels of "transgender" and "non-binary."
*see also:* TRANSGENDER; NON-BINARY

**PANSEXUAL** — Attraction to multiple genders. Attraction to all genders. Attraction to people regardless of gender. An alternative term to "bisexual."

Pansexual as a term is criticized for its biphobia and transphobia, in the implicit suggestion that bisexual doesn't encompass trans people and the misunderstanding that bisexual means attraction to the "same and opposite" genders. Both bisexual and pansexual can include attraction to trans, and non-binary, people.

In most cases, pansexual and bisexual essentially mean the same thing; but people will choose different labels to define their experience based on cultural connotations and personal preference. Other words which describe attraction to multiple genders include "omnisexual" and "polysexual," which likewise have their own subcultures and connotations.

*see also*: BISEXUAL; BIPHOBIA

**PANSY** — Pejorative meaning an effeminate man.

Pansy is used as an insult, along the lines of queer, nancy, and sissy. Its use highlights the connection between gender non-conformity and (assumed) sexuality.

*see also*: EFFEMINATE; GAY; NANCY; MASCULINITY

**PARAPHILIA** — Pathologized sexual desire.

Paraphilias are often very common desires, practiced consensually, but they are still framed as "abnormal" or "dysfunctional."

The *DSM-5* labels the desire to be an attractive woman as a paraphilia: "autogynophilia." This pathologizes trans women, but not cis women who have the same (very common) fantasy. There is also no inverse "androgynophilia" for trans men. This is very telling of the psychiatric community's transmisogyny and willful misunderstanding of trans issues. Also telling is that trans women are pathologized with a paraphilia, but pedophiles aren't.

*see also*: AUTOGYNEPHILIA; TRANSMISOGYNY

**PASS, PASSING** — To be correctly perceived as your gender; to be perceived as cis; or to be perceived as straight. Passing has connotations of success.

Cisnormativity demands that trans people try our best to pass, because transness is a shameful error to be erased. Radical queers think we should place less emphasis on passing, and more on allowing all trans people access to basic needs (safety, housing, employment, healthcare) which are currently only afforded to trans people who pass.

At the same time, there's no shame in trying to pass—being trans is already difficult and passing eases that difficulty, not only on a systemic level but often on a personal level too. Passing can mitigate dysphoria. You shouldn't feel guilty for trying to pass, so long as your politics don't dictate that passing should be required for trans people to be valid. Transness is valid whether or not it is interested in passing.

Passing is about seeking external validation for your gender, or your performance of gender/sexuality. One manifestation of this is trans people seeking sexual interest from monosexual cis people: a trans man might think, "If he's gay and only interested in men, and he's interested in me, then he really sees me as a man." But we should gently interrogate this mode of thinking, because cis approval will not magically make dysphoria disappear, nor should it be inherently more validating than approval from other trans people, or ourselves. It's also tempting to dismiss bisexuals in this regard because we can't be sure they're seeing us as we want to be seen, but we should believe them if they say they're attracted to us as our gender.

*see also:* PASSING PRIVILEGE; STEALTH

**PASSING PRIVILEGE** — The absence of discrimination and violence afforded to people who "pass" as straight and/or cisgender.

Passing privilege is, I contend, not actually a privilege, because the absence of violence is conditional on hiding your queerness. This is erasure, which is a different kind of violence. Genuine privilege is not conditional. However, we can recognize that there is a (multi-axis) scale of violence, where passing/erasure tends to be less painful than not passing.

*see also:* ERASURE; ASSIMILATION; PASSING

**PATRIARCHY** — A social system of gendered norms and expectations, in which men have relative power over everyone else.

Patriarchy, like all systems of power, is produced and reproduced through both individual behavior and institutions, including non-tangible institutions of social norms (patriarchy itself is a social institution).

Patriarchy is intertwined with capitalism and white supremacy, to privilege rich white men over poor men and men of color. There is not a single axis of power in our society—a rich white woman has systemic power over a working-class Black man, because she is likely to be seen as more "respectable" than he is. Patriarchy and misogyny are also bolstered by transphobia and queerphobia, ableism, fat phobia, and other systems of oppression which delineate the boundaries of "acceptable" gender, to create subjects which are either respectable or deviant.

Patriarchy hurts men too, with its gendered expectations. Hegemonic masculinity is toxic masculinity. Men assimilate into toxic masculinity for survival, because the punishment for deviation from prescribed gender norms is very high. Women are afforded more gender deviance (e.g., wearing trousers) than men (who are not, for example, allowed to wear skirts) because patriarchy is deeply misogynistic, and therefore it's permissible for women to behave "like men." However, for a man to behave "like a woman" is an incomprehensible denial not only of social expectation but also of his privilege. How could he stoop to the lower status of femininity? It's scandalous.

see also: MISOGYNY; CISNORMATIVITY; GENDER; OPPRESSION; RESPECTABILITY; ASSIMILATION

**PEP** — Post-Exposure Prophylaxis, an HIV prevention drug taken after possible exposure to the virus.

PEP is likened to the "morning after" pill but for HIV. It's not to be confused with Pre-Exposure Prophylaxis (PrEP).

PEP is a 28-day course of two pills a day, and when taken correctly it is very effective at preventing HIV infection.

PEP is only designed to be used in emergency situations—within 72 hours of exposure to HIV (the sooner the better). Emergency situations might include potentially being exposed to HIV during sex, sexual assault, or sharing needles for intravenous drug use. It is not a substitute for safer sex practices, like condom use or PrEP.

PEP has uncomfortable side effects such as nausea and headaches, but it is safe to take.

PEP is an important medical development in queer health activism, like all HIV-related treatments. Thirty years after the AIDS crisis began, and we're finally not just left to die anymore.

see also: PrEP; SAFER SEX; HIV/AIDS

**PERVERT** — One whose sexuality is morally bankrupt.

There is a strong connection between sexual deviance and queerness; in cisheteronormative society, queerness simply is sexual deviance.

see also: DEVIANT; NONCE; QUEER CODING

**PHARMASEXUAL** — A term for transgender or transsexual, which refers endearingly to the use of hormone replacement therapy. An alternative term is "testojunkie" (a person who takes testosterone).

*see also:* TRANSSEXUAL

**-PHOBIA (SUFFIX)** — Fear of.

The -phobia suffix is used to describe systemic oppressions and individual bigotries, such as homophobia, transphobia, Islamophobia, biphobia, and lesbophobia. The connection between "fear" and bigotry is in the perceived threat of difference to the status quo.

Its utility is mainly in its common usage; but -phobia unhelpfully conflates clinical phobias with bigotry.

*see also:* -MISMIA

**PINK** — The color pink is associated with queerness, femininity, and effeminacy.

During the Third Reich, the Nazis criminalized queerness. In the concentration camps, queer prisoners were marked with a pink triangle. This symbol has since been reclaimed by queer activists, and featured prominently in AIDS activism in the 1980s and 1990s.

Pink and black are the colors for queer anarchism.

Pink was the "boy's" color until the 1930s, and blue the "girl's" color. Now pink is the girl's color, illustrative of the shifting meaning of colors and fashions and gender throughout time.

*see also:* PINKWASH; RAINBOW FLAG; FASCISM; QUEER ANARCHISM

**PINKWASH, PINKWASHING** — Using the language or ideals of gay rights and queer liberation as justification for, or obfuscation of, capitalism or imperialism.

Pinkwashing primarily refers to shifting the narrative of gay rights away from queer liberation, and toward assimilation into capitalism and imperialism. An example of this is taking the protest out of Pride: the 2017 London Pride was led not by a queer organization, but by Barclays bank, and the marketing for the parade literally focused on straight people.

The particular manifestations of pinkwashing which justify racist colonialism through the rhetoric of "gay rights" are called "homonationalism" or "transmilitarism."

Pinkwashing takes its name from "greenwashing," the tactic of making capitalism and corporations more appealing through tokenistic environmental concessions which do nothing to significantly address the role of big business and the profit motive in polluting the Earth, unsustainably and wastefully burning through natural resources, and contributing to climate change and immense human suffering.

*see also:* HOMONATIONALISM; TRANSMILITARISM; CAPITALISM

**PIV** — Acronym for "Penis In Vagina," referring to the sex act.

In our cisheteronormative society, PIV sex is regarded as the only form of "real" sex or intercourse, and all other sex acts are "foreplay" or "perverse." PIV is extremely phallocentric and has the implicit goal of male ejaculation, with little or no emphasis on the woman's pleasure (of course, it is taken as granted that the man has a penis and the woman has a vagina and they are both cis and straight).

Of course, there are innumerable other sex acts, which are all just as legitimate and potentially pleasurable as PIV.

*see also:* SEX (v.); HETERONORMATIVITY; SCISSORING

**PLATONIC** — A relationship or attraction without sex or romance.

Platonic relationships could be described as friendship or kinship, and may have high levels of intimacy and strong bonds. Platonic relationships are no less legitimate or significant than romantic and sexual relationships.

*see also:* QUEERPLATONIC; AROMANTIC

**POLARI** — A gay slang language, spoken in 19th- and 20th-century Britain.

Polari is a form of cant slang, which is slang used by a particular group with the intention of excluding and misleading people outside the group. This was a survival strategy for queer people in a time when queerness was criminalized.

Polari's roots are disputed, and possibly date back to the 16th century. It is a mixture of Romani, Italian, Yiddish, London slang, back slang, rhyming slang, and thieves' cant. Polari was spoken by circus performers, merchant navy sailors, professional wrestlers, and sex workers. It became a part of gay subculture because many gay men worked in theater or in the merchant navy; it was further developed by queers to hide their queerness from a homophobic, hostile public and undercover police.

Polari declined in use in the 1960s, when a popular radio program called *Round the Horn* made much of the secret language public knowledge; and when homosexuality was decriminalized in 1967.

Many Polari words have entered mainstream slang; for example, "naff," "trade," "mince," "cottaging," "camp," "butch," "slap," and "ogle."

*see also:* GAY CULTURE

**POLICE (N.)** — An institution which uses force in the name of maintaining public order and upholding the rule of law.

The police as an institution was created to protect property and wealth and manage crowd control; now their role also includes "social welfare." Modern police are increasingly militarized.

In Polari, a gay slang dialect in 19th- and 20th-century Britain, there are multiple words for police—"charpering omi," "Lilly Law," "sharpy," among others—which goes to show how often queers were talking about the cops. Police would raid queer spaces (e.g., bars, clubs) to enforce anti-cross-dressing and anti-queer laws.

Police still disproportionately target and harass queers, especially racialized queers, poor queers, and queers who are trans women or perceived to be trans women.

In recognition that police, and the larger state surveillance-police-prison system does not do justice for queers (or most people), many queers have turned to alternative, community-based methods of justice for conflict resolution.

*see also:* POLICE (v.); POLARI; TRANSFORMATIVE JUSTICE

**POLICE (v.)** — To control with violence, oppression, and gatekeeping. To maintain the boundaries of a border (tangible or abstract).

Policing is a tactic used to deny marginalized groups access to material resources as well as discourses, and it's a problem both within and outwith queer communities. Feminism has been—and continues to be—policed to exclude women of color, disabled women, poor women, lesbians and women who love women, and now trans women.

Trans healthcare is policed so only respectable trans people are allowed access, denying access to the most vulnerable. Queer spaces are often policed to explicitly exclude ace and aro people and opposite-gender couples (or couples who are assumed to be opposite-gender); and they largely implicitly exclude disabled people, poor people, older people, and people of color.

*see also:* TONE POLICING; VIOLENCE; OPPRESSION; ASSIMILATION; POLICE (n.)

**POLITICAL LESBIAN, POLITICAL WOMAN** — Someone who identifies themselves as a lesbian or a woman for the purposes of political organizing, but has a different (possibly more complicated) relationship to their gender or sexuality in their daily, private life.

The "political woman" or "political lesbian" is an attempt at reconciling strategically reductive politics and complex personal lives.

The political lesbian is a feminist who thinks heterosexuality undermines her feminism. The political lesbian might not be attracted to women, or exclusively to women, but she wills herself to abandon men in an attempt to undermine patriarchy in every aspect of her life. The blame for patriarchy then falls not with men, but with women who "enable" it by simply trying to live livable lives. This tends to also be "TERFy," ironically, because you would think that political lesbians would welcome trans women into womanhood as even greater examples of eradicating maleness than cis lesbians—lesbian trans women abandon not only the men in their lives, but their lives as men! But to moralize desire and gender identity, even in defense of trans lesbians, is a mistake.

The political woman is someone who will identify as a woman for "political purposes," such as organizing and protesting, but they might have a different identity in their private life. It's useful to unify under a single term (e.g., "woman") but it's not ideal to erase and reduce our varied experiences of patriarchy into a single monolith, especially when the people most likely to experience gendered violence won't fall easily into that category (e.g., assigned male at birth non-binary femmes). "A woman for political purposes" is also alienating to people who experience violence "as women" but are not women (e.g., non-passing trans men). If your feminism doesn't adequately account for trans people, you're doing it wrong.

*See also:* FEMINISM

**POLYSEXUAL** — Sexual attraction to multiple genders.

This is an alternative label to "bisexual," which essentially describes the same thing. People choose different labels for themselves based on their cultural connotations, and their personal preferences.

*see also*: BISEXUAL; OMNISEXUAL; MONOSEXUAL; BIPHOBIA

**PONCE** — A British pejorative for a posh, effeminate gay man.

Ponce was historically used to refer to a pimp, again making a connection between queerness and perversion, which further entrenches marginalization.

Ponce has connotations of Southern England: a scathing critique of the arrogant, limp-wristed, insufficiently masculine wealthy upper classes which never get their hands dirty.

*see also*: NANCY; PANSY; GAY; SEX WORK; CASTRO CLONE

**POSITIVE** — HIV positive, often written as "HIV-positive."
*see also*: POZ

**POZ** — HIV positive, or HIV-positive.

Poz is a word around which people living with HIV/AIDS can foster community support and solidarity, and combat stigma around being HIV-positive.

*see also*: HIV; AIDS; SOLIDARITY

**PRE-OP, POST-OP** — The status of a trans person's medical history regarding gender-specific surgeries.

There are numerous surgeries a trans person might undergo in relation to their gender. There is no single operation, despite what people euphemistically suggest when they ask if you've "fully transitioned." It's generally inappropriate to ask a trans person about their surgical status. Medical history is deeply vulnerable, especially for anyone with dysphoria.

No surgical status invalidates a person's gender. Lots of trans people don't get any medical intervention for their genders at all.

*see also*: NON-OP; TRANS HEALTHCARE; GENDER REASSIGNMENT SURGERY; DYSPHORIA

**PrEP** — Acronym for "Pre-Exposure Prophylaxis," a drug used to prevent HIV infection. Not to be confused with PEP ("Post-Exposure Prophylaxis"), a drug taken *after* exposure to HIV.

PrEP is the generic name for the drug Truvada, which contains tenofovir and emtricitabine, which are also used for treating HIV.

The availability of PrEP is a massive victory in HIV/AIDS activism. It has been available in the US since 2012, and in the UK since late 2016. HIV transmission rates have remained relatively stable for years, and widespread access to PrEP for people most at risk of getting HIV could drastically reduce transmission rates.

"High-risk" or "at-risk" groups are demographics which are statistically more likely to contract HIV. This is not because these groups are negligent with their sexual health, but because they face barriers to accessing sexual healthcare and information due to homophobia, whorephobia, and stigma surrounding drug use. High-risk groups include: men who have sex with men (MSM), and the other people they have sex with; trans people; African communities in the UK; intravenous drug users; and sex workers.

PrEP is over 90% effective at reducing risk for HIV through sexual contact when taken daily (figures vary, but "over 90%" is often cited); the protection PrEP offers is comparable to condom usage. For intravenous drug users, PrEP reduces the risk of HIV transmission by more than 70%. PrEP is one tool for HIV prevention which can be used in tandem with others like condoms, depending on your circumstances and risk.

PrEP can be taken daily, or, 24 hours before and 48 hours after having unprotected sex, a method called "event-based dosing." Event-based dosing works reliably for people having unprotected anal sex, but not for people having unprotected receptive vaginal sex.

There is slut-shaming in the gay community about taking PrEP. On some apps, like Grindr, you can add your HIV and PrEP status to your profile.

Access to PrEP is still limited in the US to people who can afford it, or whose insurance covers it; the same is true for people in Northern Ireland and Canada, where it is not publicly funded. At the time of writing, PrEP is being trialed through public healthcare in Australia and Wales, and in England it is limited to a trial of 10,000; to buy PrEP privately in England costs £400 a month. It is widely available through the NHS in Scotland. PrEP is currently not widely available across Europe—according to a PrEP summit in Amsterdam in February 2018, this is largely due to the ignorance of politicians, healthcare workers, and potential users about how it could benefit them.

The argument against making PrEP widely available to anyone who would benefit from it is cost—there are no medical reasons why it shouldn't be made accessible; and, as usual, the cost of a preventative drug like PrEP is far lower than the cost of treating HIV.

PrEP does not protect against other sexually transmitted infections, or pregnancy. PrEP shouldn't be taken by people who are HIV-positive, and does not benefit people who are never exposed to the virus (e.g., people who always use condoms with new partners); and people who are monogamous with an HIV-positive partner who is undetectable, or an HIV-negative partner. PrEP has some side effects like nausea and headaches, but for most people these subside after a month of daily dosing. There are no known long-term side effects, but people taking PrEP should get their kidney function tested regularly, as well as regularly testing for HIV and other sexually transmitted infections.

*see also:* PEP; HIV; AIDS; UNDETECTABLE; BAREBACK; SAFER SEX

**PRIDE, PRIDE PARADE** — A movement to celebrate queer culture and combat stigma around queerness. An annual parade to this end, and to commemorate the Stonewall riots and other moments of queer resistance.

The first Pride celebration was in 1970, to celebrate the one-year anniversary of the Stonewall riots on the weekend of 28 June 1969, a spontaneous uprising of gay and trans people at the Stonewall Inn in Greenwich Village New York City in response to homophobic policing.

The first UK Gay Pride Parade was in London in 1972, with fewer than 1,000 people marching from Trafalgar Square to Hyde Park, and it was very much a protest. The marchers were met with heavy policing and public condemnation.

Pride is (in many places) no longer treated like a protest, an expression of solidarity with ongoing queer liberation struggles, or a commemoration of past protests; it is treated like a street party. This pinkwashing is particularly insulting when police, government departments, and corporations who directly contribute to queer suffering are allowed to march in so-called "Pride" celebrations.

*see also:* STONEWALL RIOTS; PINKWASHING; RAINBOW FLAG

**PRIVILEGE** — Systemic advantages and rights given on the basis of an aspect of identity. The lack of systemic oppression.

Privileged identities include: whiteness, cisness, heterosexuality, maleness, wealthy and middle- and upper-class people, abled and neurotypical people, citizens, and thin people.

Privileged identities are unmarked, "default," hegemonic, normalized. Minority groups and groups oppressed by systems are scrutinized, while the privileged group is not. Privileged groups are not always the majority, but they do hold the majority of literal capital and cultural capital. Having a privileged identity does not mean that you don't have difficulties in your life; but it does mean that you are not being systemically oppressed on the basis of that identity.

Our identities are not discrete; most people have both privileged and oppressed identities, which intersect. It is generally not useful to try to quantify how oppressed someone is, because that creates a false hierarchy and flattens out the nuances of our complex lives and experiences.

*see also:* OPPRESSION; VIOLENCE; ERASURE; INTERSECTIONALITY

**PROBLEMATIC** — A catch-all word to denote something bad, oppressive, wrong, and disagreeable.

Problematic is euphemistically used to gloss over specific wrongdoings or bad behavior.

Problematic is a product of call-out culture and purity politics, which tend to not have much nuance. We are all problematic and have learning to do, and a culture of ostracizing people for saying something incorrect is toxic. However, call-outs are often appropriate, and sometimes the only recourse that marginalized people have to highlight either a pattern of harm caused by an individual, or a systemic iteration of oppression. An alternative to call-outs are call-ins, which invite the problematic person to self-criticize ("selfcrit") and learn from their mistakes; but call-ins also require lots of effort and patience, usually from the people directly harmed by the original problematic behavior, and the expectation that they politely educate problematic people is unreasonable.

see also: TRANSFORMATIVE JUSTICE

**PROJECT 10** — The first organized effort to provide support to LGBT+ youth in the US.

Project 10 was based started in Los Angeles, named after the widely circulated statistic that 10% of men are "exclusively homosexual." There are known chapters in California and Canada. The facilitators discussed issues of drug and alcohol use, safer sex, and mental wellbeing with the aim of supporting LGBT+ youth.

see also: GAY–STRAIGHT ALLIANCE; SAFER SPACE

**PRONOUNS** — A word used in place of a noun which has already been referred to, or is implied.

| Traditional | She won | We like her | Her smile beams | That's hers | She loves herself |
|---|---|---|---|---|---|
| | He won | We like him | His smile beams | That's his | He loves himself |
| | They won | We like them | Their smile beams | That's theirs | They love themselves<br>They love themself |
| | It won | We like it | Its smile beams | That's its | It loves itself |
| Spivak | Ey won | We like em | Eir smile beams | That's eirs | Ey loves emself |
| Neopro-nouns | Ze won | We like zir<br>We like hir | Zir smile beams<br>Hir smile beams | That's zirs<br>That's hirs | Ze loves zirself<br>Ze loves hirself |
| | Zie won | We like zir<br>We like hir | Zir smile beams<br>Hir smile beams | That's zirs<br>That's hirs | Zie loves zirself<br>Zie loves hirself |
| | Xe won | We like xe<br>We like xyr | Xyr smile beams<br>Xer smile beams | That's xyrs<br>That's xers | Xe loves xemself |
| | Ne won | We like nem | Nir smile beams | That's nirs | Ne loves nemself |
| | Ve won | We like ver | Vis smile beams | That's vis | Ve loves verself |

Pronouns are not "preferred," they are mandatory. Saying "preferred pronouns" implies that they are an alternative to a "real" set of pronouns.

Pronouns do not necessarily correlate to gender. Just because someone uses "she/her" pronouns does not mean she is a woman; she could be agender, for example. We should endeavor to divorce pronouns from gender, just like we should divorce body parts and clothes and jobs from gender.

In English, the most commonly used pronouns are gendered; but there are many gender neutral alternatives.

People are given pronouns when they are born to "match" their assigned sex at birth. Some people change their pronouns, and some don't. Some people use different pronouns in different contexts; for example, at work versus at home, or online, or amongst people who are more familiar with non-traditional pronouns. Some people will indicate that they use a mix of pronouns (e.g., she/they). This could mean they are happy with either she or they; or it can mean they deliberately switch between multiple pronouns. Some people don't mind at all what pronouns are used to describe them.

The above is true of cis queers as well as trans people. Queer people have swapped pronouns for themselves, their partners, and people in their social group since queerness has been pathologized and criminalized. We still see this in queer communities where some men are "she" and some women are "he." This practice both cloaks queerness and makes it invisible to hostile straight people, and builds a shared subcultural language around gender bending. While it's a subversive practice, it can also reify patriarchal condescension when queer men dismissively refer to each other, or to adult women, as "girl."

Changing pronouns is a common part of transitioning for trans people. Many trans people feel hesitation in changing their pronouns because we feel like we're asking a lot of people to change the language they use to describe us, especially if we're using pronouns other than he/him or she/her. It takes some time to get used to it, but changing the pronouns you use for someone is a small and important gesture in showing them respect and support; failing to use the right pronouns is misgendering, which is painful.

That said, misgendering someone accidentally is not an unforgivable act, just a mistake that should be corrected and avoided; you don't need to make a big deal out of it, just apologize and move on. The difficulty that you feel in changing what pronouns you use for someone is nowhere near the difficulties they're feeling in managing everyone's fragility about their pronouns.

Ask people what their pronouns are—not just people who are trans, or who you suspect are trans. There is a lot of hesitation for cis people to ask about pronouns because it's seen as rude, but this is rooted entirely in the cisnormative idea that we're expected to correctly guess people's gender based on their appearance, and if we can't, it's a failure on the part of that person to adequately signify their gender. Asking about pronouns isn't rude; it invites people to tell you how they want to be referred to. The simplest way to ask is to offer your own pronouns when you introduce yourself: "Hi, I'm Morgan and my pronouns are he/him. And you are?" You can also pay attention to where people have already indicated their pronouns, on online profiles, email signatures, and by how their friends refer to them.

Practice using people's pronouns when they're not around. Getting people's pronouns right is important and shows a basic level of respect and decency, but it is not the only thing required of you to be avoid being transphobic. The heavy emphasis on pronouns makes trans people look like we're fussy and nit-picking about language, and "too fragile" to handle something as "inconsequential" as words. But I don't care if you're getting my pronouns right while detaining me, and I don't care if you get my pronouns wrong while interrupting the street harassment I get for wearing a dress. The liberal focus on inclusive language obscures the daily material kinds of violence trans people face.

*see also:* GENDER NEUTRAL LANGUAGE; MISGENDER; THEY/THEM; SPIVAK; THON; XE; ZE; IT; INCLUSION THEATER

**PUSSY** — Slang for vagina. It is also a derogatory word meaning feminine, effeminate, or weak.

Pussy is also used by some people to describe their anus, because it affirms their gender in a reclamation of their body and the ways they have sex.

Pussy was a term of endearment for girls and women, and effeminate men, in use since at least the 1580s. "Puss" has been in recorded use for "cat" since 1520s (but this use is probably older than records show). Since c.1600 it applied to girls and women as having the negative qualities of a cat, but by the 1800s it was used affectionately.

*see also:* MISOGYNY; PATRIARCHY; BOY PUSSY

**Q** — The Q in LGBTQIA+ is for QUEER and QUESTIONING.
*see also:* LGBT+

**QTIPOC** — Acronym for Queer, Trans, and Intersex People Of Color.

Queerness and transness are extremely whitewashed; it's valuable and important for queer, trans, and intersex people of color to have community without the burden of the white gaze, and for their contributions to the larger queer community to be named and recognized.
*see also:* QUEER; CULTURAL APPROPRIATION; RACISM

**QUEEN** — An exaggerated expression of femininity, typically subversive because it's being performed by people who are not allowed to access it (queer and trans people, sometimes cishet men). A description of someone queer.
*see also:* DRAG; GAY; KING

**QUEER (ADJ., N.)** — A deliberately elusive word to describe a non-heterosexual or non-cisgender identity. It can mean gay or LGBTIA+, or be in direct opposition to them. A reclaimed slur.

There is no consensus on what queerness means or where the boundary of queer is.

Queer can be someone whose gender identity is externally politicized. For simplicity, "queer" can be taken to mean anyone who is not both cis and heterosexual (cishet). Under that definition, anyone who is trans can be queer, anyone who is asexual can be queer, anyone who is LGBTIA+

can be queer. I say "can be" rather than "is" because queer is a term of self-definition, and many people are uncomfortable with it given its still-recent historical use as a slur. Others are uncomfortable with "queer" because it is associated with radical politics, which brings us to the more complicated (but probably more accurate) definition:

Queer can mean subversive, Other. One is made queer by their marginalization, by their inability or refusal to assimilate into cisheteronormativity. The category of "Other" is constantly shifting and therefore so is "queer." With the legalization of same-sex marriage in the US, white cis gay middle-class people were largely relieved of their Otherness and formally allowed to assimilate into the legal and social institution of marriage, which consolidates resources like wealth and citizenship among the rich and so reproduces systems of oppression. A middle-class white cis gay man might, however, still face gendered oppression for wearing a dress in certain contexts. As we expand the boundaries of who is to be included, who is allowed to participate in society and public life, so too do we more clearly delineate the boundaries of who is excluded and punished; who is Other.

Queer has been in use since the 16th century, meaning strange or illegitimate. Its earliest known use as slur was in an 1894 letter by the Marquess of Queensberry, who believed that "queers like [the Earl of] Rosebery" were corrupting his sons. Queensbury also accused Oscar Wilde of "posing as a somdomite [sic]" having an affair with his son. That accusation eventually led to Wilde's very public trial, conviction, sentencing to hard labor, and early death. Queer became a slur for same-sex sex, and people with same-sex attractions, especially effeminate men.

Since the 1980s, queer has been reclaimed by many in an act of empowerment and positive self-definition. However, it is still used as a slur and shouldn't be coercively assigned to anyone, even in communities where queer is the collectively preferred term. In the 1990s and 2000s, gay replaced queer as the main homophobic slur, so many people eschew gay in favor of queer for that reason.

Maybe "queer" should not only be measured by disenfranchisement and systemic oppression. You don't need to get gay-bashed ten times to earn your Gay Card. I want a world where queer kids aren't defining themselves by violence suffered.

Queer is often in opposition to "LGBT+," "gay," and "homosexual." While each of these terms could be used to describe the same person, they all have different socio-political connotations. "LGBT+" is a banner under which we can politically organize for inclusion and civil rights (assimilation); "gay" is a more culturally focused term which helps us identify sameness and foster community; "homosexual" has connotations of the psycho-medical establishment, but it is also reclaimed by some as a less respectable term than "gay"; and queer is an anti-identity. "I'm not gay as in happy, I'm queer as in fuck you." Queer challenges the idea that sexuality is an inherent, essential part of the self. Queer is a practice more than it is an identity. It is about decentering and destabilizing and disrupting cisheteronormativity; therefore it is a politically radical position. Of course, queer is also an identity, despite the contempt it holds for identity categories.

Queer culture can have an unhealthy relationship with purity politics. As queers, we're held to higher standards in our political thinking than cishets are, and if we are not extremely rigorous and articulate in defending our rights, we're denied our humanity. However, we often replicate this within our communities; claiming a queer identity is itself a luxury not afforded easily to many queer people, who cannot be out or politicize their identity for fear of abandonment or discrimination.

Queerness is hypersexualized, by cishets and queers. Contrary to popular belief, queerness isn't about the kind of sex we have; we can't fuck away patriarchy. Talking openly about queer sex and having empowering queer sex are great and can be radical but that's not the whole point. Queer sex can still be abusive, traumatic, and boring. Queers can not want sex.

It is not for me to say who is queer and who is not; if you think you're queer, you probably are. Lots of queers are invested in policing queerness because if we let straight people into it, they will make it ("it" being either just the word "queer" or the whole subculture of queerness) less queer (notice how these insecure queers ignore the possibility for straight trans people, who are absolutely entitled to claim queerness). However I am more interested in expanding the boundaries of queerness to deliberately let more people in, with the hope of decentering and ultimately destroying cisness and straightness.

*see also:* QUEER (v.); GAY; BUGGERY; IDENTITY

**QUEER (v.), QUEERED, QUEERING** — To make queer(er).

There is no single way to queer a text, an idea, a field of study, or anything. Simply being queer within an institution queers it. Part of queering is to recognize that there is not a simple truth, not a single way of being, and not an essence to be understood.

Moments of queering can be experienced by anyone, queer or not—cishetness is so fragile, it's constantly cracking.

*see also:* QUEER THEORY

**QUEER ANARCHISM, QUEER LIBERATION** — A political ideology aimed at the liberation of queer people from all forms of queerphobic violence, based on anarchist principles of solidarity, individual and bodily autonomy, collective and non-hierarchical decision-making, and mutual aid.

Queer anarchism and queer liberation movements see the liberation of all oppressed people as intrinsically linked; so they are also anti-racist, anti-imperialist, anti-capitalist, feminist, and anti-ableist.

Anarchism has a long queer history. The first publication dedicated to gay issues was *Der Eigene*, published by anarchist Adolf Brand between 1896 and 1932 in Berlin. Notable early queer anarchists include Oscar Wilde, Emma Goldman, and the Mujeres Libres.

*see also:* FASCISM; PINK; ACTIVISM

**QUEERBAITING** — To suggest, but not explicitly depict, queerness in the media.

A character's queerness is hinted at for the cynical purpose of attracting a queer audience, which is starved of representation; but the character will never be fully "realized" as queer—and may be "revealed" to be straight or cis after long plot-lines suggesting otherwise.

Queerbaiting is a cruel and cowardly tactic to deliberately ensnare a queer audience without the backlash of "alienating" a cishet audience (cishet audiences feel alienated by the presence of a single queer character or couple, despite the majority of media focusing on cishet characters). Queerbaiting is not genuine representation. Perhaps the most poignant example is J.K. Rowling's regular "reveals" that characters in the Harry Potter universe are queer or otherwise marginalized—Dumbledore is gay and asexual, minor character Anthony Goldstein is

Jewish, Hermione Granger is (maybe?) Black, Remus Lupin's werewolf condition is a metaphor for being HIV+—despite those identities not being written or represented explicitly in the texts.

Queerbaiting not only disappoints queer audiences, but it contributes to the idea that queerness is "unpopular" and impossible to represent outside of niche "special interest" media. It implies that queerness is shameful, too "explicit," and must remain hidden.

*see also:* QUEER CODING; VISIBILITY; REPRESENTATION; FAN FIC

**QUEER CODING** — Implying that a character is queer without explicitly naming their queerness.

Queers have very little representation in the media. Queer coding has been used to further stigmatize queerness by coding villains as queer—generally, hinting that they might be queer with gender non-conformity or pairing them with another villain of the same gender. Villains are queer coded in everything from Disney movies to Bond films, where they are a negative contrast to the protagonists' positive, manly, heterosexual heroes and delicate feminine damsels in distress.

In times of censorship when queerness could not be explicitly depicted, some positively portrayed characters were queer coded as well: Sherlock Holmes and John Watson are the key example. When censorship isn't an issue and characters are coded as queer (subtext) rather than explicitly named as queer (text), this is called "queerbaiting."

*see also:* REPRESENTATION; QUEERBAITING

**QUEERCORE** — A punk subgenre with queer politics.

Punk was led by queer people of color throughout the late 1960s, 1970s and early 1980s (e.g., Kid Congo Powers), and then it became more commercial (think David Bowie). Punk was whitewashed and made heteronormative for mainstream audiences, but it was always gay. In the beginning of punk, gay clubs were the only places where punks could go. Queercore developed as a distinct subgenre in the mid-80s.

Early punks were not politicized, and rejected political labels and calls to organize. Then the AIDS crisis hit and it was impossible for queers to maintain an apolitical stance. Queercore stepped up as explicitly political, in support of queer rights and AIDS activism.

*see also:* QUEERUPTION

**QUEER HETEROSEXUALITY** — A dubious claim to queerness made by straight people who occupy non-traditional gender roles. It was used in the 1990s.

Straight trans people exist and they have a solid claim to queerness, but queer heterosexuality is not about accounting for them; it's about expanding the definition of queerness to include cisgender heterosexuals who want to feel progressive and deny their compliancy in heterosexism.

*see also:* QUEER; HETERONORMATIVITY

**QUEERPHOBIA** — Fear of, or contempt for, queer people. Behavior based on those feelings; and a system of oppression in which queers are marginalized and subject to violence.

Queerphobia affects anyone who is not both cis and heterosexual, and can be viewed as an umbrella term for more specific forms of anti-queer bigotry such as transmisogyny, lesbophobia, biphobia, transphobia, aphobia, and homophobia.

Queerphobia uses biological essentialism (gayness is "unnatural," "God made Adam and Eve, not Steve") and then socialization arguments ("The gay agenda in schools is turning kids gay") to create a grotesque tapestry of contradictory bigotry.

Throughout history, different aspects of queerness have been criminalized, pathologized, and punished by society. Sometimes it was sodomy laws, sometimes it was cross-dressing, sometimes (like now) it's about gender performance and expression in public. Looking through records of laws and mental institutions is only one aspect of queer history which tells us the state's approach to queerness and what is considered a threat to the family and society, but doesn't necessarily tell us about queer resistance. Sometimes queerness was permissible if you were in a man-woman marriage and had children; sometimes it's more about making queerness invisible (to cishet people—queers would still flag to each other) in public life (e.g., during Section 28).

Like all systems of oppression, queerphobia intersects with other marginalizations: classism, racism, ableism, agism, and fatphobia.

*see also:* HOMOPHOBIA; APHOBIA; LESBOPHOBIA; BIPHOBIA; TRANSPHOBIA; TRANSMISOGYNY; BEARD; SECTION 28

**QUEERPLATONIC** — An intimate, significant, and non-sexual relationship which does not follow traditional romantic norms or the bounds of traditional friendship.

Queerplatonic relationships, and the language used to describe them, are an alternative to heteronormative relationships and the amatonormative assumption that everyone wants romantic and sexual relationships. Asexual and aromantic people might find utility in naming their significant relationships queerplatonic instead of using words which imply a sexual and romantic connection.

Queerplatonic intimacy might look like platonic physical affection— literally sleeping together, living together, co-parenting, or being naked around each other.

Queerplatonic relationship structures tend to be non-exclusive, but can follow any model which feels right for the people involved. Queerplatonic partners sometimes refer to each other as "zucchinis," rather than "friends," which downplays intimacy, or "partners," which suggests a romantic or sexual relationship.

*see also:* PLATONIC; AMATONORMATIVITY; HETERONORMATIVITY; ASEXUAL; AROMANTIC; ZUCCHINI

**QUEER STUDIES** — A multi-disciplinary subject concerned with queer genders and sexualities, including in the fields of sociology, history, geography, media studies, literature, psychology, music, and art history.

*see also:* QUEER THEORY

**QUEER THEORY** — The interrogation of hegemonic assumptions about sexuality and gender, especially relating to binaries and fixed identities. Rather than a single theory, queer theory is a critical lens through which to inspect discourses on gender and sexuality.

Queer theory examines power relations, drawing on post-structuralism. It destabilizes dominant understandings which claim to be "normal" or "natural" and exposes how sex, sexuality, and gender identities are constructed and performed.

Teresa de Lauretis gave a conference on gay and lesbian sexualities at the University of California in Santa Cruz in 1990, where she is credited with coining the term "queer theory". This is widely considered to mark the birth of queer theory (though others such as Gloria Anzaldúa used the term earlier). Lauretis has since rejected the term queer theory because it has become too apolitical.

Queer theory itself is non-static. There are many queer theories, like there are many feminisms. Queer theory uses "queer" primarily as a verb: something we do, something we constantly produce and reproduce, not an identity or something we are.

Queer theory sees normative and non-normative ideas as equally subject to scrutiny. It challenges the gender binary (men and women); sexuality binaries (gay or straight; same-sex attracted or "opposite"-sex attracted); the binary between normal and "abnormal" sexual practices; and even the binary between queer and not queer. Queer theory critiques "regimes of normativity" and the power structures upon which these regimes are founded and which they uphold/reproduce, and resists the categorization of people. There is a heavy emphasis on the importance of context, the relationship to power, and the understanding of identities as fluid and context dependent. Good queer theory has an ethics of research accountability.

Existentialism is an important precursor to queer theory. Theorists Albert Camus, Jean-Paul Sartre, Simone de Beauvoir, and Maurice Merleau-Ponty argued that there is no "essence": no one is fundamentally anything, and they can choose to be any way they please in a constant process of self-creation. De Beauvoir highlights that there are limits to our freedom to be anything/anyone, placed on us depending on our genders. Gender is something we do, and our genders are things we become, not something we are born as.

Queer theory isn't just queering existing texts—"text" meaning any source material, including writing, film, music, and visual art—it's also queer people producing their own texts. Queer art tactics are not always obvious, because they are not always able to be. Some good places to find modern queer theory include parodies of heteronormative music videos, gender-bending fan art, slash fic shipping (pairing characters together in non-canon romantic or sexual relationships), and trolling misogynistic branding on social media.

Queer theory can be justly criticized for being very white and "minority-world" focused. Other queer theories which combat this include queer diasporas, queer globalization, homonationalism, and many queer activisms in practice.

Queer theory has also been criticized for being inaccessible, using its own complex language, and being opaque and just generally difficult. Other fields of study, like the natural sciences, however, are not criticized in the same way.

*see also:* QUEER; QUEER STUDIES; FAN FIC

**QUEER TIME** — The non-normative time scales in which queer people reach or evade milestones.

The normative timeline constructed for cishet people's lives is puberty, early adulthood, love, marriage, children, divorce (optional).

Queer people are often not able to access the same traditional milestones as cishet people. We don't have access to resources which allow us a stable trajectory (queer precarity), and by virtue of being queer we fail at being heteronormative (though many queers do their best to imitate it and assimilate).

Instead of following the cishet timetable, queers often live a prolonged adolescence—because we can't afford adulthood, or because we were denied teenage self-discovery until we were adults. Trans people often measure their ages by time since beginning transition. Queers may follow a normative pattern of courtship and relationship building; or we may avoid romantic relationships and build "families" of friends; or, we might fast-track intimacy with a partner and move in with them after two dates.

Queer time is also skewed because we feel like we have no future—we literally want to die, or cannot see ourselves having a livable life. We assume we will be dead before we're adults.

*see also:* QUEER; TRANS TIME; RESPECTABILITY; ASSIMILATION

**QUEERUPTION** — An anarchist movement opposed to the lack of diversity in mainstream gay culture and its embrace of consumerism.

*see also:* QUEERCORE; QUEER ANARCHISM

**QUESTIONING** — One of the Qs in LGBTQIA+, along with "queer." Questioning can refer to questioning sexuality or questioning gender.

Some people adopt the questioning label before they feel sure about which gender or sexuality label best fits them; and some people use questioning as a space when they're not ready, for whatever reason, to claim a less "safe" label. That said, all gender and sexuality labels should be treated as potentially fluid; people are entitled to refine the vocabulary they use to self-define, go through phases, and change their minds.

Questioning is a non-committal process of self-exploration, which should be encouraged, regardless of the "outcome."

*see also*: LGBT+; BI-CURIOUS; HETEROFLEXIBLE; GENDER

**QUILTBAG** — An alternative acronym for LGBTQIA+, which stands for "Queer/Questioning Intersex Lesbian Transgender/Transsexual Bisexual/Bigender Asexual/Aromantic Gay."

*see also*: LGBT+

**RACISM** — Fear of, or contempt for, people of color. Behavior based on those feelings. A system of oppression in which people of color are marginalized and subject to violence.

Racism is not necessarily overt. It is also an implicit bias, and assumes that whiteness is the default or raceless.

Race emerged as a "scientific" category around the late 18th century. Race analysis must be intrinsic to any decent queer theory because all queers are racialized, as white, non-white, people of color, Black, brown, and other terms which may or may not reflect a "truth" about their identity (and which certainly don't reflect a truth about their biology). Further, Black feminists were the first to highlight that there aren't single, stable categories of identity which are separate from others, and this analysis is a central aspect of queer theory. Critical race theory and decolonial theory are extremely compatible with queer theory.

Gender is also extremely racialized. Whiteness holds the hegemonic norms on gender: rational, strong, successful white men; and pure, beautiful, nurturing, innocent white women. Black men are stereotyped as hyper-masculine, aggressive, and dangerous; Black women as hyper-sexual and angry. East Asian men are assumed to be effeminate and non-sexual, and East Asian women are assumed to be submissive and docile. All people of color are subject to racialized gender stereotypes.

Queerness generally is whitewashed, and it's assumed that people of color are straight and cis, because overwhelmingly the representation we see of queer people is white. People of color are also assumed to be more homophobic than white people, because whiteness is "progressive" and "liberal" in contrast to the "backwardness" and "incivility" unfairly attributed to people of color. Religion is a relevant factor here because religion is racialized too; for example, despite all relying on the same texts, Islam is assumed to be more queerphobic than Christianity, because Islam is associated with people of color and Christianity with whiteness.

Like all systems of oppression, racism intersects with other marginalizations: classism, agism, ableism, misogyny, queerphobia, transphobia, and fatphobia.

see also: CULTURAL APPROPRIATION; AAVE; ANTI-BLACK RACISM; FASCISM; VIOLENCE; WHITEWASHING; ISLAMOPHOBIA; ANTI-SEMITISM; OPPRESSION

**RAINBOW FLAG** — The iconic rainbow flag has been a symbol of the LGBT+ movement since its creation in 1978 by artist Gilbert Baker.

The rainbow flag is an instantly recognizable symbol for LGBT+ and queer people to rally around. It is also flown by allies to show their support for LGBT+ people and LGBT+ rights.

Depending on its context, the rainbow flag can be a very contentious, politically charged symbol, or a tepid, palatable symbol of "love" stripped of its political meaning and history. The White House lit up with the rainbow colors to celebrate the legalization of same-sex marriage in the US in 2015 (I'll let the reader decide if this falls into the former category or the latter, or both).

Baker was living in San Francisco and an active part of the gay community, and designed the flag at the request of Harvey Milk and other community members who wanted a symbol for the LGBT+ movement. Part of Baker's inspiration for the rainbow design was the story of Noah's ark, where God sent the rainbow to show that the flood was over.

In 2017, a version of the rainbow flag was used in Philadelphia. It included one black and one brown stripe at the top, to highlight people of color in the LGBT+ community. It has since gained traction elsewhere, such as on Lena Waithe's 2014 Met Gala rainbow flag cape. There are many additional flags since Baker's first rainbow flag, but the one for Black and brown people is the one everyone gets mad about, in a perfect display of the racism and anti-Blackness still rampant in LGBT+ spaces.

see also: PRIDE; ACTIVISM; PINKWASHING

**RAPE CULTURE** — The systemic normalization of rape, the encouragement of people to rape, and the dismissal of survivors of rape.

Queer and trans people are more likely to be targeted for rape, sexual violence, intimate partner violence, and familial abuse.

Rape culture makes survivors feel doubt, guilt, and fear about their experiences and the idea of disclosing or reporting. This is made even more difficult because rapists and abusers are afforded more protections than survivors, both socially and legally.

The best immediate intervention anyone can take to interrupt rape culture is to believe survivors.

*see also*: CONSENT; PATRIARCHY; POLICE (n.); SURVIVOR; TRANS-FORMATIVE JUSTICE

**REAL-LIFE EXPERIENCE TEST (RLE)** — A barrier to accessing trans healthcare by which the healthcare provider requires that the trans person "live as" their gender for an arbitrary (but long) period of time before allowing treatment, usually one or two years.

Proof of "real-life experience" is arbitrary. Wearing traditionally gendered clothing, being out, using a new name; none of these things indicate gender or transness, or "commitment" to a new gender expression/identity, or have any bearing on regret rates.

The real-life experience test undermines the concepts of informed consent and bodily autonomy, and does more to ease cis fears about trans people transitioning than to do anything positive for trans patients.

*see also*: TRANS HEALTHCARE; GATEKEEPING; CONSENT

**REN, RENNY, RENTHERHOOD** — Gender neutral shortened words for parent and parenthood. Renny is an alternative to "Mommy" and "Daddy." Rentherhood is an alternative to "motherhood" and "fatherhood."

*see also*: GENDER NEUTRAL LANGUAGE

**REPRESENTATION** — When we see people, real or fictional, who reflect an aspect of our own life experience back to us.

"Good representation" shows these people as being complex and whole. "Bad representation" shows them as being flat, reduced to this single aspect of themselves, often through an unflattering stereotype.

Representation is important, because "you can't be what you can't see" (a quote by Marie Wilson speaking about the representation of women in tech). If people, especially young people, don't have any positive representation of themselves in their lives or the media they consume, they might feel alienated and abnormal and ashamed of the things that make them different. They might not even know that being different is a possibility.

Queer children who don't have access to representation don't grow up not being queer; they grow up not knowing that being queer is okay.

In the 42,000-member Facebook group "sounds gay, i'm in," they did a poll: "What is gay culture?" The top result was "taking literally any word, gesture or clothing choice, of literally any person, as proof that they are also gay." Gay culture is filling the void of representation by creating our own (and calling everything gay).

Historically, queer representation was disallowed and censored. The Motion Picture Production Code, or Hays Code, was in effect in the US from 1930 to 1968; it implicitly forbade same-sex couples on screen through disallowing "any inference of sexual perversion." The Hays Code also explicitly forbade the portrayal of mixed-race couples.

The first American film representation of bisexuals, and maybe trans people, is *A Florida Enchantment*, directed and produced by Sidney Drew in 1914. This is a historic piece of art and representation, but it also employs blackface; art can be both important and racist, and should be appropriately critiqued.

*see also:* QUEER CODING; FETISHIZE

**REPRODUCTIVE RIGHTS** — The rights for people to have autonomy over their own bodies, especially regarding contraception, abortion, reproductive healthcare, family planning, and sex education.

Reproductive rights are a site of struggle for all women and all trans people. All queer people are denied comprehensive sex education and family planning.

Reproductive rights are about bodily autonomy as much as they are about reproduction, and therefore have a great deal of overlap with other trans and queer rights issues.

Reproductive rights should also consider all aspects of family planning, including pregnancy prevention (sex education, access to a variety of contraceptives), abortion, fertility treatment, and adoption.

Healthcare providers must consider that many of their patients will be trans and queer, which means that they will have a variety of bodies, non-cisheteronormative relationships, and concerns. There are men with vaginas and women who will store sperm. While reproductive healthcare is a very gendered issue, we must endeavor to divorce body parts from gender.

One aspect of family planning and contraceptives is sterilization. Trans and queer people have been historically (and in some places, continue to be) forcibly sterilized, either explicitly or implicitly; for example, being forced to have bottom surgery before they can change their gender markers, thereby effectively being sterilized. In the UK, unlike other procedures which affect fertility (e.g., chemotherapy), trans people are denied public healthcare for storing their eggs or sperm, and private storage is prohibitively expensive.

Forced sterilization violates basic human rights and bodily autonomy. Likewise, many people who have uteruses want to be voluntarily sterilized but are denied treatment on the patriarchal assumption that they will someday change their minds, or "find a man" who wants to use them to bear his children. Rather than simply deny adults the right to decide whether or not they reproduce (it is very common for sterilization to be denied to anyone under the age of 30), doctors should ensure that patients have given informed consent.

*see also:* BODILY AUTONOMY; SEX (n.); TRANS HEALTHCARE

**REPRODUCTIVE SEX** — Sex which can result in pregnancy, not necessarily between a cis and heterosexual couple.

*see also:* REPRODUCTIVE RIGHTS; SEX (v.)

**RESPECTABILITY, RESPECTABILITY POLITICS** — The notion that people must be "respectable" in order to deserve dignity and basic human rights.

Respectability politics are weaponized against all marginalized people to suggest that we are too angry, too violent, too aggressive to be afforded equal rights. The suggestion is that we would be deserving if only we didn't make people uncomfortable about it. This is a tactic used to encourage oppressed people to be docile, forcing us to be polite and articulate in demanding that people stop discriminating against us and killing us. It undermines the whole concept of human rights being fundamental to all people, regardless of how agreeable or respectable they are.

Some allies will suggest that angry or violent protestors are "hurting the cause," or "giving bigots ammunition." If people only want to give us rights when we're "good" protestors, they aren't real allies. These are false flags used to deny us legitimacy, when in reality the standard of "good" is deliberately impossible to reach—it doesn't matter how good we are, because they aren't interested in our liberation.

In modern "post-factual" debates, it doesn't matter how correct or respectable we are; the people who propagate hate speech are not interested in facts or being reasonable. They don't care how much evidence we throw at them because their ideology is fact-proof; it's about feelings (read "fragility"). They "just know" that men have penises and are violent and dangerous, they "just know" that Black people are scary and angry, they "just know" that fat people are lazy and unhealthy.

Giving them "ammunition" is irrelevant because even if we are on our most reasonable "best behavior," they will invent ammunition to use against us.

Instead of politely engaging hateful bigots in "debate," we should be asking why we are debating the validity of trans women's lives, of Black peoples' right to basic safety in public space, of queer peoples' right to bodily autonomy.

*see also:* ASSIMILATION; POLICE (v.); ACTIVISM

**RLE** — Acronym for "Real-Life Experience."
*see also:* REAL-LIFE EXPERIENCE TEST

**S** — The S in BDSM is for submission (opposed to the D for Dominance), and SADISM (opposed to the M for Masochism). The S in "submission" is traditionally kept lower-case in deference to the D; as a pair, they are stylized as D/s.

*see also:* BDSM; SADISM

**SADISM, SADIST, SADISTIC** — Sexual interest in being cruel, or inflicting pain or humiliation.

The concept of sadism was named by Kraff-Ebing and pathologized along with masochism, bisexuality, and all non-procreational sex. Its inverse is masochism, the sexual interest in receiving pain or humiliation. Together, sadism and masochism make up the S&M (also written as S/M and SM) in BDSM.

BDSM practices were pioneered by queer people and other sexual deviants, and continue to be a safe site to explore non-cisheteronormative gender expressions and sexualities.

The etymology comes from the Marquis de Sade, who practiced and wrote about sadism in great detail.

*see also:* MASOCHISM; BDSM

**SAFE/R SEX** — Informed sexual practice which accounts for pregnancy prevention and mitigates the risks of sexually transmitted infections (STIs).

Safer sex stands in contrast to the idea of "safe sex," which is misleading—no sex is absolutely safe. All sexual behavior carries risks. The goal of safer sex is to educate ourselves about the risks so we can mitigate them, and focus on enjoying ourselves.

Safer sex practices include using barriers (e.g., condoms, dental dams, and gloves); taking preventative medication (e.g., PrEP); diligently cleaning sex toys; using new barriers for each orifice and partner; using contraceptives such as the birth control pill or an intrauterine device (IUD); and getting tested for STIs frequently.

*see also:* SEX (v.); CONSENT; PrEP

**SAFE/R SPACE** — A positive space which explicitly does not tolerate homophobia, transphobia, or any queerphobia. An autonomous space that is safe for LGBT+ people and other marginalized groups to discuss their marginalizations.

Safe spaces have been around in the US since at least 1989, when teachers and student bodies created them in response to widespread bullying of LGBT+ students.

No space is guaranteed to be "safe" because safety is not a stable state of being; it is constantly produced and reproduced and repaired. This is why the phrase "safer space" is preferred to "safe space." Safer spaces which do not engage with this difficulty run the risk of reproducing the racist, ableist, heterosexist norms of wider society. Safer spaces still have power hierarchies within them, and a good safer space should be continually re-assessing the group dynamics: who has positions of social or institutional power, who is being marginalized or silenced or less able to speak freely, who is less or more supported by the group, and who the group is for?

What makes a safer space? A zero tolerance policy on hate speech and harassment; content notes or trigger warnings; explicit acknowledgement of power hierarchies; the desire to center marginalized people, followed through with action; and accountability agreements and processes with room for people to raise complaints or address problems or abuse within the space without fear of repercussion for naming a problem.

*see also:* TRANSFORMATIVE JUSTICE; VIOLENCE; ACTIVISM

**SAME-GENDER ATTRACTED (SGA)** — Someone who is attracted to the same gender as their own. The term is used primarily to discuss "Women who have Sex with Women (WSW)" and "Men who have Sex with Men (MSM)."

Some people prefer to describe their sexual attractions extremely literally rather than with the LGBT+ identity words, presumably to distance themselves from the heavy cultural connotations of those labels. Same-gender attracted doesn't carry the same stigma, or history, as words like "gay," "bisexual," and "queer." It also focuses on the attraction, rather than on using that attraction as a defining aspect of identity.

Medical doctors and researchers might refer to patients and potential patients in studies as being "same-gender attracted" rather than "LGBT+" or "queer" because same-gender attracted is more politically and culturally neutral, and therefore patients are more likely to be honest about their sexual attractions rather than affirming a queer identity.

More specific acronyms include "Women who Love Women (WLW)," "Women who have Sex with Women (WSW)," "Men who Love Men (MLM)," and "Men who have Sex with Men (MSM)."

*see also:* WOMEN WHO LOVE WOMEN; MEN WHO LOVE MEN

**SAME-SEX MARRIAGE** — Access to the legal institution of marriage for same-sex couples.

Same-sex marriage, or marriage equality, has been made the focus of the LGBT+ civil rights struggle since the AIDS crisis.

Same-sex marriages are recognized and performed in the Netherlands (since 2001), with the exception of Aruba, Curaçao, and Sint Maarten; Belgium (2003); Canada (2005); Spain (2005); South Africa (2006); Norway (2009); Sweden (2009); Argentina (2010); Portugal (2010); Iceland (2010); Denmark (2012); Brazil (2013); France (2013); New Zealand (2013) with the exception of Niue, Tokelau, and the Cook Islands; the UK (2013) with the exception of Northern Ireland, Sark, and the Caribbean territories; Uruguay (2013); Ireland (2015); Luxembourg (2015); twelve states in Mexico (2015); the US (2015) with the exception of American Samoa and some Native American tribal jurisdictions; Colombia (2016); Australia (2017); Austria (2017, due to take effect 2019); Finland (2017); Germany (2017); and Malta (2017).

*see also:* LGBT+ RIGHTS; ASSIMILATION; CIVIL UNION; MARRIAGE EQUALITY

**SAPIOSEXUAL, SAPIOSEXUALITY** — A "sexuality" where sexual attraction is premised on intelligence.

Sapiosexuality is generally classist, sexist garbage used by sad cishet people who want to feel superior and like a "sexual minority" for fetishizing intelligence. It relies on racist understandings of "intelligence" and is predicated on the false idea that intelligent women are rare.

*see also:* MOGAI; CISHET

**SAPPHO, SAPPHIC** — Sappho was a Greek lyric poet who wrote about passionate sexual and romantic relationships between women. Sapphic refers to women who love or are attracted to women.

Sapphic is not just another way of saying "lesbian." Sapphic includes all women who are attracted to women, while "lesbian" can mean Sapphic, or more specifically women who are attracted exclusively to women, depending on the context.

The UK lesbian magazine *Sappho*, first published in 1972, was a politically committed feminist magazine written for and by lesbians. It connected UK lesbians with local groups and activities, and discussed issues such as motherhood and workplace discrimination.

*see also:* LESBIAN; WOMEN WHO LOVE WOMEN; QUEER; BISEXUAL; GAY

**SAUNA** — *see:* BATHHOUSE.

**SCISSORING** — A sex act which has gained notoriety from the confusion and phallo-centric false assumptions of straight cis men trying to understand how sex between women "works."

Scissoring is when partners position themselves between each others' legs and rub their genitals together. Scissoring is not only for lesbians, or queer people, or women; and it's absolutely not the only way that women have sex with each other. Anyone can scissor.

*see also:* SEX (v.); LESBOPHOBIA

**SECTION 28 (CLAUSE 28)** — Section 28 of the Local Government Act 1988 stated that local authorities "should not intentionally promote homosexuality" or promote the "acceptability of homosexuality as a pretend family relationship" in England, Wales, and Scotland. It was enforceable until 2003.

The issue of the "promotion" of homosexuality reached government because the *Daily Mail* newspaper reported on the book *Jenny Lives with Eric and Martin* being found in a local authority library in the

City of London in 1983, and lambasted local councils for "promoting" homosexuality to children at the taxpayer's expense. The *Jenny* book was not a promotion of gayness as much as a normalization of gay family structures, actually in a quite normative (homonormative) way. At the time, Labour-controlled areas were adopting anti-discrimination policies toward LGBT+ people, which agitated homophobic voters who saw it as an attack on heterosexual family values, as did the solidarity campaigns between LGBT+ groups and the miners who were on strike, and the 1985 election of the UK's first openly gay mayor, Margaret Roff of Manchester. In the 1987 election, the Conservative party (led by Margaret Thatcher) published posters saying that Labour wanted book titles like *Young, Gay and Proud*, *The Playbook for Kids about Sex* and (fictional title) *Police: Out of Schools!*, and to be read in schools, "glorifying" homosexuality. The AIDS crisis in the 1980s made homophobia even more politically viable.

In 1987 the government was concerned that "promoting" homosexuality would undermine heterosexual marriage and the heterosexual family, and that children were being "indoctrinated" into believing that homosexuality was superior to heterosexuality, with graphic details about same-sex sex. Despite being vaguely worded and effectively unenforceable, Section 28 was enacted in 1988.

Section 28 stopped schools from mentioning gay people or history, never mind teaching safer sex education that included queer bodies. It ostensibly only prohibited the "promotion" of homosexuality, not "legitimate discussion" about it, but in practice prevented any discussion, because people who work with children are likely to be subject to witch-hunts. Homosexuality was seen as sexually deviant, making it especially dangerous for teachers to discuss with children lest they be labeled "pedophiles."

Section 28 was combated by activist groups including Black Lesbians and Gays Against Media Homophobia, who organized protests in the late 80s. It was finally repealed in 2003.

*see also:* BIOPOLITICS; REPRESENTATION

**SELF-DIAGNOSIS** — When someone diagnoses themselves with an illness or injury, including mental illness or a mental health condition.

Self-diagnosis is very important to trans and queer people, and anyone who doesn't have access to healthcare to get a formal diagnosis from a doctor. It's belittled as less "legitimate" than a formal diagnosis, but generally people who are self-diagnosing are doing so because they are trying to better understand their symptoms, and their experiences should be taken seriously.

see also: BODILY AUTONOMY; GENDER DYSPHORIA

**SEX (N.)** — A binary division of people based on their perceived possible role in biological reproduction. Sex is a socially constructed category, not an objectively scientific one.

Sex alleges to differentiate between "female" and "male," but those categories are not discrete. Sex ostensibly describes reproductive organs, genitals, chromosomes, hormone ratio, gametes, and secondary sex characteristics (e.g., breast tissue and facial hair). Sexual dimorphism is a rough guide but not strictly accurate. Many trans and intersex people have a combination of sex traits; and for each trait there is a spectrum on which traits fall, rather than being binary.

Does biology influence gender? Yes, hormones obviously influence our gender, which is why so many trans people feel more "at home" in their bodies after starting hormone replacement therapy. The brain does not have a "sex," but it is influenced by sex hormones. Even if it did have a sex, it would exist along a spectrum like all other sex characteristics. Our brains also physically change in response to our environments and experiences. Our time spent being gendered changes our brains; gender influences our biology, and biology influences our gender. The mind and body are not separate.

Sex is assumed to be binary and essential. Gender is built on this understanding of sex, and our desires as either "heterosexual" or "homosexual" are built upon that gender. All of this is flawed.

Male and female are both gender-coded words, not objective biological realities. To insist that a trans person is "biologically fe/male" is to suggest that there is a "real" sex beneath a facade of gender expression and identity. Best practice is to let people describe themselves, and trust that they will give you the necessary information when it's genuinely relevant (e.g., in certain medical contexts).

Thinking about sex in binary terms, or assuming that genitals equate to sex, is medically dangerous. Medical practitioners would do well to learn to ask trans people the questions they want the answers to. Instead of "Are you biologically male?" or "Have you had the surgery?" they might ask, "Do you need regular breast exams?" or "Do you know your hormone levels or do we need to test them?"

Some people assume that sex is knowable through secondary sex characteristics, but it just isn't. You can't tell what chromosomes or genitals someone has by looking at them in public; you can't tell if someone has had genital reconstruction surgery. Most oppression based on sex is actually based on the perceived sex, not on an "actual" knowledge of someone's chromosomes, genitals, hormone levels, or other biological characteristics.

All trans people, regardless of their genitals, suffer from oppression based on their sex (because their genitals are under constant gaze and discussion, and their transness is the basis for denial of healthcare). This is worse for trans people assigned male at birth. Everyone with a uterus is also oppressed for their sex, and denied bodily autonomy via reproductive healthcare. Cis women and all trans people are routinely dismissed by medical professionals.

*see also:* BIOLOGICAL ESSENTIALISM; TRANS HEALTHCARE; REPRODUCTIVE RIGHTS

**SEX (v.)** — Any act which involves genital stimulation for pleasure.

Sex is normatively assumed to involve penetration, especially "Penis-In-Vagina (PIV)" penetration; but sex also includes non-penetrative acts such as oral and hand stimulation, and masturbation ("solo sex").

We should shift our focus from "normal" (acceptable) sex acts to consent and communication between partners, with consideration and without coercion.

*see also:* CONSENT; SAFER SEX; PIV; SEX POSITIVE

**SEXISM** — The systemic discrimination of women on the basis of their gender under patriarchy.

Some sexism targets biology associated with women, such as slurs for breasts and vaginas, and gatekeeping reproductive healthcare. Most sexism targets gender: deriding femininity, "women are too emotional" or not smart, women are objects to be gazed at, men are entitled to women and sex from women, women are expected to do all the emotional and domestic and care labor, and so on.

Trans women face sexism, specifically transmisogyny. They are more likely to be harassed or attacked for their womanhood than cis women.

It's not possible to be sexist toward men because there is no institutional power which buttresses discrimination against men on the basis of their gender.

*see also:* MISOGYNY; TRANSMISOGYNY; SEX (n.)

**SEXOLOGY** — The scientific study of sexuality. The field emerged in Germany and England in the 1880s, and shifted sexuality from a set of behaviors (what you do) to identity (who you are).

Sexology divided sexual behavior into "normal" and "abnormal." This lead to vilifying people as deviant, as well as the "born this way" understanding of sexuality being something you are and can't change, so therefore you deserve rights and protections.

Richard Freiherr von Krafft-Ebing is an early sexologist who thought that the purpose of sex is procreation, and that any recreational sex is perverse. He's credited with the first recorded use of "sadism," "masochism," "analingus" and "bi-sexual" in its modern sense in his psychiatric book *Psychopathia Sexualis* (1886). It was one of the first books which studied sexual behavior and sexual identity. His views on same-sex activity were largely forgotten in favor of Freud's, and because he garnered animosity from the Catholic Church for associating martyrdom with hysteria and masochism.

In the early 1900s, Sigmund Freud popularized "sexuality" as a modern idea. He also popularized the idea that the main function of sex was pleasure, not procreation. He thought that sexuality "develops" and is not innate in the subject, and you make a sexual "object choice" to go for either "same" or "opposite" sex attractions based on your Oedipal complex; social environments shape your existing innate drives. He strongly suggested that some sexual practices were "healthy" and "mature" compared to others. Freud didn't champion conversion therapy, but many psychoanalysts who build on his work have and continue to do so.

Oscar Wilde's trial and prosecution in 1895 sparked widespread public interest in homosexuality and the scientific study of sexuality in the UK. British scholars Havelock Ellis, John Addington Symonds, and Edward Carpenter advocated for an understanding of sexuality as innate rather than a lifestyle choice. The British Society for the Study of Sex

Psychology was established in July 1914, with Edward Carpenter as its first president. Its founders sought to provide a scientific understanding of sexual behavior, with the aim of legal reform and public education. The Society published 17 pamphlets on sexual psychology, which included feminist politics. There was an implicit solidarity between the women's suffrage movement and sex reform, which were understood to be part of the same political struggle.

The *Institut für Sexualwissenschaft* (Institute of Sexology) was a pioneering private sexology research institute in Berlin from 1919 to 1933. Headed by Magnus Hirschfeld, the Institute campaigned for trans and gay rights and tolerance on conservative and rational grounds, as well as advocating for sex education, contraception, women's emancipation, and the treatment of sexually transmitted infections. Hirschfeld coined the word "transsexualism," and worked with police to stop the arrest of trans people under anti-cross-dressing laws. The Institute had trans people on staff. The first modern gender reassignment surgery was offered there, as well as hormone replacement therapy. The Institute was harassed by the police for "sexual immorality" beginning in 1932, was smashed up by Nazi students on 6 May 1933, and four days later was more systemically attacked in the Nazi book burnings when the Institute's archives were burned in the street, forcing it to close. Hirschfeld was abroad on a speaking tour at the time of the burnings, and spent the rest of his life in exile as both a queer sexologist and a Jew.

William Masters and Virginia Johnson were modern sexologists who studied the physiology of sexual activity in laboratory conditions in the 1950s and 1960s. They theorized that sex occurs in four stages: excitement; plateau; orgasm; resolution. Their research prioritizes and normalizes penis-in-vagina heterosexual sex, frames sex as a linear activity, and suggests that sex which doesn't follow that linear development is "dysfunctional." The Masters and Johnson Institute ran a conversion therapy program from 1968–1977 which alleged to convert homosexuals into heterosexuals with a 71.6% success rate.

Alfred Kinsey pioneered the idea that sexuality is a scale, not a binary; and that sexuality can shift throughout one's lifetime. John Gagnon and William Simon, who worked at the Kinsey Institute in the 1960s and 1970s, posited that the social world produces (not just shapes) sexuality and desire, on three interacting levels: cultural, interpersonal, and intrapsychic (conversations with ourselves).

In the 60s and 70s, Sandra Bem studied how children internalize gender roles. She radically suggested that strict adherence to prescribed gender roles of "masculinity" or "femininity" is unhealthy, and it's better for people to be androgynous. She argued that gender is not a useful way to categorize people.

While all the aforementioned researchers did groundbreaking work on the study of sexuality, their biases, motivations, and positions as "experts" over their patients should be challenged.

*see also:* BORN THIS WAY; BIOLOGICAL ESSENTIALISM; KINSEY SCALE; SEXUALITY; FASCISM

**SEX POSITIVE, SEX NEGATIVE** — The sex positive movement embraces sexuality and sexual expression. Sex negativity can refer to a normative set of repressive conditions under cisheteropatriarchy, or a nuanced critique of sex positivity.

Sex positivity is liberating in a culture which slut-shames and attaches stigma to promiscuity; but it is also uncritical of the problems with centering sex as a purely positive, and universal, experience.

There are two strands of sex negativity. The first is normative and prescriptive, anti-porn, anti-queer, anti-kink, and sometimes anti-man. The second is a nuanced response to sex positivity which allows space for trauma and complicated feeling around sex and asexuality.

Sex positivity has created a new norm of a happy, uncomplicated relationship to sex and sexuality: pressure to perform desire, to be dating actively, to be having great or certain kinds of sex. Unfortunately, we can't masturbate away patriarchy and rape culture. We need space to not be into sex, to not want it, to not be interested in changing that. As long as we live under patriarchy, our relationships to sex will always be influenced by sexism. Compulsory sex/positivity isn't radical.

*see also:* FEMINISM; SEX (v.); CONSENT; KINK

**SEX REASSIGNMENT SURGERY (SRS)** — The previous name for what is now called "genital affirming surgery," a set of trans-specific surgeries to change the patient's genitals.

Sex reassignment surgery involves a dubious use of the word "sex"; it's also called "gender reassignment surgery," which is problematic for similar reasons. Colloquially it's called "bottom surgery," which avoids those problems.

*see also:* GENITAL RECONSTRUCTIVE SURGERY; SEX (n.); BOTTOM SURGERY; GENDER AFFIRMING SURGERY; TRANS HEALTHCARE

**SEXUAL INVERSION** — *see:* INVERT.

**SEXUALITY** — An identity based on sexual attraction or lack thereof.

Sexuality is not innate, but fluid and contextually defined. People's sexual preferences can change over time. Even if they don't, the labels which people use to describe those preferences can change or be interpreted differently in different situations.

The concept of sexuality as we understand it is relatively new, coming from the sexologists of the late 19th and 20th centuries.

Philosopher Michel Foucault published *The History of Sexuality* in 1976, which suggests that sexuality is produced by certain forms of knowledge (e.g., religion and science); there is no "truth" about it to be uncovered. Foucault argues that sexuality became an identity category as a tool of post-industrial power relations, which shifted from sovereign power to "biopower" (power over bodies: labor); sexuality was a means of archiving and cataloging normalcy in bodies.

*see also:* SEXOLOGY; BIOPOLITICS

**SEXUAL MINORITIES** — An out-of-favor term which includes LGBT+ people along with people with "unusual" sexual preferences which are not related to gender (e.g., BDSM, age gaps, and mixed-race fetishization).

It does not include non-consensual sexual preferences such as pedophilia (sexual attraction to children), necrophilia (sexual attraction to dead bodies), and zoophilia (sexual attraction to non-human animals).

*see also:* MOGAI; SEXUALITY

**SEXUAL OFFENCES ACT** — An Act of Parliament which decriminalized sex between consenting adult men in private in England and Wales on July 27, 1967. This excluded anyone in the armed forces, the merchant navy, and anyone cruising in a public park or public space.

Scotland decriminalized sex between men with a Criminal Justice Act in 1980 which took effect on February 1, 1981. Northern Ireland decriminalized same-sex sex with the Homosexual Offences Order in 1982, as a result of a European Court of Human Rights case, *Dungeon v. United Kingdom* (1981), which ruled that the criminalization of same-sex sex violated Article 8 of the European Convention of Human Rights.

The age of consent for same-sex couples was set at 21 across the UK with this legislation, while the age of consent for different-sex couples remained at 16 (17 in Northern Ireland). This gave police a reason to continue raiding and policing gay spaces, looking for queer men under the age of 21. Sex between women was never a crime in the UK.

The age of consent for sex between same-sex couples throughout the UK was lowered to 18 in 1994, and equalized to 16 in 2000.

The Sexual Offences Act 2003 removed buggery and gross indecency as crimes from statutory law, and decriminalized sex between more than two men throughout the UK.

Between 1967 and 2003, 30,000 men were arrested for same-sex behavior that wouldn't have been a crime if their partner had been a woman.

In 2017 in England and Wales, the Alan Turing Law pardoned all men prosecuted under the anti-queer gross indecency laws and the unequal age of consent under the pre-2003 Sexual Offences Act. This was a seemingly benevolent gesture, but to accept a pardon is to admit wrongdoing. Activists suggest that the government should have instead offered an apology. The governments of Scotland and Northern Ireland have yet to pardon or apologize for their discriminatory sex laws.

*see also:* SECTION 28; BUGGERY; CONSENT; GROSS INDECENCY

**SEXUSOCIETY** — A term to mark the centrality of sex and sexuality in our society, and how sex is placed at the center of our love, relationships, and conceptions of fulfillment.

*see also:* ASEXUALITY; HETERONORMATIVITY; SEX-POSITIVE

**SEX WORK** — Any work where money or resources are exchanged for sex, including full service sex work (escorting, prostitution), stripping, webcamming, and pornography.

The demographics of sex workers are largely unknown because the research methodology of many studies focuses on the workers' personas rather than their out-of-work identities. Many queer and trans people do sex work, often "as" a gender or sexuality other than their own.

Discrimination, economic, social, and immigration barriers stop people from getting "civilian" jobs, so they choose sex work. This is especially true of trans people.

Sex work is not trafficking, and the conflation between sex workers and trafficking victims harms both groups.

*see also:* WHOREPHOBIA; CONSENT

**SHE/HER** — A third-person pronoun.

"She" emerged in Middle English in the mid-1100s. In Old English, "he" was a genderless pronoun used for everyone.

*see also:* PRONOUNS

**SHE-MALE** — A slur used to describe trans women and "Assigned Male At Birth (AMAB)" trans people. It has been reclaimed by some.

In the early 1800s, she-male was used in American English to mean female. By 1972 it was in use to describe masculine lesbians, and by c.1984 it was used to describe trans women (sometimes incorrectly labeled "transsexual males").

Being a slur, people who aren't affected by transmisogyny should not use it.

*see also:* TRANSMISOGYNY

**SILENCE (N., V.)** — Silence (n.) is the absence of noise and discussion. To silence (v.) is to quiet someone, stop them from talking or drawing attention to an issue.

Silence is an important activist issue. It highlights what's being talked about, what's being ignored, and who's talking. Silence shows us who is complacent, who is spoken over, who is not invited to the conversation, and who is not able to participate because they are working or child-minding or dead.

The act of being silenced is extremely distressing, especially when you're speaking about injustices which directly affect your life. HIV/AIDS activist group ACT UP used the motto SILENCE = DEATH; refusing to be silent is a political act.

*see also:* POLICE (v.); ASSIMILATION; RESPECTABILITY; ACT UP

**SKOLIOSEXUAL** — Sexual attraction to non-binary people.

Skoliosexual is a fetishizing term, basically interchangeable with "chaser." It only has positive utility when used by non-binary people themselves.

*see also:* NON-BINARY; FETISHIZE; CHASER

**SOCIALIZED FE/MALE, SOCIALIZED AS A WO/MAN** — The implication that children are "socialized" into the gender they are assumed to be (usually their gender assigned at birth).

Trans people aren't "socialized as" their gender assigned at birth; everyone is socialized into gender norms. Everyone learns how girls and boys are supposed to act (and that being neither a girl nor a boy isn't a socially acceptable option). The "socialized as" argument is mainly used to delegitimize the womanhood of trans women.

Trans women are not "socialized as men." They are rewarded and punished for assimilating into hegemonic masculinity or not, but they do not have the same gendered "socialization" as cis men. Cis men internalize entitlement and toxic masculinity, whereas trans women internalize transmisogyny, including the pain of masking their transness.

Trans women did not grow up "as boys"; they grew up as trans girls, which is a distinct experience from cis girlhood or cis boyhood. Trans men likewise do not grow up "as girls," but as trans boys. Non-binary people's experience of their gendered childhood is also distinct from a binary person's girlhood or boyhood.

Regardless of our gender, or whether or not we're trans, the consequences of straying outside of our assigned gender roles are strongly enforced. We learn from a young age that to be a girly boy, to be a boyish girl, or to be any iteration of trans, is wrong.

*see also:* MALE PRIVILEGE; TRANSMISOGYNY

**SOCIAL TRANSITION** — *see:* TRANSITION.

**SOCK PUPPET, SOCKPUPPET, SOC** — A fake or disingenuous on-line account used for the purposes of deception, which often takes "social justice" narratives to extremes for the purpose of discrediting them.

Sock puppets will insert themselves into dialogues and online spaces, sometimes simply through discussion and sometimes purporting to represent a community and then make outrageous claims. Some sock puppet tactics include creating pedophile "Pride" events, suggesting that "love is love" applies to human-animal relationships, and creating forum pages for trans support and then outing all of the members with the intention of causing harm.

Sock puppets are designed to appear sincere in order to create divisions within marginalized communities. They are a very effective tool in anti-LGBT+ movements for finding the most exploitable divisions within the "community." The clearest current example is between trans women and their supporters, and trans-exclusionary radical feminists (TERFs).

Because there is lots of infighting in queer communities about definitions of terms, political aims, legitimate tactics, and political priorities, it can be difficult to spot the difference between a sock puppet and a genuine (though perhaps clumsy or cruel) account.

Critical engagement is useful and important, and we should not be avoiding difficult conversations simply because they are "divisive"; but we must also ration our energies and remember that we are not obliged to constantly engage in emotionally taxing dialogues which personally affect us.

*see also:* TERF; TROLL

**SODOMY, SODOMITE** — Sodomy is any sex act which is criminalized as being "unnatural" or immoral. Sodomy is rarely legally defined, but is understood to include anal sex and bestiality. In practice, sodomy laws are used to target queer men.

In England, sodomy and buggery are used interchangeably as both slang and legal terms.

Legally, sodomy is often ill-defined as "the abominable and detestable act against nature" or some variation, which made it easier to prosecute specific sex acts deemed "immoral" by the judge.

The earliest known criminalization of sodomy is in the Middle Assyrian Law Code, which states "If a man have intercourse with his brother-in-arms, they shall turn him into a eunuch" (c.1075 BCE). In the Roman Republic, it was permissible for men to act on homoerotic desire, as long as the top was of higher social standing than the bottom. Sodomy was widely criminalized across Europe in the 13th century as the Roman Catholic Church rather suddenly targeted sodomites, especially men who had sex with men. During this European period of anti-gay brutality, there was also violent intolerance of Jews, Muslims, women, and witches.

The French Revolutionary Penal Code (1791) decriminalized many victimless crimes, including sodomy. This was carried forward into the Napoleon Penal Code (1810), which was imposed on Europe across the French Empire, effectively decriminalizing sodomy on most of the continent. However, sodomy laws were imposed by European empires to their colonies; for example, the British Empire outlawed being *hijra* in India.

Sex between men was decriminalized in Russia during the Russian Revolution (1917) and codified following the Russian Civil War (1917–1922) under Lenin and Trotsky, but re-criminalized under Stalin in 1933. Sex between men was not decriminalized again in Russia until 1993, and Russia continues to repress LGBT+ rights through anti-"propaganda" laws.

Laws about sodomy in the US were created by states, rather than the federal government. In June 2003 in *Lawrence v. Texas*, the US Supreme Court ruled that it is unconstitutional for states to criminalize private, consensual, non-commercial sex acts between adults on grounds of morality.

*see also:* BUGGERY; GROSS INDECENCY; SEXUAL OFFENCES ACT; CONSENT; NATURAL, UNNATURAL

**SOFFA** — Acronym for "Significant Others, Friends, Family, And Allies." It refers to the loved ones of LGBT+ people. It is often used for support groups (e.g., LGBT+ people and SOFFA).

*see also:* LGBT+; ALLY

**SOFT BOY** — A modern term to encourage making room for boys to be "soft" and feminine: floral, chubby, gentle, tender, vulnerable.

It is also used by boys as an excuse to be misogynist—because the bar for a "feminist" boy is so low, the soft boy gets away with murder.

*see also:* PANSY; FEMINISM

**SOLIDARITY** — Communal interests or responsibilities, mutual stake holding, and mutual aid.

Solidarity is a key concept in anarchist activism, along with direct action. Solidarity means that all oppressed people are mutually invested in the liberation of each other, because our struggles are interconnected.

*see also:* ACTIVISM; TRANSFORMATIVE JUSTICE

**SPIVAK** — A set of invented, gender neutral pronouns.

| E smiles | I waved at em | Eir heart warmed | That's eirs | E loves emself |
|---|---|---|---|---|

*see also:* PRONOUNS; GENDER NEUTRAL LANGUAGE

**SQUISH** — A platonic, or aromantic, crush.

The term was developed by the aromantic and asexual communities to describe their non-romantic and non-sexual feelings of attraction, and to highlight that love and infatuation are not necessarily tied to romance or lust.

*see also:* AROMANTIC; ASEXUAL; QUEERPLATONIC; ZUCCHINI; AMATONORMATIVITY

**SRS** — *see:* SEX REASSIGNMENT SURGERY.

**STEALTH** — A trans person who passes as cis and is not out as trans.

Being stealth is distinct from being closeted—a closeted trans person would be presenting as their gender assigned at birth, rather than presenting as their actual gender without disclosing their trans status.

Being stealth is a survival tactic for many trans people, whose safety is conditional on them hiding the fact that they are trans.

*see also:* OUT; PASSING; CLOSET

**STONEWALL, STONEWALL RIOTS** — A seminal moment in queer history when queer people rioted in response to police raids and police brutality.

The Stonewall riots happened on June 28, 1969 at the Stonewall Inn in New York City in response to a police raid. The Stonewall Inn was a bar in Manhattan where people could dance with other people of the same gender expression without facing police raiding/harassment (because of alleged mafia ties).

Stonewall is considered a decisive moment in LGBT+ rights movement and history, when patrons resisted arrest and rioted against the police. The following year, the first Pride parade commemorated the Stonewall riots.

While Stonewall has became a central, landmark "moment" for LGBT+ rights, is has been whitewashed, its trans actors have been pushed to the margins, and it has been stripped of its political significance as an act of resistance against a racist and transphobic police state. This whitewashing can be seen in modern Pride parades which include (still queerphobic, still racist) police forces, and in the 2015 film *Stonewall*, which erased the contributions of the Black and brown trans people who started the riots, and who continue to fight for queer youth and LGBT+ rights.

*see also:* PRIDE; WHITEWASH; PINKWASHING; COMPTON CAFETERIA RIOTS

**STP** — Acronym for "Stand To Pee," a device used by people with vaginas to urinate whilst standing up.

STPs can be phallic and look like realistic penises, or can be a more utilitarian cup and chute mechanism.

STPs can help relieve bottom dysphoria and bathroom dysphoria for people who want to but couldn't otherwise urinate whilst standing up. Some STPs also function as packers, worn by the user as a penis which can provide a visible bulge. When used to alleviate dysphoria, STPs should be considered an aspect of trans healthcare.

*see also:* PACKING; TRANS HEALTHCARE

**STRAIGHT** — A heteronormative word for heterosexual.

Straight positions heterosexual as normal, as though anything not-straight is crooked, skewed, abnormal, wrong.

Straight emerged as a slang word for heterosexual in the 1940s.

*see also:* HETEROSEXUAL; HETERONORMATIVITY

**STRAIGHT ACTING** — A queer person (usually a man) who actively avoids giving cues to their queerness.

Many queer men advertise themselves as being straight acting on dating and hookup apps. What does it mean to "act straight"?

A performance of hegemonic masculinity, including shaming all things feminine. Effeminate boys and men are still seen as inferior to masculine ones, even in gay and queer communities.

It is not a compliment to be called straight acting, because it implies that acting queer is unattractive or wrong.

*see also:* MASC 4 MASC; FEMMEPHOBIA; STRAIGHT; HETERO-NORMATIVITY; CLOSET; GAY CULTURE

**STRAIGHT GAZE** — The way straight people objectify and fetishize queerness, queer bodies, and queer relationships.

Most obviously the straight gaze targets queer women and non-binary people, especially trans women; but it also targets queer men. Straight people fetishize transness as an exaggeration of gayness; straight men fetishize lesbian and bisexual women for their attraction to other women; straight women fetishize gay and bisexual men for their attraction to other men.

*see also:* FETISHIZE

**STRAIGHT PASSING** — *see:* PASSING.

**STRAIGHT PRIDE** — A response by social conservatives to gay Pride, suggesting that LGBT+ people shouldn't be holding public events to combat stigma around queerness or have a social space to meet each other, because heterosexuals don't "shove their sexuality in our faces."

Of course they do shove it in our faces—heterosexuality is compulsory and any deviance from it is punished.

*see also:* STRAIGHT PRIVILEGE; PRIDE; HETERONORMATIVITY

**STRAIGHT PRIVILEGE** — The relative ease through which straight people are able to navigate heteronormative society. The absence of systemic discrimination of heterosexuals based on their sexuality.

For straight people, there is no expectation to come out. There is an abundance of heterosexual media representation. There is no common parlance which attacks straight sexuality (e.g., "That's so gay"). Everyone is constantly told that straightness is normal.

Privilege is not always clear-cut. Straight people who are assumed to be queer based on their gender expression are not afforded the same level of privilege as their straight peers who perform hegemonic gender roles; but this does not mean that gender non-conforming straight people face the same levels of discrimination as queer people, even queer people who are "straight passing."

Heterosexuality is a privileged identity, but it requires a lot of upkeep. Straight people constantly need to reify their straightness, because it's flimsy. It collapses under the slightest same-sex attraction, or struggle with penetrative sex, or if they do not have or want sex at the "normal" frequency. Straight people are expected to adhere to rigid gender roles, but they are also allowed more deviance from them than queer people are. This makes it easy for straight people to co-opt queer aesthetics and queer culture.

Because sexuality is so intrinsically tied to gender, and trans people are seen as gay or queer even when they are straight, straight trans people are largely denied straight privilege.

see also: HETERONORMATIVITY; PRIVILEGE; PASSING

## STREET TRANSVESTITE ACTION REVOLUTIONARIES (STAR)
— A direct action group which worked with and aided sex workers and homeless queer youth in New York City.

STAR began as a caucus in the Gay Liberation Front, and was founded by drag queens/trans women of color and Stonewall veterans Marsha P. Johnson and Silvia Rivera in 1970. It was an extremely important organization because it centered the most vulnerable people in society, and took direct action to house them and offer them support.

Johnson and Rivera opened STAR House, a shelter for LGBT+ youth, in 1970: a trailer in a parking lot in Greenwich Village. The trailer was removed, and they opened a more permanent house in a four-bedroom apartment in a building with no electricity in the East Village. Johnson and Rivera learned how to fix electricity, plumbing, and the boiler whilst operating the house, and worked as sex workers in order to fund the project. STAR House was the first LGBT+ shelter in North America, and would house up to 25 trans women at one time; it also served as a social space for queer youth. It was also the first organization in the US to be led by trans women of color, and the first trans sex worker labor organization. It was only open until July 1971, when the landlord was arrested and the building was acquired by the city, and all tenants were evicted. Johnson went on to organize within ACT UP. She was found dead in 1992 under suspicious circumstances, and is thought by friends and family to have been murdered. Rivera continued to agitate and fight for homeless queers, especially those affected by HIV/AIDS and substance dependency, despite being pushed out of Pride activism by cis gays who thought drag was misogynistic. STAR House now serves as a blueprint for other activists and queer shelters.

The politics of STAR were outspoken and uncompromising: they demanded nothing short of freedom, and condemned transphobia, sexism, racism, mass incarceration, police harassment, and the exclusion of trans people within gay and feminist movements. Their specific demands included the right to self-determination and self-declaration of name and gender marker, an end to employment discrimination, free healthcare, free education, free food, and other social goods to be free at the point of access. STAR declared that their personal freedoms are dependent on the freedoms of all oppressed people.

*see also:* STONEWALL; ACTIVISM; ACT UP

**STUD** — A queer masculinity.

The term is preferred by some queer women to "butch."

*see also:* BUTCH

**SURVIVOR** — Someone who has survived sexual violence, intimate partner violence, or familial violence (the latter two are often referred to as "domestic violence"). It can be more broadly used to describe anyone who has suffered sexual, physical, emotional, or psychological abuse.

Queer and trans people are disproportionately likely to experience sexual violence, intimate partner violence, and familial violence.

"Abuse" is a broad category of violence, and includes:

· Sexual violence—any sexual interaction where consent is absent or lacking, including when the victim is asleep or too intoxicated or unwell to consent, and when the victim is coerced

· Financial abuse—stealing or controlling the victim's money or spending

- Threatening to use systems of oppression to gain power, such as threatening to call immigration control or threatening to out someone as queer
- Physical abuse—beating, choking, using physical intimidation or threatening physical violence including gun violence
- Emotional abuse—verbal abuse, isolation, threats of self-harm or suicide as a manipulation tactic, guilt as a tool for coercion, withholding the victim's important documents from them
- Psychological abuse—gaslighting, stalking, cyberstalking, blackmail, childhood neglect

Many survivors don't report their abuse, and under-reporting is likely to be a bigger problem for queer people because the police and the criminal justice system are more likely to fail us. Queer people have legitimate concerns that the police will be prejudiced, and the more marginalized a survivor is, the less likely they are to know their rights, to have access to victims' advocacy services, and to have time and emotional energy to report. Queer survivors may also worry about being outed in reporting, or judged for the context of the abuse (e.g., dating apps or sex work).

Survivors are not a monolith: some have experienced a single incident of violence; some have suffered sustained and long-term violence; some are traumatized and some aren't; some have post-traumatic stress disorder (PTSD) or complex PTSD as a result, some don't. Queer identities which are the "result" of trauma are still valid.

Survivors cope with their experiences in different ways. There is no wrong way to be a survivor. Coping strategies are diverse: substance use, finding community, faith, immersion in hobbies, meditation, exercise, self-harm, excessive or not enough sleeping, emotionally withdrawing, minimization of event/s, therapy, and support groups, to name a few. Rather than moralizing different coping strategies, we should support survivors to process their experiences in all their complexity, and give them as much agency as possible.

Survivors may need sustained support and access to resources to recover, including emergency medical care, safe emergency housing, long-term housing assistance, protection orders and safety planning, legal services, victim advocate services, time off from school or work, financial assistance, assistance with childcare, and prolonged therapy or support groups.

Survivor is a not uncomplicated term. It can be more empowering than "victim," but it also implies a strength that some don't feel is appropriate, and they might prefer the term "victim." Claiming either term can be an important step in the process of recovery, allowing the person to name their experience of abuse or violence and their relationship to the perpetrator.

Neither "survivor" nor "perpetrator" are terms used lightly; hopefully in naming people with these terms, we are starting a conversation which will support the survivor and facilitate their recovery, and allow the perpetrator to be held accountable. But there are limits to the language, and the binary of survivor/perpetrator. Consent is constantly negotiated, boundaries are moving lines, and we are all capable of being both survivors and perpetrators. Sexual assault, intimate partner violence, and familial violence are common and extreme manifestations of boundaries being crossed.

Assault and abuse are not the only breach in boundaries which should be taken seriously. If someone's consent is violated in a way which is "less serious" than sexual assault or abuse, they might not feel able to use the language of survivor/perpetrator because it carries so much weight. Hesitation to use the language of sexual assault is understandable, given the stigma and drama which can ensue from using it, but that shouldn't mean that consent violations go unaddressed. It is very common for survivors to take time reflecting on and processing their abuse before naming it as abusive, or naming themselves as victims or survivors. The dominant narratives about sexual violence suggest that it's only serious or legitimate if it is named as violence during or immediately after the event, but this assumption must be challenged.

The criminal justice system reifies gendered violence. The criminal justice system criminalizes surviving abuse, if you use any force to defend yourself or escape, or if you later speak about your experience when your abuser has not been convicted.

You might notice that I'm deliberately avoiding calling abusers and perpetrators "criminals." A criminal is only someone who is prosecuted and deemed guilty of a crime. Many abusers are never prosecuted, and many survivors are criminalized for surviving; many survivors also have criminal records. It's important to question the label "criminal." Criminals include street sex workers, undocumented migrants, substance dealers, and thieves, all of whom might commit their crimes to survive. There is no binary between "survivor" and "criminal." Survivors do not need to fit a "perfect victim" narrative in order to be supported. We must expand our template for what a survivor looks like in terms of race, gender, class, and criminal record, lest we fall into racist narratives of innocent white femininity threatened by aggressive Black masculinity.

The survivor/perpetrator binary also reduces people into categories of essentially "good" and "bad," instead of focusing on harmful behavior. Abusers shouldn't be afforded good faith at the expense of validating a survivor's experience; but also casting people as simply "bad" makes them disposable, turns accountability processes into popularity contests, and, should perpetrators be socially exiled, just moves the problem elsewhere.

There is a myth that all abusers are themselves survivors. Many abusers are survivors, but that does not excuse their abusive behavior. Many abusers are not survivors. Most survivors do not become abusers.

There is a difficulty of abusers claiming victimhood themselves. Abuse requires a power imbalance, and I think the idea of "mutual abuse" is dubious at best, though I recognize that people may have power over each other on different axes.

Usually this means that one person will get access to social support and the other one won't, and will be ostracized and gaslighted. Supporting survivors should not be about discerning an "objective truth" about what happened; it is possible that two people exit an interaction with both of them feeling abused. Rather than try to diminish either of their experiences, we should support them in processing their feelings and living dignified lives, as well as understanding how they may have caused harm and how to prevent causing harm in the future.

Considering identity is important because structures of power impact how likely we are to face violence, how likely we are to be believed or disbelieved, and how likely we are to be seen as victims. Queers are more likely to suffer from gendered violence and intimate partner violence, but because the gender dynamics are different than the "default" narrative of domestic violence with a violent man and a battered woman, our experiences are minimized by society and within our communities.

Activism should be survivor-centered but not necessarily survivor-led, because survivors shouldn't have to do all the work. Survivors also shouldn't be expected to know what their needs are immediately, or to name their experiences immediately, and their needs may change over time or not fit the template survivor narrative. Survivor-centered means taking supportive action (which might be inaction) which helps the survivor rather than burdens them or puts them at risk.

This is more important than justice for the abuser, although that is important too.

"Support survivors" is something people say, but I want to explicitly name what that means to me. It means practically offering support; and fostering a culture of support.

Practical support can look like emotional support: "I believe you, thank you for confiding in me." It can also be: listening; cooking for them; financial assistance; legal assistance; childcare; housing; restoring agency; letting them control the narrative of their experience, and validating that narrative; organizing with survivors' support and advocacy groups; asking what the survivor wants to happen to their abuser, and if you can help action that; and implementing formal structures of accountability so people can safely and anonymously make complaints in your groups and you know what you'll do when someone is named as abusive. Let the survivor lead the conversation, offer them the support you can without pressuring them, be clear about what you are and aren't able to offer in terms of support, and don't disclose their experience to anyone else without asking them first.

Fostering a culture of support for survivors means creating safer spaces, having accountability processes, and no purity politics. Having suggested actions is great because it alleviates the burden of imagining an action from the survivor, but allows them to feed back whether it's good or not; for example: "We think they need to be asked to leave the space now. What do you think?" and "We'd like to check in with you in a few days. Would you find that helpful?"

Supporting survivors is difficult and tiring work. If you're in that position, make sure you have your own support network where you can discuss your feelings about it, without putting your feelings about supporting the survivor onto the survivor themselves.

see also: TRAUMA; VIOLENCE; TRANSFORMATIVE JUSTICE; RAPE CULTURE

**SWITCH** — Someone who is both a sadist and a masochist, or dominant and submissive, and can derive pleasure from either role(s).

Switch is a liminal space; a challenge to the binary, and a constant becoming. A switch is either dominant or submissive, depending on the context of the scene. Switch isn't really a role: it's an adaptation, a state of flux, a dynamism depending on their relation to the partner(s), their mood, the environment, and the scene. The relationship to power is constantly renegotiated, fostering good consent and agency.

Switch isn't both; it is the possibility of either.

*see also:* BDSM; KINK; VERS; BISEXUAL

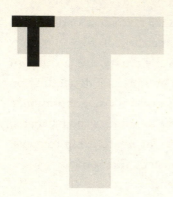

**T** — The T in LGBT+ is for TRANSGENDER. It's also short for TESTOSTERONE.

**T-GIRL** — Short for "Transgender Girl."
  *see also:* TRANSGENDER; TRANS WOMAN; TRANSFEMININE

**TEA ROOMS** — *see:* COTTAGING.

**TERF/TERFS** — Acronym for "Trans-Exclusionary Radical Feminism/Feminists."

TERF ideology is a specific strand of transphobia. It is a subset of feminism which actively denies the legitimacy of trans people and insists that gender is predetermined by biology. Some TERFs actively advocate for the eradication of trans women (and by extension, all trans people, though their focus is overwhelmingly on trans women). TERFs see trans women and AMAB trans people as a direct threat to cis women and cis womanhood. Although TERFs claim to be "radical feminists," they're closer to the right-wing than the left. They share several key ideological viewpoints with Nazis, and have adopted many of the same (modern Nazi) trolling and (historical and modern) rhetorical strategies, building on the fascist legacy of vilifying queer people.

TERFs have been a part of the discourse around trans people and feminism since the 1960s, when hormone replacement therapy became widely accessible for trans people (those who could afford it). TERFs saw trans women as stereotypes of femininity (a parody or mockery of womanhood), who reinforced sexist ideas about what it means to be a woman. Trans women were (and largely still are) forced to perform exaggerated femininity in order to access transition-related healthcare—only trans women who wear traditionally feminine clothes, are heterosexual, and behave in a stereotypically "ladylike," respectable way were/are allowed to medically transition. This isn't the fault of trans women; it's the fault of psychiatric and medical establishments, which themselves are extremely sexist and transphobic. But instead of analyzing the systems which harm all women, TERFs have instead attacked (and continue to attack) trans women.

In 1979 Janice Raymond published *Transsexual Empire: The Making of the She Male*, which said: "All transsexuals rape women's bodies by reducing the real female form to an artifact, appropriating this body for themselves... Transsexuals merely cut off the most obvious means of invading women, so that they seem non-invasive." She concluded that "transsexualism should be eradicated through denial of medical care." In 1980 Raymond was hired to write a US government white paper for the National Center for Health Care Technology on transsexual healthcare. It was called "Technology on the Social and Ethical Aspects of Transsexual Surgery" and was used as the basis to stop gender affirming surgery being covered by Medicare; private insurance companies followed suit. Transition-specific healthcare was only covered again in the US under Obama's Affordable Care Act, which required insurance companies to include it, beginning 1 January 2017.

TERFs deny that trans women are women, that trans men are men, and that non-binary people are non-binary. TERFs are biological essentialists: they equate genitals and internal reproductive organs with gender. They actively misgender trans people and claim to be "pro-science," despite the fact that biologists have long since acknowledged that both biological sex and gender exist on spectrums. Amusingly, TERFs online often put "XX" in their usernames as a declaration of their chromosomes (as if the connection between womanhood and chromosomes is obvious and undeniable). There is a shared TERF and Nazi obsession with genetics and "scientific reality," a positivist "truth" about bodies which is beyond critique. TERFs use "XX" to signify womanhood, like Nazis used "race science" to "prove" the superiority of whiteness. These views have been so thoroughly debunked that there is no need to explain them here. In all likelihood, most TERFs haven't had their chromosomes checked, and most Nazis haven't had their ancestry professionally traced (e.g., the "purity" of their whiteness confirmed). The point here isn't that some TERFs aren't XX and some Nazis aren't "purely" white (an imaginary category); it's that their bigotry rests on assumptions about biology and genetics which are scientifically lazy, as if you can "see" race and gender in a meaningful yet simplistic and binary way. TERFs and Nazis both suggest that people who are "genetically undesirable" should be sterilized, or worse.

Both TERFs and Nazis police and punish deviations from the majority identity groups—this begins by dehumanizing an entire class of people and denying them access to public space. Giving basic civil rights to a minority group (trans people) is framed as a threat to the dominant majority group. (TERFs are not a majority group, but they claim to represent and protect the views of a majority group which they belong to: cis people.) Identity is heavily policed, and the minority group is denied access to public life to "protect" the majority group. Opposition to violent rhetoric and policy is dubbed "silencing legitimate concerns"; hate speech is coded in dog whistles (TERFs use "gender critical," "transgenderism," "transwoman" instead of "trans woman") and concern trolling ("protect our women and girls," a line used by both TERFs and white supremacists). Biological essentialism is used to justify denial of rights based on social categories. Mental illness is vilified, and the minority group is coded as dangerously unstable.

TERFs fan the flames of moral panic on the far right—the same moral panic that vilifies many of them for being lesbians. TERF rhetorics are violent because they encourage a transphobic culture where trans people are denied agency and "rationality"; denied access to medical care, public life and support services; and ultimately denied personhood. Some TERFs directly encourage violence against trans women, including physical attacks and corrective rape.

TERFs declare that all trans people are pedophiles, carrying on a long tradition of categorizing proximity to queerness as child abuse. The minority group is painted not only as a threat that needs to be contained; it also needs to be exterminated in order to guarantee the safety of the majority. Today, this is most often weaponized with fear-mongering about sexual violence—trans women are labeled as inherently hyper-sexual, perverse, and a dangerous threat to (cis) women and girls.

The vilification of mental illness is another theme shared by TERFs and the far right. TERFs not only dismiss trans people as being mentally ill (thereby delegitimizing our genders) but they code us as dangerously unstable, using the pathologizing language of "sexual perversion" and linking transness to sexual violence, without evidence. They fan the flames of moral panic on the far right—the same moral panic that vilifies many TERFs for being lesbians. These are all rhetorically violent positions because they encourage a transphobic culture where trans people are denied agency and "rationality"; denied access to medical care, public life and support services; and ultimately denied personhood.

TERFs are only noticable online, and in the UK, where they are a small but loud and dedicated group. The same 100 or so people will tour the country to attend anti-trans events, which often get shut down or moved at the last minute due to public pressure to no-platform their hate speech. While they occasionally host anti-trans seminars and protest outside of trans events or events with trans speakers, the majority of their activism takes place online (under pseudonyms because their position is increasingly considered unacceptable).

One notable counterexample was London's 2018 Pride parade, where a handful of TERFs hijacked the parade and were allowed to lead it with transphobic and transmisogynistic banners. (Though Pride London [the corporation] failed to adequately deescalate or later address the TERF protest, subsequent UK Pride marches that year were often led with explicitly trans-inclusive banners.) Outwith the UK, trans rights are not positioned as oppositional to feminism.

Modern TERFs are defined as much by their ideology as their relationship to trolling. Their praxis is doxxing, harassing, outing, lurking, publishing pre-transition photos of trans women, creating fake accounts, creating accounts whose sole purpose is to index trans accounts and harass them, sabotaging surveys about trans people, and generally vying for space in online forums, especially on Tumblr, Twitter, Reddit, and Mumsnet. Rather than do anything meaningful to help cis women and girls, TERFs essentially terrorize trans women and try to force them out of physical and digital spaces. There are some explicit connections between UK TERFs and white nationalists on Twitter: mutually following each other, retweeting each other, and discussing attending each other's events (e.g., Women's Space UK events and UKIP).

TERFs are only able to push legislation when their goals align with the goals of Nazis, fascists, and other white supremacists (e.g., the Bathroom Bills, the Stop Enabling Sex Traffickers Act (SESTA) and Fight Online Sex Trafficking Act (FOSTA) in the US).

TERFs insist that it is their "free speech" right to be given a platform to espouse their ideology, whilst actually silencing the free speech rights of the minority group. Being granted an audience (e.g. on a university campus or in the national press) is neither a right nor an aspect of free speech. However, facing expulsion for starting a petition to no-platform a hate group (as is currently the case with a trans student at the University of Bristol), is a violation of free speech rights. TERFs are very vocal about how "silenced" they are by being no-platformed, despite several high-profile TERFs enjoying regular columns in international newspapers. In the UK, TERFs hold influential cultural positions within the media, community organizing, NGOs, government, and academia; the same cannot be said for trans people.

TERFs position themselves as victims of a powerful "trans lobby" which threatens to "replace" them, when in fact they have heaps of structural power over the groups they claim to be threatened by. The victim narrative is particularly noteworthy: TERFs claim to be victims of silencing and violence, with no attention paid to how their ideologies structurally silence and incite violence against marginalized people. For example, if a trans person allegedly punches a TERF at a counter-protest, the focus is then on the legitimacy of punching as a tactic (even in self-defense, assuming the punch actually happened). Centrists and fair-weather "allies" are quick to pick up on this narrative, claiming a middle ground of non-violence, not realizing that they're legitimizing an extremely violent ideology. This takes the heat off TERFs' tactics and their ideology, which are of course both extremely violent and about protecting abstract ideas of womanhood at the expense of actual living people who are not threats in the first place. Their ideology and tactics are indefensible, so they'd rather we talk about the merits and drawbacks of counter-tactics, like punching oppressors. The bullying is overlooked and the focus is on the victims' response to bullying. Victims are scrutinized for being less than perfect, but the bullies are not under any such scrutiny. Instead of playing into their victim narratives, we should stay focused on their tactics and goals: to deny trans people healthcare (trans-specific and otherwise), to bar us from public space, to harass us, and to terrorize us.

TERF arguments are predicated on the false idea of a monolithic womanhood that trans women aren't women because they don't "live as" women and they have a "male experience." But what is a "female experience"? The experience TERFs refer to is white, cis, and middle-class; the experience of a citizen, of people who have access to respectability, and in the UK, access to national media platforms. There is no universal experience of womanhood; suggestions otherwise mimic racist rhetoric which positions the experience of whiteness as "default" and "authentic" and "normal" while people of color are dehumanized and their experiences are "special interest." Many TERFs hate butch cis women for "role-playing" masculinity, but also hate very feminine women for "performing" for the male gaze.

Lesbian TERFs exclude trans women from their spaces and their analyses of feminism, lesbianism, and womanhood. Lesbian TERFs sometimes exclude trans men as gender traitors; others fetishize them as butches who need saving from being "transed," erasing and ignoring their genders as men. TERFs sometimes trawl trans message boards looking for young trans men to groom, feeding into insecurities that AFAB trans people have about abandoning womanhood and being bad feminists.

TERFs are terrified that trans women are men seeking not only to "co-opt" the struggles of women, but to gain access to women's spaces and, most terrifying of all, to deceive and fuck them as lesbians. This is essentially gay panic; they are absolutely horrified at the possibility of being attracted to a trans woman because it would undermine their status as the bastion of lesbian separatist feminists, being attracted to someone they incorrectly consider a "man."

TERFs say that the "trans lobby" refuses to acknowledge the differences between trans women and cis women, which is ironic because trans people are quick to talk about how being trans greatly affects our experiences of patriarchy, sexism, and gender. Trans people are acutely aware of the biological differences between us and cis people; that's a huge part of why many of us medically transition. Trans people aren't trying to "erase" biological differences, we're trying to secure our basic rights, and highlight shared struggles when we talk about activism and justice. Trans people not only belong in feminism; we are leading it.

*see also:* FEMINISM; TRANSMISOGYNY; AUTOGYNEPHILIA; VIOLENCE; FASCISM; BIOPOLITICS; BIOLOGICAL ESSENTIALISM

**TESTOSTERONE (T)** — A hormone used by some trans people in hormone replacement therapy (HRT) to alleviate dysphoria, to masculinize, and/or to de-feminize the body. It is used by some trans men and other trans people who were assigned female at birth.

The most significant effect of taking testosterone is an increased sense of confidence and a stronger, more comfortable sense of self.

The reversible physical effects of testosterone, which require ongoing treatment to maintain, include: redistribution of body fat to a more "masculine" pattern, including reduction in breast size; increased muscle retention; change in body odor; coarser skin; increased red blood cell count; and cessation of menstruation.

The irreversible effects of testosterone, which start to manifest after about three months of treatment, include: increased body hair; facial hair growth; receding hairline and possible hair loss; enlargement of the clitoris; thickening of the vocal cords and a "drop" in the voice; growth of an Adam's apple; and growth spurt in height, if taken before an estrogen-dominant puberty.

There are some short-term effects which are similar to going through puberty: change in mood, energy levels, and appetite; acne; and an increased sex drive. These subside within a few months, though the acne can be stubborn.

Autistic people taking testosterone also report noticing the "symptoms" of their autism more, which is probably because our diagnosis criteria is geared toward boys and men rather than accounting equally for women and girls and non-binary people.

There are myths that taking testosterone, or having testosterone as your dominant hormone (like many trans women do), makes you angry, aggressive, and violent. This is unsubstantiated; HRT does affect your mood, like going through puberty, but it does not dramatically change your personality.

Trans people who take testosterone are given a dosage to mimic the hormone levels of cis men; they do not have higher testosterone levels than cis men.

*see also*: HORMONE REPLACEMENT THERAPY; TRANSGENDER; AUTISM; ESTROGEN

**TG** — Short for TRANSGENDER in certain online spaces, especially dating apps and personals.

**THEY/THEM** — A pronoun, which does not imply or assign gender to its subject.

They/them pronouns are used by lots of people, for different reasons.

It's best practice to use they/them for people whose pronouns you don't know (which is everyone who hasn't told you their pronouns). However, it's insulting to continue to use they/them for someone once they've told you that they use different pronouns.

| They called | I smiled at them | Their skin glowed | That's theirs | They love themselves They love themself |
|---|---|---|---|---|

Despite what transphobic pedants claim, they/them have been in recorded and regular use as a singular third-person pronoun since at least the 14th century.

People complain that they/them is confusing since it can be both singular and plural, but it's much less clunky than saying "he or she," and respecting people's pronouns is worth the minor effort.

*see also*: PRONOUNS; GENDER NEUTRAL LANGUAGE

**THIRD GENDER** — A gender category which is outside of the man/woman gender binary.

Third gender is often employed as a catch-all term for anyone whose gender is neither man nor woman. It can describe anyone who is non-binary, gender fluid, agender, demi-boy, demi-girl, and any non-Western non-binary genders like *hijra*, Two-Spirit, or *fa'afafine*. In some places, third genders are given the gender marker X instead of the male M or female F; but in most places, there is no legal recognition of third genders.

Because it is such a broad category, third gender is not typically used by individuals to describe their specific experience of gender, and it should not be applied to people in place of other words that they choose themselves.

*see also:* NON-BINARY; GENDER BINARY; TRANSGENDER; X

**THON** — An invented gender neutral singular third-person pronoun, never recorded in actual use.

Thon is thought to be a contraction of "that one," coined in 1858 by attorney and composer Charles Crozat Converse. It was first included in a dictionary in 1903, in the *Funk & Wagnalls Supplement to a Standard Dictionary of the English Language*. It was included in several other dictionaries in the 20th century, and remains a subject of academic curiosity, but has never caught on in verbal language.

Some people complain about "they/them" being confusing since it is both singular and plural, but thon is a testament to how difficult it is to introduce new words into language, especially commonly used words like pronouns.

*see also:* PRONOUNS; THEY/THEM; GENDER NEUTRAL LANGUAGE

**TMA** — Acronym for TRANSMISOGYNY AFFECTED.

**TME** — Acronym for TRANSMISOGYNY EXEMPT.

**TOKEN, TOKENIZE** — Token means a singular example of "diversity" or "inclusion" in a sea of hegemony and privilege. Tokenize means to only include in order to demonstrate inclusivity.

To be tokenized is to be objectified so as to prove someone's progressiveness (e.g. the token Black friend, token gay, token woman). It flattens marginalized identities, as if all people with that marginalization are the same, and reduces the token's complexity as a person to a stereotype of their marginalized identity.

People can't be tokenized for their privileged identities; it doesn't work in reverse. There is no "token white person" in a group of people of color, or a token cis person in a group of trans people. There might be jokes made about that, but the single person with the structural power is not being marginalized by being a "minority" in that circumstance.

*see also:* FETISHIZE; OPPRESSION; VIOLENCE

**TOMBOY** — Socially acceptable gender deviance in girls. It is usually expected that they will grow out of it.

The concept of the tomboy is currently widely used in debates to suggest that trans boys should not be allowed to take hormone blockers because they're "just tomboys." This is a conflation of gender expression with gender identity. Rather than declare all gender-variant assigned female at birth children are "tomboys," we'd do better to ask them if they feel like they're girls, or boys, or neither. Do they want to be a boy because they want to do things they think girls can't do, or because they feel like they're a boy? In either case, hormone blockers are a safe option for gender-questioning children since they essentially postpone puberty while the children decide what they want.

Some queer women call themselves tomboys.

The term emerged in the 1550s to mean "rude, boisterous boy"; its opposite was "tomrig," for "rude, wild girl." The first recorded use meaning "wild, romping girl, girl who acts like a spirited boy" is from the 1590s.

*see also:* GIRL; BOY; GENDER

**TOMMY** — Slang for homosexual women in 18th-century England. It is the counterpart to "Molly," for homosexual men.

*see also:* MOLLY

**TONE POLICING** — The suggestion that the (angry or "uneducated") tone of an oppressed person's righteous anger invalidates their feelings or argument.

Tone policing is based on the implication that marginalized people should make their anger palatable; that they should politely request basic human rights and dignity instead of seizing it.

*see also:* POLICE (v.); RESPECTABILITY

**TOP** — Gay and kink slang for the complementary role to bottoms. A queer identity.

The top takes the decisive role in a sexual encounter with a bottom.

Topping is associated with dominance, masculinity, and penetrating, but none of these aspects are definitive characteristics of tops.

The language of top/bottom/vers is used by some as an identity label, but it doesn't have to be. The purpose of these labels is to make it easier for queer people to find sexual partners, not to define your identity (unless you want it to).

*see also:* BOTTOM; VERS; GAY; KINK

**TOP SURGERY** — A set of trans-specific surgeries to alter the appearance of the chest, either by removing breast tissue or adding breast implants.

Top surgery is not cosmetic; it is considered medically necessary for trans people with dysphoria about their chests.

There are multiple kinds of top surgery. The top surgeries for people who need to remove breast tissue are double incision, inverted T or T-anchor, peri-areolar, and keyhole. Each has different levels of scarring and sensation retained. The type of surgery used depends on chest size, skin elasticity, and the surgeon's and patient's preference. The double incision and inverted T surgeries leave two horizontal scars underneath the pectoral muscles, following the natural contour of the muscles. These top surgery scars are recognized by other trans people as signifiers of transness, almost like battle scars of honor.

Top surgery for people who need breast implants have variations too: the type of implant (silicone or saline), the shape, the projection (low, moderate, high), the placement of the implants (under or over the chest muscles), and the incision placements (at the breast fold, around the areola, or under the arm).

The requirements for getting top surgery depend on where you live and the surgeon you choose, but commonly surgeons require letters from therapists, a diagnosis of gender dysphoria, and proof of hormone replacement therapy. The medicalization of transness allows people access to surgery and legitimizes it as medically necessary instead of cosmetic, but it also pathologizes trans genders and places authority about our genders with cis doctors and "experts" rather than allowing us to self-declare and self-determine our genders and needs relating to our dysphoria.

*see also:* TRANS HEALTHCARE; TRANSITION; BODILY AUTONOMY

**TOXIC MASCULINITY** — Norms about masculinity which encourage toxic behavior and attitudes about gender, sex, sexuality, and power. Toxic masculinity is a feature of patriarchy.

Toxic masculinity is a culture; it is something we are all born into, and which we all learn and must unlearn.

*see also:* HEGEMONIC MASCULINITY; PATRIARCHY

**TRADE** — Polari slang for sex. Still in use, it also means a sexual partner.

*see also:* POLARI

**TRANNY** — A slur for trans people, especially those who were assigned male at birth. It has been reclaimed by some.

The long history of conflation between gender and sexuality meant that men who cross-dressed or did drag performances were called "tranny"; but now that term is targeted at trans people, especially trans women and people assumed to be trans women.

It's frankly insensitive for people who aren't affected by transmisogyny to use this slur at this point. While there is a shared history of stigma and struggle between cis queers and trans people, the cis LGB movement has absolutely left trans people behind. Cis queers do not face the same struggles or stigmas as trans people today, because as a group they deliberately separated themselves from trans people in order to be more palatable to the cishetero mainstream.

*see also:* TRANSMISOGYNY

**TRANS** — Short for transgender or (less often) transsexual. It is also used as an adjective to describe transgender people (e.g., a trans man, or a transfeminine woman).

Trans encompasses transgender (including non-binary), transsexual, and gender non-conforming.

In most cases there is a space between "trans" and its following noun (e.g., "trans man" not "transman"), similar to "gay man" rather than "gayman."

While "trans" is an adjective it is sometimes used by trans people as a noun, referring to themselves as "a trans." This is a humorous reclamation and reference to uneducated medical professionals and members of the public Othering trans people with this language. The same is true for queer and gay people using "a queer" and "a gay." However, "a transgender" is still weaponized, dehumanizing language and shouldn't be used by cis people.

*see also:* TRANSGENDER; OTHER

**TRANS\*** — Sometimes "trans" is given an asterisk in order to be "more inclusive." This is based on the misguided belief that "trans" alone is binary and does not already include non-binary people. The \* is also sometimes used to include people who are not trans, but are broadly gender variant or gender non-conforming, such as cross-dressers and drag performers.

*see also:* TRANSGENDER; TRANS; INCLUSION THEATER

**TRANS-EXCLUSIONARY RADICAL FEMINIST** — *see:* TERF.

**TRANSFEMININE, TRANS FEMME** — Someone who is transgender and assigned male at birth.

All trans women could describe themselves as transfeminine or trans femmes, but not all transfeminine people and trans femmes would choose to describe themselves as women.

The language is clunky, because not all transfeminine people are feminine or femme; but it describes a shared experience (and importantly, shared violence and oppressions) of transness when assigned male at birth. Common features of this experience include hyper-visibility and hyper-sexualization, frustration with cis people, and physical and sexual violence.

Many individual trans people will describe themselves as transfeminine, but when referencing all trans people who could be described as transfeminine, the term "transmisogyny affected" is often more appropriate.

*see also:* TRANSMISOGYNY AFFECTED; TRANS WOMAN; TRANSGENDER; WOMAN; TRANSMISOGYNY; NON-BINARY; ASSIGNED MALE AT BIRTH

**TRANSFEMINISM** — Feminism which centers trans women, and a trans/queer understanding of gender, in its politics.

Transfeminism stands in contrast to trans-exclusionary radical feminists (TERFs), who are neither radical nor feminist.

Transfeminism explicitly acknowledges that trans women are women, and that they face particular struggles under patriarchy due to their trans status.

Feminism should center the most marginalized (poor trans women of color), rather than the most privileged (middle-class white cishet women); not to create an "oppression Olympics," but to make a meaningful effort to focus on the people who are most disenfranchised, and suffer the most violence, under patriarchy.

*see also:* FEMINISM; TERF; PATRIARCHY; TRANSMISOGYNY

**TRANSFORMATIVE JUSTICE** — A community-based alternative to the criminal justice system which prioritizes safety and accountability rather than isolation, punishment, and perpetuating systemic and state violence.

Transformative justice seeks to acknowledge and address harm, interrupt the perpetuation of harm caused, and empower both the victim and the perpetrator to heal.

Transformative justice is not "restorative" or "reparative" justice, because we can't restore things to a state where harm was not caused, and we can't simply "fix" it; instead we must try to transform the situation. One key goal of transformative justice is harm reduction. Other goals include: empowering survivors by centering them and their goals, giving them agency, and prioritizing their safety; accountability and transformation for the person(s) who have caused harm; community action, accountability, and healing; and transformation of the social conditions which perpetuate violence.

Criminal justice focuses on punishment and exclusion, and is rooted in white supremacy, classism, and ableism. The criminal justice system—which includes the legislator, state surveillance, police, courts, prisons, immigration control, and detention centers—purports to solve violence through fear of consequences, which are extreme: isolation, the social stigma of being a prisoner, and the loss of freedom. Navigating the criminal justice system requires resources like time, money, knowledge, respectability, support, and collaboration. The people most likely to be targeted by it are also most likely to lack these resources.

Transformative justice is an important part of activism and community healing for trans and queer people because we are disproportionately harmed and not helped by the criminal justice system.

In practice, transformative justice is survivor-centered. The survivor is assumed to be telling the truth, and is supported and believed, rather

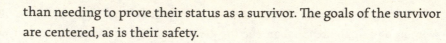

than needing to prove their status as a survivor. The goals of the survivor are centered, as is their safety.

This is all in contrast to the criminal justice system, which doesn't believe survivors, doesn't center their goals, and forces them to reify trauma by engaging with doubtful police and juries. On top of disregarding their mental health, the criminal justice system also puts survivors' safety at risk because it does not actively protect them— naming an abuser is a risky act, and abusers and their apologists retaliate. Survivors are also more likely to be criminalized themselves if they engage with the criminal justice system. They are liable to lose custody of their children, be prosecuted for defending themselves against their abusers, be imprisoned if they have unpaid debts, be charged with "harassing" their abusers in naming them, and be detained and deported if they have unstable immigration status. State violence is, to many survivors, more of a threat than violence from an abuser. State forms of violence are racialized; Black women are especially likely to be failed by the criminal justice system.

Abusers are everywhere: in the police, in the juries, in the judges' chambers. The criminal justice system protects them. The criminal justice system uses many of the same tactics that the abusers use: controlling movement and how time is spent; isolation from community; surveillance of communications; control through power and fear; and verbal, physical, and sexual harassment from guards. Prisons also abuse prisoners through forced sterilization of inmates, solitary confinement, and denial of medical care. Transformative justice seeks to interrupt rather than perpetuate cycles of abuse, in tandem with movements seeking to abolish the criminal justice and immigration systems.

Abolition includes dismantling prisons and detention centers, and getting rid of police, deportation, and state surveillance, while simultaneously building institutions which ensure actual safety and justice. The only reforms to the current system that are welcome are ones which diminish the reach of the state and private institutions, rather than expand them. We want to reduce the number of people incarcerated.

Transformative justice is also strongly opposed to the disposability attitude of the prison system, and the idea that people should be scared into good behavior under threat of punishment, or that it is acceptable to exile and lock people in cages for having made mistakes. Putting people in prison does not keep "good" people safe and punish "bad" people; it perpetuates state violence and provides no meaningful safety for survivors.

What do we do with violent criminals who are "dangers to society"? We need to examine our assumptions about who is considered a violent criminal and whose violence is socially sanctioned (e.g., military generals and arms dealers). Next we must consider if locking up violent people genuinely prevents future violence, by them or anyone else. Aside from being inherently inhumane, is incarceration an effective strategy compared to, say, preventative intervention for people at risk of being violent? I have yet to find evidence that incarceration works effectively as a deterrent, a punishment, a process of rehabilitation, or a method of keeping vulnerable people safe.

Transformative justice only works in a community setting where relationships are fostered and built on mutual aid and solidarity. It also only works if the perpetrator is open to the process, and willing to engage with the fact that they've hurt someone and may be in the wrong.

Everyone is capable of making mistakes and causing harm. There is no good/evil, safe/dangerous dichotomy. Recognizing this helps us see the systemic conditions which cause harm and encourage violence (rape culture) and hopefully will inspire us to collective solutions which do not rely on purity politics.

The responsibility of the harm caused is primarily with the person who caused harm, and secondarily with the community for re/producing the conditions under which harm is caused; it is never with the victim/survivor. Too often the work of accountability falls on the victim/survivor and mimics the criminal justice system: if there's no survivor to bear witness, there's no crime. How do we center the survivor's needs without necessarily placing them at the center of an accountability process (unless they want to be involved at that level)?

Accountability processes fail, and often. To have any chance at succeeding, they need to be collective rather than individualized processes. They cannot rest on a single individual to arbitrate who is right and who is wrong.

We should try to create an environment where it's less stressful for survivors to name harm caused to them: right now, naming the problem makes you the problem (Sara Ahmed). We also need to make it easier for perpetrators to acknowledge and address the harm they caused. Regardless of how a court would interpret the evidence, perpetrators should be held accountable for their actions and their lack of communication or sensitivity, and the priority should be making sure that harm caused is reduced, and that it doesn't happen again.

Feminist pro-survivor language is often weaponized against people; the person with the most social capital, sometimes gained through knowing the most political vocabulary or being most active in the discourse, wields power, which can be abused.

Assaulters are not doomed by default. Being called out (told you've made a mistake) or called in (invited to examine your problematic behavior, in good faith) is a gift. If you have hurt someone, the first step in transformative justice is to recognize that you hurt them, and to apologize. Ask them how they feel, and how they felt, and what they want or need going forward in order to reclaim their agency and feel empowered. Respect these needs, and ask for help if you need it. Get support from your friends to help you be accountable for your actions.

Thank the person you hurt for calling you out. This is a chance for you to grow as a person.

Yes, it's lots of work to empathize with perpetrators, and to hold them accountable, to work through their feelings of defensiveness and guilt with them, to support survivors/victims. Exclusion is a last resort, because it pushes the problem elsewhere. But it still happens, often not because the survivor or community wants to exile someone but because they don't have the resources to engage in a properly done accountability process.

Safety is a process you create through relationships, not a stable state of being. Safety should prioritize the people for whom society is unsafe: survivors, people of color, trans people, women and non-binary people, disabled people, neurodivergent people.

Community leaders should be held to higher standards, not be given more leeway. They benefit from a position of power (whether it is purely social, or institutional as well) and have increased access to resources, and are treated as authority figures. They have more power to control the narrative around events and to look "reasonable" or "right" or "sane" if there is a dispute or accusation made against them. They also have to deal with more scrutiny and pettiness, but their position of power is chosen and they could always relinquish it, step back. To seek status within a radical community is to profit from the unnamed, unappreciated work of marginalized people before you. Community leaders then have a responsibility to be more careful, and to treat others with more care.

This work falls disproportionately on survivors of violence, on women and non-binary people, and on people of color. It is care work; it is emotional labor; it is very tiring.

*see also:* ACTIVISM; VIOLENCE; POLICE (v.); POLICE (n.); EQUITY; EMOTIONAL LABOR; TRAUMA

**TRANSGENDER** — An adjective to describe someone who does not unambiguously identify with the gender they were assigned at birth. Transgender is an umbrella term which includes binary trans men and trans women, and non-binary people including gender fluid and genderqueer people, agender people, and anyone else who does not identify as (and only as) the gender they were assigned at birth. Transgender is often shortened to "trans."

Transgender is often associated with gender dysphoria and body dysphoria, but these are not "required" symptoms to be trans; neither is transition.

Not everyone who falls into this definition calls themselves trans, and it should not be coercively applied to anyone. "Transgender" as a label includes non-binary people (which is itself an umbrella term that includes any gender which isn't strictly and consistently either "man" or "woman"). However, lots of non-binary people feel that they aren't trans even though they aren't cis either. Because "transgender" is associated with transition (social or medical) and dysphoria, there are some people are who aren't cisgender but don't feel comfortable claiming a transgender identity. Claiming transness is very political and subversive and some non-binary people are weary of "appropriating" that struggle when they have relative comfort (e.g., if they don't need to fight for access to trans healthcare, or they are comfortable enough being gendered as the gender they were assigned at birth even if it's not always quite right). However, I would posit that part of the political project of transgender is dismantling cisness, and that calling yourself "trans" does not materially redirect vital resources away from people who are "more trans."

Some people who have transitioned see themselves as no longer transgender, but having a transgender history.

Trans people may change their names, their pronouns, and/or their gender expressions to better reflect their genders. Their trans status is not indicative of anything regarding their bodies: many trans people are not interested in medical intervention.

The assertion that trans people "reinforce gender norms" or "reinforce the gender binary" is misguided and harmful. Trans people are often forced to perform exaggerated gender norms in order to be recognized as their gender. Being seen "as" your gender is not only a matter of comfort and preference but a matter of safety when navigating public space or intimate relationships. The suggestion that trans people should "expand" the roles of their gender assigned at birth places the burden with us instead of with cis people, and completely misunderstands the feeling of dysphoria.

Transness is often reduced to either an illusion of choice, or the "born this way," "trapped in the wrong body" narrative. Both are overly simplistic and neither is right.

Trans women are not very gay effeminate men; trans men are not very gay butch women. There is an undeniable overlap in history, and sometimes gender expression, between these groups but they are not the same.

Trans women are women; trans men are men. It's up to individuals to define their narratives, but a common one is: "I'm assigned female at birth and I want to be a man." Current politics say, condescendingly, "No, you already are a man." However, that's dysphoria: they may not feel like a man until they have hormone replacement therapy, or until they pass and society treats them like a man. We don't transition for abstract, academic reasons, but because we want, we desire, we feel, and we cannot stop wanting.

There is no requirement to totally abandon your "old" self in order to be trans. You can carry contradiction in you. You are allowed to grieve your old self whilst becoming your new self, the same way we are allowed to grieve childhood as we grow into adults.

Transness is constructed not only in opposition to cisness, but through community, which is built on shared experiences of gender, dysphoria, trying to access healthcare and resources (changing gender markers, names, coming out, gendered clothing, having sex in ways which feel good, bathrooms). Some people who don't feel like a part of that community feel they aren't trans, even though they might fit the "definition" of transgender. We can recognize that there is a scale of dysphoria or gendered aggression people receive, while not gatekeeping or policing the boundaries of "trans" to exclude people who aren't cis. Claiming a trans identity is still very much an act of subversion. It is a challenge to cisheteronormative patriarchy and its related oppressive structures.

While people in non-Western cultures, or different time periods, could legitimately describe themselves as transgender by today's definitions, it's important to respect their autonomy and not coercively describe anyone as transgender.

Colonialism was (and remains) extremely damaging and contributed to erasure and stigma about non-cis genders, and culturally specific terms for people's genders should be respected, such as *hijra*, Two-Spirit (and the particular terms within different tribes), and *il femminiello*.

Marsha P. Johnson and Sylvia Rivera, veterans of the Stonewall riots and founders of the Street Transvestite Action Revolutionaries (STAR), described themselves as transvestites rather than transgender, and we would be remiss to erase the complicated histories of these words and, more importantly, the autonomy of the subjects we're describing, by insisting that we call them "transgender."

Transgender as an umbrella term has great utility; but by flattening out all gender non-conformity under a single word, especially without taking into account other marginalizations or privileged positions that an individual holds, the struggles and experiences of women like Johnson and Rivera are co-opted by the most privileged within the transgender community (if such a community can be said to exist). Johnson and Rivera were both not only gender variant, but impoverished women of color who refused to assimilate into what we'd today call settler-colonialist homonormativity.

There is no wrong way to be trans. Some trans people have body dysphoria, some don't; some see transness as mental illness or disability, many don't. Medicalization is a path to legitimacy but we shouldn't need that. While some of the language to describe ourselves is new, transgender people have always existed.

*see also*: NON-BINARY; TERF; TRANS HEALTHCARE; GENDER

**TRANSGENDERISM** — Allegedly the ideology of transgender people, who supposedly seek to propagate that ideology at the expense of cis women. It is not really a word.

TERFs and other transphobes suggest that the existence of trans people is a matter of modern ideology, rather than a historical and cross-cultural fact. Trans activism is framed as ideology which threatens (cis) women's rights, rather than a struggle for civil rights such as access to healthcare and public space, protection from discrimination under the law, and self-determination and bodily autonomy.

*see also*: TERF; GENDER CRITICAL; TRANSPHOBIA

**TRANS HEALTHCARE** — Trans-specific medical intervention for medical aspects of transition. Treatment which mitigates gender dysphoria. All healthcare which trans people need (e.g., non-trans specific things).

Trans-specific healthcare includes:

· Hormone replacement therapy
· Chest reconstruction or augmentation
· Tracheal shave
· Facial feminization surgery
· Laser hair removal
· Vocal surgery
· Genital reconstruction surgery (a broad range of surgeries)
· Hysterectomy (removal of the uterus)
· Vaginectomy (removal of the vagina)
· Oophorectomy (removal of the ovaries)

Other treatment (which should broadly be considered part of trans healthcare, because it mitigates gender dysphoria) includes:

· Change of legal name
· Change of gender marker on identification documents

- Counseling and other mental healthcare
- Voice therapy
- Reproductive healthcare: fertility, gamete storage, family planning, abortion, gynecological exams, prostate exams, trans-inclusive safer sex resources
- Use of prosthetics, wigs, bras, and binders

According to the World Professional Association for Transgender Health (WPATH), the leading international body on best practice regarding trans people:

> *Neither genital appearance nor reconstruction is required for social gender recognition, and so no surgery should be a prerequisite for identity document or record changes; changes to documentation so that identity documents reflect the individual's current lived expression and experience are crucial aids to social functioning, and can be a necessary component of the social transition and/or pre-surgical process. Delay of document changes may have a deleterious impact on a patient's social integration and personal safety.*

WPATH also recognize that not every patient will require the same treatment.

Transness is pathologized as a mental illness in the DSM-5 under gender dysphoria. This classification is embraced by some trans activists because it gives us social and political legitimacy regarding medical transition; it's also embraced by some individual trans people who feel that their transness is disabling in a cisnormative society, or that the medicalized narrative of gender dysphoria matches their experience. In the US, healthcare is often only covered by insurance if it is deemed a "medical necessity": in accordance with standard medical practice, clinically appropriate, and not primarily for the patients' convenience. In order for trans healthcare to be considered a medical necessity, gender dysphoria must then be pathologized and classified as an illness or disease.

WPATH notes: "These medical procedures and treatment protocols are not experimental: decades of both clinical experience and medical research show they are essential to achieving well-being for the transsexual patient." Hormone replacement therapy and gender affirming surgeries are the only treatments which have been empirically proven to effectively treat gender dysphoria in large-scale clinical studies.

The pathologization is criticized because it positions transness as something undesirable to be cured, rather than noting transness as a natural reflection of human diversity and seeking to change the bigotry of society. While many trans activists want gender dysphoria depathologized (because it will reduce stigma, and allow people to self-declare their genders without an "expert" medical or psychiatric opinion), we also recognize that it's currently politically necessary for access to healthcare that it be considered a disease.

There is unfair expectation that trans patients must be 100% sure of their pursuit of hormone replacement therapy or surgery—this burden of certainty is not placed on cis people regarding their genders. This assumes that being 100% sure is possible: that anyone can ever truly know themselves in an objective way. The self is a constant work in progress. Instead, medical professionals should focus on what the goal of healthcare is: to alleviate dysphoria, to be more comfortable in our bodies, to change how we look, to change the ways we are perceived, to explore our bodies and gender(s). It's also imperative to remember that transitioning isn't an on/off switch; there are many aspects of transition, many of them reversible, and we should be free to pick and choose which ones suit us.

*see also:* TRANSGENDER; DYSPHORIA; TRANSSEXUALISM; TERF

**TRANSITION** — A process (social and/or medical) by which a trans person changes their life or body to better reflect their gender.

There are multiple trans trajectories, none of which are more valid than the others.

Medical transition includes (but does not necessitate): hormone replacement therapy, chest surgery, genital reassignment surgery, tracheal shave, facial feminization surgery, laser hair removal, and vocal surgery.

Other aspects of medical transition which do not involve surgery or procedures include: binding, using packers, using padded bras, and tucking. Access to these resources must be considered as important as access to hormones and gender-related surgeries.

Medical transition for trans people with dysphoria, who want it, is deemed medically necessary by trans activists and the World

Professional Association for Transgender Health (WPATH), the leading international organization on trans health. It is not cosmetic or optional.

Social transition might include changing name (legally and in daily life), changing pronouns, changing gender marker on documents, changing wardrobe and physical appearance, altering body language, using different gender-segregated spaces, and coming out.

None of the above is required to be "really" trans. Trans people may or may not pursue social or medical transition, and the procedures or changes they make will vary depending on their dysphoria, access to healthcare, and personal preferences.

Transition is a becoming. We are constantly producing and reproducing ourselves as subjects. There is no linear transition, or a finite end. There is always uncertainty about the future. The becoming is a process, a constant unknowing but doing it anyway. It's okay not to know.

Transition is not necessarily about hating the body. Sometimes we bond with the body even though it feels alien, and we grieve the loss we feel through changing it, whilst also deciding that we want that change (sometimes desperately needing it).

*see also:* TRANSGENDER; HORMONE REPLACEMENT THERAPY; BRAVE; TRANSITION REGRET; TRANSPHOBIA; TRANS HEALTHCARE

**TRANSITION REGRET** — The false notion that most trans people regret medically transitioning.

The phrase "transition regret" flattens out medical transition to a single moment, when it's actually a plurality of medical procedures and interventions. In the case of hormone replacement therapy, transition can be ongoing throughout the trans person's entire life.

Nearly every study done on the subject puts transition regret (for top or bottom surgery) at less than 5%, and most studies place it between 2% and 4%.

Some people who have mild or no physical gender dysphoria, but who want to be seen as a different gender from the one they were assigned at birth, decide that the effort of getting people around them to use different pronouns or names is too exasperating and they "revert" back to the gender they were assigned at birth.

This is a failure of society, not of them as trans people.

Transition regret is a questionable use of the word "regret." "Detransitioners" are assumed to have transition regret, but often don't. Some detransitioners regret their transition, but many desist just to delay it until a better time in their life; some never re-transition but see their transition as an exploration of themselves which they don't regret.

In the UK, 5% of trans people who have medically transitioned in some way report having lowered mental health since before they transitioned: but the reasons they give are loss of family and friends, lack of appropriate support, difficulties finding employment, and other reasons which are "not directly related" to having transitioned. Yet, they are likely to be considered "transition regretters."

The hysteria around transitioning allows no room for trans people to express legitimate fear, anxiety, and concern over their transitions, or anything other than positive feelings about having transitioned, for fear of fueling anti-trans narratives.

Rather than regret, the overwhelming majority of trans people report gender euphoria as the result of transitioning, medically or otherwise.

All surgeries pose risk of regret, but trans-specific surgeries have much lower regret rates than other surgeries: for example, 65% of cis people who get cosmetic surgery regret it. The best practice is to make sure that trans patients can give informed consent, and are supported whether or not they want to medically transition.

*see also:* DETRANSITION; TRANSITION; GENDER DYSPHORIA; TRANS HEALTHCARE

**TRANS MAN** — A man who is transgender. A man who was assigned female at birth.

Trans men are men and are male. Some trans men are also non-binary.

Trans men can have any sexuality or none. Trans men may use any pronouns, and their pronouns do not necessarily indicate anything about their gender.

Note that "trans" here is a modifier word; we do not say "transman."

*see also:* MAN; TRANSGENDER; MALE; TRANS; AFAB; TRANS-MASCULINE; MAN OF TRANS EXPERIENCE

**TRANSMAN** — An incorrect spelling of trans man; "trans" is a modifying adjective.

*see also:* TRANS MAN

**TRANSMASCULINE, TRANS MASC** — Someone who is transgender and assigned female at birth.

The term does not necessarily imply "masculine" or "masc." We should abandon the assumption of gender as a linear spectrum where trans people start at the gender they were assigned (female) and then move toward the "other side" (masculinity).

Despite having problems as a term, like "trans feminine," trans masculine has utility in describing a shared experience (and shared oppressions) of transgender people who were assigned female at birth. Common features of this experience include: erasure and invisibility, frustration with cis people, and sexual violence.

*see also:* TRANSMISOGYNY EXEMPT; TRANS MAN; TRANSGENDER; NON-BINARY; TRANSMISANDRY; ASSIGNED FEMALE AT BIRTH

**TRANSMILITARISM** — The association of transgender civil rights with militaristic objectives, especially imperialism.

Transmilitarism is using transgender rights to signal ostensibly progressive, positive views about the military as a site of public life and public service instead of a racist murder machine. It's holding back critique of military service for fear that the critique will somehow delegitimize the rights of trans people to be free from discrimination.

The phenomenon of transmilitarism can also be seen in other areas of public discourse, where a trans person takes a morally reprehensible stance and trans activists are divided over how to respond because critical response is assumed to undermine the personhood and basic civil rights of the trans person. We're put in a very uncomfortable position of defending people we disagree with because their personhood is being attacked on the basis of their transness. Trans people are held as a monolith which must be supported at all costs, even when we're wrong, which is patronizing.

In the US, in June 2016 the Department of Defense lifted its ban on military service of transgender people, and began to offer hormone and surgical therapies for active duty and reserve service members. In August 2017, the Trump administration proclaimed that transgender people would no longer be allowed to be in the military, but this has essentially been ruled illegal by the US district federal court.

*see also:* HOMONATIONALISM; PINKWASHING

**TRANSMISANDRY** — The specific transphobia and gendered types of violence faced by gender non-conforming masculine or butch trans people who were "Assigned Female At Birth (AFAB)."

This transphobia is created from the assumption that trans men are "really" women, either because they're read as women or because their trans status is known and disrespected.

Transmisandry is a particularly contentious term because it implies that AFAB trans people face oppression on the basis of their maleness or masculinity. I'm asserting that—because all trans genders are inherently gender non-conforming—they do face a gendered oppression. There is no "butch privilege" for masculine, gender non-conforming people; instead they face what I'm calling transmisandrist violence. However, I'm not suggesting that misandry is an axis of oppression faced by cis people.

Trans men face a different kind of transphobia than trans women and transfeminine people, and the current lexicon fails to accurately name this. Trans men and transmasculine people don't experience misogyny, because they are not women—but when they are read as women, they experience gendered discrimination and sometimes violence. I don't think it's appropriate to call it misogyny, even if on the surface it looks the same, because trans men and transmasculine people will not internalize it in the same way as women. But it also feels inaccurate to simply call that "transphobia" because it's specific to assigned female at birth trans people, and I don't want to suggest that the masculine experience is the default for all trans people as "transphobia" implies.

"Misdirected misogyny," "misdirected transmisogyny," and "homophobia" are other ways of framing the gendered violence that AFAB trans people face. There are no perfect terms to describe the gendered types of violence faced by AFAB people who are not women, because the experiences of AFAB trans people vary widely depending on whether or not they are men, how well they pass, how aggressively they assimilate into hegemonic masculinity, and their other visible (or erased/invisible) identities.

Transmisandry is a problematic term because it is weaponized against trans women by TERFs and some trans men. The suggestion is that trans women are trying to silence trans men. This is part of a wider tactic to divide trans people within modern discourse, but it's not trans women who perpetuate transmisandry, it's cis people.

The implication that trans men and trans women face inverse oppressions is dangerously reductive. Trans women don't structurally benefit from "male socialization," and trans men who spend their lives being misgendered as women don't have "male privilege" in a comparable way to cis men. All trans people face gendered violence on the basis of their transness, to different degrees depending on their genders, their gender expressions, their assigned gender at birth, and other aspects of their identities. Visibility in the media is one example: trans men are invisible, and trans women are hyper-visible. The objectifying hyper-visibility of trans women puts all trans women at risk of physical violence; the erasure and invisibility faced by trans men is also oppressive, but relatively less violent.

Transmisogyny and transmisandry are asymmetrical types of violence. Any claim of transmisandry which is used to vilify trans women and other assigned male at birth trans people should be heavily interrogated if not simply dismissed outright.

*see also*: TRANSMISOGYNY; TRANSPHOBIA; TRANSGENDER; TRANS MAN; TRANS MASCULINE; TERF

**TRANSMISOGYNOIR** — The intersecting oppression faced by Black transgender women of color and transfeminine people.

Black trans women and trans feminine people are subject to extreme structural violence and discrimination on the basis of their race and their genders. They are more likely to be: street harassed; fetishized, hyper-sexualized, or de-sexualized; denied access to employment and housing and healthcare; denied access to other aspects of public life; stopped and harassed by police; physically assaulted; sexually assaulted; and murdered. Black TMA people are more likely to be victims of violent crime, but the way they are racialized as Black trans women (or incorrectly as Black men) means they're perceived as being violent, aggressive, and predatory.

Black transmisogyny affected (TMA) people are not afforded complex media representation; but when they are represented (e.g., Janet Mock, Laverne Cox), they are held to exceptionally high standards and subject to relentless harassment. Their cultural and academic contributions are also likely to be diminished, whitewashed, or overlooked entirely.

Alternatively, as is the case with the Stonewall riots, their dissent is reduced to a single moment of "inspiration" porn for people who would have shunned them for their lack of respectability, but now make a profit from their legacies.

TMA people of color, and especially Black trans women and other Black assigned male at birth trans people, are among the most vulnerable in the queer community; yet their oppression also plays out among queers. We must hold ourselves to higher standards of eradicating transmisogynoir both within and outwith the queer community.

The term transmisogynoir is a combination of "misogynoir" (coined by queer Black feminist Moya Bailey) and "transmisogyny" (coined by transfeminist Julia Serano).

*see also:* TRANSMISOGYNY; TRANSMISOGYNY AFFECTED; INTERSECTIONALITY; OPPRESSION; ANTI-BLACKNESS

**TRANSMISOGYNY** — The intersecting oppression of transphobia and misogyny, faced by transgender women and transfeminine people. The majority of transphobia is directed at trans women and transfeminine people.

Transmisogyny is a term coined by transfeminist scholar Julia Serano in 2007 to describe the particular discrimination faced by trans women based on "the assumption that femaleness and femininity are inferior to, and exist primarily for the benefit of, maleness and masculinity."

There are many manifestations of transmisogyny, both structural and personal. Transfeminine people not only face transphobia, but added scrutiny and violence because of their deviance from the maleness they were assigned at birth.

Cisheteropatriarchy punishes transness, it punishes womanhood and femininity, and it especially punishes gender non-conformity in people who are expected to be men.

Transmisogyny affected (TMA) people face increased levels of personal violence and discrimination, are hyper-visible and gazed upon, are patronized as women and non-men, and in a horrible twist of cruelty are told that they have "male privilege" or that their transness is indicative of "male arrogance and violence."

All women experience misogyny and sexual violence, at the very least on a structural level. Many women are groped and harassed; trans women are more likely to be physically attacked or killed by a man who gropes or harasses them if he realizes or suspects that they are trans. Trans women are more likely to be victims of violent crime than cis women, and are far more likely to be victims than perpetrators of violent crime—yet trans women are told they are rapists by virtue of their transness, either because their transness is seen as an intention to gain access to women's spaces for predatory reasons, or because their femininity is a perverse "raping" of womanhood. Conflating trans women with cis men is not only disrespectful and a violent denial of trans women's genders, but it bars them access to resources that they need even more than their cis women counterparts.

Some transmisogynists argue that trans women are not women but male parodies of women arrogantly performing a shallow femininity. This reduces all trans women to a monolith of femininity, which isn't accurate; it vilifies all feminine women as agents of patriarchy reinforcing stereotypes, trans or otherwise. It ignores the fact that trans women are coerced into performing a high femme aesthetic and "lady-like," demure demeanor in order to be read as women and believed to be women (especially when trying to access healthcare), and to ensure their survival in spaces where they feel unsafe if they don't pass. Trans women are forced by wider society to "prove" their dedication to womanhood through a feminine gender expression, and then they are demonized for it.

Trans women don't transition in order to be feminine—boys can be feminine—they transition because they have dysphoria which is alleviated by transitioning, socially and/or medically. There is no implication from trans women that "being a woman" means "wearing a dress," just like there isn't that implication when a cis woman is feminine; it's just a personal expression of gender and taste.

Trans women are represented in the media as tragic figures, sex workers (often dead sex workers), mentally ill, drag queens ("pretend women"), or a punch line to a cheap joke; they are usually played by cis men in films and on television. Trans women are more likely to be sex workers and mentally ill than cis women, because our rotten society is so hostile to them and they are denied other kinds of employment—but the representations of trans women as sex workers or mentally ill are not based on the experiences of trans women in these situations, but on cis assumptions and stereotypes. This is an example of hyper-visibility, where trans women are not in control of their own representation and are not afforded nuance or even humanity, but are under a constant gaze and extreme scrutiny.

Biological essentialism hurts all trans people, but is especially targeted at TMA people. It equates womanhood with vaginas, establishing a hierarchy of womanhood where cis women are at the top, trans women and assigned male at birth (AMAB) trans people who have access to genital reassignment surgery (GRS) are in the middle, and trans women and AMAB trans people who can't have or don't want GRS are at the bottom. Reducing womanhood to genitals is misogynistic and, when done by self-proclaimed feminists, logically inconsistent. We need to recognize that people born with vaginas are oppressed and their bodies are policed, and that trans women are oppressed and their bodies are policed, usually more rigorously than assigned-female bodies.

Transmisogyny can also be more subtle and patronizing; for example, saying "Welcome to womanhood" when a trans woman or assigned male at birth trans person tells you they've experienced sexism or sexual harassment, on the assumption that they have never been attacked for their gender expression before realizing that they are trans. Other small but persistent examples include: misgendering trans women as "he" or "they" when they've clearly expressed using "she"; excessively fawning over them, their clothes, or their makeup, perhaps like you would a small child; excessively praising their femininity as "fierce" or "goddess" or "werk girllll," as though they are constantly offering you a performance of gender rather than simply trying to live; expecting them to do asymmetrical emotional labor; fetishizing them as sexual objects; and generally ignoring or speaking over trans women and other TMA people.

There is a transmisogynist assumption that trans women are "taking up too much space," in discourse or in funding or media; that cis women or trans men are being "pushed out" because we're spending too much time on trans women. Trans women face the majority of the gendered violence under patriarchy, so we should absolutely be prioritizing them and their needs—not only because that's the kind of feminism that I'd hope we want (one which protects the most vulnerable), but because helping trans women will help cis women too. The blame for being bad systems should never fall on the people who are most victimized by them. Instead of attacking trans women for their coping strategies under cisheteropatriarchy, let us dismantle the systems which oppress us all, and attack those who benefit from and uphold them.

Transmisogyny intersects with other forms of structural violence: racism, anti-Blackness (transmisogynoir), classism, ableism, agism, and fatphobia.

*see also:* TRANS WOMAN; TRANSMISOGYNOIR; TRANSPHOBIA; TERF; MALE PRIVILEGE; SOCIALIZED AS A WO/MAN

**TRANSMISOGYNY AFFECTED (TMA), TRANSMISOGYNY EXEMPT (TME)** — The terms are used to describe people who are affected by transmisogyny, in contrast to people who are exempt from transmisogyny.

Trans women, other trans people who were assigned male at birth, and some other groups like third genders in non-Western cultures are transmisogyny affected (TMA).

Trans men, other trans people who were assigned female at birth, and all cis people are transmisogyny exempt (TME); they do not experience transmisogyny. They might experience violence if they are wrongly assumed to be trans women, but this shouldn't be called transmisogyny because they are still exempt from the structural and internal violences of transmisogyny. Some people use the term "displaced transmisogyny" or "misdirected transmisogyny" to describe this; but depending on the context of the violence and the victim, it could also be described as "transphobia," "homophobia," or "misogyny." Our vocabulary here is clunky and insufficient, but it's key to remember that even if a TME individual is subject to violence on the false assumption that they are a trans woman, they are not subject to the same pressures, violences, and discriminations as TMA people, and our focus in these conversations needs to be on the most vulnerable.

*see also:* TRANSMISOGYNY; TRANSPHOBIA; TRANSMISANDRY

**TRANS PANIC** — A legal defense used to justify violence against trans people.

Trans panic defense is most commonly invoked when a man reacts violently to a trans woman or transfeminine person when he learns or assumes her trans status; either because he is intimidated by the existence of trans people or because he was attracted to her and incorrectly thinks that his attraction makes him gay, unless he kills her to prove that he isn't (the violent fragility of masculinity and heterosexuality). It is suggested that the violence is justified by the alleged "deception" of trans people who do not disclose their trans status to their assailants and killers.

This "defense" suggests that it is acceptable to hurt or kill trans people during temporary insanity, and places the blame for the violence with the victim. It is usually invoked in cases where the guilt of the suspect is not in question, in order to play on the transphobia of judges and juries to get a lenient sentence.

Trans panic is considered a valid legal defense in all US states except California, Illinois, and Rhode Island.

The trans panic defense mirrors the gay panic defense.

*see also:* GAY PANIC; TRANSPHOBIA; TRANSMISOGYNY

**TRANSPHOBIA** — Fear of, or contempt for, trans people. Behavior based on those feelings. A system of oppression in which trans people are marginalized and subject to violence.

Trans people face external systemic transphobia and external transphobia on a personal level, which both contribute to a sense of internalized transphobia and self-loathing. Transphobia affects all people who are trans, including non-binary people and anyone who does not unambiguously identify with the gender they were assigned at birth, some of whom may not call themselves transgender. Like all systems of oppression, transphobia intersects with other marginalizations: classism, racism, ableism, misogyny, agism, queerphobia, and fatphobia. Trans women and other assigned male at birth trans people face persistent and considerable transphobia which is particular to their lives as women, called "transmisogyny"; and Black trans women face racialized transmisogyny, called transmisogynoir. Trans men and other assigned female at birth trans people face particular flavors of transphobia as well, which I discuss under the entry "transmisandry" (though this term is extremely contentious).

Statistics are relatively sparse, and sampling the trans population is a difficult task, but the following stats come from the Trans Equality Survey (US, 2015, with 27,715 respondents), a survey launched by the UK government (2011, with 1,275 respondents), and a Scottish Trans Mental Health Study (UK, 2012, with 889 respondents). There is probably overlap between the participants in the UK government study and the Scottish mental health study, though the Scottish study provided considerably more data than the UK government survey. These statistics do not give a complete picture of trans life in the US and UK but do offer insights into the scope of transphobia.

Trans people face rejection from their families for coming out or being gender non-conforming. Many trans people are forced to move away from their friends and family because they are trans and rejected (US 8%, UK 25%). In the UK, 49% of trans people experienced some form of abuse in childhood. In the US, 10% of trans people have faced violence from their family members; 19% have been rejected by their religious community. In the UK, trans parents report seeing their children less after they come out (19%), losing contact with their children as the result of being trans (18%), and having custody issues (8%).

Trans people suffer high levels of harassment, at work, at school, and in public space. Trans people face silent harassment (UK 81%), verbal harassment (US 46%; UK 50% and 73%, from different sources), sexual harassment (UK 38%) and objectification (UK 50%), physical intimidation and threats (UK 38%), and physical violence (US 9%, UK 19%) for being trans.

Trans people are constantly under the public gaze, and we are expected to come out and disclose our trans status to anyone curious enough to ask or unfortunate enough to find us attractive. In the UK, 72% of trans people feel that their trans status is not private and secure from disclosure, and 54% have experienced at least some difficulty from their local community based on their trans identity. Also in the UK, 92% of trans people have been told that being trans is not normal, and 43% say their trans status has actively prevented them from participating in civic and public life.

Trans people are justifiably anxious about being harassed or being the victim in a violent crime (47% UK), and avoid public space (US 20%, UK 25%) and social situations (UK 51%) as a result. In particular, trans people avoid gendered spaces such as bathrooms and gyms (UK 50%, with 77% of trans men avoiding bathrooms).

Trans people also face extremely high levels of sexual violence. In the

US, 47% of trans people have been sexually assaulted at some point in their lives, and 10% were sexually assaulted within the last year. In the UK, trans people report being sexually assaulted (17%) and raped (6%) specifically because they are trans. In the UK, 58% of trans people worry about their safety in relation to having sex. Trans people in the US who have done sex work (77%), experienced homelessness (65%), and have disabilities (61%) were more likely to have been sexually assaulted in their lifetime.

Trans people also suffer very high levels of intimate partner violence (US 54%), many experiencing severe physical violence from an intimate partner (UK 17%; US 24%, compared to 18% of the general population).

Gender dysphoria is a serious and distressing condition, and the only affective treatment is transition into the desired gender role (which may or may not include medical intervention). However, trans healthcare is gatekept and extremely difficult to access due to excessive cost, confusing bureaucracy, and misinformed and bigoted medical professionals. In the UK, 80% of trans people deliberately withheld information from their clinicians and 40% deliberately lied at Gender Identity Clinics (GICs) for fear of being denied care. In the US, 55% of trans people have been denied trans-specific surgeries, and 25% were denied hormone replacement therapy. In the UK, 75% have had delays in accessing treatment for gender dysphoria, and 24% had treatment refused to them. Also in the UK, 29% of trans patients said their GPs refused to address a trans-related health concern, and 54% of trans people were denied trans-related care because their GP did not know enough about the care to provide it—this is both a failure of the healthcare system and a violation of best practice; the onus is on the doctors to educate themselves about the care their patients need.

Further, trans people will often forgo seeing a doctor for issues unrelated to their transness for fear of being mistreated: in the US, 23% reported not going to the doctor when they needed to for fear of being mistreated on the basis of their transness, and 33% said they couldn't afford to go to the doctor when they needed to. In the UK, trans patients report GPs using insulting language about trans people (24%), belittling trans patients for being trans (18%), showing unprofessional curiosity about the trans patients' body (16%), using the wrong name or pronoun on purpose (26%), asking inappropriate questions about their genitals (7%), and asking questions which make the trans patient feel like they're educating the GP (61%).

Trans people are more likely to have disabilities, chronic health conditions, and mental health conditions than the general population. In the UK, 58% of trans people have a disability or chronic health condition, with 36% having a mental health condition and nearly 20% having a learning impairment or some other neurodiversity.

Despite the clear need for trans people to access them, medical and clinical environments are extremely unwelcoming to trans people— often from the very first interaction on a form: "Are you M or F?"— if not outright hostile. To combat this, trans healthcare must be understood holistically rather than only being about procedures which alleviate dysphoria.

Trans people also suffer violence at school and university. In the US, 77% of trans people experienced mistreatment at a K–12 school (ages 5–18), such as being verbally harassed (54%), prohibited from dressing according to their gender (52%), being disciplined for fighting back against bullies (36%), being disciplined more harshly than their cis peers (20%), or being physically attacked (24%) or sexually assaulted (13%); 17% left their K–12 school because they were so severely mistreated. At US colleges and universities, 24% who were out or perceived as being trans were verbally, physically, or sexually harassed.

Trans people have high levels of homelessness over their lifetime (US 30%, UK 19%). In the US, 23% of trans people had experienced housing discrimination in the past year; 26% of those who have been homeless avoided staying at a shelter because they feared mistreatment, and 70% who did stay in a shelter reported mistreatment such as harassment, assault, and being kicked out due to being trans. Trans people in the US are nearly four times less likely to own a home (16%) than the general population (63%).

Trans people suffer economic violences as well. In the US 15% of trans people are unemployed (compared to 5% of the general population), with trans people of color facing higher unemployment rates (up to 35% for Middle Eastern trans people). In the US, 29% of trans people live in poverty (compared to 12% of the general population).

Trans people also face excessive discrimination at work. Trans people are more likely to be fired, denied a promotion, or experience another form of mistreatment at work due to their trans status (US 30%, UK 52%). In the UK, 50% of trans people have faced harassment at work, and 32% said the main source of harassment came from colleagues or employers; 63% said they raised complaints within the organization, and 30% who complained said their complaint was handled poorly. In the US, 77% of trans people took steps to avoid workplace mistreatment such as hiding their gender, delaying their transition, or quitting their job—this would undoubtedly cause high levels of stress. In the UK, 86% of trans people cite employers' anxieties over the possible backlash they'd get from customers if they employed a trans person as an employment barrier; this means that trans people are not only suffering from employment discrimination, but that the work of reassuring our potential employers that we're worth the possible harassment we might face has fallen upon us. In the UK, 7% of trans people have left a job due to transphobic harassment even though they had no other job to go to.

Because trans people are less able to access "legitimate" employment, we often participate in underground economies. In the US, 20% of trans people have done exactly that: 19% have done sex work (with higher rates among trans women of color), 11% have earned money through drug sales, and 2% have made income from another form of criminalized labor.

Sex work is a means of survival for many trans people who cannot access other work; but being a sex worker makes trans people more vulnerable to violence from the state, from partners, and from clients. In the US, 77% of trans people who have done sex work have experienced intimate partner violence, and 72% have been sexually assaulted, a much higher rate than among trans people who have not done sex work. In the US, 86% of trans sex workers, and trans people suspected of doing sex work, who had interactions with the police reported harassment, assault, sexual violence, or other mistreatment from the police.

The state is extremely harsh toward trans people, and the criminal justice system utterly fails us. Trans people report high levels of harassment (14% UK) and mistreatment (58% US) when we interact with the police, on the basis of our trans status. In the US, 22% of trans people arrested in the last year believe they were arrested simply because they are trans. Of the trans people in the US who reported being arrested whilst suspected of doing sex work, 44% said carrying condoms was the basis of the evidence for their arrest.

Trans people in a US prison are over five times more likely to be sexually assaulted by staff than the general prison population, and over nine times more likely to be sexually assaulted by other inmates.

Trans women in the US are much more likely (3.4%) to be HIV-positive than trans men (0.3%), non-binary people (0.4%), and the general population (0.3%). Living with HIV while trans presents its unique barriers to HIV-specific healthcare (such as being denied access to clinics on the basis of transness or gender), trans healthcare (such as being denied surgery, or surgery costs being doubled), and public life generally (people are pressured to "come out" both as trans and as HIV-positive).

Because we suffer so much systemic violence and discrimination, being trans is extremely stressful. In the US, 39% of trans people experienced serious psychological distress in the past month (compared to 5% of the general population). In the UK, trans people have extremely high levels of depression (88%), stress (80%), anxiety (75%), and alcohol dependency issues (62%) at some point in their lives. It is worth noting that most trans people find their mental health greatly improves upon realizing they're trans or receiving a diagnosis for gender dysphoria, and getting their desired clinical treatment (if any).

Trans people have extremely high rates of attempted suicide (US 40%, compared to 4.6% of the general population; UK 45%), with that number slightly higher for trans people under 26 (UK 48%). In the US, 7% have attempted suicide in the past year (compared to 0.6% of the general population). In the US, those whose main income came from criminalized work such as sex work or drug sales were much more likely (27%) to have had a suicide attempt in the past year; and those with supportive families were much less likely (6%) to have attempted suicide in the last year than those with unsupportive families (13%). In the UK, a staggering 84% of trans people report having suicidal thoughts at some point in their lives, with 27% having considered suicide within the last week; yet 25% report not being able to access mental health services. In the UK, suicidal ideation dramatically decreases after transition to 3%.

Trans adults have comparable levels of post-traumatic stress disorder (PTSD) to war veterans—trans people are hyper-vigilant to the possibility of misgendering, social rejection, confrontation, and violence. This not only impacts us when we encounter discrimination and violence; the constant threat is extremely tiring and emotionally taxing.

The legitimacy of trans people is constantly being debated, which allows the political right to use a divide-and-conquer strategy toward feminism and LGBT+ issues. Our lives and our access to public goods (like healthcare and bathrooms) should not be up for debate.

Trans people are falsely accused of reinforcing gender stereotypes and the gender binary. Being trans doesn't enforce the binary; transitioning—claiming an identity which is different from the one you were assigned at birth—is extremely subversive and shows that the gender binary is not a rigid biological reality but a malleable social construct. Many trans people don't conform to gender norms, and often when we do, it's for survival (passing, getting access to healthcare). Trans people do not "codify" norms of binary gender, and this false assumption completely ignores that trans people, non-binary and otherwise, are the pioneers in disrupting the gender binary. Julia Serano satirically suggests that cis people, by their refusal to change sex, reinforce the gender binary and patriarchal system of gender-based oppression.

Trans children face particular mistreatment: they are more likely to be subjected to conversion therapy and be denied medical care based on misinformation about hormone blockers; and they are unlikely to have any viable options for housing outside of their families. This makes trans youth especially vulnerable to homelessness and abusive relationships where they are dependent on someone for money or housing.

On a personal level, trans people suffer individual transphobia from people in our lives. This often happens in a projection of cis insecurity about their own genders, or their ossified ideas about gender. Comments like "But you have male energy," or "You'll always be a woman" reflect a rudimentary understanding of gender as a concept and a bigoted unwillingness to show trans people basic respect; and these comments aren't made until the offending cis person learns that the trans person is trans.

Many cis people assume they understand trans experiences. When they're in positions of power, there is an assumption that they know more about the subject's gender than them. Similarly, cis people will declare that trans people (especially trans women) claim to "know" what it's like to be a cis woman: trans women don't make that claim, but cis women claim to understand the motivations for transitioning.

Cis people might use the idea of "genital preference" to mask their transphobia. Having a preference is fine, but the assumption that all trans people of a certain gender have the same body is transphobic, and a tiring notion that trans people constantly contend with. Many trans people have genital reassignment surgery; many don't. Saying you wouldn't date, for example, a trans man purely because you're "not into vaginas" is transphobic because you're assuming that all trans men have vaginas. It's also telling that trans people's genitals are preemptively scrutinized to a much larger extent than cis people's.

The media representation of trans people is dreadful. We're barely ever represented at all, and when we are it's as flat stereotypes, a tragic plot device, or a cheap joke. Trans women are much more likely to be depicted in the media than trans men and non-binary people, but it's not representation: it's caricature, overwhelmingly written and portrayed by cis people. Poor representation (where we get any) further entrenches stigma and misinformation about trans people which contributes to our increased marginalization.

Given all the structural violences trans people face, you would hope that the cis allies in our lives would be supportive; but trans people are regularly put in a position to comfort cis people who learn about transphobia, centering cisness rather than supporting the trans people actually affected by it. Individual trans people are assumed to be ambassadors of the entire trans population; we are assumed to have an academic interest in gender theory, to be absolutely certain of an imaginary "trans party line," and to be open to answering any and all invasive questions from curious cis people. We are held to extremely high standards, and should we fail to meet them, we're used as an example to tarnish trans people as a group.

Even in LGBT+ groups, trans people are the lowest priority despite being the most vulnerable. Some LGB people suggest we "drop the T from LGBT+," as though trans women of color didn't start (and continue to lead) the whole movement. Erasing trans people from the queer civil rights movement has material consequences, such as the Gill Foundation defunding the fight against anti-trans bathroom bills.

Other examples of cis LGB people failing trans people include the suggestion that trans people don't belong in a group with LGB people because gender and sexuality are different (rather than intrinsically linked); and the suggestion that queer sexuality is different from transness because transness is medicalized and gayness and bisexuality "just are" (as if queer sexuality hasn't been medicalized and pathologized, as if all trans people medically transition, as if gay and lesbian and bisexual trans people don't exist). Some LGB people try to distance themselves from trans people because transness is "too much": too controversial, too confusing, too subversive, too threatening.

Trans people are blamed for the rise of identity politics, and by extension the alienation of "politically incorrect" people on the right and the rise of Donald Trump and neo-Nazis. It's wildly unfair to blame a marginalized group for the rise of their oppressors, but it's also plainly incorrect. Trans people have always existed, and our uncompromising demands for civil rights are not to blame for the recent popularity of fascism: the combination of neoliberal politics and toxic masculinity is. In such an environment, it's even more important that we are unyielding, and that we see the struggles of trans people as inherently linked with other oppressed groups.

*see also:* TRANSMISOGYNY; PINKWASHING; SOCIALIZED AS A WO/MAN; CONVERSION THERAPY; SOCK PUPPET; REPRESENTATION

**TRANSRACIAL** — Someone who is raised in an environment culturally different from their ethnicity.

Transracial people are generally adopted children who are raised by parents of a different race. This has significant emotional consequences: feeling torn between two cultures, being disconnected from your ethnicity and denied intimate knowledge of your birth culture, and carrying the weight of intergenerational trauma within a family context that does not share it. Transracial is a very politically charged term and should only be applied to people who choose it for themselves.

Transracial does not mean "someone born in the wrong race" or someone who feels "dysphoric" about their racial identity. In this context, gender and race are not politically comparable or interchangeable.

*see also:* RACISM; CULTURAL APPROPRIATION; INTERGEN-ERATIONAL TRAUMA

**TRANSSEXUAL** — A generally out of favor term for someone who is not the gender they were assigned at birth. There is an implication of medical transition (previously, and reductively, referred to as a "sex change").

Transgender is now the preferred term, but transsexual is still in use by older trans people who have always used it, and anyone who appreciates the confrontation of the word.

Transsexual became a legitimate and named identity in the Anglophonic world when Christine Jorgensen, an American trans woman, had genital reassignment surgery in Denmark in 1952.

Because there is stigma attached to trans people and it is suffixed with "sexual," transsexual implies a sexual deviance. It's become a somewhat anti-assimilationist term, unapologetic about the link between sexual desire and gender. It plays into the genuine fear of many transphobes of the "scary transsexual" with levity.

see also: TRANSGENDER; TRANS HEALTHCARE

**TRANSSEXUALISM** — A disease according to the *International Statistical Classification of Diseases and Related Health Problems, (Tenth Revision)*, published by the World Health Organization.

see also: TRANSSEXUAL; TRANS HEALTHCARE; TRANSPHOBIA; PATHOLOGIZE

**TRANS TIME** — A trans-specific experience of time and aging. This is not so much a phrase which is in use (like queer time), but it's a phenomenon which I'd like to explore.

Trans kids who use hormone blockers have a delayed puberty. Trans people who start hormone replacement therapy as adults go through a second puberty. Trans people enter physical adulthood late, and sometimes twice. Trans adults sometimes let themselves live a childhood in their correct gender by insisting that they are, for example, "a boy" but not "a man"; in practical terms, trans people who transition as adults and want to change their gender expression need to learn how to do that: how to apply makeup, or shave, or dress differently, or do their hair differently. And then, they must learn to navigate society with a different gender presentation: how to respond to street harassment, norms about socializing with different genders, unspoken rules about gendered public spaces like bathrooms which are different for different genders; all while they are going through radical self-exploration. This can all feel very adolescent.

Anecdotally, it's very difficult to guess the age of trans people, whether or not they are on hormones. The trans people that I know all look about a decade younger than their actual age. Perpetual disbelief about our ages is amusing but probably contributes to a strange sense of time. As I alluded above, we often don't "dress our age," either because we don't yet know how, or we don't want to. Being queer gives us license to be more flamboyant into adulthood, but beyond that we're also exploring the "younger" aspects of our gender, fully, for the first time; sometimes well past adolescence.

Of course any stigma about this largely falls on women and feminine-presenting people because men are afforded a sloppy masculinity throughout their entire lives, whereas a woman who wears a skirt too short or a lipstick too bright loses respectability (women are not allowed to dress young, nor to age—there's no winning!). Trans women are judged even more harshly for this than cis women. Their femininity is held to a higher standard because they are expected to "prove" their sincerity and the legitimacy of their genders. Trans men and masculine trans people are also expected to conform to gender norms, but deviance from those norms is not as widely punished, partly because our genders are invisible: a trans boy wearing makeup isn't punished for deviating from masculinity because he's not seen as man.

Like queer time generally, trans people don't necessarily hit cisheteronormative milestones, or at least we don't necessarily hit them on time and in order. We're disenfranchised from public life, so less able to cultivate a stable life through a secure and comfortable career and stable housing, which impacts our personal lives and ability to have relationships, get married, and raise a family—assuming we want any of that.

see also: QUEER TIME; TRANSMISOGYNY; TRANS HEALTHCARE

**TRANSVESTITE** — An alternative term for CROSS-DRESSER.

There is a great deal of historical overlap between cross-dressers, drag performers, LGBQ+ people, and trans people. Many people who have previously identified as transvestites might identify themselves as transgender today, but we should honor the labels they chose, and the imperfections of our language.

see also: CROSS-DRESSER

**TRANS WOMAN** — A woman who is transgender. A woman who was assigned male at birth.

Trans women are women, and are female. Some trans women are also non-binary and might feel affinity for other genders as well. Trans women can have any sexuality or none. Trans women may use any pronouns, and their pronouns should not necessarily be taken as an indication of their gender.

Trans women face particular oppressions at the intersection of their transness and their womanhood. This is called "transmisogyny."

Note that "trans" here is a modifier word; we do not say "transwoman."

*see also:* WOMAN; FEMALE; TRANSGENDER; TRANS; AMAB; TRANSFEMININE; TRANSMISOGYNY; WOMAN OF TRANS EXPERIENCE

**TRANSWOMAN** — An incorrect spelling of trans woman, sometimes used deliberately to dehumanize and set trans women apart from cis women.

*see also:* TRANS WOMAN

**TRAP** — A derogatory term for trans people, especially trans women, who are alleged to "deceive" straight men into finding them attractive.

The idea of a trans person deceiving you into fucking them is a sexual fantasy, with no basis in reality. Trans people are not trans because they fantasize about "trapping" or tricking straight people into sex. The cultural obsession with this reveals much more about cis insecurities and fetishes than it does about trans intentions.

*see also:* PASSING; TRANSMISOGYNY; HOMOPHOBIA

**TRAUMA** — A disordered psychological or emotional state or behavior as the result of a severely stressful mental or emotional or physical event or series of events.

Not all potentially traumatic events leave people traumatized. People respond to traumatic events in different ways depending on how they're best able to cope.

Both personal and collective trauma are normalized aspects of the lives of many queer people. Queer people are liable to experience collective trauma from persistent queerphobia in our culture: homophobia, transphobia, transmisogyny, and aphobia all compound with other systems of oppression.

Historic queerphobia—for instance pathologization, criminalization, the AIDS crisis and the effective mass murder of queers by negligence, social intimidation through violence, and the Holocaust—creates a tapestry of collective intergenerational violence against queers, which many queers find traumatizing.

Queer people are also more likely than cishet people to experience personal traumas: sexual violence, conversion therapy, physical violence and intimidation, police violence, eviction and homelessness, familial violence, domestic and intimate partner violence, and discrimination and social ostracization. Public space and the body are both likely sites of violence and trauma for queer people.

While trauma can be a key factor in the lives of many queer people, queerness is not defined solely by its relationship to trauma and violence. Queer people are more than the sum of their scars.

*see also:* VIOLENCE; SURVIVOR; AIDS; TRANSFORMATIVE JUSTICE

**TROLL** — Someone online who posts inflammatory comments with the intent of provoking an emotional response, often for the troll's amusement.

Trolls are deliberately antagonistic. Trolling tactics include using "devil's advocate" and bad faith arguments, derailing discussions, insisting on the dictionary definition of sociological terms, blatant harassment, "Wouldn't it be ridiculous if...?," pedophile genders, and use of irony to obfuscate and normalize bigoted positions.

Trolls are typically best ignored. They are not interested in a genuine discussion or debate, and engagement only gives them a bigger platform while exhausting the person they're targeting.

*see also:* SOCK PUPPET; CONCERN TROLLING

**TROUSER ROLE** — A woman actor playing the role of a man, wearing men's clothes. It's also called a "breeches role."

Trouser roles were especially common in opera where cis women would play the parts of pre-adolescent boys, because they had the appropriate vocal ranges for the part. Trouser roles also came out of Victorian pantomime's "principle boy," or the boy protagonist, traditionally played by a woman in boys' clothes—child labor laws meant that adults had to play the parts of children.

Subverting gender roles—allowing women actors to engage in "masculine" behavior and dialogue, but still sexualizing them as gender deviants and sex treats in disguise—was very tantalizing to audiences, especially when the actor's legs would only be covered in masculine tights.

Today, a man performing in women's clothes is much more controversial, sensational, and novel than a woman performing in man's clothes, but that wasn't always the case. When women started performing trouser roles in the 1660s it was a scandal. Predictably, as the difference between men and women's clothing became less exaggerated, crossdressing women have become less shocking.

As a concept in theater and opera, it is assumed that the audience accepts the character as a man even if they know that the actor is not. There's something queer about this: the fluidity of gender as a performance, that with the right cues anyone can signal (and change) their gender role, and the audience will not only understand and accept it but applaud it. It's a shame that trans and queer people aren't afforded such a warm reception unless we are on stage, entertaining.

Sometimes characters who are men will be played by women actors as a production decision, but that doesn't make it a trouser role; a genderqueered Hamlet doesn't make Hamlet a trouser role. Peter Pan could be considered a modern trouser role or "principle boy."

*see also:* CROSS-DRESS; DRAG

**TRUSCUM** — People who insist that transness is a medical condition defined by physical dysphoria, and that without physical dysphoria and the desire to "fully" medically transition, one is not trans.

Truscum are often trans people themselves, and are invested in the medicalization of transness because they believe it lends them legitimacy when arguing with transphobes. Truscum deny the existence of non-binary people and insist that anyone who doesn't want to medicalize their transition is "fake" and a "transtrender," allegedly only claiming a transgender identity for attention or social capital.

*see also:* TRANSGENDER; GATEKEEP; GENDER DYSPHORIA; POLICE (v.); RESPECTABILITY; TRANS HEALTHCARE

**TS** — Short for TRANSSEXUAL, in use in some online spaces.

**TUCKING** — A technique for adjusting the penis and testicles so there is no visible bulge through clothing.

Tucking involves gently pushing the testicles up into the inguinal canal and pulling the penis backwards between the legs. A tuck is maintained with tight clothing and/or medical tape.

Tucking is done by trans people, drag queens, cross-dressers, and anyone who wants to flatten the appearance of their genitals.

If you want to try tucking, go slowly and gently. Please don't dehydrate yourself because you can't be bothered to undo your tuck to pee.

*see also:* PACKING; TRANSGENDER; DRAG; MUFFING

**TV** — Short for TRANSVESTITE, in use in some online spaces.

**TWINK** — A gay archetype. A queer who looks boyish, thin, waifish, hairless, and effeminate.

Twinks are associated with effeminacy, vulnerability, boyish mischief, and youth. Twinks are also associated with bottoming, but like anyone they could favor any sexual position or role.

Twink can be both an empowering declaration of effeminacy and an insult hurled to disparage a failure of hegemonic masculinity. Gay slang has made space for queer people to define ourselves, but its borders are also heavily policed—until very recently, only white men could be considered twinks. Men of color were, and largely still are, denied the nuance of sexuality afforded to white men. Black men in particular are hyper-sexualized as dominant and aggressive, and never allowed to have youthful innocence, which excludes them from twinkdom. Anyone who doesn't fit into the dyadic body types of slender twink or muscled jock is made to feel undesirable.

Because it captures an aesthetic, a relationship to other bodies/ power, and gendered characteristics, twink is itself a gender.

Any use of the word twink to describe people who aren't queer is simply ahistorical—twink is a queer word, to describe queer people. There is no "straight twink" because twink is more than a body type; it's a positionality in relation to other queer bodies, as old as ancient Greece.

Queers today are still pressured to define themselves as twinks (bottoms) or daddies (tops), as if these are discrete categories capable of capturing the complexity of our gendered and sexual experiences.

There has been some media coverage of twinks suggesting that this archetype could "save" masculinity. Moralizing body types is an incredibly dodgy political project, but that besides, twinks won't save us. The modern "crisis of masculinity" comes from a collective realization that toxic masculinity is unsustainable; but this has nothing to do with hairlessness, and everything to do with men repressing their emotions, a lack of empathy, and masculine entitlement.

*see also:* GAY CULTURE; BEAR; OTTER; CUB; ANTI-BLACKNESS

**U = U** — Undetectable = Untransmittable, a contemporary health campaign by Prevention Access Campaign to educate the public about HIV and reduce stigma about living with HIV.

The US Center for Disease Control, under pressure from the U = U campaign, released a statement in September 2017 saying that "People who take ART [antiretroviral therapy] daily as prescribed and achieve and maintain an undetectable viral load have effectively no risk of sexually transmitting the virus to an HIV-negative partner." It's commonly accepted that once a patient's viral load has been undetectable for six months, they are at no risk of transmitting HIV.

*see also*: UNDETECTABLE

**UNDETECTABLE** — An HIV status, where the person is HIV-positive but has a viral load which is low enough not to appear in HIV tests, and is therefore extremely unlikely or not at all likely to transmit the virus.

Once a patient has reached an undetectable viral load for at least six months, there is no risk of them transmitting the virus.

Undetectable status can be reached for HIV-positive patients who undergo antiretroviral therapy. About half of the people living with HIV in the US are undetectable. In the UK, over 90% of people diagnosed with HIV have reached an undetectable viral load.

*see also*: HIV; POZ; AIDS; PrEP; PEP

**UNISEX** — Gender neutral, designed for anyone to use.

Many products marketed as being unisex are actually quite masculine, because masculinity is afforded the "default" status while femininity is gendered. There is an implication that women will use masculine-coded items and clothing, but men will not use anything in proximity to femininity lest it undermine their masculinity and heterosexuality.

*see also:* GENDER NEUTRAL

**UNNATURAL** — *see:* NATURAL.

**URANIAN** — A 19th-century term for "third sex," or someone with a "male body and female psyche" who is attracted to men.

The uranian is an early pathology of (straight) trans women, later expanded to include butch women who had sex with women, and other sexual deviants of the time.

Uranian was first used in print by Karl Heinrich Ulrichs in a series of five books published 1864–1865. The term was derived from the goddess Aphrodite Urania, who was created out of the testicles of the god Uranus. The Uranian's heterosexual opposite is Dionian, derived from Aphrodite Dionea.

Uranian is a German word, but I'm including it because it was used by prominent Anglophonic scholars on gender and sexuality, and was maybe the first identifying term for homosexuals as an identity instead of denoting sexual behavior.

Uranian predates the first public use of "homosexual," first published in an anonymous pamphlet in 1869. Uranian was adopted into Victorian academic and activist language and was used to advocate for homosexual emancipation. It was suggested that Uranian love was comradely, and would unite the estranged ranks of society and bring about a true democracy without class or gender barriers.

Already we see the marriage of gender and sexuality, though Ulrichs eventually learned that not all men attracted to men are feminine (or trans). He later divided people on three axes: sexual orientation (male-attracted, bisexual, or female-attracted); preferred sexual behavior (active, no preference, passive); and gender characteristics (masculine, intermediate, feminine). It's interesting to note that Ulrichs did not define sexual orientation as a position of "same" or "opposite" gender attraction and based it on the gender only of the object of attraction, not the subject. Ulrichs himself was a *"Weibling"* or "feminine homosexual" who preferred an active role in sex.

Below is the taxonomy or uranismus, by Ulrich, with expanded modern terms (note that "-in" in German is a feminine suffix).

| Ulrichs' taxonomy | Gender identity | Gender characteristics | Sexual orientation | Modern taxonomy |
| --- | --- | --- | --- | --- |
| Urning | Assigned male, with a female psyche | | Attracted to men | Straight trans woman |
| Urningin | Assigned female, with a male psyche | | Attracted to women | Straight trans man |
| Dioning | (Cis) man | Masculine | Attracted to women (heterosexual) | Cishet masculine man |
| Dioningin | (Cis) woman | Feminine | Attracted to men (heterosexual) | Cishet feminine woman |
| Uranodioning | (Cis) man | Masculine | Bisexual | Bi butch man |
| Urano-dioningin | (Cis) woman | Feminine | Bisexual | Bi femme woman |
| Zwitter | Intersex | | | Today we recognize that intersex is not itself a gender |

Ulrichs later expanded on *Urningthum* (male homosexuality) using the following terms (with some amusing, roughly equivalent modern terms):

| Ulrichs' taxonomy | Gender identity | Gender characteristics | Sexual orientation | Modern taxonomy |
| --- | --- | --- | --- | --- |
| Mannling | Feminine psyche | Masculine appearance | Attracted to effeminate men | Butch gay |
| Weibling | (Cis) man | Feminine appearance | Attracted to masculine men | Queen |

*cont.*

| Ulrichs' taxonomy | Gender identity | Gender characteristics | Sexual orientation | Modern taxonomy |
|---|---|---|---|---|
| Manuring | (Cis) man | Feminine appearance | Attracted to women | Effeminate straight man |
| Zwischen-Urning | (Cis) man | Androgynous | Attracted to "young normal chaps" | Twink |
| Conjunctive | | | Romantically and sexually attracted to men | Gay |
| Disjunctive | | | Romantically attracted to men, but sexually attracted to women | Bromance |
| Virilisietre Mannlinge | Urnings | Feminine, but masculine-behaving | Attracted to men but pretend to be attracted to women | Straight acting, cis acting |
| Uraniaster | A Dionings i.e., (cis) man | Masculine | Attracted to women but situational homo-sexuality, e.g., homo-social spaces like the military | A "no homo" straight man who has same-sex experiences |

see also: PATHOLOGY; TRANSGENDER; INVERT; BORN THIS WAY

**VE/VER** — A gender neutral neopronoun.

Like ne/nir, ve/ver is derivative of both he/him and she/her, to create a gender-balanced, gender neutral pronoun.

Like all pronouns, the use of ve/ver doesn't necessarily indicate anything about the user's gender; anyone can use gender neutral pronouns.

| Ve is nice | I smiled at ver | Vis friends are cool | That's vis | Ve loves verself |
|---|---|---|---|---|

*see also:* PRONOUNS; NEOPRONOUNS; GENDER NEUTRAL LANGUAGE

**VER** — *see:* VE/VER.

**VERSATILE, VERS** — Gay slang to describe someone who sexually enjoys both topping and bottoming.

Vers, as a category, destabilizes the false binary between top and bottom. It also disrupts the assumptions which get packaged with position and gender expression: that tops are dominant, large, and butch, while bottoms are submissive, small, and femme.

The language of top/bottom/vers is used by some as an identity label, but it doesn't have to be. The purpose of these labels is to make it easier for queer people to find sexual partners, not to define your identity (unless you want it to).

*see also:* TOP; BOTTOM

**VICTIM** — Someone who has suffered violence.

Queer and trans people are made into victims by violence enacted upon us. We're more likely to be physically assaulted, but also denied access to life-sustaining resources like housing and healthcare and employment. We are also victimized and denied agency in dominant narratives and microaggressions.

Some people who are victimized prefer to label themselves as survivors rather than victims; but either label can be empowering, depending on the feelings of the individual using it.

While queer people are routinely victimized, it's important to note that the queer experience is not solely defined by victimhood. There is also queer joy, queer love, queer family, queer success, and gender euphoria.

*see also:* SURVIVOR; VIOLENCE; TRANSFORMATIVE JUSTICE

**VIOLENCE** — A wide range of harms, both structural and personal.

Violence exists on a large scale. It is not especially useful to try to quantify violence and figure out who is "more oppressed" based on a checklist of their identities. Violence has many forms, including: physical, emotional, sexual, psychological (coercion), spatial (crossing boundaries between living space and work), collective social (bullying, weaponized activism, cultural violence), economic (poverty), and financial (withholding money, controlling spending).

Violence can be direct; or indirect, like silencing, erasure, disenfranchisement, structural negligence (e.g., no healthcare or housing), denial of resources, fetishization, hate speech, and respectability politics.

When it happens to entire groups of people, we experience collective violence which can result in inter-generational trauma, such as slavery, poverty, and the AIDS crisis.

Violences are both events and conditions, which are constantly reproduced. Everyone is capable of perpetuating violence, and to varying degrees we all participate in violent systems (such as capitalism); purity politics are of little use. But if we have principles of harm reduction, we can work to diminish the scale of violence.

The rhetoric of "violence on both sides" creates a false equivalence of power between self-defense (sometimes preemptive) and harmful people with structural power. "Queers bash back!" and "Kill all men" are violent (fantasies) but are not the same as structural violence because they do not pose a structural threat.

The "both sides" rhetoric also suggests that both sides are worthy of the same attention, and the same platform. But when we give violent speech (e.g., transmisogyny or white supremacy) a platform for "debate," we're legitimizing hate as a reasonable political opinion,

**V**

and it becomes normalized. Hate speech should not be dignified with a response. When people demand that we respond "reasonably" and politely to hate speech, they are demanding exhausting emotional labor from the people most affected by that hate speech. We shouldn't have to justify our existence; our basic human rights are not up for debate.

The "both sides" debate also assumes that both sides are equally invested in being reasonable, fact-checking, and listening to each other with empathy. It's unfair to expect marginalized people to empathize with people who dehumanize us. That besides, it's a total lost cause trying to debate with people who hold hateful views, because they are not interested in telling the truth, or adjusting their views to reflect facts or the experiences of other people. That energy would be better invested in living a dignified and compassionate life, highlighting the shared violences different groups face and working together to combat them; that is, instead of debating hate speech, we might lead by example.

see also: OPPRESSION; SILENCE; TRANSFORMATIVE JUSTICE; RESPECTABILITY; POLICE (v.); POLICE (n.)

**VIRGIN** — Someone who has never had sex.

Virginity is not a physical state; it's a social concept used to describe sexual experience, and can only be defined by the individual.

see also: SEX (v.); PATRIARCHY

**VIS** — see: VE/VER.

**VISIBILITY** — The ability to be seen, witnessed, recognized, and understood; to be given a platform on which to be visible.

The hegemonic culture is the most visible. Anything which deviates from the norm needs to fight to be visible.

Visibility brings representation, which can be positive or negative. Trans visibility, for example, has exponentially increased (largely for trans women). This allows other trans people to see that we're not alone, and that being trans is a possibility; but it has also left us vulnerable to hate speech, public "debate" about our personhood, harassment, and trolling.

The opposite of visibility is "erasure." Hyper-visibility is when a group is gazed upon but not afforded their own voice or agency.

see also: INVISIBILITY; ERASURE; VIOLENCE; RESPECTABILITY; REPRESENTATION

# W

**WHITEWASHING** — Erasing the contributions and identities of people of color in order to center white people.

Queer culture and mainstream culture are both extremely whitewashed.

*see also:* RACISM; ERASURE; PINKWASHING

**WHORE** — Pejorative (some would say slur) to describe full-service sex workers, anyone profiled as a full-service sex worker, or anyone (usually women) deemed too promiscuous or too provocative in their dress.

Using whore as a slur is part of wider culture of misogyny, slut-shaming, and whorephobia.

Some sex workers police the borders of who's allowed to use the word "whore," suggesting that people who are racialized and assumed to be street sex workers (e.g., Black trans women often face this stigma) shouldn't use it. Others think that if someone is targeted by the violence of a word (and the material consequences which go with it), regardless of whether they hold the identity that goes along with the word or are just perceived to hold that identity, they should be allowed to use it.

Whore has its etymological roots in a 1530s spelling alteration of Old English "hore," which meant prostitute, from Proto-Germanic *horaz* (fem. *horon-*), "one who desires." The Middle English homonym "hore" meant "physical filth, slime," or "moral corruption, sin." It has been a general term of abuse for an unchaste or lewd woman (without regard to money) from at least c.1200, and of male prostitutes since the 1630s.

*see also:* WHOREPHOBIA

**WHOREPHOBIA** — Violence toward and stigma surrounding sex workers.

Sex workers are disproportionately queer and trans, because queer and trans people are denied access to "civilian" jobs (jobs outside of the sex industry).

Whorephobia includes the direct threats of violence that sex workers face from the state, their partners, their clients, and the public, as well as a culture of stigma and shame surrounding sex work, especially full-service sex work.

Sex work has long been an area of debate in feminism: "Is sex work feminist?," and "Is sex work work?" Rather than critiquing the choices made by vulnerable people to survive in a hostile world as "unfeminist," our feminism should endeavor to give everyone the agency to make meaningful choices about the kind of work they do (if any). This means creating conditions where people aren't economically forced into work they don't want to do. Sex work is positioned as being uniquely coercive and undignified, but under conditions of capitalism all work is coercive and much of it is undignified. Sex workers are not a monolith: many enjoy their jobs, many don't, and most fall somewhere in the middle. Forcing sex workers to reduce their experiences to a sound bite of "happy hooker" or "tragic victim" is one aspect of whorephobia.

Whorephobia also conflates sex work with sex trafficking—the definitive difference between the two is consent. Many sex workers are organized into unions and collectives, many of which have members who have also been victims of sex trafficking. We would do well to listen to them, rather than speak over them in clumsy and dangerous attempts to "rescue" them. The key things that modern sex worker collectives are campaigning for are the decriminalization of sex work (in contrast to legalization and the so-called Nordic model which criminalizes clients and by extension makes sex work less safe), and the importance of net neutrality without state surveillance.

*see also:* WHORE

**WLW** — Acronym for WOMEN WHO LOVE WOMEN.

**WOMAN** — An adult human who identifies with womanhood.

Gender is sloppy and evasive—womanhood is defined by a connection to femininity, a connection to other women, and its relationship to power.

Womanhood could also be defined in opposition to manhood, but this is largely tautological. Womanhood is not a coherent, monolithic group.

Womanhood is not defined by body parts or genetics.

*see also:* GENDER; MAN; FEMININITY; PATRIARCHY

**WOMANISM** — A strand of feminism born out of the limitations of second-wave feminism, particularly its failure to account for Black women and other marginalized women.

Womanism was first used by Black feminist author Alice Walker in 1981.

*see also:* FEMINISM; INTERSECTIONALITY

**WOMAN OF TRANS EXPERIENCE** — The preferred term for many women who are not cis but don't necessarily center their transness in their womanhood.

Alternative terms include "trans woman," "assigned male at birth," or "assigned-male," "transfeminine," and "trans femme." The terms any individual uses to describe themselves will be based on personal preference and subcultural connotations, and should be respected.

*see also:* TRANS WOMAN; TRANSFEMININE

**WOMEN AND NON-BINARY SPACES** — A safe(r) space for anyone who isn't a man, in recognition that men hold a position of privilege over women and non-binary people. They are also called "women and gender variant spaces."

Safer spaces are important sites of healing and organization for marginalized people. But are these women and non-binary spaces actually safe and inclusive for trans women and trans femmes? This is an especially relevant question regarding trans women and femmes who don't pass, or don't care about passing, or don't medically transition.

We must also acknowledge that cis women also perpetuate gendered violence, and that trans men are often allowed into spaces under this name even though they are men; privilege and oppression, and the capacity to perpetuate violence, do not exist on only a single axis (gender).

*see also:* SAFER SPACE; WOMAN; NON-BINARY

**WOMEN'S LIBERATION** — The struggle for emancipation for women from patriarchy and intersecting systems of oppression.

Some feminists viewed queer issues and lesbianism as a distraction from women's liberation, while anyone half-decent sees them as inseparable. In the 1970s, the key demands of the women's liberation movement were: equal pay; equal education and job opportunities; free contraception and abortion on demand; free 24-hour nurseries; financial and legal independence; and an end to discrimination against lesbians and a woman's right to define her own sexuality.

Feminism and women's liberation has had a conflict between race and white feminism: Black feminists Audre Lorde and bell hooks, among many others, challenge the idea of a universal (white) womanhood.

*see also:* FEMINISM; WOMAN; INTERSECTIONALITY

**WOMEN WHO LOVE WOMEN (WLW)** — Women who are sexually or romantically attracted to women. They are sometimes called "Women who have Sex with Women (WSW)," and also "Sapphic."

Women who Love Women is different from gay, bisexual, queer, and other sexuality labels because it's not centered on identity but on behavior. This makes room for women who are hesitant to claim queerness to describe their sexual and romantic life; accounting for this is especially important in a sexual health setting.

Women who Love Women also flattens out different queer identities, which is useful for solidarity, highlighting the shared experience of being a woman who loves women.

*see also:* SAPPHIC; WOMAN

**WOMYN, WOMBYN** — Alternative spellings of "woman" and "women," used by some feminists to reject the "-men" suffix and by extension the definition of women as relational to men. Wombyn is an alternative spelling which equates womb with womanhood.

Womyn and wombyn are criticized as terms for being transphobic and biologically essentialist.

Womyn first appeared in print in reference to the Michigan Womyn's Music Festival.

*see also:* WOMAN; TERF; FEMINISM; CAMP TRANS

**WSW** — Acronym for "Women Who Have Sex With Women."
*see also:* WOMEN WHO LOVE WOMEN

# X

**X** — A third gender alternative to M (male) or F (female) on identifying documents.

At the time of writing, Australia, Canada, Germany, India, Nepal, New Zealand, Pakistan, and some places in the US allow X gender markers or other third-gender markers.

The link between legal gender recognition and social acceptance and freedom from discrimination is strong, but not absolute. Legislation codifies and reproduces social hierarchies. But, just because some countries allow for legal recognition of a third gender on certain documents, it does not mean that the material conditions for trans people in those places are better, and access to changing your gender marker will depend on other socio-economic factors such as administrative fees, time cost, ease of navigating bureaucracy, and safety regarding being out.

*see also:* GENDER RECOGNITION; NON-BINARY; OUT

**XE/XEM** — A gender neutral pronoun, pronounced the same as "ze."

Xe pronouns can be used by anyone—using gender neutral pronouns or language does not necessarily indicate anything about the user's gender.

Xe represented an aesthetic change away from the feminine leanings of "ze" pronouns. The X has a "Z" sound, but this is not immediately obvious to people unfamiliar with the pronouns, which makes them fairly uncommon.

| Xe sighed | I smiled at xe | Xer friend is nice | That's xers | Xe likes xemself |
|-----------|----------------|--------------------|-------------|------------------|
| | I smiled at xyr | Xyr friend is nice | That's xyrs | |

*see also:* ZE; PRONOUNS; GENDER NEUTRAL LANGUAGE

**X**

**XEM** — *see:* XE/XEM.

**XENOFEMINISM** — A feminist politic focused on biohacking, post-capitalism, and gender abolition.

Xenofeminism was developed by the feminist collective Laboria Cuboniks in Xenofeminism: a politics for alienation (2015). Xenofeminism is anti-naturalist, unconcerned with respecting the so-called laws of nature. It's a call to arms to change nature, which "has nothing to offer us" if we are women, queer, trans, and/or disabled: "If nature is unjust, change nature!" Nothing is too sacred to hack and wield in the struggle for emancipation, including our languages and our bodies.

Xenofeminism positions itself after post-modernity and is less focused on identity politics; in fact, it chastises the puritanical virtue signaling and fetishization of oppression on modern social media. Xenofeminism does not strive for purity, but for "better corruption."

Gender abolitionism here is not shorthand for homogenizing or "ending" gender, but ending the asymmetrical power relations of gender under patriarchy.

Xenofeminism builds on cyberfeminism—the virtual and the material are understood as interconnected and equally real. It also incorporates aspects of queer theory, critical race theory, and Marxist-feminism. Critiques of xenofeminism highlight that humanity is not afforded or denied equally, and that xenofeminism should more explicitly account for these differences.

*see also:* BIOPOLITICS; GENDER; FEMINISM

**XER** — *see:* XE/XEM.

**XYR** — *see:* XE/XEM.

**YONI, YONIC** — A stylized representation of a vagina.

Yoni is Sanskrit for "vagina," "womb," "uterus," "vulva," "abode," and "source." In Hinduism, the yoni is a symbol of the goddess Shakti. Along with yoga, in which the Yoni mudra (hand symbol) is central, the yoni symbol has been appropriated by non-Hindu white people in the West. The yonic symbol is often associated with feminism.

The yoni is used by TERFs and biological essentialists to suggest a "sacred femininity" which is inherent to vaginas. Linking vaginas to femininity not only excludes trans women from womanhood, but it reduces cis women to their genitals. The conflation of gender with genitals is not only alienating but dangerous, because it gives license for transphobic people to police and violate trans genders and trans bodies.

*see also:* BIOLOGICAL ESSENTIALISM; TERF; TRANSMISOGYNY; CULTURAL APPROPRIATION

**ZE/ZIR, ZE/HIR** — A gender neutral pronoun, alternatively spelled "zie."

Anyone can use ze pronouns—the use of gender neutral pronouns does not necessarily indicate anything about the user's gender.

Ze is derived from the earlier neutral pronoun "sie" and "hir," which fell out of use because they lean toward feminine: "*sie*" and "hir" mean "she" in German and Middle English, respectively.

Ze is used with "hir" (pronounced like "here") or "zir," as in ze/hir/hirs, or ze/zir/zirs:

| Ze smiled | I called hir | Hir phone rang | That's hirs | Ze likes hirself |
|---|---|---|---|---|
| | I called zir | Zir phone rang | That's zirs | Ze likes zirself |
| Zie laughed | I hugged hir | Hir dog jumped | That's hirs | Zie likes hirself |
| | I hugged zir | Zir dog jumped | That's zirs | Zie likes zirself |

*see also:* PRONOUNS; HIR; XE; GENDER NEUTRAL LANGUAGE; GENDERQUEER

**ZIE** — *see:* ZE/ZIR.

**ZIR** — *see:* ZE/ZIR.

**ZUCCHINI** — A non-romantic noun to describe someone you're in an intimate, non-sexual relationship with.

Zucchini started as a joke term in the aromantic and asexual communities in the 2000s to highlight how there are no appropriate terms for describing significant, intimate relationships and love which are not romantic or sexual. The creation of zucchini shows a frustration with amatonormativity, or the assumption that romantic and sexual relationships are universally desired and the most important intimate bonds we form.

Zucchini is an alternative to "friend," which suggests a ceiling on intimacy, and "partner," which implies a romantic or sexual relationship. It's used by some queerplatonic partners to describe each other as in: "Ronald is my zucchini."

*see also:* SQUISH; QUEERPLATONIC; AMATONORMATIVITY; AROMANTIC; ASEXUAL; APHOBIA

# BIBLIOGRAPHY

Ahmed, S. (2017). *Living A Feminist Life*. Duke University Press: Durham, NC, US.

Alyson, S. & Yamaguchi Fletcher, L. (1980). *Young, Gay & Proud!* Alyson Publications: New York, NY, US.

American Psychological Association (2001). "Guidelines on Psychotherapy with Lesbian, Gay and Bisexual Clients".

American Psychological Association (18 May 2013). "Autism" in *Diagnostic and Statistical Manual of Mental Disorders: fifth edition (DSM-V)*. Washington DC: US.

American Psychological Association (18 May 2013). "Autogynephilia" in *Diagnostic and Statistical Manual of Mental Disorders: fifth edition (DSM-V)*. Washington DC: US.

American Psychological Association (18 May 2013). "Gender Dysphoria" in *Diagnostic and Statistical Manual of Mental Disorders: fifth edition (DSM-V)*. Washington DC: US.

Anzaldúa, G. (1987). *Borderland/LA Frontera: the new mestiza*, Aunt Lute Books: San Fransisco, CA, US.

Bailey, M. (14 March 2010). "They Aren't Talking About Me..." *The Crunk Feminist Collection*, crunkfeministcollective.com.

Barker, M.J. & Scheele, J. (2016). *Queer: a graphic history*. Icon Books Ltd: London, UK.

Baroque, F. & Eanelli, T. (ed.s) (2012). *Queer Ultraviolence: an abridged Bash Back! anthology*. Ardent Press: Berkley, CA, US.

de Beauvoir, S. (1949). *Le Deuxième Sexe [The Second Sex]*. Éditions Gallimard: Paris, France.

Bellwether, M. (October 2017). *Fucking Trans Women (FTW)*, issue 0.

Bem, S. (1974). "The Measurement of Psychological Androgyny" in *Journal of Consulting and Clinical Psychology*, volume 42, pp.155–62.

Benjamin, H. (1966). *The Transsexual Phenomenon: a scientific report on transsexualism and sex conversion in the human male and female*. The Julian Press Inc., US.

BiNet US (retrieved 2018). "The Mission of BiNet US" in "About BiNet US", www.binetusa.org.

Blank, J. (1981). *The Playbook For Kids About Sex*. Down There Press: San Fransisco, CA, US.

Bösche, S. (1983). *Jenny Lives with Eric and Martin [originally published as Mette bor hos Morten og Erik (1981)]*, Gay Men's Press: London, UK.

Boston Bisexual Women's Network (1983–present). *Bi Women Quarterly*. Boston, MA, US.

Boswell, J. (1979). "The Church and the Homosexual: an historical perspective", keynote address to the Fourth Biennial Dignity International Convention: San Diego, CA, US.

Brand, A. (1896–1932). *Der Eigene [The Unique]*, Berlin, Germany. British Library (Summer 2017). "Gay UK: love, law and liberty" exhibition, including a memo from Lord Chamberlain's Office on censoring homosexuality in theatre (31 October 1958), London, UK.

The British Society for the Study of Sex Psychology (1918). The BSSSP published pamphlets which linked sex reform to women's suffrage, such as Havelock Ellis' "The Erotic Rights of Women, and the Objects of Marriage: Two Essays", no. 5, Battley Bros. for the Society: Battersea, London, UK.

Burns, K. (17 January 2017). "The Left's Long History of Transphobia", *Medium*, medium.com.

Butler, J. (1993). *Bodies that Matter: on the discursive limits of "sex"*. Routledge: New York, NY, US.

Campaign for Homosexual Equality (CHE), Scottish Minorities Group, & Union For Sexual Freedoms in Ireland (1975). *No Offence: the case for homosexual equality in law*. Union For Sexual Freedoms in Ireland: UK.

Camus, A. (1942). *L'Étranger [The Stranger]*. Gallimard: Paris, France. Cárdenas, M. (2010). "Trans Desire", Atropos Press, New York, NY, US.

Carpenter, E. (1912 [1908]). *The Intermediate Sex: a study of some transitional types of men and women*. Mitchell Kennerley: New York, NY, US.

Chicago Women's Liberation Union (1971). *Lesbianism and Feminism*. Pamphlet, Chicago, IL, US.

Chu, A.L. (Winter 2018). "On Liking Women: the Society for Cutting Up Men is a rather fabulous name for a transsexual book club", *Motherland*, issue 30, nplusonemag.com.

Clinton, H. (25 January 1996). "Super predators" speech for Bill Clinton's presidential campaign. Keene State University, Keene, NH, US.

Committee of Friends on Bisexuality (Quaker group) (June 1972). "Ithaca Statement on Bisexuality". *The Advocate*, US.

Cooper, C. (2016). *Fat Activism: a radical social movement*. HammerOn Press: Bristol, UK.

Crenshaw, K. (1989). "Demarginalizing the Intersection of Race and Sex: a Black feminist critique of antidiscrimination doctrine, feminist theory and antiracist politics" in *University of Chicago Legal Forum*, issue 1 article 8.

*Daily Mail* (1983), unspecified article referenced in "Jenny, Eric, Martin...and me", Susanne Bösche, 31 January 2000, *The Guardian*, theguardian.co.uk.

Davis, G. (2015). *Contesting Intersex*. New York University Press: New York, NY, US.

Derrida, J. (1967). *De la Grammatologie [Of Grammatology]*, Les Éditions de Minuit: Paris, France.

Do Or Die (2001). "Give Up Activism", issue 9, 160–166. Also online at http://eco-action.org/dod/no9/activism.htm.

Doyle, A.C. (1887–1927). Sherlock Holmes canon, comprising four novels and 56 short stories. Various publishers: UK.

Dreger, A., Chase, C. *et al.* (August 2005). "Changing the Nomenclature/Taxonomy for Intersex: a scientific and clinical rationale". *Journal of Pediatric Endocrinology and Metabolism*, volume 18 issue 8, pp.729–733.

Drew, S. (dir. and producer) (1914). *A Florida Enchantment*. Vitagraph Studios: Brooklyn, New York, NY, US.

*Dysophia*. "What About The Rapists? Anarchist approaches to crime & justice", *Dysophia*, issue 5, Leeds, UK, dysophia.org.uk.

Ellis, H. & Symonds, J.A. (1896). *Das Konträre Geschlechtesgefül [Sexual Inversion]*. Wigand: Leipzig, Germany.

Emmerich, R. (dir.) (2015). *Stonewall*. Centropolis Entertainment: Los Angeles, CA, US.

English Birth Rate Commission (1666).

Gabrielis Falloppii [Gabriele Falloppio] (1564). *De Morbo Gallico Liber Absolutissimus [The Disease Free Supreme*, known as Falloppio's treatise on syphilis]. Bertellus: Padua, Italy.

Filar, R. (8 May 2017). "F.E.M.M.E." interview with Victoria Sin, Juno Mac, and Travis Alabanza, *#KilljoyFM*, Novara Media, London, UK.

Fleming, V. (dir.) (1939). *The Wizard Of Oz*. Metro-Goldwyn-Mayer: Los Angeles, CA, US.

Fornssler, B. (2010). "Affective Cyborgs", Atropos Press, New York, NY, US. Forster, J. (ed.) (1972–1981). *Sappho*, weekly magazine. London, UK. Foucault, M. (1975). *Surveiller et Punir: naissance de la prison [Discipline And Punish: the birth of the prison]*, Éditions Gallimard: Paris, France.

Foucault, M. (1976–1984). *Histoire de la Sexualitié [The History of Sexuality]*. Éditions Gallimard: Paris, France.

Freud, S. (1905). *Drei Abhandlungen our Sexualtheorie [Three Essays on the Theory of Sexuality]*. Franz Deuticke: Leipzig, Germany.

Funk & Wagnalls (1903). *Supplement to A Standard Dictionary of the English Language*. Funk & Wagnalls Company: New York, NY, US.

Fuss, D. (1991). *Inside/Out: lesbian theories, gay theories*. Routledge: Abingdon-On-Thames, UK.

Gagnon, J. and Simon, W. (1973). *Sexual Conduct: the social sources of human sexuality*. Aldine Publishing Co.: Chicago, IL, US.

Glyn, E. (1909). *It*. Macaulay: New York, NY, US.

Glyn, E. (story and adaptation) (1927). *It*. Paramount Pictures: Los Angeles, CA, US.

Gould, R.E. (January 1988). "Reassuring News About AIDS: a doctor tells why you may not be at risk". *Cosmopolitan*, Hearst Corporation: New York, NY, US.

Halberstam, J. (2011). *The Queer Art of Failure*. Duke University Press: Durham, NC, US.

Hall, R. (1928). *The Well Of Loneliness*. Jonathan Cape: London, UK. Helen Hester (2018). *Xenofeminism*, Polity Press: Cambridge, UK.

Hirschfield, M. (1910). *Die Transvestiten: eine untersuchung über den erotischen verkleidungstrieb mit umfangreichem casuistischen und historischen material [The Transvestites: an investigation of the erotic disguise drive with extensive casuistic and historic material]*. A. Pulvermacher: Berlin, Germany.

hooks, b. (1981). *Ain't I A Woman? Black women and feminism*. South End Press: Brooklyn, NY, US.

Hubbard, J. & Schulman, S. (producers) (6 June 2012). *United in Anger: a history of ACT UP*. New York Council on the Arts: New York, NY, US.

INCITE! Women of Color Against Violence (2008). *Law Enforcement Violence against Women of Color & Trans People of Color: a critical intersection of gender violence & state violence*. Redmond, WA, US, incite-national.org.

INTO (15 December 2017). "A Brief His and Herstory of Butch and Femme", intomore.com.

Karkazis, K. (2008). *Fixing Sex: intersex, medical authority, and lived experience*. Duke University Press: Durham, NC, US.

Kertbeny, K.M. writing anonymously (1869). *Paragraph 143 of the Prussian Penal Code of 14 April 1851 and its Reaffirmation as Paragraph 152 in the Proposed Penal Code for the North German Confederation: an open and professional correspondence to His Excellency Dr. Leonhardt, Royal Prussian Minister of Justice.*

Kinsey et al., A. (1948 and 1953). *Sexual Behavior in the Human Male* and *Sexual Behavior in the Human Female* [known collectively as the *Kinsey Reports*]. Saunders: Philadelphia, PN, US.

Kipling, R. (1904). "Mrs. Bathurst" in *Traffics and Discoveries*. Doubleday, Page & Co.: New York, NY, US.

Klein, F. (1982–present). *Journal of Bisexuality*. Routledge: Abingdon-on- Thames, UK [first published in New York, NY, US].

Richard von Krafft-Ebing, Charles Gilbert Chaddock (trans.) (1892 [1886]).

*Psychopathy of Sex: a clinical-forensic study [Psychopathia Sexualis: eine klinisch-forensische studie]*, Ferdinand Enke: Stuttgart, Germany.

Laboria Cuboniks (2015). *Xenofeminism: a politics for alienation*. laboriacuboniks.net.

Lessius, L. (1605). *De Iustitia et Iure [On Justice and Law]*, Lovania [now Leuven], Netherlands.

Liberman, A. (2008). *An Analytic Diction of English Etymology: an introduction*. University of Minnesota Press: Minneapolis, MN, US.

Lorde, A. (April 1980). "Age, Race and Class: women redefining difference", Copeland Colloquium, Amherst College, MA, US.

Marchant, D. (1974). "A Fragment Out Of Time", *Grup*, issue 3.

Masters, W. & Johnson, V. (1966). *Human Sexual Response*. Bantam Books: Toronto, ON, Canada.

Masters, M. & Johnson, V. (1979). *Homosexuality in Perspective*. Bantam Books: Toronto, ON, Canada.

McKay, C. (1928). *Home to Harlem*. Harper & Bros.: New York, NY, US.

Merleau-Ponty, M. (1945). *Phénonénologie de la Perception [Phenomenology of Perception]*. Edition Gallimard: Paris, France.

Mitchell, L. (1977). *Faggots and their Friends Between Revolutions*. Calamus Books, New York, NY, US.

Motion Picture Producers and Distributers of America (MPPDA) [rebranded as the Motion Picture Association of America (MPAA) in 1945] (1930–1968). *The Motion Picture Production Code of 1930 ["The Hays Code"]*. Los Angeles, CA, US.

National Bisexual Liberation Group (1972). *Bi-sexual Expression*, pamphlet/newsletter. New York, NY, US.

North, G. (1988–?). *Bisexuality: news, views, and networking*, US.

Parker, T. (1970). *The Frying Pan: a prison and its prisoners*. Faber & Faber: London, UK.

*Police Review* (1984). Jane's Information Group: London, UK.

Jasbir K. Puar (2007). *Terrorist Assemlages: homonationalism in queer times*. Duke University Press: Durham, NC, US.

Marquess of Queensberry (1 November 1894). Letter to Alfred Montgomery. Marquess of Queensberry (February 1895). "Somdomite" calling card for Oscar Wilde, the Albemarle, London, UK.

Raymond, J. (1979). *Transsexual Empire: the making of the she-male*. Beason Press: Boston, MA, US.

Rich, A. (Summer 1980). "Compulsory Heterosexuality and Lesbian Existence", *Signs: Journal of Women in Culture and Society*, volume 5 no 4, 631–660. University of Chicago Press: Chicago, IL, US.

Gerulf Rieger, et al (1 August 2005). "Sexual Arousal Patterns of Bisexual Men", *Psychological* Science, volume 16 issue 8, pp.579–584.

Robinson, T. (1976). "Glad To Be Gay", first performed at a gay pride parade in London, UK.

Roche, J. (2018). *Queer Sex: a trans and non-binary guide to intimacy, pleasure and relationships*. Jessica Kingsley Publishers: London, UK.

*Round The Horne* (1965–1968). BBC Light Programme: London, UK.

Rowling, J.K. (1997–2007). Harry Potter canon, comprising seven books. Bloomsbury Publishing: London, UK.

Rowling, J.K. (19 October 2007). "Dumbledore is gay" reveal during a Q&A session, Carnegie Hall, NY, US.

Rowling, J.K. (8:06 PM 16 December 2014). ".@benjaminroffan Anthony Goldstein, Ravenclaw, Jewish wizard", twitter.com.

Rowling, J.K. (10:41 AM 21 December 2015). "Canon: brown eyes, frizzy hair and very clever. White skin was never specified. Rowling loves black Hermoine", twitter.com.

Rowling, J.K. (6 September 2016). *Short Stories from Hogwarts of Heroism, Hardship, and Dangerous Hobbies*. e-book, Pottermore Publishing.

de Sade, D.A.F. [Marquis de Sade] (1791). *Justine, ou les Malheurs de la Vertu [Justine, or Good Conduct Well-Chastised)*, 2nd version, J.V. Giroaurd: Paris, France.

Sartre, J.-P. (1946). *L'existentialisme est un Humanisme [Existentialism is Humanism]*. Les Editions Nagel: Paris, France.

Sears, C. (2015). *Arresting Dress: cross-dressing, law, and fascination in nineteenth-century San Fransisco.* Duke University Press: Durham, NC, US.

Serano, J. (2007). *Whipping Girl: a transsexual woman on feminism and the scapegoating of femininity.* Seal Press: Boston, MA, US.

Serano, J. (19 November 2012). "Bisexuality and Binaries Revisited", juliaserano. blogspot.com.

Serano, J. (26 May 2015). "Reconceptualizing 'Autogynephilia' as Female/Feminine Embodiment Fantasies (FEFs)", juliaserano.blogspot.com.

Sontag, S. (1964). "Notes On 'Camp'", in *Partisan Review*, volume 31 issue 4, New York, NY, US, pp.515–530.

sounds gay, i'm in [closed facebook group] (21 October 2017). "What is gay culture" open poll by admin Noah Butsch, facebook.com.

Spivak, G.C. (1988). *Can The Subaltern Speak?* Macmillan: Basingstoke, UK.

Stryker, S. (2008). "Transgender History, Homonormativity, and Disciplinarity", *Radical History Review*, volume 100, pp.145–157.

Ulrichs, K.H. (1864–1865). *Forschegen über das Räthsel der Mannmännlichen Liebe [Research into the Riddle of Man-Male Love)*, I–V, Gelbftverlag des Berfaffers: Leipzig, Germany.

Vogel, L. (13 June 2005). Interview with Amy Ray from "Michigan's Womyn's Fest Interviews: interview #3", indigogirls.com.

Vogel, L. (11 April 2013). "Letter To The Community", *Michigan Womyn's Music Festival*, michfest.com.

Vyāsa (c.400 BCE). *Mahābhārata [The Great Tale of the Bhārata Dynasty].*

Walker, A. (1979). "Coming Apart" in *You Can't Keep a Good Woman Down: Stories* (1981) Harcourt Brace Jovanovich: San Diego, CA, US.

Warner, M. (1991). "Introduction: fear of a queer planet", *Social Text*, volume 9 issue 4, pp.3–17.

Wilson, M. (7 April 2010). "You can't be what you can't see" speech, White House Project EPIC Awards, IAC Building, New York, NY, US.

Winters, K. (1 November 2016). "The Gill Foundation & NCTE choose money over trans lives", *The Transadvocate*, www.transadvocate.com.

Wittig, M. (21 April 1979). "The Straight Mind", keynote address at "The Scholar and the Feminist Conference, the Future of Difference", Barnard College Women's Center, Columbia University, New York, NY, US.

World Health Organization (1948–1990). "Homosexuality", first appearing in the *International Classification of Diseases*, 6th revision, under Pathological Personality under the sub-category Sexual Deviations as code 320.6. It remained there in the 7th revision (1955), and in the 8th revision (1965) was moved to Sexual Deviations and Disorders and became code 302.0.

World Health Organization (1990). "F64.0 Transsexualism" in *The International Statistical Classification of Diseases and Related Health Problems*, 10th revision (ICD-10).

World Professional Association for Transgender Health (21 December 2016). "Position Statement on Medical Necessity of Treatment, Sex Reassignment, and Insurance Coverage in the U.S.A.", wpath.org.

## Citations for statistics

Savas Abadsidis (22 October 2017). "CDC Officially Admits People with HIV who are Undetectable Can't Transmit HIV", *HIV Plus*, hivplusmag.com.

Government Equalities Office (2011). *Transgender E-Surveys*, UK Government, UK. This survey received 2,172 responses and was the largest survey of the UK's trans population at the time it was completed.

Joanne Herman (13 March 2007). "Transsexual Regret", *The Advocate*, advocate.com.

Zinnia Jones (18 December 2017). "When 'Desisters' Aren't: de-desistance in childhood and adolescent gender dysphoria", *Medium*, medium.com. This piece cites many relevant studies and statistics.

Medical Accident Group (28 May 2014). "Two Thirds of Brits Regret Having Cosmetic Surgery", medicalaccidentgroup.co.uk.

National Center for Transgender Equality (December 2016). *The Report of the 2015 U.S. Transgender Survey*, Washington DC, US. This survey received 27,715 responses.

P. Pathela, A. Hajat, et al. (19 September 2006). "Discordance Between Sexual Behavior and Self-Reported Sexual Identity: a population-based survey of New York City men", *Annals of Internal Medicine*, volume 145 issue 6, pp. 416–425.

Pew Research Center (13 June 2013). *A Survey of LGBT Americans: attitudes, experiences and values in changing times*, Washington DC, US, pewresearch.org.

Scottish Transgender Alliance (September 2012). *Trans Mental Health Study 2012*. This survey had 889 responses.

Terrence Higgins Trust (27 July 2018). "Viral Load and Being Undetectable", tht.org.uk.

## Citations for legislation and government communications

* starred legislation has its own entry

### Argentina

22 July 2010 — Congreso de la Nación Argentina [National Congress of Argentina]. "Marriage for People of the Same Sex" bill, Buenos Aires, Argentina. Argentina was the first country in Latin America to legalize same- sex marriage.

25 November 2010 — Congreso de la Nación Argentina [National Congress of Argentina]. "Salud Publica: derecho a la proteccion de la salud mental" ["Public Health: the right to the protection of mental health"], ley 26657 [law 26657], published in el Boletín Oficial [the Official Gazette], no. 32041, 3 December 2010, Buenos Aires, Argentina. This law bans conversion therapy for registered health professionals, and declares that mental health diagnoses cannot be made on the basis of sexual orientation.

### Assyria

c.1075 BCE — "The Code of the Assura", Aššur, Nineveh; sourced from J.S. Arkenberg, California State Fullerton, CA, US. The Middle Assyrian Law Code is the earliest known example of criminalizing homosexuality, noting that if a man in the military has sex with a fellow soldier he will be turned into a eunuch.

## Australia

27 April 2016 — Victorian Parliament. "Health Complaints Bills 2016", Victoria, Australia. This bill, which came into effect 1 February 2017, made Victoria the first and (so far) only state to ban conversion therapy.

8 December 2017 — Parliament of Australia. "Marriage Amendment (Definition and Religious Freedoms) Act 2017, Act no. 129, Canberra, Australia. This legalized same-sex marriage across Australia.

## Austria

4 December 2017 — Verfassungsgerichtshof Österreich [Austrian Constitutional Court]. Ruling that the ban on same-sex marriage is unconstitutional, no. G 258-259/2017-9, Vienna, Austria. Same-sex couples will be able to marry in Austria on 1 January 2019.

## Belgium

28 February 2003 — Federaal Parlement van België / Parlement Fédéral Belge [Belgian Federal Parliament]. Article 143 of the Belgian Civil Code, Book I, Title V, Chapter I, Brussels, Belgium. "Two persons of different sex or of the same sex may contract marriage." It came into effect 1 June 2003.

## Brazil

22 March 1999 — Conselho Federal de Psicologia (CFP) [Federal Council of Psychology]. "Resolução CFP N° 001/99 de 22 de Março de 1999: estabelece normas de atuação para os psicólogos em relação à questão de orientação sexual" [CFP Resolution No. 001/99 of 22 March 1999: establishing norms of performance for psychologists in relation to sexual orientation"], Brasília, Brazil. This provision banned conversion therapy on the basis of sexuality, making Brazil the first country in the world to ban conversion therapy. In September 2017, a federal judge in Brasília approved the use of conversion therapy thereby overturning the CFP ban, but in December 2017 the same judge changed his decision; the ban remains in place.

14 May 2013 — Conselho Nacional de Justiça [National Justice Council]. "Resolução N° 175, de 14 de Maio de 2013" ["Resolution No. 175 on 14 May 2013"], São Paulo, Brazil. The Council ruled that notaries (who officiate marriages in Brazil) can't refuse to marry same-sex couples; and it allows existing civil unions to be converted into marriages. It came into force 16 May 2013.

29 January 2018 — Conselho Federal de Psicologia [Federal Council of Psychology]. "Resolução N° 1, de 29 de Janeiro de 2018: estabelece normas de atuação para as psicólogos em relação às pessoas transexuais e travestis" [Resolution No. 1, 29 January 2018: establishing norms of performance for psychologists in relation to transsexuals and transvestites"], Brasília, Brazil. This provision bans the use of conversion therapy on the basis of gender identity.

## Canada

20 July 2005 — Parliament of Canada. "Civil Marriage Act", S.C. 2005, c.33, Ottawa, Canada. This Act nationally legalized same-sex marriage across Canada and Canadian territories.

22 May 2015 — Government of Manitoba. "Position on Conversion Therapy", Manitoba, Canada. Manitoba became the first Canadian province to ban conversion therapy for healthcare professionals. Since then, conversion therapy has also been banned in Ontario (2015, for minors only); Vancouver (2018, in all settings); and Nova Scotia (2018, for minors).

## Colombia

7 July 2016 — Corte Constitucional de Colombia [Constitutional Court of Colombia]. "Sentencia SU214/16" ["Ruling SU214/16"], Bogotá, Colombia. This ruling states that it's unconstitutional to prohibit same-sex couples from marrying; and that civil partnerships are to be converted into marriages.

## Denmark

12 June 2012 — Government of Helle Thorning-Schmidt. "Ægteskab mellem to personer af samme køn" ["Marriage between two persons of the same sex"], L 106, Copenhagen, Denmark. Same-sex marriage is legalized, and those with civil partnerships will be automatically granted marriage status. It came into effect 15 June 2012. Greenland and the Faroe Islands, two constituent countries of the Kingdom of Denmark, legalized same-sex marriage in 2015 and 2017 respectively.

## Ecuador

2014 — Ministerio de Justica, Derechos Humanos y Cultos [Ministry of Justice, Human Rights and Cults]. "Artículo 151. Tortura" ["Article 151. Torture"] in *Código Orgánico: Integral Penal [Penal Code]*, Quinto, Ecuador, p.71. Conversion therapy is banned and considered torture; the penal code protects people on the basis of sexual orientation and gender identity.

## European Union

22 October 1981 — European Court of Human Rights. *Dungeon v United Kingdom*, Strasbourg, France. The ruling found that the Criminal Law Amendment Act 1885 which criminalized homosexuality in the UK is a violation of the European Convention on Human Rights. The case led to legislation decriminalizing homosexuality in Northern Ireland.

## Fiji

2010 — Government of Fiji. "Mental Health Decree 2010", Decree no. 54 of 2010, Suva, Fiji. This decree established a national ban on conversion therapy in the field of mental health, but only applies to registered mental health professionals.

## Finland

20 February 2015 — Väestörekisterikeskus [Citizen's Initiative]. Amendments to the "Marriage Act", Helsinki, Finland. This bill removed all gendered references in the Marriage Act, thereby legalizing same-sex marriage. It came into effect 1 March 2017.

## France

25 September–6 October 1791 — Assemblée National Constituante [National Constituent Assembly]. "Code Pénal de 1791" ["French Revolutionary Penal Code"], Versailles, France. The new penal code decriminalized sodomy along with many other victimless crimes.

3 June 1810 — Napoléon Bonaparte. "Le Code Pénal de 1810" ["French Penal Code of 1810"], Paris, France. The French empire imposed its penal code across Europe, and therefore widely decriminalized sodomy on the continent. The UK is a notable exception.

18 May 2013 — Parlement Français [French Parliament]. "Loi n° 2013-404 du 17 May 2013 Ouvrant le Mariage aux Couples de Personnes de Même Sexe" ["Law Opening Marriage to Same-Sex Couples, no. 2013-404"] known as "loi Taubira" ["Taubira law"], ACT No. 2013-404 of 17 May 2013, Paris, France.

## Germany

15 May 1871 — Reichstag [Parliament of Germany]. "Paragraph 175" of the Strafgesetzbuch [German Penal Code], §175 StGB, Berlin, Germany. criminalized homosexuality. In 1935 the Nazis redefined crimes under paragraph 175 as felonies with more severe punishments; and reinterpreted the law to include "debauched intention" (not necessarily involving physical contact) when the crime was previously only applied to penetrative anal sex. It was not repealed until 10 March 1994.

20 July 2017 — Bundestag [lower house of Germany Parliament]. "Ehe für Alle" ["Marriage for All"], Berlin, Germany. The law also included the right for same-sex couples to adopt children. It came into effect 1 October 2017.

## Iceland

11 June 2010 — Alþingi [Icelandic Parliament]. "Ein Hjúskaparlög" ["One Marital Law"), Þskj. 836 — 485 mál., amendments to nr. 31/1993, Reykjavík, Iceland. The bill provides a gender-neutral definition of marriage and grants adoption rights to same-sex couples, and came into effect 27 June 2010.

## Ireland

29 October 2015 — Oireachtas [the legislator of Ireland]. "Marriage Act", no. 35 of 2015, Dublin, Ireland. The constitutional amendment provides that marriage is recognized irrespective of the genders of the partners; it was signed into law following a referendum. It came into effect 16 November 2015.

## Luxembourg

18 June 2014 — D'Chamber [Chamber of Duties]. Réforme du Mariage" ["Reform of Marriage"], 6172A, A — N° 125, Luxembourg City, Luxembourg. This bill legalized same-sex marriage and same-sex adoption, and came into effect on 1 January 2015.

## Malta

5 December 2016 — Parlament ta' Malta [Parliament of Malta]. "Affirmation of Sexual Orientation, Gender Identity and Gender Expression Act", Valletta, Malta. This Act outlaws conversion therapy.

1 September 2017 — Parlament ta' Malta [Parliament of Malta]. "Marriage Act and other Laws (Amendment) Act, 2017", bill no. 20, Valletta, Malta. This law includes the rights to same-sex couples to adopt, and in the same session the Maltese parliament added the words "sexual orientation" to the constitution in relation to freedoms and protections from discriminations; it was the first country to specifically address protections around gender identity.

## Mexico

3 June 2015 — Suprema Corta de Justicia de la Nación [Supreme Court of Justice of the Nation]. "Matrimonio: la ley de cualquier entidad federativa que, por un lado, considere que la finalidad de aquél es la procreación y/o cue lo defina como el que se celebra entre un hombre y una mujer, es inconstitucional" ["Marriage: the law of any federative entity that, consider that the purpose of marriage is procreation and/or that define it as celebrated between a man and a woman, is unconstitutional"], 1a 43/2015, 10a época, tesis de jurisprudencia [thesis of jurisprudence], Mexico City, Mexico. This ruling declared it unconstitutional to define to exclude same-sex couples. Same sex marriage is legalized in twelve states and several municipalities, the first being Mexico City which amended the definition of marriage on 21 December 2009.

## The Netherlands

1 April 2001 — Staten-Generaal [States General of the Netherlands]. "Huwelijk tussen personen van gelijk geslacht" ["Marriage Between Persons of the Same Sex"], Article 1:30 in Burgerlijk Wetboek [Civil Code], The Hague, Netherlands. The Netherlands was the first country to fully legalize same-sex marriage; though same-sex marriages aren't performed in Aruba, Cuaçao, or Sint Maarten which are constituent countries of the Netherlands.

## New Zealand

19 April 2013 — New Zealand Parliament. "Marriage (Definition of Marriage) Amendment Act 2013, Wellington, New Zealand. This amendment changed the definition of marriage to be gender neutral. New Zealand Parliament is only able to enact marriage laws governing New Zealand proper and the

Ross Dependency (Antarctica); the territories of the Cook Islands, Niue, and Tokealu do not recognize same-sex marriage. The amended law came into effect 19 August 2013.

## Norway

1 January 2009 — Stortinget [Storting, or "the great assembly"; Norway's Parliament]. "Felles Ekteskapslov for Heterofile og Homofile Par" ["Joint Marriage Law for Heterosexual and Gay Couples"], Besler. No. 91 (2007-2008), Oslo, Norway. This bill changed the definition of marriage to be gender-neutral, and grants full parental rights to partners whose spouse becomes pregnant through artificial insemination. The law also provisions state funding for fertility treatment for woman-woman couples.

## Portugal

31 May 2010 — Assembleia da República [Assembly of the Republic]. "Lei n° 9/2010: Permite o Casamento Civil Entre Pessoas do Mesmo Sexo" ["Law no. 9/2010: Allows Same-Sex Civil Marriage"], Lisbon, Portugal. It came into effect 5 June 2010.

## Russia

December 1917 — Российская Совётская Республика [Russian Soviet Republic], Petrograd, Russia. The Legal Code of Tsarist Russia was discarded following the October Revolution, effectively decriminalizing homosexuality (though it was criminalized in the 1920s in Azerbaijan, the Transcaucasian and Central Asian Soviet Republics, Uzbekistan, and Turkmenistan).

7 March 1934 — "Статья 121.1" Уголовного кодекса Российской Советской Федеративной Социалистической Республики ["Article 121.1" of the Russian Soviet Federative Socialist Republic (Russian RFSR) Penal Code], Moscow, Russia. Under Stalin, male homosexuality was recriminalized in the Soviet Union.

29 April 1993 — Russian President Boris Yeltsin. Article 121.1 is repealed, Moscow, Russia. The decriminalization of homosexuality did not take effect until 1 January 1997, and there were cases that some people prosecuted under the old legislation had not been released from jail. Russia continues to repress LGBT+ rights through anti-"propaganda" laws.

## South Africa

29 November 2006 — National Assembly. "Civil Union Act, 2006", Act No. 17 of 2006, Cape Town, South Africa. This Act legalized same-sex marriage, and allows couples, regardless of gender, to form marriages or civil partnerships.

## Spain

2 July 2005 — Cortes Generales [Spanish Parliament]. "Law 13/2005" amending Artículo 44 del Código Civil [Article 44 of the Civil Code], Madrid, Spain. The phrase "Marriage will have the same requirements and effects regardless of

whether the persons involved are of the same or different sex," was added to the Civil Code, and the law took effect 3 July 2005.

1 June 2016 — Presidencia de la Region de Murcia [Presidency of the Region of Murcia]. "Ley 8/2016, de 27 de Mayo, de ingualdad social de lesbianas, gais, bisexuales, transexuales, transgénero e intersexuales, y de políticas públicas contra la discriminacíon por orientacíon sexual e identidad de género en la Comunidad Autónoma de la Regíon de Murcia" ["Law 8/2016, of 27 May, on the Social Equity of Lesbian, Gay, Bisexual, Transsexual, Transgender and Intersex people, and the Public Policies Against Discrimination Based on Sexual Orientation and Gender Identity in the Autonomous Community of the Region of Murcia"], Murcia, Spain. Murcia was the first autonomy in Spain to ban conversion therapy for health professionals. Bans also exist in Madrid (2017, extending to everyone including religious groups); Valencia (2017); and Andalusia (2018).

### Sweden

1 April 2009 — Riksdag [Swedish Parliament]. "Könsneutrala Äktenskap och Vigselfrågor" ["Gender Neutral Marriage and Affairs issues"], CU19 2008/09, Stockholm, Sweden. The law adopted gender-neutral language and took effect 1 May 2009.

### Switzerland

10 March 2016 — Conseil National [Swiss Federal Council]. "Interdiction et punissabilité des thérapies visant à "traiter" l'homosexualité chez des mineurs" ["Prohibition and Punishability of Therapies to 'Treat' Homosexuality in Minors"], Bern, Switzerland. The Council wrote that conversion therapy is a breach of professional duties, and are subject to prosecution at the discretion of the Swiss criminal courts.

### Taiwan

22 February 2018 — 衛生福利部 [Ministry of Health and Welfare]. "衛部醫字第1071660970號" [Ministry of Health and Welfare no. 1071660970"], Taipei, Taiwan. Conversion therapy is not legally banned, but is effectively banned by the Ministry of Health and Welfare; and anyone practicing conversion therapy would be liable to large fines and prosecution.

### United Kingdom

1533 — Parliament of England. "Buggery Act 1533", 25 Hen. 8 c. 6, London, UK. The Buggery Act criminalized homosexuality in England from 1533–1553, and again from 1563 until its repeal in 1828 when it was replaced with the Offences Against the Person Act, which provided that buggery would remain a capital offense.

27 June 1828 — Parliament of the United Kingdom. Section 15 of the "Offenses Against the Person Act", 9 Geo. 4 c. 31, London, UK. This Act replaced the Buggery Act of 1533, and kept buggery as a capital offense.

12 October 1871 — Governor-General of India the Earl of Mayo. "Criminal Tribes Act", various pieces of legislation enforced in British-occupied India between 1871–1924. The Act was repealed in 1949. These laws created still- entrenched stigmas and stereotypes about the tribes they subjected.

14 August 1885 — Parliament of the United Kingdom. Section 11 ("the Labouchere Amendment") of the "Criminal Law Amendment Act 1885", 48 & 49 Vict. c. 69, London, UK. This effectively criminalized homosexuality in the UK by making "gross indecency" a crime where sodomy (anal sex) could not be proved.

4 September 1957 — Committee on Homosexual Offences and Prostitution. "Report of the Departmental Committee on Homosexual Offences and Prostitution", better known as the "Wolfenden report", Her Majesty's Stationary Office: London, UK. The report recommended that "homosexual behaviour between consenting adults in private should no longer be a criminal offence".

27 July 1967 — Parliament of the United Kingdom. "Sexual Offences Act 1967", 1967 c. 60, London, UK. The Act decriminalized homosexual acts in England and Wales in private between two men who were both at least 21.

13 November 1980 — Parliament of the United Kingdom. "Criminal Justice (Scotland) Act 1980", 1980 c. 62, London, UK. The Act decriminalized homosexual acts in Scotland in private between two men who were both at least 21 years old, 13 years after such acts were decriminalized in England and Wales.

27 October 1982 — Northern Ireland Orders in Council. "The Homosexual Offences (Northern Ireland) Order 1982", 1982 no. 1536 (N.I. 19), Belfast, UK. This order decriminalized homosexuality in Northern Ireland and was adopted following a mandate by the European Court of Human Rights.

1986–1987 — Central Office of Information. "AIDS: Don't Die of Ignorance" [campaign of leaflets, television ads, and posters], UK.

1987 — Conservative Party. "Is This Labour's Idea of a Comprehensive Education?", election campaign posters, London: UK.

* 24 March 1988 — Parliament of the United Kingdom. Section 28 of the "Local Government Act 1988", London, UK. Section 28 stated that local authorities (which include schools and libraries) "shall not intentionally promote homosexuality" or "the acceptability of homosexuality as a pretend family relationship". It was repealed in Scotland in 2000, and in the rest of the UK in 2003.

3 November 1994 — Parliament of the United Kingdom. "Criminal Justice and Public Order Act", 1994 c. 33, London, UK. This Act lowered age of consent for same-sex couples from 21 to 18, though still not equal to the age of consent for different-sex couples.

30 November 2000 — Parliament of the United Kingdom. "Sexual Offences (Amendment) Act 2000", 2000 c. 44, London, UK. The Act equalized the age of consent across the UK to 16.

20 November 2003 — Parliament of the United Kindgom. "Sexual Offenses Act 2003", 2003 c. 42, London, UK. This Act decriminalized group sex between men,

and repealed much of the Sexual Offences Act 1967 including the crimes of buggery and gross indecency.

18 November 2004 — Parliament of the United Kingdom. "Civil Partnership Act 2004", 2004 c. 33, London, UK. This Act established same-sex civil partnerships across the UK.

17 July 2013 — Parliament of the United Kingdom. "Marriage (Same Sex Couples) Act 2013", 2013 c. 30, London, UK. This Act legalized same-sex marriage in England and Wales. It came into effect 13 March 2014.

12 March 2014 — Scottish Parliament. "Marriage and Civil Partnership (Scotland) Act 2014", 2014 asp. 5, Edinburgh, UK. This Act legalized same- sex marriage in Scotland. It came into effect 16 December 2014.

31 January 2017 — Parliament of the United Kingdom. The "Alan Turing Law" within the "Policing and Crime Act 2017", 2017 c. 3, London, UK. This law pardoned all men (approximately 49,000) who were prosecuted under the anti-queer laws.

## United States

27 April 1953 — US President Dwight D. Eisenhower. "Executive Order 10450", Washington DC, US. This EO barred gays and lesbians from working within the federal government and remained on the books until it was rescinded with the "Don't Ask, Don't Tell" policy in 1994.

18 January 1977 — Dade County Commission. "Ordinance 77-4", Miami, FL, US. One of the first US law outlawing discrimination on the basis of sexuality in employment, housing, and public services. It was repealed on 7 June 1977 after national anti-gay campaigning by Anita Bryant; and it was reinstated on 1 December 1998.

1980 — Janice Raymond. "Technology on the Social and Ethical Aspects of Transsexual Surgery", commissioned by National Center for Health Care Technology: Washington DC, US. This report was the basis for denying Medicare coverage for trans-specific healthcare.

18 December 1992 — Center for Disease Control. "1993 Revised Classification System to HIV Infection and Expanded Surveillance Case Definition for AIDS Among Adolescents and Adults", *Morbidity and Morality Weekly Report (MMWR)*, 41(RR-17), Atlanta, GA, US. This is the most recently revised definition of HIV/AIDS, updated to include women after pressure from ACT UP groups.

5 May 1993 — Supreme Court of Hawaii. *Baehr v Lewin*, no. 15689, Honolulu, HI, US. The Court determines that the state cannot demonstrate sufficient interest in denying marriage licenses to same-sex couples, and so that denial is unconstitutional.

21 February 1993 — US President Bill Clinton. "Department of Defense Directive 1304.26", known as "Don't Ask, Don't Tell", Washington DC, US. Don't Ask Don't Tell prohibited harassment and discrimination toward closeted queers in the military, but still banned LGBT+ people working in the military from disclosing their LGBT+ status.

26 April 2000 — Vermont Governor Howard Dean. "Act 91", originally introduced by the Vermont House Judiciary Committee as "H.847", Montpelier, VT, US. Vermont was the first US state to legalize same-sex civil unions.

26 June 2003 — Supreme Court of the United States. *Lawrence v Texas*, 539 U.S. 558, Washington DC, US. The Court ruled it unconstitutional to criminalize private, consensual, non-commercial sex acts between adults on the grounds of morality; the effectively decriminalized homosexuality in the US.

23 March 2010 — US President Barack Obama. "Patient Protection and Affordable Care Act (ACA or 'Obamacare')", Washington DC, US. The ACA banned discrimination of trans people by insurance companies on the federal level, which practically meant that transition-specific healthcare must be covered in the US for the first time since the 1980.

27 September 2014 — California Governor Jerry Brown. "Assembly Bill No. 2501", Sacramento, CA, US. This bill made California the first state to ban gay and trans panic defenses.

26 June 2015 — Supreme Court of the United States. *Obergefell v Hodges*, 576 U.S., Washington DC, US. The Court ruled that denying marriage licenses to same-sex couples is unconstitutional; the ruling requires all states to issue marriage licenses to same-sex couples, and to recognize same-sex marriages performed in other districts.

25 August 2017 — Illinois Governor Bruce Rauner. SB 1761, "Prohibits 'Gay Panic' Defense", Springfield, IL, US. This bill bans the gay and trans panic defenses in Illinois.

27 September 2017 — US Center For Disease Control. "HIV & AIDS in the United States: Information from CDC's Division of HIV/AIDS Prevention", email newsletter.

22 May 2018 — Rhode Island Governor Gina Raimondo. H 7066, "An Act Relating to Criminal Procedure — Trials", Providence, RI, US. This bill bans the gay and trans panic defenses in Rhode Island.

**Uruguay**

3 May 2013 — El Senado y la Cámara de Representantes de la República Oriental de Uruguay [The Senate and House of Representatives of the Oriental Republic of Uruguay]. "Ley N° 19.075" ["Law No. 19.075"], Montevideo, Uruguay. This law amends the civil code definition of marriage to include same-sex couples.

## Events referenced

* starred events have their own entry

**1526–1888** — European and American enslavement of Africans, beginning with the first transatlantic slave ship by Portugal to Brazil, and ending with Brazil banning slavery. The complete dehumanization of Black people—who were legally trafficked and sold as property, and implicitly excluded from the category of 'human'—colors the context for everything covered in this book up to and including the present moment.

**early 1600s–present** — Capitalism is the dominant socio-economic system in Europe and North America, evolving out of feudalism. Stages of capitalism include agrarian capitalism, mercantilism, industrialism, and modern or late capitalism.

**1660s** — Women started performing trouser roles, London, UK. This gender variance was likely only afforded to white women of certain classes.

**1848–1855** — California Gold Rush, US.

**1855** — The first rubber condom was produced, New England, US.

**1861–1865** — US Civil War.

**1874** — Jockstraps are invented in Chicago, IL, US.

**25 May 1895** — Oscar Wilde is convicted of "gross indecency" in London, UK.

**1914–1918** — World War I.

**1920** – Latex is invented, and latex condoms are mass produced in the US.

**1929–1939** — The Great Depression.

**10 May 1933** — Nazi book burning of the Institut für Sexualwissenschaft [Institute of Sexology] in Berlin, forcing the Institute to close.

**1939–1945** — World War II.

**1941–1945** — the Holocaust, which targeted Jews, queers, Roma, ethnic Poles and other Slavs, Soviet citizens, the disabled, the mentally ill, and communists and anarchists.

**1946–1991** — Cold War.

**1950–1964** — The Lavender Scare, in which homosexuality was conflated with communism; queer people and people suspected of being queer were purged from public office and public life in the US. The end of the Lavender Scare is difficult to pinpoint: I've opted for 1964 with the disbandment of Florida Legislative Investigation Committee whose purpose was to investigate and fire gay public school teachers, though Executive Order 10450 which barred homosexuals from working for the federal government remained in effect until 1995, and the lasting cultural impact of the Scare is ongoing.

**1955–1975** — Vietnam War.

**17 April 1965** — One of the first demonstrations for gay rights, Washington DC, US. Frank Kameny and Jack Nichols picketed the White House in protest of the anti-LGBT+ Lavender Scare policies, demanding gay rights.

**August 1966** — Compton's Cafeteria Riot, San Fransisco, CA, US. The first recorded militant resistance of LGBT+ people.

**1964–1973** — "War on Poverty" in the US, which established welfare programs through the Office of Economic Opportunity.

**28 June 1969** — Stonewall Riots, Greenwich Village, New York City, NY, US. The Stonewall Riots are considered the start of the LGBT+ rights movement.

**27 June 1970** — The first Pride parade, organized by the Chicago Gay Liberation in commemoration of the Stonewall Riots; Chicago, US.

**1 July 1972** — The first UK Pride parade, London, UK.

**8 November 1977** — Harvey Milk elected to the San Fransisco Board of

Supervisors, and was the first openly gay non-incumbent man to win public office in the US.

**1979** — "Third World Conference: When Will the Ignorance End?", the first US national conference for gay and lesbian people of color, co-organized by bisexual activist Billy S Jones.

**14 October 1979** — National March on Washington for Gay and Lesbian Rights, Washington DC, US. The first LGBT+ march on Washington, it drew between 75,000 and 125,000 LGBT+ people and allies.

**1979–1990s** — HIV/AIDS crisis across North America and Europe, which disproportionately affects queers and Black people.

**July 1984** — BiPOL, the first bisexual rally, outside the Democratic National Convention in San Fransisco, CA, US.

**8–9 December 1984** — The first BiCon UK, London, UK.

**1984** — East Coast Conference on Bisexuality in Storrs School of Social Work at the University of Connecticut, CT, US; this is the first regional bisexual conference in the US.

**1984–1985** — Miner's Strike in South Wales, UK; supported by Lesbians and Gays Support the Miners on the basis of solidarity and shared liberation.

**13 November 1985** — Margaret Roff is elected as the mayor of Manchester, making her the first openly gay mayor (after being outed by the press) in the UK.

**24 March 1987** — ACT UP's first action: a demonstration on Wall Street protesting pharmaceutical profiteering, and demanding access to AZT (an early HIV/AIDS treatment) and a coordinated national strategy for addressing the public health crisis, New York City, NY, US.

**1988** — The first national US bisexual newsletter, *Bisexuality: News, Views, and Networking*, is published by Gary North.

**January 1988** — ACT UP demonstrates at the Hearst building in protest of an article in Cosmopolitan incorrectly suggesting that heterosexual women can't get AIDS, New York City, NY, US.

**11 October 1988** — ACT UP shut down the Food and Drug Administration (FDA) in protest of their slow drug-approval policy, which resulted in thousands of deaths from lack of access to treatment, MD, US.

**3 May 1989** — Bisexual Cliff Arnesen becomes the first non-heterosexual person to testify before Congress, speaking on queer veterans' issues, Washington DC, US.

**14 September 1989** — Seven ACT UP New York members infiltrated and occupied the New York Stock Exchange to protest the high price of AZT, New York City, NY, US.

**10 December 1989** — About 4,500 ACT UP protestors occupy the Roman Catholic Church in New York City in protest of the church's homophobic and misogynistic policies on AIDS and abortion, NY, US.

**1990** — The WHO updates the International Classification of Diseases (ICD-10) which declassifies homosexuality as a disease, Geneva, Switzerland; member states began using ICD-10 in 1994.

**February 1990** — The term "queer theory" is coined by Teresa de Lauretis at a conference she organized on lesbian and gay sexualities, University of California Santa Cruz, US.

**21 May 1990** — ACT UP occupies the National Institute of Health, protesting the underrepresentation of women and people of color in clinical trials, and demanding more AIDS treatments; Bethesda, MD, US.

**2 October 1990** — ACT UP protests at Washington DC, US over the Center for Disease Control definition of AIDS excluding women, protesting "Women don't get AIDS, they just die from it".

**22 January 1991** — ACT UP storms CBS evening news and declares "AIDS is news, fight AIDS not Arabs!" on live national broadcast. The following day there were coordinated demonstrations across New York City demanding "money for AIDS not for war".

**30 June 2016** — The US Department of Defense lifts its ban on trans people openly working in the military, Washington DC, US.

**25 August 2017** — US President Trump issues a presidential memorandum that re-bans transgender people from working openly in the military, Washington DC, US.

**9–10 February 2018** — PrEP summit in Amsterdam, Netherlands.

**1 May 2018** — The Castro is established as an LGBT+ Leather cultural district by the city of San Francisco, CA, US.

## Groups referenced

\* starred groups have their own entry

**AIDS Coalition To Unleash Power (ACT UP)**, global (first formed in New York City, US), 1987–present. ACT UP is a direct action group made up of autonomous chapters, fighting for access to HIV/AIDS treatment and against HIV/AIDS stigma and misinformation.

**Bash Back!**, US (first formed in Chicago, IL, US), 2007–2011. Bash Back! were a radical network of anarchist queer groups in the US, formed to critique the assimilationist position of the mainstream LGBT+ rights movement.

**The Belfast Gay Liberation Society (GLS)**, Belfast, Ireland, 1972–early 1980s. Belfast GLS fought social prejudice against gays; lobbied for legislative change including against the Labouchere Amendment which no longer applied in England and Wales but still affected Northern Ireland and Scotland; and hosted gay nightlife parties.

**Black Lesbians and Gays Against Media Homophobia**, UK, 1988–1990s. Black Lesbians and Gays Against Media Homophobia formed to oppose Section 28 and other anti-queer propaganda.

**BiNet US**, US (founded in San Fransisco, CA, US), 1990–present. BiNet's mission is to "facilitate the development of a cohesive network of bisexual communities, promote bisexual visibility, and collect and distribute educational information regarding bisexuality."

**BiPhoria**, UK (based in Manchester, UK), 1990–present. BiPhoria is the UK's longest-running bi organization, and offers socials and support groups for bi people.

**BiPOL**, San Fransisco, CA, US, 1983–1990s. BiPOL is one of the oldest bisexual political organizations, and advocated for bisexual rights, visibility, and inclusion, organizing several national bisexual events and demonstrations.

**Boston Bisexual Women's Network**, Boston, MA, US, 1983–present. The Boston Bisexual Women's Network is a feminist collective which brings women together through the vehicles of discussion, support, education, outreach, political action, and social groups related to bisexuality.

**Call Off Your Tired Old Ethics (COYOTE)**, US (founded in San Fransisco, CA, US), 1973–present. COYOTE is a feminist sex workers' rights organization which advocates for decriminalization and the elimination of social stigma relating to sex work. They offer services for sex workers and training for social services and law enforcement.

**Camp Trans**, Oceana County, MI, US, 1992–2015. Camp Trans was an annual demonstration outside the Michigan Womyn's Music Festival, in protest of the festival's policy of excluding trans women from attendance.

**Campaign for Homosexual Equality (CHE)**, London, UK, 1964–present. CHE was formed to campaign for the decriminalization of homosexuality, and continues to fight for improved sex education in UK schools, and social equality and dignity for LGBT+ people.

**Damned Interfering Video Activists TV (DIVA TV)**, New York City, NY, US, 1989–present. DIVA TV was a lesbian video activist collective and affinity group of ACT UP which created activist media and documented ACT UP demonstrations.

**Daughters of Bilitis**, global (founded in San Fransisco, CA, US), 1955–1995. Daughter of Bilitis were homophiles and was the first lesbian civil and political rights organization in the US; conceived as an alternative lesbian bars which were subject to raids, it also educated women on their rights and gay history and published a lesbian magazine called *The Ladder* (1956– 1972). Their gay men's counterpart was the Mattachine Society.

**Fed Up Queers (FUQ)**, New York City, NY, and Arkansas, US, 1998–2001 (NY) and 2009 (AR). FUQ were a direct action group who protested police murders and held political funerals for trans and queer people.

**Fierce Pussy**, New York City, NY, US, 1991–present. Fierce Pussy are a lesbian feminist artist and activist collective, formed to highlight lesbian identity and visibility. They're known for their wheat pasting campaigns and sticker campaigns.

**Gay Liberation Front (GLF)**, US, UK, and Canada (originally formed in New York, NY, US), July 1969–1973. GLF formed immediately after the Stonewall Riots, advocating for sexual liberation.

**Gay Liberation Front Women (GLFW)**, 1970–c.1973. Women were a minority within GLF, and GLFW formed as a response to misogyny and chauvinism within GLF.

**Gay Shame**, San Francisco, CA and Brooklyn, New York City, NY, US, 1998– 2015. Gay Shame was formed in opposition to mainstream gay rights assimilation and commercialization. Gay Shame held alternative Pride events and protests.

**Gay-Straight Alliance (GSA)**, global (first started in Concord, MA, US), 1988– present. A student or community group which provides a safe/r space to LGBT+ youth, and plausible deniability as being an "ally" while seeking support.

**Gran Fury**, New York City, NY, US, 1988–1995. Gran Fury was an autonomous visual arts collective within ACT UP, who created art to support ACT UP actions, and to disseminate art as an action itself.

**The Homosexual Law Reform Society (HLRS)**, UK, 1958–1970s. The HLRS campaigned to decriminalize sex between men, using the Wolfenden Report as evidence for reform; they later campaigned on equalizing the age of consent. The HLRS were seen as more radical groups like the GLF as being too assimilationist in their aims.

**Housing Works**, Soho, New York City, NY, US (founded in New York City, with satellite offices in Albany and Brooklyn), 1990–present. Housing Works is dedicated to homeless people living with HIV/AIDS in New York City. It was set up by ACT UP activists to provide stable housing, healthcare, and legal aid services.

**Lesbian Avengers**, global (founded in New York City, NY, US), 1992–present. The Lesbian Avengers are a direct action group focused on lesbian survival and visibility, starting with an action to include queer sexualities in children's sex education. There are over 60 chapters worldwide.

**Lesbians and Gays Support the Migrants (LGSM)**, UK (founded in London), 2015–present. LGSM is founded on the same principles of solidarity and direct action as its predecessor, Lesbians and Gays Support the Miners. They oppose homonationalism and campaign for migrants' rights under the slogan "No one is illegal".

**Lesbians and Gay Support the Miners (LGSM)**, UK (founded in London), 1984–1985. LGSM was a solidity alliance between lesbians and gays who supported the 1984–1985 miners' strike. LGSM raised money for the miners' strike funds.

**Mattachine Society**, US (founded in Los Angeles, CA, US), 1950–1960s. The Mattachine Society were homophiles and one of the US' earliest LGBT+ rights organizations, founded by gay communist men; the lesbian counterpart was the Daughters of Bilitis. As the gay liberation movement became more militant, the Mattachine Society was seen to be too traditional and non-confrontational, and eventually fizzled.

**Mujeres Libres** [Free Women], Spain (founded in Madrid), 1936–1939. Mujeres Libres were queer anarchist women in Spain who worked to empowerworking class women, arguing that women's liberation and socio-economic revolution were equal and parallel goals which should be pursued in tandem. They organized women-only education, childcare, traveling libraries, a newspaper, a magazine, and material support for the revolution.

**National Bisexual Liberation Group**, US (founded in New York City, NY), 1972–1970s. The National Bisexual Liberation Group advocated for bisexual rights, published the first bisexual national newsletter (*The Bisexual Expression*), and held monthly parties and other socials for bisexuals.

**National Coalition of Black Lesbians and Gays (NCBG)**, US (founded in Columbia, MD), 1978–1990. The NCBG was the US' first organization of Black and third world gay rights, adding Lesbian to its name in 1984. They advocated for LGBT+ parental rights, HIV/AIDS prevention in the Black community, sponsored two national conferences, and published the news magazine *Black/Out*.

**OutRage!**, UK (founded in London), 1990–2011. OutRage! was a non-violent direct action group formed to protest escalating queer bashing and the persecution of queer men for consensual sexual behavior. OutRage! was the longest running grassroots LGBT+ organization in the world.

**Project 10**, North America (founded in Los Angeles, CA, US), 1984–present. Project 10 promotes the personal, social, sexual, and mental wellbeing of LGBT+ youth and young adults aged 14–25.

**Prostitute's Union of Massachusetts (PUMA)**, Boston, MA, US, 1974–1980s. PUMA was a collective organizing mutual aid among sex workers, providing arrest support; referrals to medial, legal, and childcare services; throwing Hooker Balls for fundraising; and dramatizing prostitution in the press for the purpose of advocating for sex workers' rights. PUMA was especially concerned with the needs of women who were poor, imprisoned, substance dependent, and survivors of sexual violence. PUMA was inspired by COYOTE.

**The Scottish Minorities Group**, Scotland, 1969–1978. The Scottish Minorities Group campaigned for Scotland to partially decriminalize sex between men, thereby matching England and Wales after the 1967 Sexual Offences Act which did not apply to Scotland or Northern Ireland. The term 'minorities' was used to avoid the dangers of explicit reference to homosexuality. In 1978 the group rebranded as the Scottish Homosexual Rights Group.

**Street Transvestite Action Revolutionaries (STAR)**, New York City, NY, US, 1970–2001. Originally "Street Transvestites Actual Revolutionaries", STAR began as a caucus of the Gay Liberation Front to advocate on behalf of homeless queer youths and runaways. STAR was run with a direct action, socialist revolutionary group that demanded free healthcare, free education, free food, and free public services for all oppressed people, distinguishing itself from the mainstream assimilationist LGBT+ rights organizations.

**Queer Nation**, North America (founded in New York City, NY, US), 1990–present. Queer Nation was a direct action group formed by ACT UP activists in response to homophobic violence and discrimination in the media. Their first action was a "Queer Night Out" at Flutie's Bar in New York City, a straight bar where Queer Nation parodied straight behavior and displayed a refusal to be invisible in public space, highlighting that public space had in fact been assumed to be heterosexual space. More recent Queer Nation actions took place across the US to pressure officials and corporations to divest from Russia, in response to the 2013 Russian anti-gay laws.

# Individuals referenced

**Gilbert Baker**, 2 June 1951 – 31 March 2017. Baker was an American LGBT+ rights activist who designed the iconic rainbow flag in 1978. Baker died aged 65 from atherosclerotic cardiovascular disease.

**David Bowie**, 8 January 1947 – 10 January 2016. Bowie was an influential English musician who commercialized queer aesthetics. Bowie is widely regarded as a queer icon, but it's crucial to complicate this by noting his commodification of queerness as a cis heterosexual person; his flirtation with fascism; and the multiple allegations of rape made against him. He died aged 69 from liver cancer.

**David Cameron**, 9 October 1966 – present. Cameron was the UK Prime Minister 2010–2016. His government fueled the UK's colonial white savior complex and perpetuated armed invasions of the Middle East using homonationalist rhetoric, while materially depriving queers at home through austerity politics.

**Cher**, 20 May 1946 – present. Cher is an American musician, actor, artist, and enduring camp icon.

**Laverne Cox**, 29 May 1984 – present. Cox is an American actress and LGBT+ advocate. She is one of the first openly transgender actors to gain mainstream popularity, and a trailblazer of trans rights, trans visibility, and the intersection between being Black and a trans woman.

**Don Fass**, dates unknown. Fass was a psychotherapist in New York City when he founded the National Bisexual Liberation Group on 1972, and the corresponding *Bisexual Expression* national bisexual newsletter.

Stephen Donaldson aka **Donny the Punk**, 27 July 1946 – 18 July 1996. Donny was an American bi activist who championed LGBT+ rights and prison reform. He was the founder of the Student Homophile League at Columbia University in 1966. At that time he identified as a homosexual; when he later identified as bisexual, he expressed discomfort with the biphobia in the homophile and gay liberation movements which was so disillusioning that he left activism to enlist in the US Navy. He was kicked out of the Navy after two years. Donny suffered depression, insomnia, and panic attacks, and became active in the punk and anti-racist skinhead subcultures. He wrote openly about his experiences of prison rape, and was the president of Stop Prisoner Rape. He died aged 49 from AIDS.

**Emma Goldman**, 27 June 1869 – 14 May 1940. Goldman was a Russian queer Jewish anarchist and political philosopher, lecturing on anarchism, women'srights, and other social issues. Her family immigrated to the US in 1885. She was imprisoned several times throughout her life including for illegally distributing information about birth control. In 1906, she founded the anarchist journal *Mother Earth*. Goldman was deported to Russia in 1917, and lived across Europe and Canada, influencing North American and European political thought. Goldman died at age 70 after suffering a series of strokes.

**John/James Gruber**, 21 August 1928 – 27 February 2011. Gruber was an American teacher, and bisexual homophile and early LGBT+ rights activist. He was one of the founding members of the Mattachine Society. Gruber died at the age of 82 from unspecified ill health.

**Harry Hay**, 7 April 1912 – 24 October 2002. Hay was an American communist and an activist, campaigning for LGBT+ rights, labor rights, anti-racism, and Native American civil rights. He was a founder of the Mattachine Society, and of the Los Angeles branch of the Gay Liberation Front in 1969, taking an anti-assimilationist stance on LGBT+ rights. Hay died of lung cancer at the age of 90.

**Liz Highleyman**, unknown–present. Highleyman is an anarchist bi activist, who co-founded the Boston ACT UP IV League and organized one of the first needle exchanges in the US in 1991. Highleyman continues activism in public health, HIV/AIDS, hepatitis B and C, sex education, global justice, civil liberties, censorship, and gender and sexuality.

**Brenda Howard**, 24 December 1946 – 28 June 2005. Howard is an American bi activist and considered the "mother of Pride" for her role in coordinating a rally in 1970 to commemorate the one-year anniversary of the Stonewall riots. Howard was lived on a commune of anti-war activists, was a feminist, and a militant LGBT+ rights activist. She was an active member of the Gay Liberation Front, ACT UP, Queer Nation, and other radical LGBT+ groups. Howard died at age 58 from colon cancer.

**Marsha P Johnson**, 24 August 1945 – 6 July 1992. Johnson was a Black American gay liberation activist, a sex worker, and a self-described drag queen. She was an active member of ACT UP, a founding member of the Gay Liberation Front, and the co-founder of Street Transvestite Action Revolutionaries (STAR) along with Silvia Rivera, though she is most known for her involvement in the Stonewall riots. Johnson is an iconic figure of queer history, and her activism focused on homeless trans and queer youth of color. She died aged 46. Her body was found in the Hudson River in New York City, and her death was ruled a suicide despite her having a head wound; this is contested by Johnson's family and community, and witnesses who saw

Johnson harassed and attacked. In 2012, the New York police reopened her case as a possible homicide.

**A Billy S Jones**, dates unknown. Jones was a Black bisexual activist and a founding member of the National Coalition of Black Lesbians and Gays. Jones organized the "Third World Conference: When will the ignorance end?" which was the first national gay and lesbian people of color conference; and the first Gay and Lesbian March on Washington, both in 1979. Jones also organized the first federally funded national "AIDS in the Black Community" conference, and the first Black gay delegation to meet with the White House.

**Christine Jorgensen**, 30 May 1926 – 3 May 1989. Jorgensen was an American trans women who had genital reassignment surgery in Denmark in 1952, and through her charismatic media presence she advocated for trans people and "legitmized" transsexual as an identity in the Anglophonic world. Jorgensen died at the age of 62 from bladder and lung cancer.

**Frank Kameny**, 21 May 1925 – 11 October 2011. Kameny was an American LGBT+ rights activist. He was fired from the US Army Map Service in 1957 for his homosexuality, co-founded the Washington DC branch of the Mattachine Society with Jack Nichols in 1961, and picketed the White House in 1965 in one of the first demonstrations for gay rights. Kameny died at age 86 from arteriosclerotic cardiovascular disease.

**Kid Congo Powers**, 27 March 1959 – present. Kid Congo Powers is a Mexican American queer punk and post-punk musician. His musical career began in 1979, and during the 1980s he was involved in ACT UP.

**Phyllis Lyon**, 10 November 1924 – present. Lyon is an American homophile and feminist lesbian activist, and co-founder of the Daughters of Bilitis with her wife Del Martin and several other lesbians. Lyon was also involved in the National Organization for Women, and the Alice B Toklas Gay and Lesbian Democratic Club. Her work with Martin influenced anti-discrimination legislation and culturally-sensitive healthcare activism.

**Del Martin**, 5 May 1921 – 27 August 2008. Martin was an American homophile and feminist lesbian activist, and co-founder of the Daughters of Bilitis with her wife Phyllis Lyon and several other lesbians. Martin was the editor of the DOB's newsletter *The Ladder* from 1960 to 1962. Martin was also involved in the National Organization for Women, the San Fransisco Commission on the Status of Women, and the Alice B Toklas Gay and Lesbian Democratic Club. Martin was also an associate of the Women's Institute for Freedom of the Press, working to platform women. Her work with Lyon influenced anti- discrimination legislation and culturally-sensitive healthcare activism. Martin died at age 87 from complications of an arm bone fracture.

John Sholto Douglas, 9th **Marquess of Queensbury**, 20 July 1844 – 31 January 1900. Queensbury was a Scottish nobleman and homophobe, angered that Oscar Wilde was having a relationship with Queensbury's son Alfred. Queensbury sent evidence to Scotland Yard which led to Wilde's being charged and convicted of gross indecency. He died at age 55, possibly from a stroke.

**Bob Mellors**, 1950 – 24 March 1996. Mellow was a British LGBT+ rights activist, and co-founder of the London chapter of the Gay Liberation Front while he was working at the London School of Economics, along with Aubrey Walter. Mellors was murdered at the age of 46 during a burglary of his flat in Warsaw, Poland where he was living from 1994.

**Harvey Milk**, 22 May 1930 – 27 November 1978. Milk was a gay American politician, and the first openly gay elected official in California. While on the San Fransisco Board of Supervisors, he passed a gay rights ordinance for the city of San Fransisco. He was assassinated by another city supervisor at the age of 48 and became a queer icon and a martyr.

**Janet Mock**, 10 March 1983 – present. Mock is an American writer, TV host, and trans rights activist. She is one of the most visible trans activists and Black trans women in the US.

**Jack Nichols**, 16 March 1938 – 2 May 2005. Nichols was an American writer and LGBT+ rights activist, and co-founded the Washing DC branch of the Mattachine Society in 1961 with Frank Kameny. His activism was especially concerned with forging links between the gay rights movement and the National Council of Churches. In 1967, he became one of the first Americans to talk openly about his homosexuality on national television, though he did so under the pseudonym Warren Adkins, under threat from his father who feared losing his FBI security clearance should people realize Jack was his son. Nichols died at age 67 from cancer complications.

**Gary North**, dates unknown. North was an American writer and bisexual activist, and a founder of BiNet US. In 1988 he published one of the first national bisexual newsletters: *Bisexuality: News, Views, and Networking*.

**Michael Page**, dates unknown. Page is a bi activist based in Florida, US, who designed the bisexual Pride flag (unveiled 5 December 1998). He co-created Bisexual Visibility Day (23 September, annually) to celebrate bisexuals, pansexuals, fluid and non-monosexual people.

**Reverend Ian Paisley**, 6 April 1926 – 12 September 2014. Rev. Paisley was an anti-queer campaigner in Northern Ireland, leading the "Save Ulster from Sodomy" campaign in 1977. He instigated loyalist opposition to the Catholic civil rights movement in Northern Ireland, which contributed to the outbreak of the

Troubles (late 1960s–1990s). He was the founder of the Democratic Unionist Party (DUP) in 1970 and became a peer in the House of Lords in 2010. He died of heart complications at age 88.

**Al Parker**, 25 June 1952 – 17 August 1992. Parker was an American gay porn star, producer, and director who embodied the Castro clone look. His company, Surge Studios, was one of the first studios to mandate safer sex practices when the HIV/AIDS crisis broke out. He died of AIDS-related complications at age 40.

**Veneita Porter**, dates unknown. Porter was a bisexual activist and member of the Prositutes' Union of Massachusettes, and Call Off Your Tired Old Ethics (COYOTE). She advocated for women, trans people and injection drug users during the HIV/AIDS epidemic.

**James Pratt**, 1805 – 27 November 1835. Pratt was a stable hand who lived in Deptford, London, UK. Pratt was the last person (along with John Smith) to be sentenced to death for buggery in the UK. Their sentencing was based entirely off the testimóny of a landlord who alleged to see Pratt and Smith having sex through a keyhole; they were hanged in front of Newgate Prison in London. Pratt was 30 years old.

**Silvia Rivera**, 2 July 1951 – 19 February 2002. Rivera was a Latina American trans and gay liberation activist, a sex worker, and a self-described transvestite and drag queen. She was a founding member of the Gay Liberation Front and the Gay Activists Alliance, and co-founded Street Transvestite Action Revolutionaries with Marsha P Johnson. She is primarily known for her (possible) involvement in the Stonewall riots. Her activism centered around the most marginalized in the queer community: runaway and homeless trans and gender non-conforming youth of color. She died aged 50 from complications of liver cancer.

**Alan Rockway**, 1944 – November 1987. Rockway was a clinical psychologist and bi activist who co-authored the first successful anti-discrimination legislation in the US in 1977 in Dade County, Florida. In 1978 he founded the Miami Transperience Center, which provided counseling for LGBT+ people. In 1983, he co-organized BiPol to build bisexual visibility and a bisexual political movement. He was openly HIV+ and spoke out against biphobic stereotypes and HIV stigma. He died of AIDS at age 43.

**Sappho**, c.630 – c.570 BCE. Sappho was an archaic Greek poet from Lesbos. Most of her work is lost, but she is known for her lyric poetry. Sappho has become a symbol of love between women—the word lesbian takes its name from the island where Sappho was born—though for centuries she was misread as a heterosexual poet. Many details of her life, including her death, are unknown.

**William Shakespeare**, April 1564 – 23 April 1616. Shakespeare was an English playwright, poet, and actor who made comedic and dramatic use of crossdressing and queerness. He died aged 52, possibly from fever.

**Cynthia Slater**, 1945–1989. Slater was a bi activist and HIV+ activist. She presented safer sex education in bathhouses and BDSM clubs in the 1980s, and organized the first Women's HIV/AIDS information switchboard in 1985. She was a pro domme and active in shaping the BDSM scene. She died of AIDS related complications at the age of 45.

**John Smith**, 1795 – 27 November 1835. Smith was a Londoner from Southwark Christchurch, and the last person (along with James Pratt) to be sentenced to death for buggery in the UK. Their sentencing was based entirely off the testimony of a landlord who alleged to see Smith and Pratt having sex through a keyhole; they were hanged in front of Newgate Prison in London. Smith was 40 years old.

Touko Valio Laaksonen aka **Tom of Finland**, 8 May 1920 – 7 November 1991. Tom of Finland was a Finnish homoerotic artist whose work heavily featured, and popularized, men stylized like the Castro clone. He is widely considered the most influential gay fetish artist of the 20th century. He died at age 71 from a stroke.

**Alan Turing**, 23 June 1912 – 7 June 1954. Turing was a gay English mathematician, logician, cryptanalyst, and computer scientist. He is the inventor of the Turing machine, and is widely regarded as the father of modern computer science and artificial intelligence. During World War II he was instrumental in the UK deciphering German codes. He was charged with and convicted of gross indecency in 1952 when he reported that his lover's acquaintance had burgled his house. Turing accepted chemical castration treatment as an alternative to prison. He died two years later, aged 41, from cyanide poisoning which was ruled a suicide.

**Lena Waithe**, 17 May 1984 – present. Waithe is an American actor, producer, and screenwriter. She's openly a lesbian, and wore rainbow flag (with brown and black stripes) cape in 2018 Met Gala.

**Aubrey Walter**, unknown – present. Walter co-founded the Gay Liberation Front in the UK at the London School of Economics in 1970, along with Bob Mellors. She also founded the Gay Men's Press, which published in London from 1979 to 2006.

**John Waters**, 22 April 1946 – present. Waters is a gay American filmmaker, author, actor, visual artist, and camp icon. He is known for his "trash" cult classics like *Pink Flamingos*, and for leaning in to negative stereotypes of queers being filthy and perverse.

**Oscar Wilde**, 16 October 1854 – 30 November 1900. Wilde was a gay Irish writer, poet, and playwright living in London, UK. He was prosecuted for "gross indecency" in 1895 in a highly publicized trial. He was sentenced to two years of hard labor and was imprisoned from 1895–1897. Immediately upon his release he left London for France. He died destitute in Paris from meningitis, aged 46. Wilde, a champion of aestheticism, is a queer camp icon.